T0074599

ICT and
Data Sciences

Green Engineering and Technology: Concepts and Applications

Series Editors: Brujo Kishore Mishra, GIET University, India and
Raghvendra Kumar, LNCT College, India

Environment is an important issue these days for the whole world. Different strategies and technologies are used to save the environment. Technology is the application of knowledge to practical requirements. Green technologies encompass various aspects of technology which help us reduce the human impact on the environment and creates ways of sustainable development. Social equability, this book series will enlighten the green technology in different ways, aspects, and methods. This technology helps people to understand the use of different resources to fulfill needs and demands. Some points will be discussed as the combination of involuntary approaches, government incentives, and a comprehensive regulatory framework will encourage the diffusion of green technology, least developed countries and developing states of small island requires unique support and measure to promote the green technologies.

Handbook of Sustainable Development Through Green Engineering and Technology
Edited by Vikram Bali, Rajni Mohana, Ahmed Elngar, Sunil Kumar Chawla, and Gurpreet Singh

Integrating Deep Learning Algorithms to Overcome Challenges in Big Data Analytics
Edited by R. Sujatha, S. L. Aarthy, and R. Vettriselvan

Big Data Analysis for Green Computing
Concepts and Applications
Edited by Rohit Sharma, Dilip Kumar Sharma, Dhowmya Bhatt, and Binh Thai Pham

Green Computing in Network Security
Energy Efficient Solutions for Business and Home
Edited by Deepak Kumar Sharma, Koyel Datta Gupta, and Rinky Dwivedi

Handbook of Green Computing and Blockchain Technologies
Edited by Kavita Saini and Manju Khari

Artificial Intelligence and Cybersecurity
Advances and Innovations
Edited by Ishaani Priyadarshini and Rohit Sharma

ICT and Data Sciences
Edited by Archana Singh, Vinod Kumar Shukla, Ashish Seth, and A. Sai Sabitha

For more information about this series, please visit: https://www.routledge.com/ Green-Engineering-and-Technology-Concepts-and-Applications/book-series/ CRCGETCA

ICT and Data Sciences

Edited by
Archana Singh
Vinod Kumar Shukla
Ashish Seth
A. Sai Sabitha

CRC Press
Taylor & Francis Group
Boca Raton London New York

CRC Press is an imprint of the
Taylor & Francis Group, an **informa** business

First edition published 2022
by CRC Press
6000 Broken Sound Parkway NW, Suite 300, Boca Raton, FL 33487-2742

and by CRC Press
4 Park Square, Milton Park, Abingdon, Oxon, OX14 4RN

CRC Press is an imprint of Taylor & Francis Group, LLC

© 2022 Taylor & Francis Group, LLC

Library of Congress Cataloging-in-Publication Data
Names: Singh, Archana (Data Science), editor.
Title: ICT and data sciences / edited by Archana Singh, Vinod Kumar Shukla, Ashish Seth, and Sai Sabitha.
Description: Boca Raton : CRC Press, [2022] | Series: Green engineering and technology : concepts and applications | Includes bibliographical references and index. | English with a paper in Greek. | Summary: "This book highlights the state-of-the-art research on data usage, security, and privacy in the scenarios of the Internet of Things (IoT), along with related applications using Machine Learning and Big Data technologies to design and make efficient Internet-compatible IoT systems. ICT and Data Sciences bring together IoT and Machine Learning and provides the careful integration of both, along with many examples and case studies. It illustrates the merging of two technologies while presenting basic to high-level concepts covering different fields and domains such as the Hospitality and Tourism industry, Smart Clothing, Cyber Crime, Programming, Communications, Business Intelligence, all in the context of the Internet of Things. The book is written for researchers and practitioners, working in Information Communication Technology and Computer Science"-- Provided by publisher.
Identifiers: LCCN 2021046702 (print) | LCCN 2021046703 (ebook) | ISBN 9780367501143 (hbk) | ISBN 9780367501150 (pbk) | ISBN 9781003048862 (ebk)
Subjects: LCSH: Internet of things.
Classification: LCC TK5105.8857 .I26 2022 (print) | LCC TK5105.8857 (ebook) | DDC 004.67/8--dc23/eng/20211122
LC record available at https://lccn.loc.gov/2021046702
LC ebook record available at https://lccn.loc.gov/2021046703

ISBN: 978-0-367-50114-3 (hbk)
ISBN: 978-0-367-50115-0 (pbk)
ISBN: 978-1-003-04886-2 (ebk)

DOI: 10.1201/9781003048862

Typeset in Times
by SPi Technologies India Pvt Ltd (Straive)

Contents

Preface

The editors of the book are actively involved in research areas related to ICT and data sciences. This book is a collection of relevant work of valuable contributors from the academia and industry in ICT and data sciences. ICT and data sciences is an interdisciplinary field of scientific methods, processes, and systems to extract knowledge or insights from data used in various applications. The collaboration between industry and academics has been a driving force behind the exponential rise in the usage of ICT devices. Both of these technologies, data science and ICT, have formed an interdependence which helps both domains to aid development. Data science has become crucial to understanding the external and internal forces impacting the business through data generated from social media, search engines, and government portals and can be leveraged in widespread business by including people analytics.

The chapters of the book are organized to meet the demand for data scientists with depth of knowledge and applied skills in various areas like statistics, AI, ML, deep learning, NLP, and big data in the application areas of healthcare, the cyber world, customer services, augmented reality, IoT-integrated systems like cluster-based wireless systems, and social networks.

The book is primarily focused on promotion of research and developmental activities in information communication and technology in the application areas of data science for developing business strategy and exploring security techniques in the cyber field. Another goal is to promote scientific information exchange among researchers, developers, consultants, academics, and research practitioners. The focus of our work has been to address fundamental issues that are common to many data science research practitioners.

We hope this volume finds space in the minds of the practicing world of business and IT and draws new landscapes in the future.

TOPICS COVERED

Suitable topics include, but are not limited to, the following:

Image Classification Using Deep Learning
Artificial Intelligence
Data Sciences and Modeling
Data-Centric Programming and Statistical Analysis
Machine Learning and Computational Intelligence
Social Media Analytics
Big Data Mining and Analytics
Cyber Security
Information Security
Internet of Things Systems

Feature Engineering and Tensor Flow
Knowledge Engineering
Web Databases and Information Systems
Opinion Mining and Sentiment Analysis

Editors

Archana Singh has more than 20 years' experience in academia and the IT industry. Presently, she is working as a professor, Department of IT, Amity University, Uttar Pradesh, Noida. Her research area interests include: data sciences, machine learning, artificial intelligence, ICT, business intelligence, data analytics, big data, and its applications. She has more than 60+ research papers including several SCI-indexed journals and 22+ in Scopus, Web of Science-indexed journals by the likes of ACM, Springer, Elsevier, Wiley, and others. She has reviewed many articles for international journals and conferences and is a regular reviewer for the *International Journal of Retail and Consumer Services* (Elsevier) and has been recognized for the same. She has authored eight books from national and international publishers.

She is a guest editor for special issue of *Inderscience Journal* and editor of SAGE, Macmillan Publications. She has extensively contributed for several IT meets, panel discussions, and faculty development programs. She is NPTEL-certified for many courses related to data science. She is part of various memberships like IETE and IEEE. She has been guiding many engineering graduates, postgraduates, and PhD scholars. She is easily reached at archana.elina@gmail.com.

Vinod Kumar Shukla is currently working at Amity University, Dubai, UAE in the capacity of associate professor and head of Academics, Engineering Architecture, and Interior Design. He has more than 14 years of experience. He has completed his PhD in the field of Semantic Web and Ontology and is an active member of IEEE and CSI (India chapter). He has published many research papers in various reputed journals/conferences and has also completed the General Management Program at Indian Institute of Management Ahmedabad (IIM-A). He is a certified Network Trainer CCNI (Cisco Certified Network Trainer) and is a part of multiple editorial and reviewer boards for various internationally reputed journals and publications.

Dr. Shukla has been awarded many prestigious awards internationally, to name a few, the Global Academic Excellence Award – 2021 in Global Edu-Conclave 2021, where he presented his views on the topic of UN – SDG, Sustainable Development Goal – 2030, the Inquisitive Award in Unanimity – 2020, organized and hosted by Amity University Dubai, UAE, and the Star Supporter Award 2019 presented by Manzil Center, Sharjah, UAE.

Ashish Seth is an author, consultant, researcher and teacher.

He is a professor at the School of Global Convergence Studies, Inha University, South Korea and is presently deputed to Inha University Tashkent, Uzbekistan. He is also a visiting faculty member at TSI, Riga, Latvia. He is senior member of IEEE, life member of CSI, and an active member of international societies like IACSIT, IAENG, and more. Dr. Seth also serves as the ACM-Distinguished Speaker in the ACM-DSP program and holds a PhD (computer science) in information systems from Punjabi University, Patiala, Punjab, India. He has published more than 40 research papers in indexed journals. He has authored eight books and several book chapters. Dr. Seth has also edited a number of books and indexed journals. His research interests include service-oriented architecture, cloud computing, and blockchain technologies. He finds interest in reading and writing articles on emerging technologies.

A. Sai Sabitha, BE (CSE), ME (CSE), PhD (CSE), served as an associate professor and HOD (IT), ASET, at Amity University Uttar Pradesh. She has more than 20 years of experience in teaching and industry. Her areas of interests are e-learning, knowledge management, data mining, artificial intelligence and web technologies. Dr. Sabitha has handled several B. Tech and M. Tech projects, and has published more than 60 research papers in international conferences and reputed journals. She is a member of ISTE, IEEE, ACM, and more and is also a reviewer of various national/international journals of repute.

1 Impact and Analysis of Machine Learning and IoT Application in People Analytics

Praveen Mohan Kulkarni and Santosh Saraf

CONTENTS

1.1 INTRODUCTION TO PEOPLE ANALYTICS

The technology and functions of human resource management (HRM) are making efforts to combine experience and concepts of HRM for people analytics [1, 2]. People analytics supports HRM to understand the workgroups and also individuals working in the organization. Data is collected and transformed into meaningful information about the employee's attributes, behavior, and performance, which support effective human resource decision-making [3]. Association of people analytics with HRM aims to improve recruitment, retention, assessment, promotion, salary, employee turnover, and other functions of human resource management [4].

DOI: 10.1201/9781003048862-1

1

The backbone of people analytics includes technology which is reformed and redefined to support people analytics. The Internet of Things (IoT) is one of the major technologies to support human resource practices for effective people analytics, as it is convenient for collecting information and supporting effective decision-making for human resource professionals [5, 6]. While the role of machine learning in human resource practices provides an opportunity for processing data analytics related to human resource departments in organizations, this technology collects information in advanced algorithms that predicts employee information related to human resource practices, through deep learning neural networks that are transformed for meaningful results and conclusion of data. The convergence of machine learning and IoT paves the way for improved efficiency, accuracy,productivity, and overall cost-savings for resource-constrained IoT devices. Using a combination of machine learning algorithms and IoT, we can achieve improved communication and computation, better controllability, and improved decision-making [7]. Therefore, employees are the most important resource for an organization, hence companies must make the right people-oriented decisions.Therefore, initiatives combining machine learning and the IoT with people analytics could bridge the gap between the existing judgment-based approaches with a data-driven approach for HRM.

1.2   PURPOSE AND MOTIVATION OF MACHINE LEARNING AND INTERNET OF THINGS (IoT) IN PEOPLE ANALYTICS

1.2.1   MACHINE LEARNING AND PEOPLE ANALYTICS

Machine learning, which includes the subset of artificial intelligence, is embraced with the tools of statistics and support of computer science. Machine learning systems are instructed by programs to learninteractive data and provide meaningful information through the application of statistical interventions. This data generated through machine learning aids with decision-making for managers and other employees in anorganization [8]. Likewise, IoT supports machine learning in collecting data from various self-directed devices through nodes. These nodes have the capability to collect information through sensors and communicate with other sensors and generate data. These data are connected with machine learning algorithms, which generate meaningful information for an organization's decision-makers [9].

Machine learning technology applies different algorithms for analysis of the data collected through IoT. Machine learning algorithms and methods of data processing for people analysis are presented in Table 1.1 [10].

1.2.2   INTERNET OF THINGS AND PEOPLE ANALYTICS

IoT is internet-based smart technology which connects people and devices, and generates meaningful information for decision-makers. As IoT becomesmore integral to employees, its relationship would be more related to human resource practices. IoT enables one to influence anorganizational culture by understanding employees from remote locations, monitor performance, and also provide flexibility on work-timings to employees [11]. The application of IoT in HRM is presented in Table 1.2.

TABLE 1.1

Machine Learning Algorithms and Data Processing Tasks for People Analytics

Sr. No.	Machine Learning Algorithms	Data Processing Tasks	People Analytics
1	K-Nearest Neighbors	Classification	Employee turnover, employee demographics, salary grades
2	Naive Bayes	Classification	Employee performance, talent management, leave management
3	Support Vector Machine	Classification	Talent classification, abilities, skills, knowledge
4	Linear Regression	Regression	recruitment, selection, training, compensation
5	Support Vector Regression	Regression	Working hours, employee productivity analysis, training effectiveness
6	Classification and Regression Trees	Classification/ Regression	Succession planning, leadership management
7	Random Forests	Classification/ Regression	Human resource (HR) planning, job analysis
8	Bagging	Classification/ Regression	HR process, training performance
9	K-Means	Clustering	Personal management systems, employee engagement
10	Density-Based Spatial Clustering of Applications with Noise	Clustering	Talent evaluation and management, Performance management systems, job descriptions
11	Principal Component Analysis	Feature extraction	Salary survey, performance productivity analysis
12	Canonical Correlation Analysis	Feature extraction	Analysis of past performance to present performance of employee
13	Feed Forward Neural Network	Regression/ Classification/ Clustering/ FeatureExtraction	Employee performance forecasting, human resource forecasting
14	One-class Support Vector Machines	Anomaly detection	Job turnover analysis, HR decision-making, strategic HRM

1.3 CHALLENGES OF IMPLEMENTING MACHINE LEARNING AND INTERNET OF THINGS IN PEOPLE ANALYTICS

The next part of the chapter will cover problems related to acceptance of machine learning and IoT for people analytics. Accompanying the major advantages of people analytics through machine learning and IoT, there are challenges that need addressing to enhance the effectiveness of this technology. Novel interaction techniques are needed to fully support seamless intuitive visual communication with the system. The analyst should be able to fully focus on the task at hand and not be distracted

TABLE 1.2
IoT in People Analytics

Sr. No.	IoT in HRM	Descriptions
1	Recruitment	Employees are more likely to have a real experience of their future office spaces, before taking a major step. IoT-enabled artificial intelligence can make the selection process more impartial and introduce more diversity of employees.
2	Measuring Employee Behavior and Identification	However, these badges can serve as sociometric badges and are used to track workplace, or employee stress levels with their voice and heart rate, etc. In the service delivery industry, it can help to track the speed of driver monitoring, eliminate downtime between delivery, gauge efficient and secure routes, etc., in all with IoT software.
3	Enabling an Insightful and Agile Organization	IoT will also enable organizations to make real-time employee statistics possible. It will give them insight into employee productivity, their time horizons and skill sets, among others. This will also improve HR performance and HR response to staffing issues.

by overly technical or complex user interfaces and interactions [12]. Gaps in training exist and ethical issues are rarely considered, despite risks to employees and organizations [7]. One critical issue regards members' privacy. Concerns for privacy are liable to pre-empt the willingness and ability to implement a full model, thus impeding the full realization of our method's potential. We must therefore guarantee that the privacy of individuals and groups is meticulously preserved, by taking one or several of the following measures [13]. The selected professional networking web source is Stack Overflow and multivariate statistical data analysis was used to test the correlations between skills and competences in the job offers dataset. The present work falls into a relatively new field of research, concerning the competence mining of peopleware data with special focus on software development [14]. One reason many organizations have found it difficult to successfully adopt people analytics is the disparate skills and capabilities required to do the work. Creating and honing a clear and repeatable methodology focused on producing actionable insights is a clear differentiator between those that are successful and those that struggle with people analytics. People analytics initiatives require investment, time, and best practices [15].

These challenges include connection to different devices for, firstly, flow of data related to human resources; secondly, selection of right sensors, applications for data collection related to human resource practices; thirdly, availability of internet to the employees and to human resource professionals; and fourthly, development of an effective ecosystem for acceptance of this technology by human resource professionals. In addition, effective segregation of data for classification of data into descriptive analytics, predictive analytics, prescriptive analytics, and adaptive analytics. Therefore, this section highlights on these challenges, problems, and gaps while applying machine learning and IoT in people analytics.

1.4 RESEARCH DESIGN AND METHODOLOGY

In this section of the chapter, systematic literature review methodology would be undertaken to understand the problems related to implementation of machine learning and IoT in people analytics. The data would be collected from systematic and content centric literature review based on the multiple stage approach of Webster and Watson. The initial systematic search would apply two electronic databases namely Web of Science and Scopus to identify the key academic papers. Further, the initial systematic search would also include the Google search engine to understand the key industrial and commercial repots on application of machine learning and IoT in people analytics. Finally, careful review and application of exclusion criteria through the method of Liao would be applied for understanding the gaps in the application of this technology.

1.4.1 DATA SOURCES

In the first stage, the study searched electronic database through keywords applied for searching the database on (1) machine learning and people analytics, and (2) machine learning and people analytics.

1.4.2 SCREENING

The study included premier database source, these include EBSCO, Google Scholar, Emerald, IEEE Xplore Digital Library, JSTOR, ProQuest Dissertations and Theses, Science Direct, Taylor & Francis, Scopus, and Web of Science. The study has excluded the proceedings of the conference from systematic literature review to focus on the most cited literature on (1) machine learning and people analytics and (2) machine learning and people analytics. This process is more focused on the understanding of the concept of the study [16]. A literature review protocol based on Popay et al. [17] was developed to limit the systematic error and bias in the screening of papers for review. This protocol summarized the scope, strategy, and data extraction method for the review, as shown in Figure 1.1. This research used the protocol to obtain the final sample of articles. The first step was a broad search of the literature review to find abstracts that met the screening criteria, i.e., machine learning and people analytics and IoT, in the title or abstract of the article. The titles and abstracts were analyzed. It helped in removing the duplicates. The remaining abstracts were screened using the inclusion/exclusion criteria mentioned earlier. The full articles were then read to ensure they met the inclusion/exclusion criteria. The reference list of articles was read to further improve the search criteria. The total number of articles, along with the breakup, is shown in Figure 1.1.

1.4.3 DATA ANALYSIS

As the primary goal of this research was to explore the key ingredients for assessing machine learning and people analytics and IoT, it was decided to identify the patterns, directions, similarities, and differences in key ingredients within the sampled

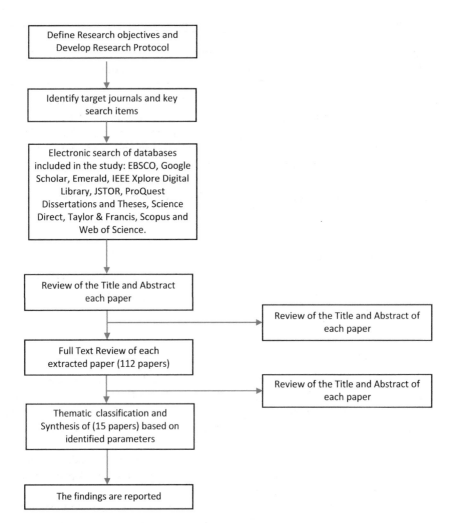

FIGURE 1.1 Search of articles for literature review for the study.

articles [18]). In total, 15 articles were extracted after review considering the research objective of the study. To ensure that the identified papers really dealt with the objective of the research, the papers were read by both the authors independently. The papers were reflected on in terms of themes of machine learning and IoT for people analytics in the studied literature. The themes were further analyzed independently by both the authors and classified into master themes. The rationale of the classification scheme was to meet the goal of parsimony to explain the key ingredients of (1) machine learning and people analytics and (2) machine learning and people analytics. The objective of the study was to find the master theme behind these large numbers of factors. The master theme reflected the categorical classification of the theme as a higher order cluster or categorization The process of data analysis is presented in Figure 1.2.

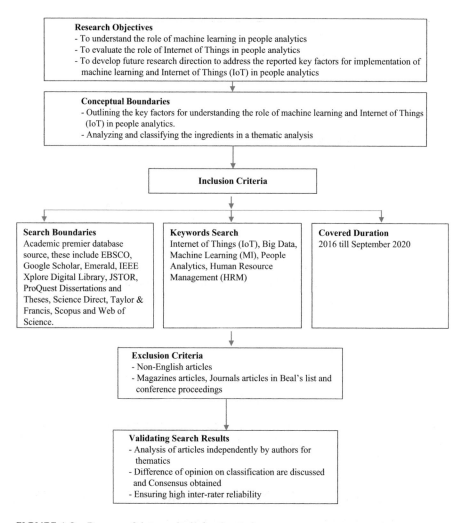

FIGURE 1.2   Process of data analysis for the study.

1.4.4   DESCRIPTIVE ANALYSIS OF LITERATURE

The descriptive analysis of articles was conducted and shows distribution of articles. In total, 30.77 percent of the articles are from USA, followed by India 23.08 percent, Israel 7.69 percent, the Netherlands 7.69 percent, Romania 7.69 percent, UAE 7.69 percent, Qatar 7.69 percent, and Germany at 7.69 percent. As expected, the USA is in the lead; however, other countries are catching up.The distribution of articles by country is presented in Table 1.3.

In total, 23.08 percent of the articles follow a conceptual viewpoint, 15.38 percent are case studies, quantitative methods like survey accounted for 46.15 percent, and literature review 15.38 percent. The quantitative and conceptual dominate, suggesting the area of machine learning and people analytics and IoT is just building up. It

TABLE 1.3
Country-Wise Distribution of Articles

Country	No	Percentage
India	3	23.08
USA	4	30.77
Israel	1	7.69
Netherlands	1	7.69
Romania	1	7.69
UAE	1	7.69
Qatar	1	7.69
Germany	1	7.69
	13	100.00

TABLE 1.4
Research Method-Wise Distribution of Articles

Research	No	Percentage
Conceptual	3	23.08
Case Study	2	15.38
Quantitative	6	46.15
Literature Review	2	15.38
	13	100.00

also further submits the huge need for future research to test the viewpoint and theories suggested in case studies. Details with regards to research method-wise articles are presented in Table 1.4.

1.5   RESULTS THROUGH THEMATIC ANALYSIS OF LITERATURE

In this section, the themes extracted from the review of academic research on the key ingredients for (1) machine learning and people analytics, and (2) machine learning and people analytics. are enumerated and explained to achieve the research objective of the study.

1.5.1   ROLE OF MACHINE LEARNING IN PEOPLE ANALYTICS

The studies related to machine learning in people analytics indicate that machine learning has supported effective decision-making in organizations' human resource processes by making these decisions data-driven and transparent [5]. This technology also supports recruitment processes by reducing recruitment timesand matching the right candidates for the organization, changing the face oftraditional recruitment and candidate selection methods in an organization [19]. One of the most advantageous aspects of machine learning in people analytics is that it collects a largeamount of data with regards to the knowledge, skills, and behaviors of employees and prospective employees.This datahelps devise effective talent management strategies [20]. Another wing of HRM is the training and development of employees' competencies, as machine learning and people analytics can help create a database and directions with regards to the newskills required for a job profile. It canalso forecast the required skill-set of employees for the future, helping an organization design and develop effective training programs for its employees [21]. Apart from recruitment and talent management, another application formachine learning technology is for the performance management of employees, as information related to employees' performance can be collected through the tools of artificial intelligence (AI). This reduces the bias in employee appraisal [22]. However, for effective implementation,the role of the stakeholder for people analytics needs to be considered, which include employees and HR professionals. Apart from the involvement of employees and HR professionals, the right technology also needs to be developed in organizations which can support the technology of machine learning in people analytics [23, 24].

1.5.2 ROLE OF INTERNET OF THINGS (IoT) IN PEOPLE ANALYTICS

The technology of IoT provides an opportunity for automation of HR processes which results in improving the human resource process and practices in the organization [25]. Technology sensors of face recognition and neural network technology provide information on the communication, behavior and performance of the employees, which support development ofappropriateHR practices to match the requirements of the employee'srole [26]. This data onemployees' behavior is also applied to developing effective teams in the organization, to create synergy among an organization's team members [27]. IoT technology provides an opportunity for data collection through advanced sensors which provide deep information about the human resourceswithin an organization; this data thus supports development of effective HR practices in the company [28]. From the perspective of organization culture, technology-enabled human resource practices also influence anorganization's culture; therefore, special attention to device application and practices needs to be made for employees to acceptthese technologies [29, 30].

1.6 PRACTICAL IMPLICATIONS

The present study provides key directions for effective implementation of machine learning and IoT for people analytics. The domain of machine learning supports the collection of large amounts of data on employee behavior, communication, and performance, and of information related to recruitment and selection. This data supports helps and supports HR professionals' decision-making. However, there are other factors (such as the involvement of employees and HR professionals during the designing, development, and implementation stages) which are critical for gaining full benefit of this technology.

Another factor associated with IoT and people analytics is that of organizational culture.IoT has an influence onorganizational culture; hence,employees' involvement and awareness of this technology would support in reducing resistance to change in the organization. Apart from these two factors, organizations need to design and develop training programs on the benefits of IoT and machine learning for the employees to provide clarity. These training programs also help reduceemploy-ees' privacy-relatedconcens(these technologies collect information about human behavior).Hence,an awareness of security and confidentiality needs to be communicated to employees for their acceptance of this technology.

1.7   CONCLUSION

Overall, the studies discussed in this chapter show that machine learning and IoT provides an opportunity to understand employees better than the traditional methods of HRM and people analytics. However, caution needs to be applied by an organization about awareness among the employees of these technologies. Confidence also needs to be built among the workforce that their privacy is maintained. The most crucial factor is that caution is applied regarding these technologies'influence on a company's organizational culture. Hence, there are a number of factors that need to be considered for the effective implementation of machine learning and IoT in an organization's use of people analytics.

REFERENCES

1. T. Rasmussen and D. Ulrich, "Learning from practice: How HR analytics avoids being a management fad," *Organizational Dynamics* 44, No. 3 (2015): 236–242.
2. J. Van der Togt and T.H. Rasmussen, "Toward evidence-based HR," *Journal of Organizational Effectiveness: People and Performance* 4, No. 2 (2017): 127–132.
3. T. Pape, "Prioritising data items for business analytics: Framework and application to human resources," *European Journal of Operational Research* 252, No. 2 (2016): 687–698.
4. N. Guenole, J. Ferrar, and S. Feinzig, "The power of people: Learn how successful organizations use workforce analytics to improve business performance," *FT Press*, 2017.
5. S. Shrivastava, K. Nagdev, and A. Rajesh, "Redefining HR using people analytics: The case of Google," *Human Resource Management International Digest* 26, No. 2 (2018): 3–6.
6. J.W. Boudreau and P.M. Ramstad, "Beyond HR: The new science of human capital," *Harvard Business Press*, 2007.
7. A. Tursunbayeva, S. Di Lauro, and C. Pagliari, "People analytics—A scoping review of conceptual boundaries and value propositions," *International Journal of Information Management* 43 (2018): 224–247.
8. D. Handa Garima, "Human resource (HR) analytics: Emerging trend in HRM (HRM)," *International Journal of Research in Commerce & Management* 5, No. 6 (2014): 59–62.
9. A. Sheth, "Internet of things to smart IoT through semantic, cognitive, and perceptual computing," *IEEE Intelligence System* 31, No. 2 (2016): 108–112.
10. M.S. Mahdavinejad, M. Rezvan, M. Barekatain, P. Adibi, P. Barnaghi, and A.P. Sheth, "Machine learning for internet of things data analysis: A survey," *Digital Communications and Networks* 4, No. 3 (2018): 161–175.
11. B.C. Vaught, R.E. Taylor, and S.F. Vaught, "The attitudes of managers regarding the electronic monitoring of employee behavior: Procedural and ethical considerations," *American Business Review* 18, No. 1 (2000): 107–115.

12. R. Netzel, B. Ohlhausen, K. Kurzhals, R. Woods, M. Burch, and D. Weiskopf, "User performance and reading strategies for metro maps: An eye tracking study," *Spatial Cognition & Computation* 17, No. 1–2 (2017):39–64.

13. R. Gelbard, R. Ramon-Gonen, A. Carmeli, R.M. Bittmann, and R. Talyansky, "Sentiment analysis in organizational work: Towards an ontology of people analytics," *Expert Systems* 35, No. 5 (2018): 12289.

14. C. Huang, L. Yao, X. Wang, B. Benatallah, and X. Zhang, "Software expert discovery via knowledge domain embeddings in a collaborative network," *Pattern Recognition Letters* 130 (2020): 46–53.

15. D. Green, "The best practices to excel at people analytics," *Journal of Organizational Effectiveness: People and Performance* 4, No. 2 (2017): 137–144.

16. S. Scott-Findlay and C.A. Estabrooks, "Mapping the organizational culture research in nursing: A literature review," *Journal of Advanced Nursing* 56, No. 5 (2006): 498–513.

17. J. Popay, H. Roberts, A. Sowden, M. Petticrew, L. Arai, M. Rodgers, N. Britten, K. Roen, and S. Duffy, "Guidance on the conduct of narrative synthesis in systematic reviews," a Product fromthe ESRC Methods Programme Version, *Institute of Health Research Lancaster* 1 (2006): 92.

18. L.A. Burke and H.M. Hutchins, "Training transfer: An integrative literature review," *Human Resource Development Review* 6, No. 3 (2007): 263–296.

19. D. Pessach, G. Singer, D. Avrahami, H.C. Ben-Gal, and E.I. Ben-Gal, "Employees recruitment: A prescriptive analytics approach via machine learning and mathematical programming," *Decision Support Systems* 134 (2020): 1–18.

20. K.C. Saling and M.D. Do, "Leveraging people analytics for an adaptive complex talent management system," *Procedia Computer Science* 168 (2020): 105–111.

21 J. Fernandez, "The ball of wax we call HR analytics," *Strategic HR Review* 18, No. 1 (2019): 21–25.

22. M. DiClaudio, "People analytics and the rise of HR: How data, analytics and emerging technology can transform human resources (HR) into a profit center," *Strategic HR Review* 18, No. 2 (2019): 42–46.

23. T. Peeters, J. Paauwe, and K. Van De Voorde, "People analytics effectiveness: Developing a framework," *Journal of Organizational Effectiveness: People and Performance* 7, No. 2 (2020): 203–219.

24. S.-C. Necula, and C. Strîmbei, "People analytics of semantic web human resource résumés for sustainable talent acquisition," *Sustainability* 11, No. 13 (2019): 1–18.

25. B. Sivathanu and R. Pillai, "Smart HR 4.0 – How industry 4.0 is disrupting HR," *Human Resource Management International Digest* 26, No. 4 (2018): 7–11.

26. P.M. Kumar, U. Gandhi, R. Varatharajan, G. Manogaran, R. Jidhesh, and T. Vadivel, "Intelligent face recognition and navigation system using neural learning for smart security in Internet of Things," *Cluster Computing* 22, No. 4 (2019): 7733–7744.

27. G.C. Kane, "People analytics through super-charged ID badges," *MIT Sloan Management Review* 56, No. 4 (2015): 1–18.

28. K.T. Kadhim, A.M. Alsahlany, S.M. Wadi, and H.T. Kadhum, "An overview of patient's health status monitoring system based on Internet of Things (IoT)," *Wireless Pers Communnication* 114 (2020): 2235–2262.

29. M. Al-Hitmi and K. Sherif, "Employee perceptions of fairness toward IoT monitoring," *VINE Journal of Information and Knowledge Management Systems* 48 No. 4 (2018): 504–516.

30. S. Strohmeie, "Smart HRM – A Delphi study on the application and consequences of the Internet of Things in Human Resource Management," *The International Journal of Human Resource Management* 31, No.18 (2020): 2289–2318.

2 Augmented Reality in Online Shopping

Chetna Choudhary and Anmol Sharma

CONTENTS

2.1 INTRODUCTION

Augmented reality (AR) is the upgraded version of today's technology in which a person can view things through a device and can examine objects. Meanwhile, virtual reality (VR) is a different experience in which a person can see objects in a virtual environment. But in augmented reality it is real environment. Three-dimensional (3D) movies are virtual reality and game named Pokémon go is augmented reality. This development has comfort us. Rather than going out people are ease at their homes. Innovation plays a most important role when it comes to technology.

A new way of shopping is implemented. E-commerce converted the way of living. Online shopping has made people see and feel the products. AR commerce innovations mix the trust level of a physical store with the comfort of online shopping as shown in Figure 2.1. It has converted customers' habits, thanks to the rapid growth of the IT sector [1]. Online shopping is a widely used e-commerce form which can allow users to purchase goods online. U.S. retail e-commerce sales for the third quarter of 2012 was reported at \$57 billion, which was greater than the third quarter of 2011 [2]. Online websites help people by easily presenting them the choices. Anyone will be comfortable when they are at home/working and can know what they want to buy besides being at a store. Websites nowadays provide plenty of information. There's quantity as well as quality types, which satisfies customers' wishes.

Technology's main motive is to make things easy for people. E-commerce enables visualization for a better customer experience. When a person wants to buy things online, they want to see how that product looks but AR has taken things

FIGURE 2.1   Using augmented-reality interactive technology (ARIT) in a real environment.

FIGURE 2.2   IKEA's example of an AR app.

further – with the help of AR, anyone can see how an item fits. Clothing shopping has been effortless for this generation. As per Figure 2.2, IKEA has built an AR catalog app in which consumers can see the furniture in their own home dimensions. With other apps (like Asian paints), you can view paint or wallpaper on your wall. One more notable example is the Sephora visual artist app in which you can examine lipstick, eye shadow, eyeliner, and many more make-up products on your skin. Physical try-on of clothes is a time-consuming procedure in retail shopping. It takes the try-on of several clothes before the shopper can make decision on design, color, and size of the apparel that satisfies. Virtual try-on can help to speed-up the process as the shopper can see the clothes on their body without actually wearing them or narrow down selections before physical try-on [2]. This makes shopping simple, avoiding time wastage, and offering more satisfaction to customers. Many measurements are considered with virtual try-on. The app must be adapted for all types of skin color, body customization, 3D preview, clothes alignment – all the aspects are studied based on usability of technology.

In this chapter we have discussed what is AR, its advantages, disadvantages, and the differences between VR and AR. Our proposed framework is that everything needs to be online when there is a crisis, like the coronavirus pandemic of 2020, as is knowing what AR applications will help keep customers safe in times of lockdown. They can take advantage of this technology and in the long term, it will be beneficial for both businesses and their customers.

2.2 LITERATURE REVIEW

AR has made people think creatively. More ideas are being considered. Some have expressed their perspective toward this technology, and some have made new projects for benefit of customers, especially in the fashion retail industry, the utilization of computer-generated innovation in stores has the potential to refresh the customer experience. But users must gain experience of and compatibility of new services. To know what changes and comment surveys are taken by which, we can figure out the change and outcome and make a better improve version of innovation. AR technology can immensely increase the worth and image of a brand among the users and engage them in a more efficient manner. The major difference has been made by the smart/digital mirrors and virtual fitting rooms. Smart mirrors are capable of producing an image of what a customer might look like in an outfit without them trying it on. A smart (virtual) fitting room identifies the exact articles a customer brings into the fitting room; it then indicates which colors, varieties, and sizes are available directly in the store or in the web shop.

Different researchers have published different articles on e-commerce relations with AR. Wang et al. [2] proposed a survey which experimented with a task for participants – the participant underwent a session of AR and gave their review. The results showed that people liked this technology and were satisfied with it. Chakraborty et al. [1] conducted a survey in which 127 people participated – they wanted to see how people have adopted AR technology in India. The results revealed that people who are gadget lovers are more likely to try AR. Adhikari et al. [3] proposed a framework in a mall in which they presented an IntelligShop which will automatically recognize the retailers and fetch their online reviews from various sources (including blogs, forums, and publicly accessible social media) to display on the phones. They demonstrated the system effectiveness via a test bed established in a real mall of Singapore. Huynh et al. [4] conducted a study of products recommended in AR and the results revealed that the majority of people chose AR over browser product images, as products were more clearly visualized in AR.

Recent research has shown the advantages of such technologies as AR in retail contexts, as they are media that enrich the customer's experience [5]. AR combines the real and virtual worlds, supplementing the real world with computer-generated virtual objects in real-time [6–10]. According to a study in the *Journal of Retailing*, some customers research products before buying, while others are more impulsive. Strong visual presentations can help guide purchasers toward the company or product. The data from an AR app can help retailers know more about their customers and their buying decisions. According to the study, retailers that do not embrace technology could be left behind. Some customers resist purchasing online because they lack product information, and being inadequately informed about products makes a purchase decision risky [11]. AR can compensate for this lack of product information, and also the inability to handle products, by creating a 3D augmented experience [5, 12–14]. Direct contact with the desired products is important to shoppers because they acquire product information through the sensory shopping experience – visual, audio, touch, and so on – which assists them in the process of decision-making [14]. The technology is, however, yet to fully permeate the Indian retail system, with only a handful of retailers in India being bold enough to adopt this dynamic solution to beat the challenges of long queues outside dressing rooms and more importantly, provide an enriching shopping experience. The research conducted shows that AR technology has the potential for further development in fashion retail stores. This is because the advantages and beneficial uses of AR features are able to engage the customers in the purchasing process and help improve their buying experience in various aspects. Furthermore, in an attempt to provide actual experience with the product and environment, and to minimize the risk of receiving a faulty product, a few online retailers in India have also started to provide virtual try-on (VTO). VTO plugins act as 3D virtual showrooms and fitting rooms by allowing e-shoppers to swirl (i.e., rotating) a product or try it virtually on themselves, by using a picture or by using it live with AR [15]. The consumers can try apparels and other accessories before purchasing any product, thereby reducing the returns due to unfitting or faulty products while increasing online retailers' commercial performance [16]. Since VTO is still a novel technology in developing markets, it still requires further validation in such settings. Also, the opportunities are so much more than the challenges, as AR is accepted in terms of various aspects like comfort, availability of stocks, variety, time-saving, hassle-free, expert advice and suggestions, avoiding long queues and fitting room queues over factors like security and privacy.

2.3 METHODOLOGY

2.3.1 COMPARISON BETWEEN AR AND VR

The virtual reality (VR) and augmented reality (AR) applications have been widely used in a variety of fields; one of the key requirements in a VR or AR system is to understand how users perceive depth in the virtual environment and augmented reality [17, 18]. Both are known for changing our way of life in the twenty-first century. VR replaces the environment with a fictional world, whereas AR is based in the real world. Both are important in changing the future. These technologies are able to engage our mind as another real version of life. They have been used in every kind of field to fascinating effect. VR is used with headset, goggles, and there can be some visual and auditory experiences. You can experience AR with your smartphone. The study revealed that VR faces more issues than AR, however. The precision of AR is better than VR. The accuracy of detailed knowledge in AR is better than VR. The setup cost of AR is more than VR, but has relevance to a wide variety of fields. But extreme involvement in both can harm mental health or cause major healthcare issues.

2.3.2 ADVANTAGES AND DISADVANTAGES

There are numerous benefits from AR as a technology of the modern era we are living in. Several sectors are affected by it; for instance, the health sector, education sector, business sector, etc. provide profit and loss. AR is used in a wide domain and has sensors, user input devices, and many more devices. In general, AR means an upgraded perspective on reality through increasing the parts or components in context to nature. Through the help of this application's filter, clients presently end up in as focal point of a carefully controlled and intuitive experience which could be of benefit to this present reality.

It is also of help to medical doctors as it helps in maintaining records of patients and also in surgery. AR application development has simplified their work as they receive support and can see more clearly for operating on a patient or for computerized tomography scans.

Online and offline shopping has been advanced because of AR. It is currently conceivable that virtual fitting rooms advantage customers in getting the suitable size, lessening the number of losses. This advantage can also be applied to the shade of a new vehicle or furniture inside your home. Sellers could now create exceptionally expanded reality applications which are customized to their brands so as to cut off the improved encounters to their customers. Notwithstanding, it mustn't be forgotten that one could utilize AR innovation for advertising efforts too, just by consolidating AR as an advantage. AR helps in travel apps; it tells the tourist about their destination and gives a brief specification of their sightseeing. It can be used by anyone as per their need. Life has become fun because of AR. Electronics have become smart and more information can be gathered to the new inventions. Users can interact with real world in real-time. Time utility is also a main concern. Freehand gesture is comfortable to customers, their electricity is indeed saved. College students are showing a huge interest in this.

However, it is expensive to build an app as well, as it is high maintenance and the devices are costly. For the younger generations it is also addictive, it can make one unwell when used obsessively. Illnesses like headache, eye problems, obesity, and backache are more common side effects. AR is also a drawbacks in the case of cybercrime. People can misuse your details or can use your bank details for transaction. Hackers can have access to your camera, gallery, privacy, etc., which is not safe. That is why it requires some learning to use AR. AR, despite everything, has a few difficulties to confront. For example, individuals who might not have any desire to depend on their cell phones often have little screens on which to superimpose data. Consequently, wearable gadgets like expanded reality fit contact focal points and glasses will furnish clients with progressively advantageous, extensive perspectives on their general surroundings. Screen land will never again be an issue. Sooner rather than later, you might have the option to play a continuous technique game on your PC, or you can welcome a companion over, put on your AR glasses, and play on the tabletop before you. This can also lead to loss of the sense of distinguishing between the real world and virtual world.

2.3.3   RESEARCH OBJECTIVE

The previous studies provide us with information that state having this future reality is very beneficial. In every field it has come to be profitable. Shopping online has been lot easier. When e-commerce came, customers did not like buying online because the products from certain producers were sometimes not exactly what was ordered. Unethical online sellers created trust issues, but now technology has been advancing, customers are more reassured. A virtual fitting room enables a person to try on clothes online and new technology has changed the Internet of Things. AR has enabled one to see stores' clothes on you while at home, on your smartphone. There is no worry of size, color, fitting, length; all the necessary details are provided like type of cloth, material, etc. Moreover, every item is available.

Now when there is a global pandemic going on (i.e., COVID-19), everyone is following lockdown and has made themselves quarantine. Until we receive our coronavirus vaccines, we will not be able to go out like we used to do. Everyone will be scared to shop at crowded places. Nowadays, everyone is only buying online. From taking classes online, working from home, to shopping, everything is done through the internet. Offline retailers and shop owners will need to make their business online compatible. With e-commerce, they make themselves accessible to all.

2.3.4   CONCEPTUAL MODELS

Human traits as depicted in Figure 2.3, that indicate adoption of AR for online purchase:

* Personality: Customers who value seeing the object rather than other factors will be easily attracted toward AR.
* Innovative viewers: People who like innovation have become influenced by it and are thought to be influenced by new technologies.
* Technology expert: Well-informed about technology, computer enthusiasts are most likely to adopt AR.
* Shopaholics: People who are addicted to shopping are more likely to pursue new potential purchases through AR.
* Age factor: Younger people prefer development and are most likely to be drawn toward AR.
* Satisfaction from certain facilities: Product/service facilities are an important factor as it describes satisfaction from customers.

2.3.4.1   Virtual Fitting Room (VFR) Application

This application as shown in Figure 2.4 is now available to stores and homeworkers via our smart gadgets. VFR needs a perfect body fit which is necessary for customers to see how an outfit will look on them. Information like gender, height, weight, and other will help clothes be a more accurate fit. Another alternative system is that in which a 3D avatar is shown with outfit/accoutrements on them, which tries to show how the product will look. The application is made so that it can be easily run though

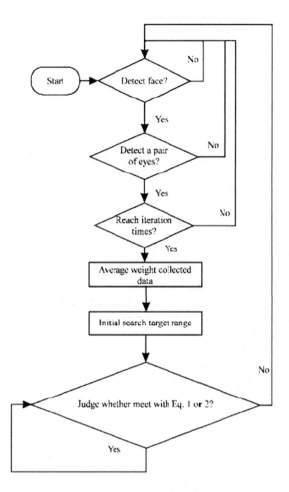

FIGURE 2.3   Process of face detection and tracking algorithm.

FIGURE 2.4   Virtual fitting room examples. (https://orltechblog.wordpress.com/2011/02/01/virtual-dressing-room-a-new-way-to-shop-online/)

smartphones. The main factor with AR is that it has increased the sale opportunities and these applications are helpful for humans.

2.4 CONCLUSION

AR and relation with e-commerce has increased the demand of production. Gadget lovers as well as every other human who has used AR interactive technology have liked the advancement in today's life. AR has made shopping and many more internet market attractive and creative. It's much easier to shop online than it was before. Many customers prefer to purchase online and have products delivered to their home. All the data related to things one wants to buy is available and there are a lot of websites to go through and make choices with. AR is an involved process that improves visualization. Growth in smartphone usage has increased rapidly. Humans cannot spend their time or work without help from their cellphone. This computer-based technology is used by everyone nowadays, most people are dependent on e-commerce. To make it effortlessly simple, customers should be given detailed information of how to use AR and VR to their best advantage. During times such as pandemics and when individuals have to maintain social distancing and quarantine themselves, online business, online shopping, working from home. and students having their classes online is the only way to maintain everyday functionality. There will be purchasing of goods online. AR is advantageous as it satisfies customers' needs and will be pivotal to our future, making online shopping an even safer and reliable option during challenging situations like COVID-19.

REFERENCES

1. Chakraborty, S., & Gupta, D. (2017, May). A study of the factors impacting the adoption of augmented reality in online purchases in India. In *2017 2nd IEEE International Conference on Recent Trends in Electronics, Information & Communication Technology (RTEICT)* (pp. 1526–1529). IEEE.
2. Wang, C. H., Chiang, Y. C., & Wang, M. J. (2015). Evaluation of an augmented reality embedded on-line shopping system. *Procedia Manufacturing* 3: 5624–5630.
3. Huynh, B., Ibrahim, A., Chang, Y. S., Höllerer, T., & O'Donovan, J. (2018). A study of situated product recommendations in augmented reality. In *2018 IEEE International Conference on Artificial Intelligence and Virtual Reality (AIVR)* (pp. 35–43). doi:10.1109/AIVR.2018.00013.
4. Pantano, E., & Servidio, R. (2012). Modeling innovative points of sales through virtual and immersive technologies. *Journal of Retailing and Consumer Services* 19(3): 279–286.
5. Sirakaya, M., & Sirakaya, D. A. (2018). Trends in educational AR studies: A systematic review. *Malaysian Online Journal of Educational Technology* 6(2): 60–74.
6. Akçayır, M., & Akçayır, G. (2017). Advantages and challenges associated with AR for education: A systematic review of the literature. *Educational Research Review* 20: 1–11.
7. Budiman, R. D. A. (2016). Developing learning media based on AR (AR) to improve learning motivation. *Journal of Education* 1(2): 89–94.
8. Solak, E., & Cakir, R. (2015). Exploring the effect of materials designed with AR on language learners' vocabulary learning. *The Journal of Educators Online* 12(2): 50–72.

9. Wei, X., Weng, D., Liu, Y., & Wang, Y. (2015). Teaching based on AR for a technical creative design course. *Computers and Education* 81: 221–234.
10. Kim, J., & Forsythe, S. (2008). Adoption of virtual try-on technology for online apparel shopping. *Journal of Interactive Marketing* 22(2): 45–59.
11. MacIntyre, B., Bolter, J. D., Moreno, E., & Hannigan, B. (2001). Augmented reality as a new media experience. In *Augmented Reality, Proceedings. IEEE and ACM International Symposium on* (pp. 197–206). IEEE.
12. Lu, Y., & Shana, S. (2007). Augmented reality e-commerce assistant system: Trying while shopping. In *Human-Computer Interaction. Interaction Platforms and Techniques* (pp. 643–652). Springer, Berlin/Heidelberg.
13. Papagiannidis, S., Papagiannidis, S., Pantano, E., Pantano, E., See-To, E.W., & Bourlakis, M. (2017). To immerse or not? Experimenting with two virtual retail environments. *Information Technology & People* 30(1): 163–188.
14. Pachoulakis, I., & Kapetanakis, K. (2012). Augmented reality platforms for virtual fittingrooms. *The International Journal of Multimedia & Its Applications* 4(4): 35–46. doi:10.5121/ijma.2012.4404P.
15. Zhang, J., & Tsai, W. S. (2017). What promotes online group-buying? A cross-cultural-comparison study between China and the United States. *Journal of Promotion Management* 23(5): 748–768. doi:10.1080/10496491.2017.1297986.
16. Zhang, T., Wang, W. Y. C., Cao, L., & Wang, Y. (2019). The role of virtual try-on technology in online purchase decision from consumers'aspect. *Internet Research* 29(3): 529–551. doi:10.1108/IntR-12-2017-0540.
17. Adhikari, A., Zheng, V. W., Cao, H., Lin, M., Fang, Y., & Chang, K. C.-C. (2015). IntelligShop: Enabling intelligent shopping in malls through location-based augmented reality. In *2015 IEEE International Conference on Data Mining Workshop*, 14–17 November 2015, Atlantic City: Proceedings (pp. 1604–1607). Research Collection School of Computing and Information Systems.
18. Ping, J., Liu, Y., & Weng, D. (2019, March). Comparison in depth perception between virtual reality and augmented reality systems. In *2019 IEEE Conference on Virtual Reality and 3D User Interfaces (VR)* (pp. 1124–1125). IEEE.

3 Internet of Things (IoT)
Their Ethics and Privacy Concerns

V. Lakshmi Narasimhan and Zablon A. Mbero

CONTENTS

DOI: 10.1201/9781003048862-3

3.1 INTRODUCTION

Internet of Things (IoTs) or Internet of Everything (IoE) refers to a network of sensors and actors (actuators) in devices that act individually or cooperatively to affect the way we live – most often for the benefit of the humanity, but not always. Indeed, they do impact our social life, education, health, and our awareness as human beings. For example, wearable and implantable sensor devices can monitor many important physiological events (i.e., parameters) in human beings (and their in-built IoTs) and notify patients, caregivers, and decision-makers. Sometimes this information is collected with or without the knowledge or express permission of the patients. The amount of data collected from individuals can lead to clues on how a society may behave under some circumstances and these can lead to unanticipated consequences brought about by IoTs. Considerable research has been carried out on IoTs which covers such areas as health and business, but the research on the social impacts and the corresponding security aspects of IoTs are few and far between.

This chapter addresses issues relating to ethics and privacy concerns resulting from the deployment and use of IoTs in various situations – with or without the knowledge of individuals and organizations. In healthcare, for example, IoT technologies are used to promote numerous personal health and wellness activities and to monitor the health of elderly citizens. In precision agriculture, IoTs are used to signal early alerts on moisture level and hence help in precision harvesting to maximize crop output. IoTs can also be used in cities or urban environments to provide convenience and safety. This includes criminal tracking, traffic safety, helping drivers to locate parking spaces in advance and smart shopping – all these have impacts on our day-to-day behavior in life. While all these have positive benefits, a significant amount of ethical and privacy concerns are associated with their usage. This chapter essentially argues for concern and caution on the use of IoTs. The rest of the chapter is organized as follows: Section 3.2 highlights the research methods used to draw statement and conclusions, Section 3.3 offers a review of the recent literature on IoT, while Section 3.4 provides the broad definitions for ethics and privacy, which is followed by Section 3.5, which illustrates how the use of IoTs impacts individuals. Section 3.6 details the impacts of IoTs on society and is followed by Section 3.7, which details the issues concerning the ethical aspects and privacy concerns of IoTs on individuals and society. The conclusion summarizes the chapter and offers pointers for further research in this area.

3.2 METHODOLOGY

A systematic process of searching the literature was carried out in order to obtain related research papers. A search on digital libraries such as IEEE Xplore, Google scholar, ACM DL, IEEE, and others was carried out. The search included queries such as "Ethics and Privacy concerns," "IoT in Precision Agriculture," "Ethics of IoT," "Internet of Things." These queries combined with Boolean logical operators "OR," "AND" were used in the search. We selected the related work, out of the many results, that dealt with; privacy concerns, scope, and future of internet, IoT systems, IoT use cases and other IoT-related technologies and applications.

3.3 INTERNET OF THINGS (IoT)

It is estimated that by the year 2020, around 50 billion devices will be connected to the internet [1–4]; such devices would include all home appliances (e.g., washing machine, dryer, oven, toaster, etc.), home monitoring systems, and people monitoring systems. Moving equipment such as cars will be fully controlled by IoT-based sensors that would automatically communicate with other friendly devices. An interesting aspect is the IoT-based control of personal health monitoring systems, along with sensors and gadgets that monitor an individual's health and well-being. Their signals, data, and information thereof would be transported over the internet/cloud. IoTs find themselves in factory automation, especially in vibration monitoring, as this helps to reduce equipment failures and costs of installation. IoTs are employed in many cities to enhance user conveniences and safety. Convenience in the sense that IoTs allow drivers to locate and park in designated parking spots, while safety in the sense that IoTs help law enforcement officers to track criminals in the cities – e.g., IoTs with GPS installed allow cars to be tracked very easily and in a proactive manner. IoTs are used in hospitals to monitor patients in intensive care units (ICUs) and alert doctors and nurses in case of any emergency. They are also connected to hospital systems and the integration makes hospitals become more efficient, thereby saving more lives at reduced costs. IoTs are now being used in telemedicine, e.g., IoTs are used for remote diagnostics and treatment of patients via virtual physicians.

Considerable research has been carried out on the design of IoT systems for projects such as smart cities, smart transport, smart health, smart shopping, smart homes, and smart hospitals, just to mention a few, but few efforts have been discussed in depth on the ethics and privacy impacts on human beings, and by extension, to the society they live in.

Smart City: Mitchel et al. [5] have summarized how IoTs in the form of IoE can connect people, processes, data, and things to improve the "livability" of cities and communities by bringing more "value" to "livable" connected cities, but little effort has been directed toward the ethics and privacy issues of individuals within those communities and cities. Zanella et al. [6], for example, dwell only on the framework design of a smart city with IoTs.

Smart Homes: Gould [7] describes the architecture and the growth of smart homes in Western Europe in the years up to 2022, while Greg Lindsay et al. [8] conclude that there are smart homes and not-so-smart ideas due to consumers' concern about hacking and other interference. Sangle et al. [9] also fall short of mentioning the ethical and privacy concerns of IoTs on individuals. Narasimhan [10] describes IoT-enabled smart homes and buildings in which IoTs are widely used in every aspect, and constantly monitor various conditions of rooms on an ongoing basis and make appropriate amendments.

Smart Hospitals: Lei Yu et al. [11] proposed architecture and a scheme for a smart hospital based on IoTs but make no mention of ethical and privacy issues. Hrishikesh et al. [12] dwelt on the use of IoT technology in hospitals, and Thangaraj et al. [13] concentrated on real-world scenarios of smart hospital management with IoT. Many other articles sourced from the literature deal with a number of projects but provided little information on the ethical and privacy issues of IoT.

3.4   DEFINITION OF ETHICS AND PRIVACY

3.4.1   DEFINITION OF ETHICAL ISSUES

Ethics is considered a relative issue in that different cultures view ethics from the historical view of development of their kind. Snell [14] defines ethics as "the study of moral law," while Mason [15] defines ethical issues as, *"PAPA-Privacy, Accuracy, Property and Accessibility"* and, Eysenbach et al. [16] describe ethical issues as, *"research ethics particularly concerning informed consent and privacy of research subjects, as borders between public and private spaces are sometimes blurred."* The Webster's Collegiate Dictionary [17] defines ethical issues as, *"the discipline dealing with what is good and bad with moral duty and obligation."* In this chapter, we will consider all of these aspects into consideration when dealing with IoTs or IoT-based systems.

3.4.2   DEFINITION OF PRIVACY CONCERNS

Privacy is considered a personal issue in that different people – from the same culture – view privacy concerns from their personal point of view. An old adage goes, "All human beings have things to hide and every human being makes judgments every day!". The Webster's Collegiate Dictionary [18] defines privacy as *"freedom from unauthorized intrusion and one's right to privacy."* La Quadrature du Net [19] defines privacy concerns as, *"an enabler for other fundamental rights, such as the freedom of expression and to form and join associations,"* and goes further to state that *"some powerful entities have now an interest in weakening the protection of this fundamental right to increase the surveillance of citizens and draw a profit by collecting, processing, storing and trading it."* However, Privacy International [20] describes privacy concerns as, *"no one shall be subjected to arbitrary interference with his privacy, family, home, or correspondence."* In this chapter, we will take all of these aspects into consideration when dealing with IoTs or IoT-based systems.

It is noted that IoTs have applicability to a wide spectrum of areas and, as a consequence, have a profound impact on equipment, people, and the society at large. Next we describe several issues in this context on the use of IoT-based systems in relation to their usage by individuals.

3.5   IMPACT OF IoTs ON INDIVIDUALS

3.5.1   MONITORING INDIVIDUALS

IoT devices/sensors can reveal the exact location of individuals – the smartphone is a classic example. According to Statista [21], India's smartphone users were estimated to be 760 million in 2021 and expected to exceed 3.8 billion in 2021 [22]. Wikipedia, China recorded the highest number of users at 851.2 million in 2019. The work reported in [23] describes smartphones with embedded sensors that can track, locate, and monitor vital signs. While it may not be illegal to deploy a reader, monitoring individuals without their permission and consent, does however lead to severe loss of privacy. Thus, for example: Mary has an IoT-enabled smartphone that she uses to record, track, and monitor her vital signs for her well-being. Any intruder gaining access to Mary's smartphone can alter and use the data for ulterior motives, thereby rendering Mary at risk.

3.5.2   MONITORING INDIVIDUAL'S VEHICLE USAGE

Built-in GPSs and mobile phones placed in cars record speed and direction without informing the drivers –often such functionalities are never turned off. For larger vehicles, IoTs can even be embedded in engines, so that they can inform the manufacturer about the state of the engine on an ongoing basis. For example, the Malaysian Airlines MH370 plane that vanished was said to have made its last communication from one of the engines. The engine sent periodic signals to the manufacturer, General Electric in this case, but the engine did not communicate to the crew. Other devices such as cooling systems and engines do communicate with each other. Furthermore, the IEEE Vehicle Data Communications Standards [24, 25] have called for vehicle-to-vehicle communication. The embedded IoTs inside cars can now be connected to the internet and the cloud, thereby exposing an individual's movement and location thereof, but pose a risk of privacy loss in its monitoring of an individual's movements.

3.5.3   Monitoring the Company an Individual Keeps

IoTs can be networked quite readily and once networked, their performance can be optimized through a variety of data and information interchange mechanisms. Furthermore, IoTs are designed to form automatic clusters based on various preferential parameters. The gleaning of preferential parameters exposes an "individual's company" they prefer to keep. As the old adage goes "you know a person by the company they keep"; one can glean information about a group of people based on their ability to form preferential clusters, interest groups, or birds-of=-the-same-feather networks. The loss of privacy of one's personal preferences is to be critically curtailed in such a case.

3.5.4   Monitoring User Finances and Business Interests (or Nature of Work)

IoT data can reveal a lot about the navigation pattern and hence can potentially reveal one's personal finances and business interests. It is also possible to fathom the nature of work an individual performs, thereby compromising their livelihood, profitability, and well-being – this is an antithesis in point in the case of a smart home.

3.6   MONITORING USER PREFERENCE FOR TECHNOLOGIES

It is possible to deduce the technologies one prefers to use through various innocuous IoT devices. Just as Microsoft and Google gather users' software applications and other details, IoTs can potentially gather such information on a periodic basis, which can then be sold or used to take advantage for business purposes. Furthermore, several apps offer free services through push technologies so that the users' datasets can be tied to the given technology. Getting the user datasets from the given technology so that they can be ported to another platform can be rather difficult – i.e., IoTs can facilitate dataset being tied down to a particular technology, thereby also impeding portability and interoperability.

3.7   MONITORING USER'S STATE-OF-HEALTH AND WELL-BEING

Biomedical engineering permits various electromechanical devices to be embedded inside the human body. Such devices include cardiac pacemakers (Figure 3.1), cochlear implants, brain implants (to manage diseases such as Parkinson's disease, epilepsy, etc.) and various body-part replacement devices. There are close to 3 million people in the world and almost 600,000 pacemakers implanted in people every year [26]. Such embedded devices will have IoTs contained in them – for example, the latest Siemens' heart pacemaker, viz., Siemens Elema Variopacer, and Vitatron Threshold Analyzer (Fundamentals of Cardiac pacing) [27] have a built-in wireless modem and a GPS through which a person's need for an ambulance can be inferred, based on their current heart conditions. Accordingly, the wireless modem can dial up the closest available ambulance to inform the location of the person prior to the occurrence of any heart event. While such IoT-based technology is wonderful for the

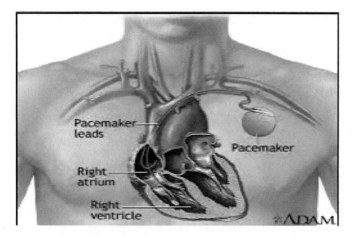

FIGURE 3.1 Pacemaker (image adapted from MobiHealthNews).

health and well-being of an individual and society, it can also expose their personal and private details also.

3.8 MONITORING USER'S PERSONAL BEHAVIOR IN AN OPEN ENVIRONMENT AND THEIR SECURITY

The behavior of a person in private – i.e., whether in an open or closed environment – may be exposed by IoT devices by a series of triangulation processes. This has implications for an individual's security. As noted in FTC Staff report [23], this includes smartphones that have sensors and GPS which can record, track, and locate an individual in any place. For example, John has such a smartphone, he leaves his place of work and joins friends in a pub instead of going straight home. His spouse can use a smartphone to locate and track John's location, drives there, and can cause commotion.

3.9 MONITORING THE SOCIETY A USER IS IN

The use of IoTs in certain communities or groups of people expose their preferential traits about certain practices, procedures, and habits. While businesses can potentially take advantage of such information in terms of advertisement and marketing, this can lead to "setting the minds of the society" that an individual might belong to, thereby raising several ethical questions.[1]

3.10 MONITORING A USER'S VISIT PATTERNS TO OFFICES AND PLACES

IoTs worn by people and/or placed in various places can potentially expose a user's presence to systems that monitor them. For example, these systems can automatically monitor – without informing the individual – about the places and offices a user visits, and the number visits as well. While this is good for surveillance in the case of national security, it raises privacy concerns. One may notice several cameras on highways and at many other public and private places too.

3.11 IMPACT OF IoTs ON SOCIETY

IoTs are being applied to a number of areas that have societal implications, as discussed next.

3.11.1 MONITORING PRODUCTION OF VARIOUS AGRICULTURAL CROPS AND THEIR PRICES

With the advent of IoTs, agriculture is becoming "precision agriculture," i.e., agricultural field's critical datasets (e.g., humidity, pH, levels of various elements like phosphorus and potassium) can be measured very accurately in real-time, transmitted, and processed. With in-plant IoTs, one can detect plant growth and thereby predict the yield from a given plant and its neighborhood. Through a series of statistical calculations, one can predict yield per acre for a given agricultural area (or village). This leads to prediction of yields and price per ton of the yields.

Furthermore, IoTs are very much employed during transportation of various agricultural goods in order to maintain humidity and temperature. These IoTs can actually be networked and can potentially provide information on the arrival of products at a given marketplace, thereby leading to market price settings and predictions ahead of time. For example, in the state of Kerala (India), the Cochin Fish Market sells the catch (fish) before it reaches the shore through a confluence of technologies such as IoTs, internet, and e-commerce. Indeed, the Cochin Fish Market is currently "silent and smell free," as opposed to a typical fish market "noisy and smelly."

3.11.2 MONITORING AVAILABILITY OF BEDS AND DOCTORS

Carefully embedded IoTs can report on the availability of beds in a hospital (typically in a non-ICU environment in the case of a smart hospital). This information could be useful for providing better services and reduce patient-wait times in a hospital. However, the availability of such information in public domain may lead to information leakage issues at critical times (e.g., in case of emergencies, such as major disasters of national significance), when such information can be misused (e.g., denial of service attack). Similarly, carefully embedded IoTs can report on the availability of parking spaces in a business environment, thereby saving fuel and time spent on locating parking spaces.

3.11.3 MONITORING THE BUYING PATTERNS OF USERS

Similar to commercial commodities, military equipment (e.g., ships, planes, and automobiles) are typically embedded with IoTs. This may cause potential problems in terms of their detectability. Furthermore, such entities (e.g., various equipment) move in patterns called ORBATs (order of battalions), which are closely guarded defense secrets of individual countries. However, IoT-enabled equipment will lead to exposure and exploitability of such ORBATS, e.g., presence of military equipment and detection of their capabilities, their grouping and usage patterns.

3.11.4 MONITORING USERS' PREFERENCES AND SOCIETAL PATTERNS

Since most commercial items in supermarkets are automatically tagged with radio-frequency identification tags (RFIDs) or equivalent technologies, their picking and purchasing patterns can be monitored (thru' IoT-based device clustering and their nature of clustering). The purchase patterns and behaviors of groups of people can also be therefore monitored. This would result in appropriate placement of relevant items at the correct shelves and at the appropriate gender-specific and age-specific heights. While such sales tactics help the vendor, these potentially expose a society's weaknesses in brazen manner.

3.11.5 MONITORING MASS MOVEMENT OF ENTITIES (E.G., DISEASES, VEHICLES, AND PEOPLE)

Embedded IoT devices in various entities (inside luggage, human beings, and almost any object one can think of) may be used to monitor diseases and this could be useful for taking preventive measures. For example, in the case of severe acute respiratory syndrome, or SARS (also known as H1N1), this virus spreads through air. The airflow pattern employed for weather modeling and predictions (for which several IoT-based air balloons are typically deployed) could well be used to monitoring of infected areas automatically in order to control the spread of the virus. This can potentially be misused if not controlled properly through appropriate legislative framework.

3.11.6 MONITORING AND MANAGING THE SECURITY AND WELL-BEING OF SOCIETY

It is now mandatory for all commercial and public entities (buses, trains, planes, and ships) to declare their travel plans and cargo ahead of time. Further, IoT-based technologies are available to verify whether a container has been opened or not during shipment. The availability of such information is helpful in monitoring and managing the security of the society – e.g., traffic analysis, train, plane, and ship data analytics. However, such large-scale monitoring would also intrude into the privacy of the society at large.

3.11.7 MONITORING SECURITY PROFILES OF ORGANIZATIONS, SYSTEMS, AND NATIONS

The presence of IoT in animate and inanimate objects can point out security holes in an organization's systems (or inside a nation). The state of the alertness of such objects can now be analyzed and upgraded when need be. For example, Stuxnet is a computer worm designed to infect industrial plants by changing the codes in their control [29]. Stuxnet infected Iran's nuclear plant centrifuges, making them unusable. Struxnet has the capacity to hijack targeted computers or systems and stealing information from them.

3.11.8 MONITORING BUSINESS PRACTICES AND BUSINESS PATTERNS

Once again, due to the presence of IoTs in many systems and subsystems, the status of an inventory can be monitored accurately. This results in better inventory control, staffing needs, and productivity management; however, if not carefully controlled, a competitor can also monitor the same and use such information to their advantage.

3.11.9 MONITORING COMPANY TRADE SECRETS

IoTs can expose the trade secrets of a company if they are not properly protected, leading to a company's security holes (vulnerabilities). Protecting such trade secrets would become part of future IoT development and this could happen through appropriate encryption mechanisms such as Bitcoin [30].

3.12 ETHICAL ASPECTS AND PRIVACY CONCERNS OF IoTs ON INDIVIDUALS AND SOCIETY

While IoTs will be able to enhance the quality of service of both individuals and society, there are profound concerns on their usage, which include the following.

3.12.1 PROGRAMMABILITY OF SOFTWARE OF IoTs

With embedded IoTs in self-driving cars, typically a set of the algorithms will control the car and make it to obey the laws of the country in which they are driven. However, coding such laws for motoring can be difficult – for example, what might happen in case of an unanticipated accident, where an oncoming Lorry/truck driving on the wrong side of the road and this self-driving car is on the same road or lane? There is likely to be a collision. Software might have been written that in such a case the car is forced to swerve right (or left) to avoid the collision. However, what happens when one encounters a small child seated on the left (or right) side, and one would have preferred a sideways knock? As these algorithms are controlled by predetermined assumptions, it would be difficult to instruct an automated system to extend the software on-the-fly in order to make a choice as per one's underlying values.

3.12.2 EMBEDDED ALGORITHMS IN IoTs

Standard algorithms, rules of law and the like can be encoded into IoT-based systems. However, embedding culturally sensitive rules, styles and regulations can be rather difficult. For example, what will happen to two IoT-based system, when they 'meet' at a common place? Specifically, the underlying query is: how can an algorithm adapt to different cultures all over the world?

3.12.3   Use of IoT Embedded Household Appliances

With the advent of IoT embedded fridges or microwaves, one can easily analyze what and when an individual might want to eat a certain type of food at a particular time. There might also be the case where the pre-programmed IoT device might give another type of food to the user, which s/he may not like. Further, such devices (i.e., fridges) might be infected with malicious codes that may increase or raise the temperature, thus spoiling the available food in the fridge.

3.12.4   Monitoring Medical Conditions

Medical conditions can be monitored in real-time through IoT-based devices, as explained next:

1. Parkinson's disease is a type of movement disorder where nerve cells in the brain do not produce enough brain chemical called dopamine. One method of treatment for Parkinson's is through DPS (deep brain stimulation) [31], wherein an IoT-enabled implant delivers stimulation to specific areas in the brain that control movement and blocking abnormal nerve signals that cause the underlying symptoms. When this IoT-enabled implant is infected by an intruder or a virus, it might send more stimulation or no stimulation at all hence putting the patient in danger.
2. Arrhythmias concerns the rhythm of the heartbeat. A pacemaker is an IoT-enabled device placed in the chest or abdomen of a human being to help control arrhythmias.

It uses low-energy electrical pulses to prompt the heart to beat at a normal rate. However, research at MIT [32] has shown that a pacemaker can be hacked to give out pulses which are not required, potentially leading to bad consequences for the patient.

3.13   ACTIVE PROSTHETICS

Active prosthetics are available to replace a variety of body parts (e.g., [33, 34]). These IoT-enabled parts are being currently used in a small scale. However, when an intruder manipulates these parts, it can lead to dangerous consequences.

3.13.1   Inequality of Access to Data of Value

IoT-based devices can potentially be misused to offer unequal data services to individuals or societies. For example, IoTs can be used for surveillance, thus curtailing or undermining employees' freedom and privacy. This effect, called the Panopticon impact,[2] is to be avoided at all cost in the IoT environment. While in a physical building, such Panopticon impact can be observed. But in the digital world of IoT, Panopticons are difficult to detect.

3.13.2   PUBLIC ATTITUDES, OPINIONS, AND BEHAVIOR

A number of devices are available that are in common use and deploy the innocuous IoTs inside them. They can monitor attitudes, opinions, and behaviors of individuals and groups of people. Such devices – e.g., transport monitoring cameras kept over many toll booths – can notify about group behaviors such as the happening of an event, an occasion of significance, etc. They are indeed useful for crowd monitoring, but would they also help criminals if they could be tampered with?

3.13.3   MONITORING WORKPLACE

With the advent of smart offices with IoTs, organizations can reap considerable benefits as work can be done as per the organization's policies and guidelines anywhere and anytime. Such profound monitoring can be misused to observe junior workers [35], as opposed to supporting the main functions of an organization. For instance, the use of RFID cards by employees for accessing workplace may be misused to monitor employees and, according to the National Parkinson's Foundation [31], most organizations do not have proper policies on use of data generated by IoT-enabled RFID systems.

3.13.4   EXPLOITING CONSUMPTION DATA BY INDIVIDUALS AND NEIGHBORHOODS

A lot of data can be generated by IoT-enabled devices; for example, in a smart city (or such complex systems) which is designed in a manner to identify where one lives, when someone is eating, watching TV, going for a date, use their car, etc. These IoT-enabled sensors have data or leave traces of data that may hurt individuals' and society's privacy.

3.14   FUTURE SCOPE

The future of IoTs is well represented in the way it collaborates with other technologies, e.g., cloud computing (Figure 3.2), and Big Data analytics. The former allows large data packages generated by the IoT to travel through the internet, while IoT-generated Big Data can be used for large-scale analytics in order to predict future outcomes.

Automotive is now enhanced, thanks to IoT-enabled/embedded safety control systems. Seamless integration of IoTs enables (relatively) easy integration of future technologies making life affordable and enjoyable (e.g., AI incorporated in IoT). IoT's contribution to economic growth (e.g., the manufacturing sector) has immensely contributed to the ease with which manufacturing sector have been producing quality products. All these should not be at the expense of taking care of

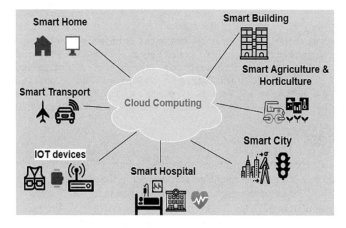

FIGURE 3.2   Cloud computing and Internet of Things.

ethical issues, however, all of them have to consider the balance of ethics and (helping) the humanity.

3.15   CONCLUSIONS ON THE PANOPTICON IMPACTS OF IoT

The IoT is the future of information and communication technology (ICT), in that very soon almost all devices, plants, animals and even humans will be tagged and "connected over the internet" whether they want or not such connectivity. Users may employ such technologies in ways other than their original intentions and data and information gathered by embedded IoTs can be used for surveillance, thus curtailing or undermining employee's freedom and privacy. It is critical that the Panopticon impact of IoT-based systems must be avoided at all cost, particularly in the digital world, where detection of surveillance is difficult. Laws must therefore be developed to ensure public freedom as guaranteed by a country's constitution.

In this chapter, we presented the impact of IoTs on individuals and society, specifically their underlying privacy issues and security concerns. An extensive review of the literature on IoTs systems, along with projects like smart city, smart home, smart hospitals are presented along with their underlying issues on ethics and privacy on individuals and society. Safety issues of IoTs depend on the technologies, protocols, security, privacy, and even ethics, if any, implemented by the manufacturers. Further, IoT use depends on the individuals and society that benefit and that their privacy should be somehow integrated into IoT-based systems by the manufacturer – as a matter of principle. These privacy-friendly procedures will help minimize problems and enhance ethical usage of such these systems. Furthermore, researchers should pay attention to appropriate legal and regulatory frameworks surrounding the privacy of use of such devices and work together with manufacturers to avoid escalating costs for innovation of new IoT-based systems. Several so-called voluntary standards for IoT security have also been proposed (see [36] for example), but none have been ratified so far by the technical community.

NOTES

1 In this context, the decision to impose a huge fine on Google Inc. by the EU Court is important to note [28]. Goggle is currently modifying its search engine software as a consequence.
2 The Panopticon is a type of institutional building designed by the English philosopher and social theorist Jeremy Benthamin the late 18th century. The concept of the design is to allow all (pan-) inmates of an institution to be observed (-opticon) by a single watchman without the inmates being able to tell whether or not they are being watched (see: https://en.wikipedia.org/wiki/Panopticon).

REFERENCES

1. "CISCO: Over 50 billion devices connected to Internet," http://blogs.cisco.com/news/the-internet-of-things-infographic/ (accessed September 2020).
2. "AutoBot," http://mavizontech.com/MeetMavia.htm (accessed September 2020).
3. "Internet of Things," https://en.wikipedia.org/wiki/Internet_of_Things.
4. D. Evans, "The Internet of Things – How the next evolution of the Internet is changing everything," *Cisco Whitepaper* (2011) (accessed September 2020).
5. "The Internet of Everything for Cities," https://www.cisco.com/c/dam/en_us/solutions/industries/docs/gov/everything-for-cities.pdf (accessed September 2020).
6. A. Zanella, et al., "Internet of Things for smart cities," *IEEE Internet of Things Journal*, Vol. 1, No. 1 (February 2014), pp. 1–4.
7. A. Gould, "Internet of Things for the smart home," *CIR Smart Homes & Cleanpower* (2013), http://www.hvm-uk.com (accessed September 2020).
8. G. Lindsay, et al., "Smart homes and the Internet of Things," *Brent ScowCroft Center on International Security*, March 2016.
9. N. Sangle, et al., "Smart home system based on IoT," *IJETAE*, Vol. 6, No. 9 (September 2016), www.ijetae.com
10. V. Lakshmi Narasimhan, "iSHAB: IoT-enabled smart homes and buildings," in *10th Intl. Advanced Computing Conf (IACC)*, 5–6 December 2020, To appear in Springer CCIS Series, 2021.
11. L. Yu, Y. Lu, and X. Zhu, "Smart hospital based Internet of Things," *Journal of Networks*, Vol. 7, No. 10 (October 2012), pp. 1–8.
12. Hrishikesh, et al., "Smart hospitals using Internet of Things (IoT)," *International Journal of Scientific & Engineering Research*, Vol. 8, No. 5 (May 2017), pp. 1–4.
13. M. Thangaraj, et al., "Internet of Things (IoT) enabled smart autonomous hospital management system – A real world health care use case with the technology drivers," in *2015 IEEE International Conference on Computational Intelligence and Computing Research*, pp. 1–8.
14. G. D. Snell, *Search for a rational ethic*, Springer-Verlag, New York Inc, 1988, pp. 221–222.
15. R. O. Mason, "Four ethical issues of the information age," *MIS Quarterly*, Vol. 10, No. 1 (March 1986), pp. 5–12. JSTOR.
16. G. Eysenbach, et al., "Ethical issues in quantitative research on Internet communications," *Medical Humanities BMJ*, October 2001, https://www.bmj.com/content/323/7321/1103.short (accessed September 2020).
17. "Webster's collegiate dictionary," https://www.merriam-webster.com/dictionary/ethics (accessed October 2020).
18. "Webster's collegiate dictionary," https://www.merriam-webster.com/dictionary/privacy (accessed October 2020).
19. "LA QUADRATURE DU NET Internet and liberties," https://www.laquadrature.net/en/privacy (accessed September 2020).

20. "Privacy International," https://www.privacyinternational.org/ (accessed October 2020).
21. "Number of smartphone users in India in 2010 to 2020, with estimates until 2040," https://www.statista.com/statistics/467163/forecast-of-smartphone-users-in-india/#:~:text=The%20number%20of%20smartphone%20users,3.8%20billion%20users%20in%202021.&text=The%20number%20of%20smartphone%20users%20worldwide%20is%20projected%20to,nearly%202.7%20billion%20by%202019 (accessed February 2021).
22. "List of countries by smartphone penetration," https://en.wikipedia.org/wiki/List_of_countries_by_smartphone_penetration (accessed February 2021).
23. https://www.ftc.gov/news-events/media-resources/protecting-consumer-privacy/privacy-security-enforcement (accessed November 2021).
24. "IEEE 802.11p," https://en.wikipedia.org/wiki/IEEE_802.11p (accessed September 2020).
25. "Performance of vehicle-to-vehicle communication," by IEEEp in Vehicular Ad Hoc Network se.
26. Mark A. Wood and Kenneth A Ellenbogen, "Cardiac pacemakers from the patient's perspective," *Circulation Journal*, Vol. 105, No. 18 (May 2002). https://www.ahajournals.org/doi/full/10.1161/01.cir.0000016183.07898.90#:~:text=There%20are%20about%203%20million,the%20recipient's%20activities%20or%20lifestyle (accessed February 2021).
27. "Fundamentals of cardiac pacing," https://books.google.com/books?isbn=940099334X, pp. 240 (accessed September 2020).
28. "Google appeals against EU's €2.4bn fine over search engine results," https://www.theguardian.com/technology/2017/sep/11/google-appeals-eu-fine-search-engine-results-shopping-service (accessed March 19, 2018).
29. "An unpresented look at Stuxnet, the world's first digital weapon," https://www.wired.com/2014/11/countdown-to-zero-day-stuxnet/ (accessed September 2020).
30. "Financial cryptography and data security," https://books.google.com/books?isbn=3662447746.
31. "National Parkinson's foundation," http://www.parkinson.org/understanding-parkinsons/treatment/surgery-treatment-options/Deep-Brain-Stimulation (accessed September 2020).
32. "MIT News," http://news.mit.edu/2011/protecting-medical-implants-0613 (accessed September 2020).
33. "Bionic Legs, i-Limbs, and Other Super Human Prostheses You'll Envy," https://www.fastcompany.com/1514543/bionic-legs-i-limbs-and-other-super-human-prostheses-youll-envy (accessed October 2020).
34. "Implants and Prosthetics," https://www.fda.gov/MedicalDevices/ProductsandMedicalProcedures/ImplantsandProsthetics/default.htm (accessed October 2020).
35. "9 to 5: Do you know if your boss knows where you are? Case studies," https://books.google.com/books?isbn=0833041126 (accessed September 2020).
36. "Australian DRAFT code of practice securing the Internet of Things for consumers," Australian Cybersecurity Centre, https://www.homeaffairs.gov.au/reports-and-pubs/files/code-of-practice.pdf (accessed September 2020).

4 Artificial Intelligence and Deep Learning are Changing the Healthcare Industry

Gaurav Singh, Anju Mishra, and Archana Singh

CONTENTS

4.1 INTRODUCTION

For some time now, we have seen artificial intelligence (AI) and its branches like deep learning and machine learning slowly penetrate the healthcare/medical industry and reshaping it with the latest technologies. Intelligent software with powerful processing gives computers the ability to read through large amounts of unstructured public health data in much less time and with higher accuracy than regular humans. AI algorithms like artificial neural networks (ANNs) let computers extract certain patterns, perform analysis on the findings, and thus make predictions. These advancements are helping healthcare professionals accurately diagnose diseases, form treatment plans and improve the future health of the patients. These systems are helping to save enormous amounts of time and resources and in doing so are saving a lot of lives [1].

DOI: 10.1201/9781003048862-4

Though these AI systems have shown a lot of potential, the mass extinction of healthcare professionals by them in the foreseeable future remains very much uncertain. But these robust AI systems surely can help in discovering valuable clinical data and patterns buried in the extensive and unorganized healthcare records collected daily around the globe. AI tools can analyze clinical data and implement methods like big data analytics and machine learning to guide and assist human physicians in making clinical decisions. Moreover, AI systems can also help in mitigating the diagnostic and treatment errors that sometimes arise by a physician's misinterpretation [2].

There has been an exponential growth of different forms of AI in the healthcare field [3]. Since the late 1990s, there has been a tectonic shift in the computer industry which has facilitated the growth of AI in healthcare. Powerful and mobile devices with smart algorithms which are interconnected by the internet have led to this phenomenon. Example of these include enhanced gene sequencing, computerized augmentation of medical images, sophisticated life-saving equipment like ventilators, numerous therapeutic treatments, collaborative drug research, procurement of various medicines, and countless others.

4.2   DEEP LEARNING IN HEALTHCARE

If one is studying the impact of AI on the healthcare industry then, deep learning is the place to start. This field of AI is starting to have a transformational effect on the industry. Deep learning-based AI systems, which offer the ability to break down huge unstructured datasets and helps in uncovering critical information, have been revolutionary and are reframing traditional practices.

4.2.1   WHAT IS DEEP LEARNING?

Deep learning is a branch of machine learning that uses a layered algorithmic framework like convolutional neural networks (CNN), recurrent neural networks (RNN), or ANN to examine data and perform analysis. The objective of the field is to emulate the thinking capabilities of the human brain with a machine. This helps the machine in processing data and identifying consistent patterns within unstructured or unlabeled data sets, and the whole process is usually self-taught by the machine and unsupervised by humans. Examples of deep learning at work include automated driving (where cars can learn to detect pedestrians, traffic signs, and other objects), virtual assistants (where devices can perform speech recognition), healthcare (where programs can diagnose and detect diseases), and more [4, 5].

4.2.2   HOW DEEP LEARNING WORKS?

Deep learning models are loosely based on the functioning of a human brain. In fact, the idea behind deep learning is to make computers as smart as humans. A human brain functions by cells, known as neurons, which connect with one another to process information and perform astonishing tasks. Information is shared across different neurons through electrochemical signals, which helps them to learn, form patterns, and make correlations. Similarly, in deep learning models, there are neural networks that essentially try to simulate the functioning of biological neurons. With computer neural networks, data is filtered through multiple layers, and each layer performs analysis on the output from the previous one. The more layers there are, the more complex a task the deep learning model is able to accomplish [6, 7].

Deep learning neural networks typically consist of thousands or sometimes millions of neurons unlike humans, which generally have billions of neurons in their brains. A deep learning model follows two steps technique to learn something: the first is training and second is inferring. There exists an input layer where data is entered, hidden layers where the model learns, corrects, and relearns the assigned data, and output layers where model outputs the new learning. To make a deep learning model learn to distinguish cats, the first step would be to expose the model to a huge dataset of cat images. The model would train itself pixel by pixel and image by image, and try to make patterns by color, size, and frame. The second step for the model would be to infer and make an educated guess on new images that might or might not contain cats [8, 9].

4.2.3 Convolutional Neural Network (CNN)

A convolutional neural network, or *Covnet* for short, is a type of deep learning model which specializes in working with two-dimensional images by applying multiple filters, channels, and layers. It is widely used for image recognition, classifications, and object detections across various fields.

In a 2018 study, it was found that a CNN-based deep learning model outperformed human clinicians in diagnosing melanoma, a skin disease, by nearly 10 percent. Results from various other studies have also shown that a CNN trained with MRI scans and X-rays is able to diagnose a tumor in brain, lung, liver, pancreas, breast, prostate, etc. with more than 97.5 percent accuracy. All these findings have clearly shown that CNN-based deep learning models are exceptionally well suited for assisting human physicians in diagnosing, treating, and preventing various diseases [10, 11].

4.3 THE CASE FOR GLAUCOMA

Glaucoma is a chronic, neurodegenerative ocular condition that can cause permanent vision loss or blindness by damaging the optic nerve. Usually, there are no symptoms and patients become aware of the disease when considerable damage has already been done. There is no cure for glaucoma but if detected early, vision could be protected from further damage by various treatments and surgeries. Glaucoma is caused when the fluid inside the eyes, known as aqueous humor, starts being collected and thus increases the eye pressure. It happens when the channels responsible for the drainage of the fluid get blocked. As the fluid builds up inside the eye, the interocular pressure (IOP) starts rising and this damages the optic nerve. Once optic nerve cells start dying, there is vision loss. As optic nerve cells don't have the ability to regenerate, once a large amount of these optic cells die the patient could become blind.

Early detection of glaucoma is key for protecting the optic nerve and consequently the vision. The most common procedure for detection of glaucoma is tonometry, where a doctor measures the IOP of the eyes with the help of a tonometer during an eye exam. If there is an increase in the IOP, the doctor suggests the patient for a visual fields (VF) test and an optical coherence tomography (OCT). A VF test measures the scope of vision and checks whether the patient has developed any blind spots because of the loss of cells in the optic nerve due to high eye pressure. OCT is a non-invasive imaging test that helps to create a 3D image of the retina with essential information like optic nerve thickness, retinal nerve fiber layer (RNFL) thinning, fundus imaging, and disc size. VF and OCT scan are the two most advanced techniques for the assessment and monitoring of glaucoma.

4.3.1 AI AND GLAUCOMA

It is estimated that about 60.5 million people were diagnosed for glaucoma in 2010 and it is predicted that over 112 million people worldwide would have glaucoma by 2040. As, >50 percent of the cases go undiagnosed [12], it is becoming increasingly important to make diagnosis and detection for glaucoma more accessible. AI together with deep learning has shown great results and the medical community has great optimism for these systems. Today, glaucoma diagnosis is highly dependent upon a trained ophthalmologist, but computer scientists are confident that AI systems would help to carry the load in the near future. Given the growing public pain around the disease, researchers have been able to make AI systems which have given breakthrough results. High-performance computers and advanced algorithms are enabling researchers around the world to develop AI systems that are able to gather information and perform accelerated analytics. Advancement in screening and monitoring of glaucoma with computer-aided tests like VF and OCT scans are assisting doctors as well as glaucoma patients. It is safe to say that AI and deep learning have the potential to play a vital role in the detection as well as management of glaucoma with high accuracy.

More and more studies have shown that AI and deep learning could have a tremendous impact on the ophthalmology field. A study conducted by Muhammad H. in 2017 identified open-angle glaucoma in 63.7–93.1 percent candidates out of 102 with hybrid deep learning model trained with standard OCT and VF metrics, and with only four false positives and three false negatives [13]. In another study, conducted by Asaoka R. and Murata H. in 2019 deep learning model trained only with OCT scans was able to detect early-onset glaucoma [14]. With 4316 OCT images from 1371 eyes, the model was able to diagnose with an accuracy of 93.7 percent.

More recently, an IBM researcher partnered up with New York University (NYU) scientists to conduct research on finding new ways to utilize OCT images with the help of AI for detecting glaucoma [15]. Their deep learning framework, which was trained with raw OCT images, was able to distinguish between eyes of 217 healthy and 432 glaucoma patients. This five-layered deep learning network after normalization just had a 2 percent error rate. Still, in the early stages, models like these show a lot of promise and researchers continue to innovate upon them.

4.3.2 GLAUCOMA MISDIAGNOSIS

Diagnosing glaucoma in the early stages of disease is crucial in preventing vision loss. Due to this, ophthalmologists almost always start glaucoma drops the moment they observe any glaucomatous pattern. However, other disorders such as thyroid eye disease or an orbital tumor can very much mimic glaucoma in VF and OCT scans. Such scenarios are difficult to manage even for experienced ophthalmologists.

When asked, *How often are patients misdiagnosed with glaucoma?*, Steven D. Vold, MD, at Vold Vision in Fayetteville, Arkansas, said: "It happens more frequently than one might presume." Other ophthalmologists also agree and note that "This is not something they see once in a blue moon. It is reasonably common to see patients who are on glaucoma medications and might not need them" [16].

Glaucoma is a highly asymptomatic condition, which makes it even more complex to diagnose. In a paper, Nikhil S. Choudhari presented the cases of six patients with neuro-ophthalmic optic neuropathies, misdiagnosed as glaucoma. They were not only treated for glaucoma with medications for years but also had undergone surgical interventions. In another 2017 study, to analyze the most common neuroophthalmological conditions that may mimic glaucomatous optic neuropathy, 101 eyes of 68 patients were enrolled with neuroophthalmological diseases, out of which 16 (15.8%) were classified as conditions that could mimic glaucoma. Based on the review of fundus images and VF tests, 25% of these were misdiagnosed as glaucoma. The study concluded, in eyes with IOP in the normal range (<21 mmHg), some neuroophthalmological disorders can mimic and be misdiagnosed as glaucoma [17, 18].

These findings indicate considerable high possibilities of misdiagnosis of glaucoma. Thus, it becomes essential to neither over-diagnose nor under-diagnose the cases of glaucoma.

4.4 FUTURE SCOPE

The ever-increasing human population continues to put tremendous pressure on the healthcare sector to provide medical diagnostics, quality treatment, and vital research. Now, more than ever, people are demanding intelligent healthcare services and smart medical devices that can fundamentally improve patient care, increase lifespan, and potentially save lives. AI, which has made considerable progress since it was first established as a field in 1956, is poised to fulfill this need. With technologies like pattern recognition, robotics, and natural language processing (NLP), AI is on its way to overhaul the healthcare sector.

4.4.1 AI FOR DIAGNOSTICS

Diagnosing patients by analyzing medical reports, organ scans, and images is a prime candidate for the application of AI-powered software/hardware in the healthcare field. By increasing both the speed and accuracy of performing diagnostics tasks AI systems could assist healthcare professionals in diagnosing diseases in a much efficient manner and further helps in eliminating the risk of human error.

Specifically, examining medical images like X-rays, MRI scans, OCT scans, etc. is ideal for these AI systems since we already have an abundance of clinical data and images, grouped and ordered together in a normalized form, stored at medical hospitals all over the world. These AI systems, which prosper in analyzing massive collections of data, are well equipped to diagnose a large number of medical issues, from diabetes to glaucoma to cancer.

4.4.2 AI FOR PATIENT MANAGEMENT

Personalized healthcare is one of the overarching goals pushing the advancement of AI systems for the healthcare industry. Virtual assistants and chatbots powered by AI and NLP can perform various tasks at clinics, hospitals, and other medical organizations with less error and far more precision. From booking patient's appointment to taking an accurate medical record, managing insurance, payments as well as assisting the healthcare professional by highlighting vital habitual details of the patient like regular consumption of tobacco or alcohol, particular allergies and other chronic medical conditions of the patient. By this approach, a virtual database of every patient can be generated and managed by these virtual assistants, which then serves the healthcare professional in the diagnosis and treatment planning. This also benefits the patient in future follow-ups and getting much more personalized treatment.

4.4.3 AI FOR DRUG DISCOVERY

The prime objective of drug discovery research is to distinguish drugs or chemical compounds that could have a healthful impact on the body, as such, they can help to treat, prevent, or manage a specific disease. Despite having numerous chemical elements and millions of chemical compounds, there exist only a few unique combinations of molecules that can successfully tackle a target anomaly or pathogen associated with a disease.

It is estimated that over USD2.6-billion is spent on the development of a new drug. This substantial figure looms over researchers looking for new medications. A large sum of that essentially goes down the drain in identifying and developing a few candidates, with the potential of one becoming a promising drug. Since nine out of ten candidates fail somewhere between phase I trials and regulatory approval and less than 10% of drug candidates making it to the market. Hardly anyone in the field questions the need to do things more efficiently [19].

With the possibility of synthesizing millions of compounds and predicting the properties of each possible compound becoming practically impossible for individual researchers. AI and machine learning systems can excel in generating new concepts for novel compounds, review them, and precisely estimate the success rates from existing databases and other biochemical factors. The development of sophisticated algorithms for these AI systems can also assist researchers in extracting hidden insights from existing datasets, and thus saving hundreds of mind-numbing hours in the lab by eliminating the need for repetitive work. AI systems can also be used by drug makers for optimizing their supply chains and streamlining their manufacturing processes, thus lowering the cost of manufacturing.

Building better drugs, in a faster and cheaper manner, thereby making more effective drugs available to patients and saving more lives. Considering this, drug discovery is one of the areas where AI could have its greatest impact in the healthcare field.

4.4.4 AI-BASED ADVANCED APPLICATIONS

As AI progresses further and more research is carried out in both artificial intelligence and the healthcare field. New possibilities of convergence of these two would arise in the future. AI in nascent stages requires a lot of structured data and supervised learning to work well. As AI systems advances and complex models are introduced which begin to function well in an unsupervised learning environment, we will start to see some real game-changing applications like robotics surgeries, genome editing, nanotechnology, etc. which will fundamentally transform the way we live and perceive healthcare.

4.5 CONCLUSION

In this study, we highlight the use of AI and its branch of deep learning in the healthcare industry with the example of glaucoma diagnosis. This study presents AI, deep learning, its working, and CNN. We examine the working of deep learning algorithms and CNN neural networks, which have huge application in the medical field. We brief about glaucoma and carefully presents the potential AI showcases in diagnosing glaucoma with clinical accuracy rate.

AI still in the early years holds a lot of promise as recent advancements have shown. The diagnostic performance of deep learning models for glaucoma indicates the potential AI has to greatly enhance the clinical experience for patients. Although, it is still a number of years away in replacing healthcare professionals, it clearly is suitable for assisting them today. Our research aims to promote the adoption of AI and deep learning in the healthcare industry.

REFERENCES

1. Fei J., Yong J., Hui Z., Hao L., Sufeng M. (2017). Artificial intelligence in healthcare: Past, present and future. Stroke Vasc Neurol 2(4). doi:10.1136/svn-2017-000101.
2. Kun-Hsingh Y., Andrew L., Isaac K. (2018). Artificial intelligence in healthcare. Nat Biomed Eng 2(10):719–731.
3. Thomas D., Ravi K. (2019). The potential for artificial intelligence in healthcare. Future Healthc J 6(2):94–98.
4. Andre E., Alexandre R., Bharath R., Volodymyr K., Sebastian T., Jeff D. (2019). A guide to deep learning in healthcare. Nat Med 25(1):24–29.
5. Yann L., Yshua B., Geoffery H. (2015). Deep learning. Nature 521(7553):436–444.
6. David N. (2018). On the prospects for a (deep) learning health care system. JAMA 320(11):1099–1100.
7. Titus J., Achim H., Jochen S., Dirk S., Carola B., Theresa S., Alexander H., Chrisof V. (2018). Skin cancer classification using convolutional neural networks: Systematic review. J Med Internet Res 20(10):e11936.

8. Gaungzhou A., Kazuko O., Satoru T., Yukihiro S., Naoko T., Toru N. (2019). Glaucoma diagnosis with machine learning. J Healthc Eng 2019:4061313.

9. Dr Gadi, W. (2014). OCT for glaucoma diagnosis, screening and detection of glaucoma progression. Br J Ophthalmol 98(Suppl 2):ii15–19.

10. Chengjie Z., Thomas V., Aakriti G., Michael V. (2018). Artificial intelligence in glaucoma. Curr Opin Ophthalmol 30(2):97–103.

11. Rahul K., Benjamin T., Lama A. (2019). The role of artificial intelligence in the diagnosis and management of glaucoma. Curr Ophthalmol Rep 7(2). DOI:10.1007/s40135-019-00209-w.

12. Quigley, H. A., & Broman, A. T. (2006). The number of people with glaucoma worldwide in 2010 and 2020. Br J Ophthalmol 90(3), 262–267. https://doi.org/10.1136/bjo.2005.081224.

13. Muhammad, H., Fuchs, T.J., De Cuir, N., De Moraes, C.G., Blumberg, D.M., Liebmann, J.M., Ritch, R., Hood, D.C. (2017). Hybrid deep learning on single wide-field optical coherence tomography scans accurately classifies glaucoma suspects. J Glaucoma 26(12), 1086–1094. https://doi.org/10.1097/IJG.0000000000000765.

14. Asaoka, R., Murata, H., Hirasawa, K., Fujino, Y., Matsuura, M., Miki, A., … Araie, M. (2019). Using deep learning and transfer learning to accurately diagnose early-onset glaucoma from macular optical coherence tomography images. Am J Ophthalmol 198, 136–145.

15. IBM (2018). AI and the Eye: Deep Learning for Glaucoma Detection. Available at: https://www.ibm.com/blogs/research/2018/10/glaucoma-detection/

16. American Academy of Ophthalmology. When It's Not Glaucoma. Available at: https://www.aao.org/eyenet/article/when-its-not-glaucoma.

17. Choudhari N.S., Aditya N., Vimal F., Ronnie G. (2011). Cupped disc with normal intraocular pressure: The long road to avoid misdiagnosis. Indian J Ophthalmol 59(6):491–497.

18. Kavitha S. (2020). Neuro-ophthalmological conditions mimicking glaucoma – A diagnostic challenge. Indian J Ophthalmol 68(6):1165–1166.

19. Scientific American. Cost to Develop New Pharmaceutical Drug Now Exceeds $2.5B. Available at: https://www.scientificamerican.com/article/cost-to-develop-new-pharmaceutical-drug-now-exceeds-2-5b/.

5 Application of Disruptive Technology in Food Trackability

Ashok Chopra and Vinod Kumar Shukla

CONTENTS

DOI: 10.1201/9781003048862-5

5.1   INTRODUCTION TO TRACKABILITY SYSTEM

There are several definitions of trackability, most of which define "trackability as
Tracing" without defining the meaning of "trace" in this case. Trackability can
access partial or complete relevant evidence through recorded identification relevant,
desired, and sought during the lifetime. It was an effort to improvise, merge, and
better the various aspects of existing knowledge and explanations while avoiding
sub-routing and vagueness. This effort was by two authors (Olsen and Borit, 2018).
A particular focus is on complete, or part evidence trackability at any stage of the
batch's life cycle. A unit of foodstuff or goods used or created by a food trade operator (FTO) or a business unit (i.e., an element of food or goods sold by an associate
and delivered) and received by another FTO. The specific term used in the domain is
the "trackable basis (resource) unit (TBU)" (Kim et al., 2005). TBU is followed by
"an entity which wants to locate" or "the unit that records information in our trackability system."

　　Internal trackability means the ability to locate in the context of a link or a company. Internal trackability is usually the trackability system's pillar; when recording
all relevant information, every chain company relies on their deployed best resources
within an organization. Chain trackability can locate desired information between
links and organizations and rely on data entered into the internal tracking system; the
same is then read and understand at the following link in the chain. For understanding the relationship between internal trackability/traceability and inner chain track-
ability/traceability, refer to Figure 5.1.

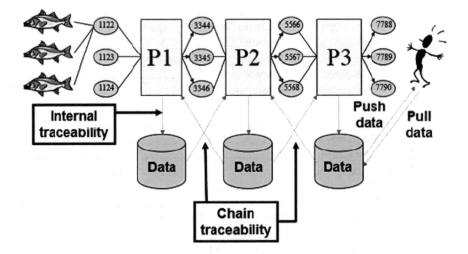

FIGURE 5.1   Trackability/traceability vs. tracking within.

5.1.1 System of Trackability and Its Integral Components

From a trackability perspective, it is crucial to link the information explained in the first link to subsequent links (or get transported to). The trackability system does the same, ensuring that the information entered is accessible elsewhere and remains safe and intact. This means that if one wants to analyze the trackability system's characteristics, one needs to differentiate between the following component types clearly:

- The comprehensive steps and methods used for identifying TBUs, including code and making decisions regarding uniqueness, quality, and uniqueness of the code while defining TBU/TRU identifier for linking to code.
- The methodology and steps related to the records of the chain's transformations include recording the TBU/TRU transformations, the part, and the related set of information that describes and gives information about other data.

The recording of the characteristics and properties of the TBU, which may initially be something that defines the TBU (e.g., production of FTO, the origin of TBU, the details and description of the TBU, the measurement taken at the TBU, the criteria for the recording process of the TBU). The elements of the trackability system are as shown as under Figure 5.2.

5.1.2 Trackability Systems' Main Drivers

Different motives/drivers for implementing trackability systems activate different expectations between manufacturers and consumers, which do not always correspond to the trackability systems used. Table 5.1 below summarizes various features of trackability systems, including drivers for their implementation, benchmarks/standards, objectives, and suitable examples.

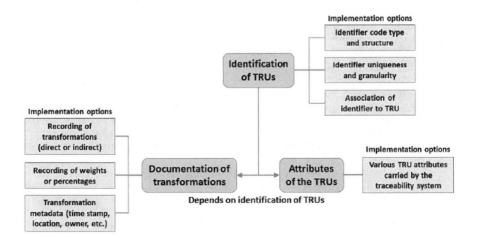

FIGURE 5.2 Elements of track ability system. (Source: Olsen and Borit, 2018).

TABLE 5.1

Trackability Systems: Depicting Objective, Drivers, Characteristics, Metrics, and Examples

Purpose/Driver	Objective	Attributes	Standard	Example
Safety	Consumer protection (through recall and withdrawal)	Specified in food and fish safety regulations	Mandatory Voluntary[a]	EU regulation US regulation
Security	Prevention of criminal actions (through verifiable identification and deterrence)	Specified m security regulations	Regulatory[b]	US Prevention of bioterrorism, regulation
		Verification of selected attributes on package and/ or food	Voluntary (no common standard)	Brand and product protection
Regulatory quality	Consumer assurance (through recall and withdrawal)	Specific attributes included in regulations	Regulatory[c]	EC labeling, mandatory consumer information
Non-regulatory quality and marketing	Creation and maintenance of credence attributes	Specific attributes included in public standards	Voluntary (common standard)[d]	Public quality seals (e.g., Label Rouge, France) Organic fish, eco- labeling
Food chain trade and logistics management	Food chain uniformity and improved logistics	Specific attributes required to food and services suppliers by contract	Private standards[d] Public standards for encoding information	Own traceability systems (e.g., Walmart) EAN.UCC 128[e], (e.g., with TRACEFISH[f] standard) SSCC[g]
Plant management	Productivity improvement and costs reduction	Internal logistics and link to specific attributes	Voluntary (internal traceability; own or public standards)	From simple to complex IT systems
Documentation of sustainability	Natural resource sustainability	Specified in environmental protection regulations	Mandatory Voluntary	EU IUU regulation FAO IPOA-IUU[h]

Source: Olsen and Borit (2018)

[a]   Recall and withdrawal can become compulsory if a responsible company does not take action

[b]   Includes the possibility of mandatory disposal, recall and withdrawal, legal and police actions but primary purpose is prevention

[c]   Includes the possibility of mandatory disposal, recall, and withdrawal and administrative actions, but primary purpose is consumer assurance

[d]   Could include voluntary (contractual) recall and withdrawal and agreed (contractual) sanctions

[e]   GS1 system standardizes bar codes (www.GS1.com)

[f]   TRACEFISH, "Traceability of fish Products" (EC-funded project) http://www.tracefish.org/

[g]   SSCC: Serial Shipping Container Code (UCC)

[h]   IPOA-IUU: I International Plan of Action to Prevent, Deter and Eliminate illegal, Unreported, and Unregulated fishing

5.1.3   TRACKABILITY AND SYSTEMATIC METHODS

It is worth mentioning that the majority of parameters and information about food products fall under the term trackability, but records are unsubstantiated mainly due to deliberate fraud and erroneous mistakes. However, there are methods to check the facts concerning biochemical food properties, and such methods have relevance concerning potential food safety implications. Depending on the type of food, these methods are not only limited to Near-Infrared Spectroscopy, Nuclear Magnetic Resonance; Metabolite Profiling, High-Performance Liquid Chromatography; Gas Chromatography-Mass Spectrometry; Chemical Profiling, Proteomics, and many more. These mentioned methodologies are collectively known as "diagnostic methods." These tests are capable of analyzing the value of food or profiling biochemical food item properties. The identified property can identify the origin, species, status (fresh or frozen), process information, origin, presence of an additive, chemical properties of food, nutrient value, the extent of organic production contribution, species, shelf life, etc. and more. Analytical testing on food items increases and improves daily, but a relatively small portion of food items are subject to these tests from a trackability perspective. It is important to mention that these analytical tests cannot give information about the farmer who grew it, the actual traceable resource unit (TBU), the route of applied supply chain followed, or adaption of fair and ethical practices followed in growing the food. Publishers and practitioners must term these analytical tests as integral parts of trackability and traceability but need to look at trackability's definition, including the one described earlier in this chapter. These analytical tests are termed as partial because they do not deal with "recorded identifications." Often, these tests may include nomenclature typically as the partial route to the trackability ecosystem, as these statements are claimed to be correct. However, in reality, we do not know the truthfulness.

5.1.4   TRACKABILITY AND CHRONOLOGY OF OWNERSHIP (COO)

Chronology of ownership, also known as CoC (chain of custody), is regularly mixed and confused with trackability. The difference between COO and trackability is that COO deals with details and control input and outputs in a supply chain. In specific terms, COO is a series of processes integrated into an implementation COO system, including characteristics preserved, isolation, and material balance. Table 5.2 depicts the difference between trackability and COO/CoC.

5.1.5   TRANSPARENCY AND TRACKABILITY

Transparency is the pivotal point in risk communication because it is directly linked to reliance and faith among involved stakeholders ( ). On the other hand, transparency is a crucial part of the supply chain, and deals with considering access of information as solicited by stakeholders with communication bias (e.g., delay, noise, or distortion) (Hofstede, 2004). It is essential to clarify at this stage that transparency and trackability are not the same; logically, rackability sets a framework for transparency (Egels-Zandén and Hansson, 2016). Thus, on the one hand, a sound trackability

TABLE 5.2

**Differences between Trackability and Chronology of Ownership (COO)/
Chain of Custody (CoC)**

	Traceability	Chain of Custody (CoC)
Objective	To associate recorded data with TRUs; to document what happens	To prevent mixing that violates the CoC requirements; to document that no such mixing has occurred
Of what?	Anything	With respect to some particular property which the CoC is in relation to, often origin or ecolabel status
The traced unit	A batch or a trade unit (the TRU)	The units with the same CoC identifier
Mix/join units	Yes, but must be documented	Only the units with the same CoC identifier
After mix/join	New unit and new identifier created	Considered same unit and receiving the same CoC identifier

Source: Olsen and Borit (2018).

system can provide unbiased, comprehensive, complete product-related information to stakeholders with hardly any business offers, but mostly unverified claims. If one wants transparency, it is apparent that one cannot have transparency without trackability. Thus, trackability can provide the comprehensive product, transformation, and process-related information, but transparency needs more components than mentioned here. Although the concept of trackability, in general, is assumed as "watching what you do in a series," transparency refers to a specific application and target audience (for example, the general public or decision-makers).

5.2   FOOD SECTOR AND USE OF BLOCKCHAIN TECHNOLOGY

5.2.1   MAJOR CONTRIBUTORS TO BLOCKCHAIN TECHNOLOGY

Blockchain is a blend of numerous advantages for source code, expandability, ease of use, adjustment, and expansion. The negative impact of the adoption of source code requires a comprehensive understanding of the code. The most impressive part of adoption is freedom and ease of specific usage in most cases. Many players have emerged in the market with specific usage and sector specialization in recent years, taking the advantages mentioned earlier. The list of the most important players with their domain expertise is as follows.

5.2.1.1   Blockchain as a Service (BaaS)

BaaS and SaaS can synonym each other as the delivery model of hosting third-party services. In this concept, a third party offers a service (application functionality), hosting its application through the internet. Such examples of such companies include WebEx by CISCO, Salesforce, Google Apps, and Dropbox. Such application is as ODS (on-demand service) and typically requires registration to start accessing and using such application. Platform as a Service and Infrastructure as a Service and other variant examples of such services' ideology prevent beneficiaries from developing from scratch the Blockchain system. Microsoft's Azure, Amazon's AWS, and IBM's BlueMix offer such services using the cloud. The advantages users under the BaaS model have are that there's no required investment in hardware for configuring and setting up Blockchain.

5.2.1.2   Blockchain Applications Offered by Amazon AWS

A variety of Blockchain applications based on an ETE (end-to-end) basis is an offer by Amazon AWS. Examples such applications are limited to Hyperleader and Sawtooth and include Hyperledger Fabric, Ethereum, and Corda. Amazon provides application makers with links to the built-in Blockchain for one-click deployments and complementary applications.

5.2.1.3   Blockchain Workbench Offered by Microsoft Azure

The unique yet effective Blockchain development system uses a Blockchain workbench, that is, Microsoft Azure propositions as modular pre-configured network infrastructure. A workbench combines capabilities and Azure services to build and set up Blockchain applications for sharing data and business processes with many organizations. Microsoft delivers and designs the infrastructure framework for building Blockchain applications providing application developers the right direction by focusing on smart contracts and business logic. A few of the known working examples of Blockchain solutions are Hyperledger Fabric, Ethereum, and Corda. Besides this, comprehensive solution architecture about supply chain trace and track is also part of an offer.

5.2.1.4   IBM BlueMix

IBM has taken the lead and provides BaaS among all Blockchain players. IBM Blockchain offering services and solutions use hyperledger technologies, which offer toolsets and frameworks. It claims that IBM has successfully developed and implemented more than four hundred dedicated solutions. IBM Enterprise-Ready Blockchain Services offers one of the best practices norms in the industry.

5.2.1.5   Blockchain First Limited

Solutions offered by Blockchain First best work with Blockchain stack and tools. The only limitation/downside in implementation is that it requires complete assembly. On the other hand, the advantages/upside is having a high level of innovation and freedom because of directly working with Blockchain. The best example to support the above argument is working with the original Bitcoin and Ethereum source code, accessible on Github.

5.2.1.6   A Large Number of Development Platforms

Currently, there are several platforms for development, focusing on swift development and implementation of Blockchain. The focus of such developmental platforms on any specific Blockchain technology but programmability potential, e.g., Blockstream (blockstream.com), BlockApps (blockapps.net), Parity, Hyperledger, Tendermint, and Monax.

5.2.1.7 Vertically Integrated Solutions

The number of vertically integrated Blockchain industry-specific solutions concentrate on private Blockchain or ledger infrastructure. Many vertically integrated Blockchain solutions are not the best and proper Blockchain solutions, but focus on distributed ledger solutions (a subset of Blockchain technology). Examples include Axoni, itBit, Clearmatics, Digital Asset Holdings, Chain, and R3.

5.2.2 OVERLAYS AND APIS (APPLICATION PROGRAMMING INTERFACE)

The main focus and approach on using the Blockchain as a strength or asset, ownership, or identity-binding infrastructure are typical of a specific purpose, e.g., (CoP) chains of proof, title registries ownership rights, or other specific services with a focus on a trust-based component. Examples include Blockstack, Open Assets, Factom, and Tierion.

5.2.3 BRIEF STATUS ON BLOCKCHAIN TECHNOLOGY APPLICATIONS AS PREVALENT IN FOOD INDUSTRY

There are currently several applications of Blockchain testing and trial in food chains looking after specific issues, including trackability and segmenting. Nevertheless, no single/standard technology succeeded in addressing different Blockchain issues in food trackability (Ciaian et al., 2018). The majority of current Blockchain systems are from 2015 onwards (Galvez et al., 2018). Table 5.3 on the next page gives Blockchain technology's brief currently being used in the food or agriculture sector and its main objectives for implementation.

TABLE 5.3
Specific Solicitations of Blockchain Technology Used in the Farming and Agri-Business Food Supply Chain

Goods/Products	Initiative/Project/Company involved	Objectives
Agri-food	AgriOpenData (Galvez et al., 2018)	Allow quality and digital identity to be certified
Agri-food	Supply chain traceability system for china based on RFID and Blockchain technology (Galvez et al., 2018)	Trusted information throughout the agri-food supply chain
Beef	"Paddock to plate" project, BeefLedger; JD.com (Kamilaris & Prenafeta-Boldu, 2018)	Food traceability
Beer	Downstream (Kamilaris & Prenafeta-Boldu, 2018)	Food traceability
Chicken	Gogochicken, Grass Roots Farmers' Cooperative; OriginTrail (Kamilaris & Prenafeta-Boldu, 2018); zhongAn (Ciaian et al., 2018)	Food traceability, food safety concerns of urban consumers
Coffee	FairChain coffee: Bext360 in partnership with Moyee Coffee (Ciaian et al., 2018)	Traceability, transparency of the value added

(Continued)

TABLE 5.3 (Continued)

Specific Solicitations of Blockchain Technology Used in the Farming and Agri-Business Food Supply Chain

Goods/Products	Initiative/Project/Company involved	Objectives
Fish	Provenance (Galvez et al., 2018)	Auditable system
Fresh food	Ripe (Galvez et al., 2018)	Enabling data transparency and transfer from farm to fork
Fruits	FruitChains (Galvez et al., 2018)	Public, immutable, ordered ledger of records
Grains	AgriDigitat (Kamilaris & Prenafeta-Boldu, 2018)	Financial
Large enterprises	IBM (Galvez et al., 2018)	Food tracking project
Mangoes	Walmart, Kroger, IBM (Kamilaris & Prenafeta-Boldu, 2018)	Food traceability
Olive oil	OlivaCoin (Ciaian et al., 2018; Kamilaris & Prenafeta-Boldu, 2018)	Financial, Small farmers support
Orange juice	Alber Heijn & Refresco (International Supermarket News 2018)	Show customers how and by whom products are made
Pork	Walmart, Kroger, IBM (Kamilaris & Prenafeta-Boldu, 2018)	Food traceability
Pork	Arc-net (Galvez et al., 2018)	Brand protection and security through transparency
Scotch Whisky	CaskCoin (Ciaian et al., 2018)	Investing in maturing Scotch Whisky
Soybean	HSBC & Cargill; ING & Louis Dreyfus Co. (Hochfelder, 2018)	Help authenticate products as well as eliminate the "paper trail" of verification at every stage of the supply chain
Sugarcane	Coca-Cola (Kamilaris & Prenafeta-Boldu, 2018)	Humanistic
Turkeys	Cargill Inc., Hendrix Genetics (Ciaian et al., 2018; Kamilaris & Prenafeta-Boldu, 2018)	Food traceability, animal welfare
Wine	Chainvine (Galvez et al., 2018), Winecoin (Ciaian et al., 2018)	Increase performance, revenue, accountability, and security

5.3 COMPARATIVE ANALYSIS OF PERFORMANCE OF CONVENTIONAL VS. BLOCKCHAIN-BASED TRACKABILITY SYSTEMS

To explain the comparative analysis, let us begin with an example. Think of a question like, "What is a Chinese sizzler lunch?" Is it still a Chinese sizzler lunch if one serves with any vegetable rather than specialized Chinese vegetables? Is it still a Chinese sizzler lunch if one does not serve it on the wooden platform instead of serving it on a non-wooden platform? Is it still a Chinese sizzler lunch if one serves it on disposable paper/plastic plates rather than on proper authentic Chinese crockery/cutlery? If asked, most respondents may respond yes to all these questions, stating it is still a Chinese sizzler lunch, even if one changes the perspective, serving, and portion options. However, it is hard for anyone to take away the sizzling sound of Chinese sizzlers, and if the sizzling sound goes away, then one may no longer call it a Chinese sizzler lunch.

Similar to the analogy mentioned here and the challenges in Blockchain, it is also essential to know that one has limited "serving options." Block indeed can be defined as a set of registered transactions. Blockchain is a linked sequence like a chain of such set of blocks where forward block refers to and draws to the previous block, which cannot change information contained in it, and if any change takes place in the previous block, then it is known to all such blocks present in the network. From a computer expert perspective, Blockchain is simply the structure of data similar to a linked list, which uses hashes rather than pointers for referring to the previous link in the chain. Like the "Chinese sizzler" analogy where if the sizzling sound is not there, it would not be called Chinese sizzler; likewise, if one does not have a particular data structure, then what one has should not be termed as a Blockchain.

Taking further the analogy of Chinese sizzler, let us see the "serving options." Any article on Blockchain implementation clarifies that Blockchain is a set of online distributed multiple copies of databases, which follow logical consensus protocol to synchronize multiple copies through a set of protocols that belongs to either public or private keys to facilitate encryption. It is applicable and accurate for Bitcoin and all public, private, and hybrid Blockchain. Usually, while developing Blockchain in standalone offline mode, a developer could program deployment based on a standalone version of the Blockchain, with no accord instrument of signing process or encryption requirement. Blockchain should address the data arrangement for the implementation. The data logged would be identical to a (single copy of) an online public Blockchain, implemented traditionally with accord management, signing protocol mechanism, and encryption using private or public keys.

Nevertheless, such a situation complicates Blockchain-based tracking systems to traditional electronic ones, typically using a relational data business management system (RDBMS) as the underlying data structure mechanism. Going by the rule, the two systems differ in fundamental database structures, which indirectly means a difference in the implementation. Such differentiation is relatively tiny and relates to the incontrovertible, intrinsically consistent Blockchain data files and structure. It appears that the difference is not looked at from a Blockchain vs. Non-Blockchain viewpoint rather than online vs. offline implantation or distributed with centralized single-copy applications or encoded with decoded signatures.

Several articles on Blockchain application in the food industry (Chopra, 2020) often have the following statement repeated: "While developing Blockchain for Walmart, it generally took approximately two seconds to pinpoint a mango farm. Without a Blockchain, it takes the retailer 6 days, 18 hours, and 26 minutes to identify the native source or original farm." Factually speaking, the first statement is apparent; however, the second statement states that it took more than 26 days using an RDBMS or any other database moderately than Blockchain. It is somewhat related to the shift from non-continuous to integrated, probably partially manual data to online, distributed, harmonized, and connected data.

Comparing a traditional RDBMS electronic system vs. a Blockchain-based food trackability system, it is worth computing some of these "serving options" referred to in Table 5.4.

At this stage, the critical question is: Should Blockchain implementation be compared to traditional trackability or compare with something of equivalent level with implementation options?

TABLE 5.4

Characteristics and Execution Choices for Conventional vs. Blockchain-Based Trackability Systems

	Traditional Electronic Traceability System	Electronic Traceability System Based on Blockchain Technology
Underlying database	Relational database (usually)	Blockchain
Immutable database?	Possible by setting "append only" flag on database, but very unusual	Yes
Single copy of database?	Normally, yes. Traditional databases often use client-server network architecture, where a single, master copy of the database is stored on a centralized server	No, normally multiple copies (but strictly speaking this is an implementation option)
Consensus mechanism?	Needed if there are multiple copies of the database, unusual	Yes (but strictly speaking, this is an implementation option)
Online? Cloud-based?	Not uncommon for large companies, and for modern chain traceability systems	Yes (but strictly speaking, this is an implementation option)
User authentication	In a client-server implementation, the server authenticates a client's credentials	Based on cryptography with private keys and public keys (but strictly speaking, this is an implementation option)

Comparing Blockchain with traditional trackability is something like comparing apples to oranges. There is no straightforward answer, and it depends on what one wants to achieve and measure. A somewhat better option would be comparing characteristics and application options on a case-to-case basis, keeping each platform's pros and cons.

5.3.1 Appropriateness of Database

While comparing traditional databases and Blockchain, one can find that a traditional database stores anything. Blockchain is well suited for storing data about food/product trackability and traceability. It saves the current state or assessment of the data records, whereas Blockchain, on the other hand, stores both transformations and transactions present in the food supply chain.

5.3.2 Records Assessment and Authenticity

It is always a challenge to assess recorded data's authenticity in both traditional and Blockchain-based systems. Unintentional errors are present, and such a change is possible equally in both types of systems. However, the chances of measured fraud are remote (but possible) in a Blockchain-based system. As the saying goes, "garbage in and garbage out" – this duplicitous statement realizes that the chances of being caught quickly are there; thus, they usually try to refrain from doing so.

5.3.3 Susceptibility, Veracity, and Pellucidity

Consistency allows one to overwrite data elements, but it is not uncommon to have a login version that shows who, where, and when they cross. Data documented on

Blockchain is an immovable strategy. In Blockchain, the data records are present once. Therefore, traditional databases do not have default consistency; it instead records the newest requested state of every data component individually. Implementing Blockchain does not save the status of every variable. Instead, all transactions to this state are safe. The feed cell, e.g., RDBMS, contains the current volume and type of feed (perhaps also added to the silo from the previous feed transaction). Implementing Blockchain does not save feed volume. Or say we complete a list of transactions with Cello only. In RDBMS, the feed level recorded in the database is a baseless claim. In Blockchain implementation, the feed's current level is arrived at by performing all recorded transactions, which improve transparency and consistency in the specific feed level's value.

5.3.4 CONFIDENTIALITY

While the implementation of Blockchain, especially private Blockchain, can provide data privacy, preferably in Blockchain implementation, layered data access and privacy protocols are present externally and uniquely. Blockchain rests upon transparency, and in this context, transparency and privacy are, to no small extent, reciprocally private; if one scores well at one time, one will not score well the other way around.

5.3.5 ASSURANCE

Assurance is not a small aspect to be evaluated in this context, as different implementations present its concept differently. In traditional tracking systems, one asks to assure the system and database owner. If something goes wrong (fabricated privileges, food deceit, the database owner's image – in practice and as name), Blockchain has a design to work with without relying on any particular organization. While this is a helpful attribute, there is no confirmation on how assurance works in the food sector. Eliminating the need to assure any organization and democratize data accuracy is relevant in the virtual system, but not the food sector. Brands and titleholders still need to rely on data delivery to produce safe, nutritious, and high-quality food. Blockchain-based system's use provides no problem for assurance, as the inherent Blockchain standard of "no one needs to be assured" does not apply to the food sector.

5.3.6 VELOCITY AND EFFICACY

Implementing Blockchain is, as of today, slower than traditional RDBMS implementation because it supports functions that support common databases (write and read data) and verifies signatures/identities using cryptography. This veracity originates at a higher price. Furthermore, there is a need to run a consensus algorithm, i.e., Which blocks add to the Blockchain with the next update? This increases instability associated with the built-in robustness present in Blockchain.

5.3.7 ROBUSTNESS

Redundancy is a visually significant result. Visibility refers to the data's sensitivity and the database to vulnerabilities, or incidents, including power outages, hacking, server failures, and malicious S/W or H/W. In traditional systems, the vision supports the peripheral processes, and these can alter. If not planned properly, a substantial number of records could be lost if something goes wrong. If defensive actions occur in a Blockchain-based system, the data state can be recreated, bypassing recorded transactions, usually to the online database and often copied. Thus, robustness in the Blockchain system has the edge over the traditional system, where robustness is Sisyphean.

5.3.8 INTEROPERABILITY

Theoretically, interefficiency is interoperability, and the methodology of exchanging information among various elements of different systems is independent of the method of selection, i.e., traditional or Blockchain. Nevertheless, there are numerous options in traditional systems in practice, as configured database options are widely used. On the other hand, Blockchain implementation is uniform because all transactions rather than data are online and irreplaceable and implemented through cryptography for identification and verification. Blockchain implementation follows uniformity as transactions themselves are recorded online instead of data item values, and these transactions are irreplaceable, employing cryptography (practice and study of techniques for secure communication) for identity verification. The homogeneity of cryptography makes Blockchain more disruptive and has proven helpful in supply chain management and data sharing rather than the Blockchain features (Chopra & Venkat, 2019). Traditional trackability system deployability depends on the pervasive adoption of electronic data interchange (EDI) and data content criteria. Incidentally, the field has very high competitive standards, so the updated compatibility level is relatively low. This section emphasizes the improved differentials in the food industry as the most crucial advantage of using Blockchain-centered electronic trackability. This advantage on a particular part of the Blockchain is not strictly because the difference between Blockchain implementations is easy. Blockchain implementations are similar to RDBMS trackability implementations in that one can build on a wide range of operating principles, system architecture, and database types.

5.4 PRACTICAL AND ECONOMIC IMPLEMENTATION ISSUES IN BLOCKCHAIN-BASED SYSTEMS

5.4.1 FOOD PRODUCT SUPPLY CHAINS IN PRACTICE

Table 5.5 in the subsequent section gives an efficiency analysis of the Blockchain system in the food products supply chain. The rows and columns in this table are using three colors, namely red, gray, and green. The careful examination would show that red remarks show the plethora of implementation problems, remarks highlighted in gray show minor benefits for the system in use, and remarks in green color indicate significant benefits. The green color remarks are those belonging to an electronic trackability system using Blockchain technology.

The first five parameter comparisons have nominal costs and benefits associated with quality, such as gray shading; on the other hand, green color points to a potential benefit. As mentioned, it is evident, the two most essential benchmarks by which the difference between trackability is most incredible are "velocity and effectiveness,"

TABLE 5.5

Economic Efficiency of Blockchain-Centered Systems Useful to Authorities

Comparison Criteria	Traditional Electronic Traceability System	Electronic Traceability System Based on Blockchain Technology
Suitability of database	Authorities can only access claims in relation to state of variables	Authorities can access the entire set of transformations that led to the current state, which makes it easier to see the origin of the stated claim
Data quality and veracity	Authorities need separate and external checks to test the data quality and veracity	Some degree of quality and veracity is provided by the blockchain-based system itself
Immutability, integrity, and transparency	It is difficult for authorities to know if recorded data has been subsequently overwritten	The immutability of the database means that the authorities know that the data has not been overwritten
Confidentiality	Not an issue for authorities	
Trust	Not really an issue for authorities (except for trust in data quality and veracity, which is better in a blockchain-based system)	
Robustness	Not an issue for authorities	
Speed and efficiency	Not an issue for authorities	
Interoperability	Lack of interoperability makes it more difficult to identify discrepancies, and to do mass-balance accounting which is sometimes necessary to identify fraud	Better interoperability and better access to comparable data from different systems makes it easier to identify discrepancies, and to do mass-balance accounting

which fully support the RDBMS system, and "Interoperability," when compared with a Blockchain-based system. When choosing between the RDBMS-based implementation of an electronic trackability system and a Blockchain-based one, it is essential to determine which system features are most important. Based on database transparency, integrity, and reliability importance, Blockchain solutions can be very relevant. On the other hand, when velocity/response and data privacy are considered essential features of a system, a traditional electronic tracking system is probably looking better.

It is essential to mention that the applicability and effectiveness of improved interoperability should not be underestimated. While traditional trackability systems allow mutual functionality between features to be technically possible, it is not easy to settle between standards and data formats for use by large and diverse corporate groups. One can get a large and dissimilar group of companies to approve all Blockchain-based systems. Mutual efficiency, which is simple yet most significant, is the most desirable side effect of the decision.

As shown, Blockchain-based detection systems' main advantage is increased interoperability, which is very problematic with RDBMS detection systems. This argument applies to all foods. Advanced interoperability is probably the most direct benefit if one chooses a Blockchain-based system (or a set of Blockchain-based systems that exchange data). As shown in the two examples above, the advantages and disadvantages of using a Blockchain-based detection system rather than the traditional detection system vary slightly depending on the product type. Blockchain-based systems clearly define and identify TBUs, if these TBUs are the size, value, and initial quality associated with tracking all transactions that lead to that TBU. However, data capture is expensive, and verification is easy. Blockchain implementations do not perform well for large products, products that do not explicitly record transactions, or products that contain fuzzy data. It means that Blockchain systems cannot handle these problems. The benefits of Blockchain-based implementations, in general, are less clear and visible at this stage; however, in the future, more application developers have expected to make Blockchain the obvious, fundamental choice.

5.4.2 Usefulness of Recorded Data in a Blockchain-Supported System

The implementation and maintenance of a one-time cost of Blockchain-based trackability systems are mainly by the food companies. The same also includes the creation and limited maintenance of the Blockchain system itself. Table 5.5 depicts the expected benefits of Blockchain systems, which are most beneficial to the executives. It is worth mentioning that the economic benefits associated with Blockchain-based systems (especially speed, efficiency, and privacy) are not particularly important to authorities. In contrast, some advantages (recording and tracing transactions and not just states, variable databases, changing interoperable systems) are most important to officers. It goes beyond the fact that officials should support Blockchain-based food trackability systems and encourage food business operators to adopt them.

5.5 INFERENCE AND RECOMMENDATION

The Blockchain-based system is sound and recommended when it comes to essential features like privacy and speed. Another important reason for this clear conclusion is data sharing, which favors the Blockchain bases system. While it is precisely possible to accomplish this between existing systems and Blockchain, the same behavior is the main obstacle to accessing data from the farm to the fork in an RDBMS system. Rather than continuing to expect widespread adoption of standards to support interoperability, many supply chain stakeholders should adopt a Blockchain-based trackability system, which in itself enhances interoperability. Realistically, it is worth emphasizing that Blockchain-based implementations cannot solve all or most of the problems associated with traditional electronic tracking system systems. The same includes:

Data quality and effectiveness remain a significant challenge as of now in Blockchain-based implementations.

Food deceit remains a problem in Blockchain-based implementations, but it is easy to identify who made the fraudulent claim when food fraud is detected.

Need for standards:

EDI standards are less relevant when using Blockchain-based systems, but more and higher standards define the meaning of recorded data items and values (ontologies). At the same time, increased interoperability means increased access to data recorded elsewhere in the supply chain. Standards are needed to define the meaning of item names and the meaning of recorded values signify. For food businesses and solution providers to know these challenges, Blockchain-based implementations are necessary to avoid future disappointments. In particular, the latter group will reduce the current technology oversold and overacting.

REFERENCES

Chopra A. (2020). Blockchain technology in food industry ecosystem. *IOP Conference Series: Materials Science and Engineering*, Vol. 872. doi:10.1088/1757899X/872/1/012005.

Chopra, A., & Venkat, S. (2019). Blockchain technology disruptions reshaping the market. *Journal of Advance Research in Dynamical & Control Systems*, Vol. 11.

Ciaian, P., Rajcaniova, M., & Kancs, A. (2018). Virtual relationships: Short- and long-run evidence from BitCoin and altcoin markets. *Journal of International Financial Markets, Institutions and Money*, Vol. 52, pp. 173–195.

Egels-Zandén, N., & Hansson, N. (2016, December 1). Supply chain transparency as a consumer or corporate tool: The case of Nudie Jeans Co. *Journal of Consumer Policy: Consumer Issues in Law, Economics and Behavioural Sciences*, Vol. 39, No.4, pp. 377–395.

Galvez, J. F., Mejuto, J. C., & Simal-Gandara, J. (2018, October 1). Future challenges on the use of Blockchain for food traceability analysis. *Trends in Analytical Chemistry*, Vol. 107, pp. 222–232.

Hochfelder, B. (2018). HSBC, Cargill successfully complete blockchain trade-finance transaction. *Supply Chain Dive*. Available at: https://www.supplychaindive.com/news/hsbc-cargill-blockchain-pilot/523554/

Hofstede, G. J. (2004). *Hide or confide?: The dilemma of transparency*. 's-Gravenhage: Reed Business Information.

Kamilaris, A., & Prenafeta-Boldu, F.-X. (2018). Deep learning in agriculture: A survey. Available at: https://arxiv.org/abs/1807.11809

Kim, H. M., Biehl, M., & Buzacott, J. A. (2005, January 1). *3rd IEEE International Conference on Industrial Informatics (INDIA). M-CI/sup2/: modeling cyber interdependencies between critical infrastructures* (pp. 644–648).

Olsen, P., & Borit, M. (2018, July 1). The components of a food traceability system. *Trends in Food Science & Technology*. doi: 10.1016/j.tifs.2018.05.004.

6 Analyzing Cyber Security Breaches

Fatima Farid Petiwala, Insha Mearaj, and Vinod Kumar Shukla

CONTENTS

6.1 INTRODUCTION

A few years back even being able to imagine a scenario where we could pick up our mobile devices and call our loved ones from across the globe, no matter how far away, would sound like a miracle. We have made a long journey from writing letters and waiting for days to receive them, to sending text messages on the click of a button within milliseconds.

But imagine that someone with the intent to harm gains access to our devices. Terrifying, right? This is where cyber security comes into action. Whether it is in regard to net banking or cloud computing, anything and everything that involves data passage over the internet is vulnerable to cybercrimes. The already rapid growth of cyber security breaches over the past years, and exacerbated by to the pandemic of COVID-19, has now accelerated its pace fivefold. The number of data breaches across the globe have skyrocketed and the number of people skilled enough to deal with it are limited.

Cyber security is an integral aspect of modern society. Its role and scope of growth is never ending especially so with the establishment of IoT. Development of telecommunication, automation, and robotics has time and time again proven than cyber security is an ever-growing field with boundless opportunities. The pace of technological advancement is boundless and has opened up more vulnerable loopholes waiting to be exploited by malicious individuals.

No organization or individual is or will ever be able to achieve 100 percent security against attacks and breaches, whether they are due to the mistake of an insider or intentionally done by a malicious outsider. This fact compels us even more to take

DOI: 10.1201/9781003048862-6

precautions to avoid such incidents and have a strategic plan in place in case it does occur.

Although it is impossible to be completely safe, steps such as providing training to employees to at the very least have basic knowledge of common forms of attacks such as phishing emails, which are currently on the rise, is extremely important. Earlier all we needed was a secure firewall and a trusted antivirus; however, our changing times have proved that we need more.

> **Reason for increased risk**: The main reason for the increased risk in terms of cyber security is due to the world being connected globally through wireless connection and widespread use of cloud services, which are extensively being used for storing sensitive personal and professional data without any extra protection. This together with emergence of organized and experienced criminals have drastically increased the rate of successful data breaches and other forms of cyber-attacks that may negatively harm an individual or an organization by various means to satisfy their personal agendas – whether it if fame, financial gain, or other motives.
>
> **Who is behind cyber security breaches?** Cyber security breaches can be facilitated accidentally by an insider, a malicious outsider (criminals or black hats), malicious insider with the intent of causing harm to the organization, or due to a lost or stolen device which lacks password protection and any data stored in it is unencrypted. The cyber attackers can thus broadly be divided into Insiders and Outsiders, and they can be accidental or malicious depending on their intent.
>
> **Why are cyber attacks conducted?** Most black hats do it for financial gain such as by the use of ransomware, where they hold data hostage and ask for a sum of money for it instead. Another reason is for fame – individuals or even organized communities conduct breaches and then release stolen data into the world without financial motive just to boost their sense of superiority and to spread terror.

White hacks do the same, i.e., hack into an organizations' servers, except their motive is to help an organization fix these loopholes. The work they do is completely legal because they have the organization's permission. Many competitor organizations may do so to gain access to future plans or ideas and thus gain an unfair advantage over their competitors in the market (espionage).

Some hacktivists may do it to raise awareness of an issue, i.e., make a political statement or social point (hacktivism).

6.1.1 Types of Cyber Security Breaches

1. *Social Engineering* – These attacks are mainly carried out by the use of human interaction. The cycle of the attack begins with targeting an individual or organization, followed by gathering adequate data about the victim which may include sensitive data that may reveal unprotected weak points suitable for carrying out the attack. The next step is to gain the victim's

trust, which makes it easier to carry out the final steps, causing harm by either releasing the victim's personal data or acquiring easy access to their sensitive data [1, 2].

2. *Phishing* – This is the most common form of security attack and is currently on the rise. It involves impersonation of a known or trustful source in order to be able to purloin the targeted victim's personal information. Phishing itself is a type of social engineering attack and is commonly used by malicious individuals to gain details such as credit card details or user ID's and passwords, etc. It can be conducted by the use of fake emails or messages or fake websites [1, 3].

3. *Malware* – This is basically any form of a malicious software that is installed in the victim's device without their knowledge to gain their sensitive data, which could further be used for financial gain or other motives. There are many types of malware such as virus, worms, Trojan horse, ransomware, etc. [1].

4. *DDoS* – This stands for Distributed Denial of Service and is mainly associated with compromising the availability of desired data to the victim. The malicious individual in this case floods the victim's servers by using specific commands, rendering the service unusable [1].

5. *Brute Force* – These attacks are mainly aimed at being able to find out secret passwords or pin codes of the victim's devices or credit cards, etc. It is a trial-and-error technique where the attacker uses all possible combinations of letters, numbers, and special characters in hopes of being able to guess the password correctly. This is also the reason why simple passwords that can be easily guessed, such as birthdates or names, must not be used. Instead, strong passwords using a variety of combinations of upper- and lower-case letters, numbers, and special characters are recommended [1, 4].

6. *Man in the Middle* – Just like the name suggests, the attacker infiltrates the communication between two devices in a way that the attacker gains access to any communication from A to B and, B to A and also alter it before it is delivered to its destination. This attack is especially dangerous as it poses the threat of not only releasing sensitive data but also potential misunderstandings and other issues in case of data alterations [1].

6.2 RELATED FACTS

The growth rate of malicious malware infections has taken a huge leap from 12.4 million to 812.67 million in just a decade as shown in Figure 6.1, not to forget the fact that technology has come a far away from what it used to be back in 2009. The increase in various device usage among individuals has opened up a fairly respectable number of ways for data breaches to occur.

This is especially true of our current situation, as people are required to work from home and BYOD (bring your own devices) has become widespread. This means users are no longer using the protected connection servers of their organization – home networks are far more easy targets for criminals. Hence the already-urgent

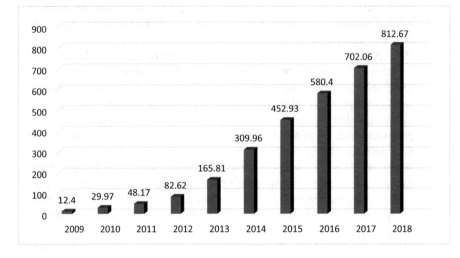

FIGURE 6.1 Growth rate of malware infections (millions) [5].

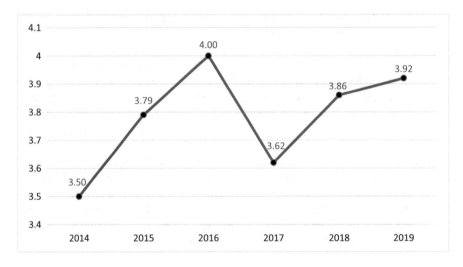

FIGURE 6.2 Average cost of a data breach globally (millions) [6].

requirement of precautionary measures to ensure cyber breaches do not occur had become even more compelling. And this is also an important reason in the rise of cyber-attack.

Cyber breaches are not just devastating in terms of gaining bad reputation for the victim organization but also in terms of resources that the organization has to utilize and is wasted needlessly (money, time, people, effort, etc.). The more sophisticated the criminals are, the harder it is to catch them and fix the damage caused. As discussed earlier, that increase in tech has accelerated the growth of cyber criminals due to the number of loopholes which, in turn, over the years has affected the cost of data breaches. This fact is clearly visible from Figure 6.2.

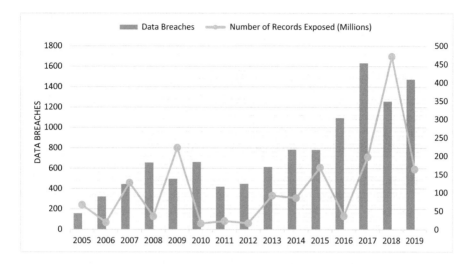

FIGURE 6.3   Annual number of data breaches and records exposed (2005–2019) [7].

It is more terrifying than alarming that the annual number of data breaches have reached a peak value of 1,473 million in 2019 (Figure 6.3). Imagining how much more this number would increase by the end of 2022 unless drastic measures are taken and knowledge about data breaches and cyber security is made widespread is petrifying. None the less, the increase in cybercrime has also caused a significant increase in the creation of more laws to protect individuals and organizations against it, as well as highlighting the need to encourage young generation to take an interest in the field of cyber security.

The global size of the cyber security market has increased from $137.63 billion in 2017 to $184.19 billion in 2020. It is further expected to reach about $248.26 billion in 2023 as depicted in Figure 6.4. No doubt that the increase in cybercrimes has led

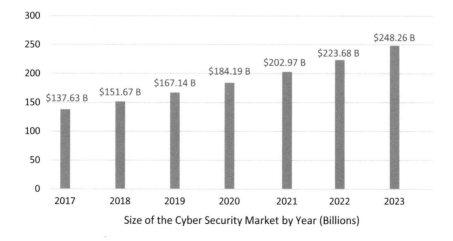

FIGURE 6.4   Size of the cyber security market by year (billions) [8].

to a rapid development in the cyber security market and will continue to do so as technology advances further in the coming years.

6.3 CASE STUDY FOR CYBER-ATTACK

In following case study, a dataset (Figure 6.5) has been taken from KAGGEL and further analyzed to understand the impact of cyber-attack and to know another possible pattern. Software used for this is **Spyder** which is an open-source cross-platform IDE for integrating scientific programming in **Python**.

Python and Spyder – Python is an extremely powerful coding language which is widely used to several general purposes unlike other languages. It can be used with ease for web development and software development as well [9]. Spyder's scientific environment itself has been written using Python. Python has several advantages that makes it a better option in comparison to other languages including the flexibility and compatibility it offers with the Spyder IDE which makes it an excellent choice. Python is user friendly, faster in terms of development, open source, has a variety of libraries, and allows the user to be able to complete a lot of processes with very less code [10].

Linear Regression – One of the important fields of machine learning is regression; linear regression is one of the statistical methods of regression. It is a statistical procedure which is used for modeling relationships between any dependent variable with another set of independent variables. We have applied regression model here for forecasts, which basically means that we use linear regression to calculate some resulting outputs based on some sample data set which will be used as input [11].

Statistical Modeling – It is a mathematical model which encompasses some statistical assumptions concerning the generation of some sample data. It basically helps us assess a scenario, understand it further, and be able to deduct some predictions about the input data [12].

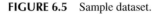

FIGURE 6.5 Sample dataset.

6.3.1 PROCESS IMPLEMENTATION

We have implemented linear regression and statistical modeling to start with linear regression (Figure 6.6) concluded that the dependent variables and independent variables are not correlated and shows no correlation. While as statistical data analytics helped in understanding the data breaches, correlation matrix (Figure 6.7) determining the level of correlation between various variables of the dataset.

We have computed the correlation matrix to evaluate the relationship and the correlation coefficient between variables. When we go through the correlation matrix we see that each cell of the matrix represents a correlation value. The correlation matrix factor tell us about the relationship between various attributes from the dataset in our case we see that the individuals affected and year of attack are slightly correlated however hold less relation and are independent or we can say there is no significant correlation between the two parameters. The same can be seen in the linear correlation graphed the X and Y plot are not linearly correlated (Figure 6.8(a) and (b)).

The execution of the code which imports several essential data processing libraries such as pandas, sklearn.linear_model, matplotlib.pyplot, seaborn, and numpy helps us structure the correlation matric and calculate the linear regression model.

- *X is a numpy array which holds individuals affected in an organization.*
- *Y holds the year.*
- *XX_test will hold 20 percent of the X value while XX_train will hold 80 percent – the same is true for yy_test and yy_train.*

```
87
88 from sklearn.linear_model import LinearRegression
89 regressor = LinearRegression()
90 regressor.fit(XX_train, yy_train)
91
92 coeff_df = pd.DataFrame(regressor.coef_, XX.columns, columns=['Coefficient'])
93 coeff_df
94
95 yy_pred = regressor.predict(XX_test)
96
97 df = pd.DataFrame({'Actual': yy_test, 'Predicted': yy_pred})
```

FIGURE 6.6 Code to implement linear regression.

```
1
2 # Correlation matrix
3 def plotCorrelationMatrix(df, graphWidth):
4     filename = df.dataframeName
5     df = df.dropna('columns') # drop columns with NaN
6     df = df[[col for col in df if df[col].nunique() > 1]] # keep columns where there are more than 1 unique values
7     if df.shape[1] < 2:
8         print(f'No correlation plots shown: The number of non-NaN or constant columns ({df.shape[1]}) is less than 2')
9         return
0     corr = df.corr()
1     plt.figure(num=None, figsize=(graphWidth, graphWidth), dpi=80, facecolor='g', edgecolor='b')
2     corrMat = plt.matshow(corr, fignum=1)
3     plt.xticks(range(len(corr.columns)), corr.columns, rotation=90)
4     plt.yticks(range(len(corr.columns)), corr.columns)
5     plt.gca().xaxis.tick_bottom()
6     plt.colorbar(corrMat)
7     plt.title(f'Correlation Matrix {filename}', fontsize=15)
8     plt.show()
9
```

FIGURE 6.7 Code to implement correlation matrix.

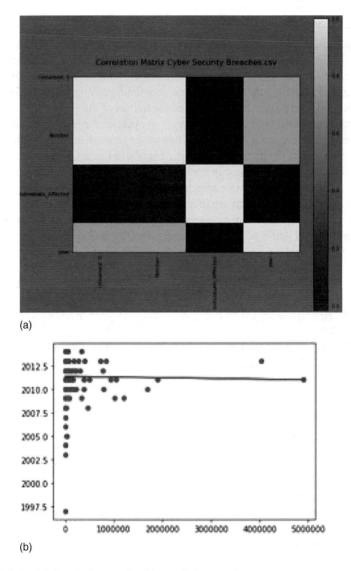

(a)

(b)

FIGURE 6.8   (a) Correlation matrix; (b) correlation graph.

```
83 from sklearn.model_selection import train_test_split
84 XX_train, XX_test, yy_train, yy_test = train_test_split(XX, yy, test_size=0.2, random_state=0)
85
86
```

We have computed the correlation matrix to evaluate the relationship and the correlation coefficient between variables. When we go through the correlation matrix, we can see that each cell of the matrix represents a correlation value. The correlation matrix factor tells us about the relationship between various attributes from the dataset in our case we see that the individuals affected and year of attack are slightly correlated however hold less relation and are independent or we can say there is no significant correlation between the two parameters. The same can be seen in the linear correlation graphed the X and Y plot are not linearly correlated. The graph represents the maximum impact is at individual level.

6.4   CONCLUSION AND FUTURE SCOPE

We have come to the point in time where data breaches have become extremely common; hence, being able to analyze data obtained from these breaches plays an important role in gaining valuable information and make further predictions in regard to future breaches. It is very important for the organization to understand their data and possible points of vulnerability. In this chapter we have explained about the types of breaches and the rise of cyber-attack during these times of COVID-19. With the help of a technical case study, an experimental discussion is represented based on the dataset taken from KAGGAL. In future, the study can be extended with different datasets from various websites and the optimization methodology can be adopted for better results.

REFERENCES

1. Bendovschi, Andreea.: "Cyber-Attacks – Trends, Patterns and Security Countermeasures", *Procedia Economics and Finance*, Vol. 28, 2015, pp. 24–31, ISSN: 2212-5671. doi:10.1016/S2212-5671(15)01077-1.
2. Imperva: "Social engineering", *Imperva* [Online], https://www.imperva.com/learn/ application-security/social-engineering-attack/.
3. Imperva.: "Social engineering", *Imperva* [Online], https://www.imperva.com/learn/ application-security/phishing-attack-scam/#:~:text=Phishing%20is%20a%20type%20 of,instant%20message%2C%20or%20text%20message.
4. Kaspersky.: "Brute force attack: What you need to know to keep your passwords safe", *Kaspersky* [Online], https://www.kaspersky.com/resource-center/definitions/brute-force-attack.
5. Purplesec.: "2020 cyber security statistics: The unlimited list of stats, data & trends", *Purplesec* [Online], https://purplesec.us/resources/cyber-security-statistics/.
6. Statista.: "Average cost of data breaches worldwide from 2014 to 2020 (in million U.S. dollars)", *Statista* [Online], https://www.statista.com/statistics/987474/global-average-cost-data-breach/.
7. Statista.: "Annual number of data breaches and exposed records in the United States from 2005 to 2019 (in millions)", *Statista* [Online], https://www.statista.com/statistics/273550/data-breaches-recorded-in-the-united-states-by-number-of-breaches-and-records-exposed/.
8. Broadbandsearch.: "Essential cyber security facts for buisiness owners", *Broadbandsearch* [Online], https://www.broadbandsearch.net/blog/business-cyber-security-facts-statistics.
9. Morris, Scott.: "Tech 101: What is Python? Plus, 13 reasons why you should learn it", *Skillcrush* [Online], https://skillcrush.com/blog/what-is-python/.

10. Basel, Krzysztof.: "Python pros and cons: What are the benefits and downsides of the programming language", *netguru* [Online], https://www.netguru.com/blog/python-pros-and-cons (accessed June, 2018).
11. Stojiljković, Mirko.: "Linear regression in Python", *RealPython* [Online], https://real-python.com/linear-regression-in-python/.
12. Sannazzaro, Roberto.: "An introduction to statistical analysis and modelling with Python", *towardsdatascience* [Online], https://towardsdatascience.com/an-introduction-to-statistical-analysis-and-modelling-with-python-ef816b67f8ff (accessed May, 2018).

7 Industrial Internet of Things (IoT) and Cyber Manufacturing Systems

Industry 4.0 Implementation and Impact on Business Strategy and Value Chain

Shreyanshu Parhi, Manoj Govind Kharat, Mukesh Govind Kharat, Sharad Chandra Srivastava, and Anju Singh

CONTENTS

DOI: 10.1201/9781003048862-7

7.1   INTRODUCTION

In the age of growing industrial digitalization and automation, companies are progressively capitalizing in tools, technological offerings and solutions that permit the integration of their systems, processes, mechanisms, machines, workforces, and even the products themselves into a single integrated network for efficient data collection, analysis, the assessment of company development, and performance improvement. The present manufacturing industry is undergoing a digital transformation driven by emerging technologies like the Internet of Things (IoT), cyber-physical systems (CPS), cloud, etc. Applying the ideas of CPSs and IoT to the industrial automation domain led to the definition of the *Industry 4.0* concept; this concept is referred to as the fourth industrial revolution or Industry 4.0. Industry 4.0 as an emerging business archetype is already gaining attention among industry technological professionals. Industry 4.0 refers to the deployment of emerging technologies to the manufacturing environment to make it highly agile, flexible, and resilient and can respond to changing demands of the customers and to various external and internal uncertainties (Xu et al., 2018). These capabilities of Industry 4.0-based manufacturing systems have resulted in the development of demand-driven processes, dynamic supply chains, and end-to-end digitalization of the systems (Karaköse and Yetiş, 2017; Liao et al., 2017).

Industry 4.0 mainly deals with applying advanced technologies such as IoT, CPS, Cloud, etc. to serve as a communication channel between people, products, sensors, and control systems. The application and successful implementation of Industry 4.0 considerably depend on the technology. The information technology domain has already started considering advanced technologies such as IoT and CPS to have the potential to revolutionize future communication and computation. IoT is considered to become the next game-changer in the Information Technology field. However, the application of IoT technology to instrument Industry 4.0 will entail a collaborative and concerted effort. In this regard, the stakeholders need to take into account the multiple aspects; these aspects can be defined as (i) effective integration of the advanced IoT sensors (things) into existing businesses and industrial activities; (ii) secure and transparent communication network and software layer to establish a link between cloud-based platforms and manufacturing data; (iii) advancement toward a standard IoT architecture; the open standard is vital to guarantee hundreds of millions of Internet-connected things are interoperable and being able to communicate with each other; (iv) Big Data storage and management capability; (v) development of efficient IoT sensors and devices.

Industry 4.0 and IoT appear promising in providing a mutual set-up that will enable communicating, intelligent, and self-controlled systems. From this perspective, Industry 4.0 is characterized by four conceptual approaches internet technology, CPSs, communication networks among different constituents, and security protection for data being transferred. In the manufacturing environment, the application of IoT and CPSs will empower automation system designers to integrate numerous sensors, controllers, and products under one common platform. The concept of Industry 4.0 has led to the digital transformation of operations and businesses, resulting in the emergence of Big Data and analytics applications in manufacturing (Tao et al., 2018).

The phenomena have completely changed the capabilities of the traditional manufacturing environment, thus making them smart. This is why smart manufacturing systems and Industry 4.0 terminologies are often used synonymously (Mittal et al., 2019). IoT dealing with intelligent objects (things) can seamlessly connect, share information, data and be able to react and respond to changes in the environment. The enhanced automation and digitization of connected objects will lead to an intelligent system in which the objects and mechanism will be able to sense the surrounding environment and communicate. This provides several benefits in industrial systems. The system will work efficiently and effectively; it will be able to predict failures, initiate self-maintenance processes, and schedule production activities. Operators, handlers, and users will be able to communicate remotely through the Internet with systems in the industry. The emergence of Industry 4.0 has expedited the creation of the digital age of the business by enabling data-driven processes and decision-making based on them. The manufacturers' competitiveness in the market has increased, which has compelled the businesses to move toward the digital revolution or Industry 4.0. The concept is rather a hit than hype, and the manufacturers have already started realizing its importance (Ghobakhloo, 2018). Hence, in the highly turbulent and hyper-competitive markets, modern businesses and manufacturers are striving to embrace this change to remain competitive and gain advantages. Unfortunately, the understanding of the technologies and the operational changes that an organization can encounter on the deployment of Industry 4.0 is highly limited (Kamble et al., 2018a; Karadayi-Usta, 2020). It is because the concept is still in its infancy, and the researchers have recently started exploring this avenue (Ghobakhloo, 2020). Moreover, there lies an ambiguity among the managers to focus on the choice of enabling technologies or the enablers while deploying Industry 4.0. To address the mentioned gaps, this research focuses on the following objectives to develop an understanding and make manufacturers aware about the emerging phenomenon:

- To identify and discuss the significant technologies for Industry 4.0, also referred to as enablers.
- To discuss a conceptual framework of Industry 4.0 based on the identified enablers.
- To determine the potential drivers for the adoption and implementation of Industry 4.0.
- Mapping the enablers with the drivers of Industry 4.0.

The purpose of this work is to present an outline about Industry 4.0 by describing its potential drivers. In doing so, the study initially presents the evolution of Industry 4.0. It is followed by a comprehensive discussion on the key enablers for Industry 4.0. The next section focuses on the discussion of the conceptual framework for Industry 4.0 based on the enablers. The subsequent section deals with the determination of the potential drivers for Industry 4.0 and a detailed discussion of them. It also deals with the mapping of the enablers with the determined drivers. The mapping will ensure the enablers that are contributing toward the development of various drivers. Finally, the discussions and conclusions are presented.

7.2   THE EVOLUTION OF INDUSTRY 4.0

In order to understand the progression, the evolution of Industry 4.0 is presented in Figure 7.1. The first industrial revolution began at the end of the eighteenth century, which is referred to as the age of mechanization powered by steam engines. The second industrial revolution began in early twentieth century and focused on the mass production of the components. It gives rise to the assembly line in manufacturing powered by electricity. The early 1970s saw the growth of electronics and automation in manufacturing. It gives rise to the emergence of robotics and mechatronic systems in the industrial environment. Finally, the present manufacturing environment is characterized by the emergence of IoT and cyber-physical systems (CPS). It has given rise to data-driven decision-making processes in the manufacturing environment, thus enhancing competitiveness. Although the third industrial revolution focused on automation and robotics in manufacturing, Industry 4.0 principal focus is on the end-to-end digitalization of the processes through integration and analytics. Primarily, Industry 4.0 is characterized by the deployment of emerging technologies, which enabled the creation of virtual networks, virtualization of the real processes, modeling, simulation, real-time data acquisition, advanced analytics, and data-driven decision-making of the manufacturing ecosystem (Xu et al., 2018). The evolution of the industries is characterized by the enhanced levels of complexity and the development of sophisticated systems that facilitate the easy execution of customer demands and market requirements. Therefore, with the evolution of the fourth industrial revolution, the flexibility and innovativeness of the manufacturing systems have increased (Wuest, 2019; Mittal et al., 2020).

7.3   ENABLERS OF INDUSTRY 4.0

The enablers are the pervasive and driving technologies for implementing Industry 4.0. We have identified key enablers based on literature review, namely: cyber-physical systems (CPS); Internet of Things (IoT); cobotics; autonomous robots; autonomous machines; horizontal and vertical integration; modeling and simulation; augmented reality; digital twin; Big Data analytics; additive manufacturing;

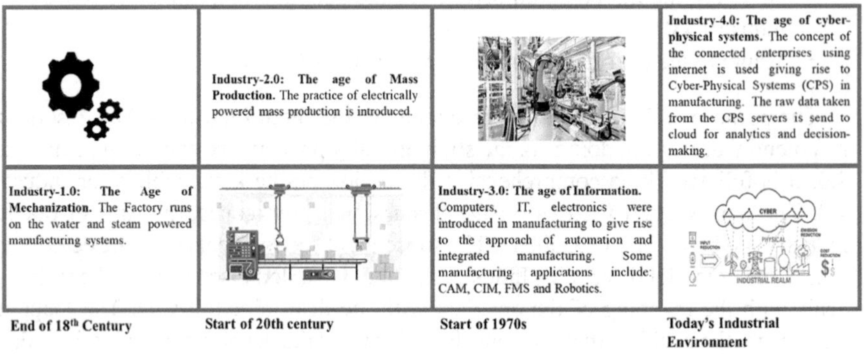

FIGURE 7.1   The evolution of Industry 4.0.

cyber-security; and cloud manufacturing (Rüßmann et al., 2015; Baur and Wee, 2015; Almada-Lobo, 2016; Lu, 2017; Sung, 2018; Fatorachian and Kazemi, 2018; Haag and Anderl, 2018). Interestingly, we found that all these enablers indicate the technologies that contribute to Industry 4.0. The prominence and relevance of these enablers will differ based on the organization's manufacturing strategy and technology adoption level. The enablers are discussed in this section especially focusing on several aspects such as the technology evolution, characteristics features, their role in the development of capabilities, their interaction with other enablers, and their effect on system performance. A representation of the enablers is shown in Figure 7.2.

1. Cyber-physical systems (CPS): CPS is an amalgamation of the cyber world and the physical world where the physical resources can interact with the cyber layer, analyze data, configure, plan, and adapt (Francisco Almada-Lobo, 2016; Letichevskyi et al., 2017; Gürdür and Asplund, 2018; Liu et al., 2018). In Industry 4.0, CPS provides a secure communication and connectivity channel among the manufacturing resources through integrated networked systems, advanced feedback control, and certified operations (Rüßmann et al., 2015; Xu, 2017). The CPS controls the physical processes by data accessing and processing services available at the Internet using

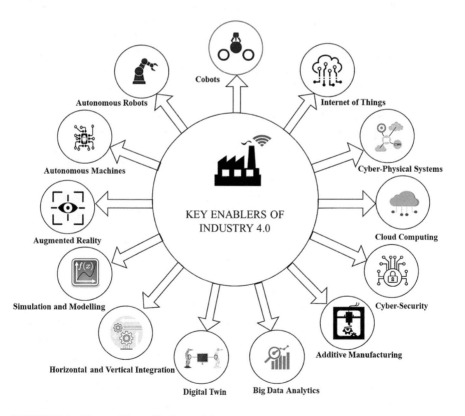

FIGURE 7.2   Key enablers of Industry 4.0.

data analytic tools, leading to enhanced efficiency, accountability, sustainability, and scalability of the systems (Frazzon et al., 2013; Xu and Duan, 2019). CPS primarily accounts for key functions like acquiring real-time information, ensuring connectivity, cyber representation of digital twin, real-time monitoring, control, and warranting agility toward varying internal as well as external choices (Monostori et al., 2016).

2. Internet of Things (IoT): It refers to the means of connecting various resources and integrating processes (Ashton, 2009; Yang et al., 2016). The IoT obtains real-time information using devices such as sensors, RFIDs, etc., forwards this data to cloud-based data centers and updates the related parameters (Gubbi et al., 2013). IoT allows the integration of the cyberspace and the physical world (Ma, 2011). It provides seamless connectivity among the entire manufacturing system to facilitate real-time data flow and better decision-making (Gubbi et al., 2013; Zhang et al., 2014). Such capability of the IoT facilitates the deployment of CPS in Industry 4.0.

3. Cobots: A cobot refers to a robot intended to physically interact with humans to establish a synergistic relationship between them and utilize their complementary abilities in accomplishing a task (Khatib et al., 1999; Djuric et al., 2016). Cobots provide higher flexibility as compared to robots due to effective man and robot interactions (Brown and Woods, 2017). Industry 4.0 demands effective workplace collaboration between human efforts and robots to complement each other to enhance the manufacturability of the product, reduce errors rates, and enhance worker productivity (Gilchrist, 2016). The high flexibility in operations makes the demand for the mass-customized product, and the cobots act as an enabler in achieving it (Cherubini et al., 2016).

4. Autonomous robots: Industrial robots have been extensively recognized to augment productivity, flexibility and minimize the 'workers' involved in physical, heavy, and dangerous industrial activities (Kopacek, 1999; Bibby and Dehe, 2018). Robots enable autonomy on the shop floor to perform a range of jobs (Day, 2018). The robotic manipulators are integrated with human sensing and cognition technology for smart robotic operations ranging from material handling to manufacturing operations (Brown and Woods, 2017; Day, 2018). It increases the flexibility of Industry 4.0. Thus, robots play a significant role in enhancing the reconfigurability, agility, and adaptability of the manufacturing systems (Pedersen et al., 2016).

5. Autonomous machines: Autonomous machines refer to the structure of a hierarchal intelligent control system consisting of three levels, i.e., the organizational level, the coordination level, and the control level (Saridis and Valavanis, 1988; Lee et al., 2015) specified that Industry 4.0 is driven by the transition of the regular machines to self-aware, self-cognitive, self-controlled, and self-learning autonomous machines. The autonomous machines are capable of performing under uncertain circumstances like tool/equipment failure, environmental changes, and incomplete and inadequate process information (Burns, 1997; Park and Tran, 2014).

6. Augmented reality: Augmented reality (AR) is an innovative human-machine interaction system that connections the virtual cybernetic computer-generated information into the real-world manufacturing scenario (Reinhart and Patron, 2003; Jimeno and Puerta, 2007). The characteristics of the AR systems are that the AR systems combine the real as well as the virtual worlds and remain interactive in real-time environments. They are highly reliable, responsive, and agile (Elia et al., 2016). Several applications of AR are in error diagnostics, safety, and security of Industry 4.0 systems, product design, system reconfiguration, process optimization, layout planning, maintenance, and human resource training (Damiani et al., 2018; Uva et al., 2018).

7. Modeling and simulation: Modeling and simulation refer to the process of creating, experimenting, and analyzing the virtualized model of a physical object by generating an artificial history of the manufacturing system (Banks et al., 2000; Chung, 2004). Modeling and simulation are the most commonly used technique in the field of operations management (Amoako-Gyampah and Meredith, 1989; Pannirselvam et al., 1999). It helps in preventing errors and is used as an optimization tool for manufacturing actions, thus acting as a potential enabler for managing complex operations in Industry 4.0 systems (Gilchrist, 2016). With the advent of Industry 4.0, modeling and simulations on real-time data are essential for effective decision-making.

8. Horizontal and vertical integration (HVI): Incorporating connectivity across the machines, physical assets, databases, human resources, and factories are referred to as horizontal and vertical integration (Ghobakhloo, 2018). It is one of the significant components of Industry 4.0 systems. The horizontal connectivity ensures data sharing capability and seamless communication networks among the manufacturing resources available on the shop floor (Anderl et al., 2018; Kusiak, 2018; Wang et al., 2018). It centers on end-to-end value chain integration across networks, thus enhancing cohesiveness, enabling cross-organizational operations, and facilitating enterprise data integration (Rüßmann et al., 2015). Vertical integration focuses on digital integration across the hierarchical levels, i.e., right from sensors level to corporate planning levels (Li et al., 2017; Xu et al., 2018). Such integration improves connectivity, resulting in well-informed decision-making and higher efficiency.

9. Digital twin: Digital twin is the technology that enables activities to be accomplished in the digital layer by cyber counterpart, which was first undertaken in the physical layer (Anderl et al., 2018; Tao and Zhang, 2017; Wang, 2018). Digital twin plays a vital role in analyzing product manufacturability by monitoring the real-time data of the product (Zhuang et al., 2018). The IoT, CPS and Big Data are unified into Industry 4.0 ecosystem for integrating the physical with its digital counterpart, introducing the digital twin concept. This is further used for modeling, simulation, optimization, and making informed production planning decisions like scheduling and shipping for improving manufacturing performance.

10. Big Data Analytics: Big Data is raw data with huge volume and variety; gathered and extracted using the modern technologies designed to extract value economically. Several dimensions of Big Data include velocity, volume, variety, veracity, value, variability, and complexity (Gilchrist, 2016). To determine value from raw data several analytics tools are implemented in Industry 4.0 systems (Lee et al., 2016). Big Data analytics is defined as the process of inspecting, cleansing, transforming, and modeling the data to generate solutions, identify patterns and draw inferences that will enable fast decision-making. Big Data analytics is classified as descriptive, predictive, and prescriptive (Xu and Duan, 2019). The use of machine learning algorithms can also facilitate the predictive and prescriptive behaviors for autonomous systems, thus enabling intelligence and smart controls without any human intervention.

11. Additive manufacturing (AM): AM is the process of manufacturing by the connection of the materials using layer-upon-layer deposition in the absence of any machining processes (Rauch et al., 2018). AM offers numerous benefits in manufacturing complex, high quality, lightweight, and highly customized products (Bibby and Dehe, 2018; Rauch et al., 2018). In manufacturing systems, AM enables the manufacturing of customized products with shorter lead times and reduced costs. Thus, AM, along with seamless connectivity, makes the Industry 4.0 environment highly responsive and competitive.

12. Cyber-security: Cyber-security acts as an important driver for Industry 4.0 systems as the enhanced connectivity has triggered more attack-prone systems. This had resulted in issues such as alteration of the tool path, change of process parameters, and wrong manufacturing controls thus affecting the quality of the product. The majority of cyber-attacks belong to three categories, i.e., availability, confidentiality, and authenticity (Alguliyev et al., 2018). The security breaches in data, especially of cyberinfrastructure, resulted in concerns for Industry 4.0 adoption and implementation. Hence, proper cyber-security measures need to be ensured while deploying Industry 4.0.

13. Cloud manufacturing: The cloud acts as a platform for storing and retrieving data for an Industry 4.0 based manufacturing system (Tao et al., 2014). Cloud-based manufacturing transfers the production-oriented manufacturing system to service-oriented manufacturing systems by focusing on offering the resources as a service in manufacturing, giving rise to the concept of manufacturing as a service (MaaS) (Liu and Xu, 2017; Bibby and Dehe, 2018). Cloud manufacturing has led to the emergence of an entire service-oriented manufacturing model by extending the roots of the conventional manufacturing concepts to modern service-oriented smart manufacturing systems (Zhang and Tao, 2016).

These enablers are the key technologies needed to adopt for implementing Industry 4.0. However, based on the organization's strategic decisions for the desired level of adoption and readiness index, the choice and level of these technologies

TABLE 7.1

The Core Technologies of Industry 4.0

Core Technologies	Description
Internet of Things (IoT)	IoT is used to integrate manufacturing resources and is responsible for real-time monitoring and quality assurance applications of the manufacturing system.
Analytics and AI	The analytics and AI are used to gain meaningful insights into the raw data acquired from the factory floor. Use of various analytics like descriptive, predictive, and prescriptive is used in various manufacturing applications like maintenance, quality control, inventory planning, etc. The AI uses the factory floor data to train the algorithm, predicts the future behavior of the resource and accordingly prescribes the necessary corrective actions to be taken in advance.
Big Data	The connected devices generate a lot of data of various types refer to as Big Data. The generated Big Data are subjected to various analytics and machine learning techniques for root cause analysis and process efficiency applications.
Cloud Computing	The cloud is used for storage and centralization to enhance the integrity and real-time accessibility of raw data collected from the factory floor. The cloud eliminates the data silos and provides a centralized service-oriented platform to integrate the various actors of the value chain, removing inefficiency and enhancing productivity.
Augmented Reality (AR)	The AR devices are used for workforce training, quality assurance, design, and prototyping applications. AR helps in improving the safety and speed of the production process by providing the workforce with dynamic information throughout the route.
Wearables	Wearable devices are used for the real-time traceability of the employees' movement and bioinformatics through the production processes. They help in tracking the operator's performance and expediting the identification of health hazards.
Advanced Robotics	Advanced robotics, also referred to as autonomous robots, can expedite operations in the factory without any human intervention. They are trained using AI algorithms and are capable enough to work alongside human operators.

may vary. The choices made among the enablers depend on the focus of the drivers that the organization needs to meet their competitive priority. A comprehensive list summarizing the core technologies out of the discussed enablers of Industry 4.0 is reviewed in Table 7.1. The technologies mentioned in Table 7.1 are an evident requirement for the deployment of Industry 4.0. The next section deals with the discussions on the conceptual framework for Industry 4.0 based on the identified enablers and the core technologies.

7.4 CONCEPTUAL FRAMEWORK FOR INDUSTRY 4.0

Industry 4.0 has been an emerging topic of interest among the academicians, managers, consultants, and strategists over the recent past. Yet, in many manufacturing areas, managers are finding it difficult to understand the implications and requirements for

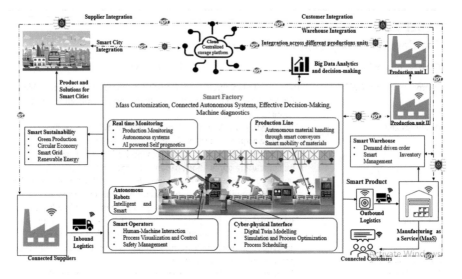

FIGURE 7.3   Conceptual framework of Industry 4.0.

Industry 4.0. Industry 4.0 is characterized by the deployment of emerging technologies, also referred to as the key enablers (Vázquez-Bustelo et al., 2007). The details about enablers are discussed in the previous section. This section deals with a conceptual framework for Industry 4.0 based on the identified enablers. The purpose is to make the practitioners and academicians aware of the basic structure and implications of Industry 4.0. A detailed description of the conceptual framework for Industry 4.0 is shown in Figure 7.3. Industry 4.0 is a transition of the traditional manufacturing systems to the connected, agile, and intelligent systems that can respond to the changing demands of the customers and the needs of the market (Karaköse and Yetiş, 2017; Kusiak, 2018). As shown in Figure 7.3, Industry 4.0 is an integrated system to facilitate healthy control, thus enhancing the efficiency and effectiveness of the value chain. Figure 7.3 goes beyond the basic concepts of the smart factory and discusses the integration of the supply chain with the processes.

The smart factory refers to the factory floor embedded with integrated and autonomous machines, robots, cobots, additive manufacturing systems, and sophisticated systems (Kagermann et al., 2013). The integration among the machines and the monitoring of the real-time data of the production processes take place through IoT. Thus, IoT forms the data acquisition systems for Industry 4.0 (Haverkort and Zimmermann, 2017). Such integration across the systems enables seamless connectivity among the manufacturing assets and facilitates data communication between the machines and the operators. It plays a significant role in enhancing the human-machine and the machine-machine interaction (Ali et al., 2015). Such capabilities lead to the creation of interoperable systems where effective communication and data sharing takes place among the manufacturing assets with low latency and jitter (Gilchrist, 2016). The autonomous systems present on the factory floor are capable of making their own decisions with less/no human intervention, which enables intelligence, leading to the development of decentralized systems (Zhong et al., 2017). Decentralized systems facilitate localized decision-making. For instance, an electronic component industry manufacturing switch gears used the concept of dynamic testing right during production. Such a feature enables testing of the components during manufacturing, and whenever there is an introduction of a new component in the line, the testing facility readjusts itself as per the specifications of the new components without any human intervention. The defective ones are sent for rework. The capability of the testing system to readjust as per the change in the component specification without any human intervention makes it autonomous and intelligent. The decision to accept or reject the components based on defect identification through a dynamic testing system enhances the decentralization of the system through localized decision-making.

The cyber-physical interface shows the confluence of the physical and digital worlds. It is responsible for visualization of the digital twin model throughout the operations (Tao and Zhang, 2017). The digital twin refers to the digital representation of the physical manufacturing asset present on the factory floor (Rüßmann et al., 2015). The digital twin facilitates the modeling and simulation of the processes on the cyber-physical interface. It helps in effective visualization, monitoring, and control of the operations taking place on the factory floor, enhancing productivity and performance. Smart sustainability is another driving capability for Industry 4.0. It is responsible for facilitating the employment of eco-friendly methods in production (Kusiak, 2018). The recycling, reuse, and remanufacturing of the components out of wastes/used components leads to suitable manufacturing phenomena (Kamble et al., 2018a). Another key aspect may be to use smart grids and renewable energy to reduce wastage and pressure on the environment. Summing up the various capabilities, the smart factory is responsible for intelligent systems, localized decision-making, transparency, effective control, sustainable, and flexible operations.

Smart factories produce and deliver products and services for the smart cities whose requirements are directly communicated to the factory over the cloud (Karaköse and Yetiş, 2017). The smart factory can be connected to the suppliers, which facilitates the inbound logistic integration of the value chain. The inbound integration enables the suppliers to digitalize their manufacturing facilities in order to work in synchronization with their clients (Karadayi-Usta, 2020). The smart and connected products, which form the output of the smart factory, are stored in a smart warehouse with smart inventory management and automated material handling capabilities. The smart warehouse is connected with the smart factories, leading to outbound logistic integration. The product is delivered to customers as per demand (Ghobakhloo, 2018). The smart products are embedded with the sensors referred to as the internet of service (IoS), which continuously tracks the product in real-time and provides the product as a service and MaaS business models (Ghobakhloo, 2020). The manufacturers track the product and deliver services to the customers giving rise to the product-service system. This integrates the customers with the value chain (Zhang and Tao, 2016). The cloud forms the centralized storage platform for all the data coming from various sources. The data can be retrieved from the cloud as per the requirements. In addition to, the cloud also acts as a means to integrate the various actors of the product value chain (Xu, 2012; Ghobakhloo, 2020). The cloud contains massive amount of real-time data from various sources; hence is characterized by high volume, variety, complexity, velocity, and veracity. Hence, the data due to the mentioned characteristics is referred to as Big Data (Gilchrist, 2016). The Big Data should be used effectively for making certain critical decisions. It is done by converting the data to information and then to knowledge through the use of various analytics algorithms (Woo et al., 2018). Depending on the type of data, the choice is made among the appropriate analytic algorithms. Due to the centralized storage and open communication among the various value chain actors, the chances of data espionage and leakage is evident. It can give rise to an increase in the probability of potential cyber threats (Alguliyev et al., 2018). Thus, proper cyber-security measures need to be ensured to prevent potential threats. It is done through the use of authentication and encryption protocols while transmitting data to make sure that the right data has been delivered to the right host (Gilchrist, 2016).

The smart factory is also connected with different production units within the plants, thus leading to inter-unit integration through a cloud. It is observed from the conceptual framework that Industry 4.0 is characterized by horizontal integration, i.e., integration across various actors of the supply chain, and vertical integration, i.e., integration across the hierarchies right from the factory floor to the enterprise level operations (Sanchez et al., 2020). Thus, both the integration leads to the end-to-end digital integration of the supply chain. Integration across various layers leads to effective communication leading to enhanced transparency. It depends on the organization to decide the level of transparency they allow within the firm (Liu et al., 2018). This section predominantly focuses on the discussion of the conceptual framework of Industry 4.0 based on the enablers. It is found that the deployment of the emerging technologies is also relevant, as enablers have made substantial digital transformations to the traditional manufacturing environment. The transformations have changed the capabilities of the manufacturing systems, thus making them "smart" (Mittal et al., 2019). The following section determines the potential drivers of Industry 4.0 based on the distinguishing smart capabilities most present in the traditional manufacturing environment.

7.5   DRIVERS OF INDUSTRY 4.0

The deployment of Industry 4.0 will transform the capabilities of the manufacturing firm. The development of new capabilities will enhance the performance of the manufacturing systems. This section deals with the determination of the drivers based on the capabilities of Industry 4.0. The drivers are the essential requirements that an Industry 4.0-based manufacturing system is required to possess. The drivers are the evident and pervasive requirement for Industry 4.0 systems (Bartodziej, 2017). Based on literature review and consultation with the domain experts, the 12 drivers are determined. A detailed discussion about the drivers along with certain examples is given next.

1. Adaptability: It accounts for the system's ability to respond to the variation in engineering, product/process design, and configuration (Brad et al., 2018). It ensures the system to reconfigure as per the change in product and process requirements. The driver will enhance the flexibility and agility requirement of the manufacturing systems (Fatorachian and Kazemi, 2018).

For instance, the robots used for material handling can be reconfigured for welding/painting operation by changing the end effector and reprogramming the motion as per the need of the process. Thus, the flexibility of the robot to accomplish multiple tasks will increase, which in turn enhances the capability to produce parts with different geometry and type at a lesser cost. Adaptability will facilitate the system to cater to the market disruptions in demand and address customer requirements efficiently and effectively without delay. This driver forms a quintessential part of Industry 4.0. It is because one of the purposes of the deployment of Industry 4.0 is to deliver flexible, customized, and innovative products at a low price, which is addressed through this driver (Karaköse and Yetiş, 2017).

2. Integrability: The traditional manufacturing environment was operating in silos. There was no proper connectivity among the manufacturing resources, and improper collaboration and coordination were observed on the factory floor. It resulted in higher work-in-process inventory, increased lead time and cost, and lower utilization of resources. Unlike traditional manufacturing, Industry 4.0 is characterized by integration across the value chain and hierarchies (Rüßmann et al., 2015). The integration ensures the system gets end-to-end connected, which enhances the communication among the various resources (Sanchez et al., 2020). The driver refers to the ability of Industry 4.0 to get integrated. The integration can be of two types, i.e., horizontal and vertical. Integrability will facilitate the easy collaboration of activities right from the design to delivery, thus enhancing the efficiency of the supply chain (Dalenogare et al., 2018). For example, the HVI made the production planners aware of the situations faced in the factory floor. Accordingly, the scheduling decisions are executed to cater to the need of the problem.

3. Interoperable systems: Industry 4.0 is described though the development of the interoperable systems that confirm the system's capability to work in synchronization with each other (Xu et al., 2018). Interoperability facilitates the human–machine and machine–machine interaction in a system (Xu, 2017). Through the use of enablers like IoT, CPS ensures connectivity among the manufacturing assets. The deployment of the connectivity infrastructure will expedite the data sharing capability among the assets, thus giving rise to communication among the humans and machines, enhancing coordination and efficiency of the system (Longo et al., 2017). For instance, interoperability will enhance the synchronization among the machines by indicating one machine in advance of the status of the next machine. Accordingly, the processing sequence and time will get adjusted to reduce delay and improve productivity.

4. Customization: One of the essential drivers for Industry 4.0 is customization. The purpose of Industry 4.0 is to deliver customized products at a low cost (Karaköse and Yetiş, 2017). It can be done through the use of contemporary methods in production. For example, additive manufacturing systems can be used to manufacture complex-shaped components of different geometries at a low cost, which was not possible to be made with the traditional

machining process (Chong et al., 2018; Kusiak, 2018). Therefore, the use of such modern and innovative methods in manufacturing will increase the degree of customization offerings of the manufacturing system. Moreover, the use of an additive manufacturing system will also decrease the production delay, and hence the lead time also gets reduced significantly. The wastage in the production process is also reduced, thus addressing the sustainability aspect of Industry 4.0.

5. Virtualization: Industry 4.0 deals with the use of the digital twin to represent the physical activities happening on the factory floor. The cyber-physical interface forms the virtual/cyber layer of Industry 4.0 (Lu et al., 2020). In the virtual space, the changes are made in the factory model and finally the actualization of the virtual model is conducted to test its real-time implementation and performance outputs. Hence, it plays a critical role in modeling and simulation of the manufacturing environment (Rüßmann et al., 2015). For instance, the AR techniques can be applied for aiding and assisting the training of the workforce based on real-time data, seeing the possibility of assembly operations for a particular part type, manufacturability of the parts in an existing facility, space management, and layout planning (Reinhart and Patron, 2003). Similarly, the degree of virtualization and the selection of potential enablers for virtualization depend on an organization's strategic interest. The virtualization can be assessed through the accuracy of the digital twin readings.

6. Intelligent systems: This refers to the capability of Industry 4.0 systems to sense the requirements of the product/processes and accordingly plan the course of actions to be taken without any human intervention (Lidong and Guanghui, 2016; Kusiak, 2018). The concept is also referred to as autonomous systems. The autonomous systems can sense, think, and execute decisions properly. It gives rise to the development of cognitive capabilities of the manufacturing systems (Wan et al., 2018). The driver enhances the decentralization or the localized decision-making capability of Industry 4.0. For instance, the machines used in the manufacturing system can be trained using the machine algorithm through the use of historical data. The training will ensure the machines behave in a way as per the product/process requirement. Thus, the machines behave in the way as trained without any human intervention. The human-machine interaction is also enhanced by reducing the intervention time (the time taken by the human to operate or control the machine) and increasing the neglected time (the time on which the machine operates autonomously without any human intervention).

7. Diagnosability: In the automated and digitized manufacturing environment, the Industry-4.0-governed systems must be capable enough to identify and diagnose an unknown problem creating an erroneous situation (tools and equipment faults, material handling system faults). The problem is then evaluated, segmented for easy understanding and analysis, and finally, the necessary corrective actions are taken (Alavian et al., 2020). This driver of Industry 4.0 enhances the maintenance capability of the systems. The system

achieves the ability to monitor health and facilitate the prognosis of the machines and resources (Lee et al., 2017). Diagnosability is characterized by the use of predictive and prescriptive analytics. For example, the historical data can be used to predict the potential time for the machine failure and based on the failure, the necessary corrective actions can be addressed by the system. Therefore, it decreases the downtime of the equipment, thus enhancing the quality rate and decreasing lead time significantly.

8. Data quality: The quality of data plays a fundamental role in the improved decision-making process. It is because the data should be complete, consistent, precise, perfect, and convertible to machine processing language to facilitate the use of analytics (Gilchrist, 2016; Li et al., 2017). The incorrect data can result in faulty decision-making, hence leading to inefficiencies and delays. The raw data acquired from the sensors should be free from any errors, and there should be fewer missing data points. The correct predictions of the system behavior can be made if the dataset is complete and correct (Zhang et al., 2015). For instance, the data of the defective or rejected parts should be correct to accurately calculate the manufacturing system's quality rate. The quality rate will allow to properly estimate the overall equipment effectiveness (OEE) of the system. Therefore, data quality plays a significant role in assessing the performance of the system.

9. Data security: Industry 4.0 is characterized by connectivity and communication among the resources. So, the chance of data leakage and espionage is very high, contrary to traditional manufacturing systems, which were primarily operating in silos (Rüßmann et al., 2015). This can increase the probability of cyber threats and attacks on the system (Alguliyev et al., 2018). In order to prevent any chances for cyber threats, proper security protocols need to be ensured. Proper encryption and authentication protocols are to be used while transmitting data so that the right data is delivered from the right server to the right host. It reduces the chances of data leakage. For example, transmission layer security (TLS) protocols are used to ensure the right communication of data to the right place at the right time (Gilchrist, 2016).

10. Manufacturing sustainability: The concept of smart, sustainable manufacturing accounts for the balanced social, economic, and environmental facets of manufacturing (Kamble et al., 2018a, 2018b). Sustainability influences the design, manufacturing processes, development of eco-friendly materials for manufacturing and logistics decisions (Kusiak, 2018). The smart, sustainable manufacturing also emphasizes on reconditioning, remanufacturing, and reusing along with eco-friendly manufacturing. It gives rise to the concept of circular economy. This will help to expand the customer acceptability of the manufactured product considering the extended producers' responsibility (EPR) in manufacturing (Gu et al., 2019). For instance, the cell phone manufacturers used the concept of the product take back after the use from the customers. The required product can be further recycled to produce new cell phones, thus reducing wastage. Additionally, contemporary manufacturing practices such as additive manufacturing reduces wastage during production hence meeting the requirements of green production.

11. Training and capacity building: Industry 4.0 deployment is characterized
    by the development of digital capabilities on the part of the human resource
    to operate the system. The human resource role in Industry 4.0 cannot be
    ignored (Kamble et al., 2018b).

Workforce and human factors play a significant role in monitoring, reconnaissance,
and decision-making of the process. Successful implementation of automation and
digitization demands the development of innovative skills and employee empow-
erment measures in order to make their technology ready and competent enough
to embrace and operate smart shop floor technologies (Karadayi-Usta, 2020). The
extensive focus needs to be made on the training, learning, and capacity building of
human resources in manufacturing.

The focus of Industry 4.0 is on the decentralization or localization of decision-
making. It is done by empowering operators to make certain decisions while operating such systems (Kazancoglu and Ozkan-Ozen, 2018). So, a human plays the role
of the problem solver rather than being mere operators. For instance, in consultation
with the experts, we found that managing human resource is the most critical thing
while deploying Industry 4.0. It is because they are the ones who are not ready to
accept the change easily. Therefore, proper training and motivation workshops on the
impact of a digital revolution, their role in innovation and productivity need to be
given to the workers to make them aware of the significance of this revolution (Fantini
et al., 2020). Besides, the operators need to be trained to perform multiple operations,
enhancing workforce flexibility.

Supplier relations: The connectivity with the suppliers plays a significant role in
the deployment of Industry 4.0. It is because Industry 4.0 systems do not operate in
silos and encourage connectivity among the systems. The supplier forms one of the
critical stakeholders of any manufacturing system. Therefore, integration and connectivity with the suppliers are essential for the proper deployment of Industry 4.0
(Karadayi-Usta, 2020). Additionally, supplier integration enhances the integration of
the inbound logistics with the value chain, thus enhancing the supply chain integration (Bienhaus and Haddud, 2018). Also, it enhances the proper coordination with
the suppliers. More accurately, the driver refers to the development of the digital
capabilities of the suppliers by making their system embed with the enablers or the
emerging technologies so that they can function in coordination with the manufacturing firm (Uygun and Ilie, 2018).

The drivers are the requirements for an Industry 4.0-based system, as inferred
from the detailed discussion. The drivers reflect the capabilities of Industry 4.0-based
systems; consequently, the drivers support the features of Industry 4.0-based systems. A comprehensive list of the features of Industry 4.0 is summarized in Table 7.2
for concrete understanding.

The details about the drivers of Industry 4.0 are now discussed. As already mentioned, the drivers are the requirements of an Industry 4.0-based system. The drivers reflect the capabilities of the Industry 4.0-based manufacturing system. It is
paramount to understand the role of the various enablers in facilitating the adoption
of drivers while deploying Industry 4.0. Therefore, the drivers are mapped with
Industry 4.0 to make the organization aware which enablers are contributing to the

TABLE 7.2
The Features of Industry 4.0

Industry 4.0 Features	Description
Information Transparency	A virtual copy of the shop floor information is created in the digital twin through the data obtained from the sensors and visualized via a cyber-physical interface. The transparency of the information shows the real-time visibility of the manufacturing processes and business operations taking place through the organization.
Decentralized Systems	The decentralization of the manufacturing systems refers to the ability to take decisions autonomously without any human intervention. The systems are trained using machine learning techniques to take certain situational decisions without any human intervention and enable the systems' self-awareness and intelligence.
Technical Assistance	Industry 4.0 systems are equipped with technical assistance systems to support the operators and the engineers in performing certain complex and difficult tasks. It enables the manufacturing system to reduce errors in operation, thus enhancing the quality and reducing the cost of the products.
Digital Presence	Industry 4.0 systems can create a digital copy of the physical system and develop a simulated environment for expediting advanced planning, decision support, and validation capability prior to its physical implementation.
Heterogeneity	It refers to the creation of the economies of scope inside the organization. It enables the system capability to produce multiple varieties of products at effective cost, facilitating customer satisfaction.
Modularity	Creating economies of scale inside the organization. It supports the system to produce a higher volume of products at an effective cost.
Proactive Systems	Industry 4.0 systems can predict the events and problems of production in advance using intelligence and situational awareness systems. Accordingly, the necessary corrective measures can be taken in advance to rectify such problems.
Information Appropriateness	One of the features of Industry 4.0 is to acquire information from multiple sources within the organization, store it, and ensure its compatibility for quality, errors, understandability, and provisioning them to the right people at the right time.
Scalable Systems	Industry 4.0 systems can adjust the plant's production capacity (i.e., increase or decrease) using reconfigurable systems at an effective cost and less time.
Distributed Systems	Industry 4.0 systems work on the concept of a distributed system that enables it to produce products at dispersed manufacturing facilities, coordinated using information and communication technologies and cloud-based systems.

development of what drivers. It will make the organization aware of the potential enablers to focus on based on the drivers they plan to adopt. The details about the mapping are shown in Figure 7.4. It can be observed from Figure 7.4 that the enabler IoT, autonomous machines, and Big Data analytics seem to be the leading contributors toward drivers facilitating the deployment of Industry 4.0. It can be due to the evident fact that Industry 4.0 is primarily driven by connectivity,

DRIVERS	A	B	C	D	E	F	G	H	I	J	K	L	M
Adaptability				√	√								
Integrability		√				√						√	√
Data Quality		√				√			√				√
Customization							√		√				
Intelligent Systems			√	√	√				√				
Data Security					√		√		√	√			
Interoperable Systems		√	√			√				√			
Virtualization	√						√	√	√				
Diagnosability		√		√	√				√				
Training and Capacity building	√		√	√	√		√	√	√	√	√		
Manufacturing Sustainability		√					√	√		√			
Supplier Relations		√				√							√

LIST OF ENABLERS

A: Cyber-physical systems (CPS)
B: Internet of Things (IoT)
C: Cobotics
D: Autonomous Robots
E: Autonomous Machines
F: Horizontal and Vertical Integration
G: Modelling and Simulation

H: Augmented Reality
I: Digital Twin
J: Big Data Analytics
K: Additive Manufacturing
L: Cybersecurity
M: Cloud Manufacturing

FIGURE 7.4   Mapping of the enablers with Industry 4.0 drivers.

intelligence, and analytics which is predominantly done through the applications of these enablers.

The choices made among the enablers and the drivers facilitate the roadmap toward the deployment of Industry 4.0 (Zheng and Ming, 2017). Adoption of Industry 4.0 does not mean implementing all the enablers and drivers. The way is to proceed in a phase-wise manner of deployment (Mittal et al., 2018). It completely depends on the organizations' strategic vision to focus on the relevant set of enablers and drivers as per their requirement (Ghobakhloo, 2018). For instance, an organization working on steel production units need not require the AR systems to the extent required by the firms working in the gaming industry. The steel production unit should initially consider the enablers like IoT, CPS, HVI to facilitate the swift flow of operations and enhance the production outputs. It is because their initial focus is on drivers like integration, connectivity, visualization. Similarly, additive manufacturing will be a paramount requirement for the organizations working in the field of industrial products, plastic, and medical implants industry. The reason pertains to the evident fact that the primary focus of such industries is on drivers like customization at low prices. Therefore, the choices made among the enablers and drivers vary from the organization and the type of market segment in which they deal. The organization can focus on other enablers and drivers when their preliminary requirement for digitalization is achieved.

The transformation to Industry 4.0 is, of course no end in itself, but this revolution must lead to enhanced resource efficiency, high value and innovative products, fast and novel services, and a short time-to-market mechanism. Specifically, the applications and potential benefits encompass:

➢ Improved predictability and cost transparency with high-resolution production

> Improvements in the adherence to delivery dates, reduction in costs, and throughput times using intelligent production planning
> Predictive maintenance, automatic fault detection, enhanced maintenance performance, reduction in maintenance costs, low tooling costs, and superior equipment effectivity
> Intelligent process control, efficient production control, enhanced resource utilization with minimal resource consumption, waste reduction, and short running-in and production times
> Reconfigurability enabling swift scale-up and change management
> Improved ergonomics and high labor productivity with advanced human-machine interaction
> Intra-organization data and feedback sharing that improves the engineering, planning, and production systems
> Value-added customized product and service delivery with the adoption of novel and innovative business models
> As programming and commissioning efforts to become a negligible transition from small batch sizes down to batch size one feasible with intelligent automation

Thus, the integration of industrial IoT, CPS, and Industry 4.0 can improve the sustainability of smart manufacturing, adding value to business strategy and the value chain. The following benefits of determining the enablers and drivers are discussed next.

7.5.1 Flexibility

Intelligent and smart production systems, processes, and self-configuration have to consider various elements such as time, quality, price, and sustainability features (e.g., avoid peak time, etc.).

7.5.2 Remote Monitoring

IoT technology enables remote access and involvement of the third party (e.g., suppliers) in the monitoring, operating, and maintenance of industrial units with new services. Production operations require minimum human intervention. Hence, this results in enhanced efficiency and reduction in errors and waste, and other resources.

7.5.3 Mass Customization

Production and industrialized processes have to meet varying requirements. Mass customization permits individual design considerations and allows high time changes. Even with low production volumes, it warrants profit. Hence, the management of the disproportion between the economies of scale and scope can be handled with the help of mass customization.

7.5.4 Proactive Maintenance

Continuous monitoring of production system and real-time performance data collection positively impact and improve proactive maintenance.

7.5.5 Optimized Decision-Making and Visibility

Right decisions at any time are a key to competitive advantage and market success. IoT offers real-time monitoring and control (e.g., production status) with end-to-end transparency, allowing for optimization across factory sites, thus improving factory efficiency and making well-informed decisions. Moreover, transparency, for example, provides data and makes aware of the energy consumption behavior of production processes, resource consumption, and resource inefficiency. Here, data can be considered in production management decisions to reduce resource usage, waste, and costs and increase efficiency. Further, minimum human intervention reduces errors and waste, and other resources.

7.5.6 Connected Supply Chain

Industrial IoT application helps to gain a superior understanding of the supply chain information that can be delivered in real-time. The automation and digitization, machines and equipment can be connected to the suppliers, "all pertinent elements can understand interdependencies, the flow of materials, and manufacturing cycle times".

7.5.7 New Planning Methods

Smart factories allow the real-time optimization of the manufacturing processes at different levels on a case-by-case basis. The IoT and CPSs digital models can help to make use of abstract planning measures with a robust parallelization in view of the planning of mechanical and electronic systems increasing resource productivity and improving efficiency; further, the ready availability of real-time consumption data from IoT can assist in minimizing consumption costs of production schedule by defining the launch time for job processing.

7.5.8 Creating Values from Big Data Collected

The analysis of large quantities of data collected by IoT devices (i.e., Big Data) and CPSs could help to make new improvements and add value. For example, understanding the machines' behavior through different periods using Big Data. Accordingly, best maintenance services can be adapted, and machines efficiency can be improved, which eventually helps to build a strong relationship with the customers.

7.5.9 Creating New Services

IoT applications will open up new ways of creating new and innovative services with values for the customers before and after.

A transparent, secure, and adaptive communication channel is essential to assure the real-time delivery of information, robustness, and other facets of quality-of-service. Although the collaborative approach offers several benefits, a specified, generally accepted, extensible infrastructure or architectural pattern is required. Hence, it should be able to support the hardware and software systems and a variety of sensors, actuators, on the one hand, while on the other hand, it should be able to manage the complexity of the system. Furthermore, such systems with decentralized structure need a higher level of automation regarding self-management and maintenance. Business analytics and artificial intelligence need to be established to expedite the aforementioned self-management and diagnosis capabilities. In addition, new optimization potentials can be revealed by making use of enormous amounts of gathered data. Moreover, the human-machine interfaces have to be adapted, reflecting the increasing complexity of these systems. The system should ensure a timely and correct display of required information. Otherwise, the mass of information cannot be handled by the human workforce and decisions cannot be made in time.

The lack of a clear digital strategy in value-creating (production and logistics) processes and a lack of support from top management acts as an impediment in the implementation of Industry 4.0. The unknown level of economic benefits of digital investments and the high costs of those investments raise concern among organizations worldwide. They appear not to be ready for this advancement. Moreover, they are also not prepared for the safe storage and handling of data, either.

7.6   CONCLUSIONS

The present study deals with Industry 4.0, the architecture for IoT and CPS-based smart manufacturing and production, and the characteristics of such factories with a focus on the business strategy and value chain aspects. The principal focus of the research work is to list the enablers and determine the drivers' facilitating deployment of Industry 4.0. Initially, the introduction and the need to conduct the research are discussed. It is followed by a detailed discussion of the enablers for Industry 4.0. A conceptual framework for Industry 4.0 based on the enablers is discussed, and it is followed by the determination and detailed discussion for the drivers of Industry 4.0. Finally, the mapping of the enablers with Industry 4.0 drivers is shown and discussed to develop an understanding regarding the potential enablers responsible for the development of drivers. The study is beneficial to the managers, consultants, and academicians working in the domain of Industry 4.0 to get a thorough understanding of the enablers and the potential drivers that characterized the deployment of Industry 4.0. Also, it gives substantial explanations through discussions on the conceptual framework and the drivers of the operational transformations that an organization can undertake while adopting Industry 4.0. The managers can use the study's findings to develop the strategy to implement Industry 4.0 in their factories. Additionally, the organizations that have already deployed Industry 4.0 can refer to the study findings to focus on their key drivers and enablers instead of all for gaining maximum benefit out of Industry 4.0 at limited investment. The study highlights that adopting the IoT-CPS paradigm at production level increases the efficiency of production systems and provides better support to industrial management. The real-time data collection from the shop floor (e.g., at the production line, machine, processes level, etc.), and providing it to the decision-makers at any place, eventually help to take well-informed decisions integrating the data in production management practices, thus enabling smart decision-making at production management level (e.g., production scheduling, and maintenance management, etc.), which can lead to enhanced industrial efficiency, through finding and reducing waste.

The application of industrial IoT, CPS, and Industry 4.0 offers a smart and efficient production, more well-organized processes with their associates, a higher level of logistic service, improved collaboration between certain logistic functions, competitiveness, and higher market performance and financial returns. Furthermore, the efficient production processes lead to achieving better productivity and economies of scale, which eventually might also result in better economic sustainability. For businesses to take advantage of the enormous opportunities of the industrial Internet and Industry 4.0 and adapt to the industrial IoT concepts, some radical changes are required in every area of their business. A thorough evaluation of the company's current position in terms of their philosophy, vision, and mission, strategy, processes, procedures, and current technologies is required, taking into account the level of adaptation they wish to achieve. Companies are required to transform their business to operate seamlessly in a digital world. Although there are several approaches for digital transformation, three key areas that need to be focused on are operational process, business models, and customer experience.

Digitally transforming businesses and adapting to the Industry 4.0 environment will build global business networks, connecting factories, machinery, and warehousing facilities as CPS, connecting and controlling each other intelligently by sharing information that triggers actions. These CPSs will thus act as smart factories, smart machines, smart storage facilities, and smart supply chains. This will drive improvements in the industrial processes within manufacturing as a whole through engineering, material usage, supply chains, and product lifecycle management, thus deeply integrating each other and providing remarkable improvements in the industrial process.

In summary, Industry 4.0 will require the integration of CPS in procurement, manufacturing, and logistics while introducing the IoT and services in the manufacturing process. This will bring new ways to create value, business models, and downstream services.

7.6.1 LIMITATIONS OF THE STUDY

The main limitation of the work is that the drivers of Industry 4.0 are determined but not any way is proposed to measure the drivers. The study generally discusses the various features, characteristics, and benefits of Industry 4.0 and does not provide any real case. The study addresses the constraints in the adoption of Industry 4.0, but to a relatively small extent, this can be addressed in-depth in future studies.

7.6.2 FUTURE SCOPE

The future work of the study should focus on the development of a metric to quantify the drivers. The metric can be further used to develop a mathematical model to optimize the manufacturing performance based on Industry 4.0 deployment. Finally, the strategic insights can be delivered from the detailed analysis of the mathematical model.

REFERENCES

Alavian, P., Eun, Y., Meerkov, S. M., & Zhang, L. (2020). Smart production systems: Automating decision-making in manufacturing environment. *International Journal of Production Research, 58*(3), 828–845. doi:10.1080/00207543.2019.1600765.

Alguliyev, R., Imamverdiyev, Y., & Sukhostat, L. (2018). Cyber-physical systems and their security issues. *Computers in Industry, 100* (April), 212–223. doi:10.1016/j.compind.2018.04.017.

Ali, S., Qaisar, S. Bin, Saeed, H., Khan, M. F., Naeem, M., & Anpalagan, A. (2015). Network challenges for cyber physical systems with tiny wireless devices: A case study on reliable pipeline condition monitoring. *Sensors (Switzerland)* (Vol. 15, Issue 4). doi:10.3390/s150407172.

Almada-Lobo, F. (2016). The Industry 4.0 revolution and the future of manufacturing execution systems (MES). *Journal of Innovation Management, 3*(4), 16–21. doi:10.24840/2183-0606_003.004_0003.

Amoako-Gyampah, K., & Meredith, J. (1989). The operations management research agenda: An update. *Journal of Operations Management, 8*(3), 250–262. doi:10.1016/0272-6963(89)90027-2.

Anderl, R., Haag, S., Schützer, K., & Zancul, E. (2018). Digital twin technology – An approach for Industrie 4.0 vertical and horizontal lifecycle integration. *It – Information Technology, 60*(3), 125–132. doi:10.1515/itit-2017-0038.

Ashton, K. (2009). That 'Internet of 'things' thing. *RFID Journal, 22*(7), 97–114.

Banks, J., Carson, J. S., Nelson, B. L., & Nicol, D. M. (2000). *Discrete Event System Simulation* (3rd ed.). Englewood Cliffs, NJ: Pearson.

Bartodziej, C. J. (2017). The concept Industry 4.0. *The Concept Industry 4.0, 2011.* doi:10.1007/978-3-658-16502-4.

Baur, C., & Wee, D. (2015). *Manufacturin's Next Act.* Available at: https://www.mckinsey.com/business-functions/operations/our-insights/manufacturings-next-act

Bibby, L., & Dehe, B. (2018). Defining and assessing industry 4.0 maturity levels – Case of the defence sector. *Production Planning & Control, 29*(12), 1030–1043. doi:10.1080/09537287.2018.1503355.

Bienhaus, F., & Haddud, A. (2018). Procurement 4.0: Factors influencing the digitisation of procurement and supply chains. *Business Process Management Journal, 24*(4), 965–984.

Brad, S., Murar, M., & Brad, E. (2018). Design of smart connected manufacturing resources to enable changeability, reconfigurability and total-cost-of-ownership models in the factory-of-the-future. *International Journal of Production Research, 56*(6), 2269–2291. doi:10.1080/00207543.2017.1400705.

Brown, S., & Woods, A. (2017). An operations management perspective on collaborative robotics. In *Proceedings of the International Annual Conference of the American Society for Engineering Management*, pp. 1–8.

Burns, R. (1997). Intelligent manufacturing. *Aircraft Engineering and Aerospace Technology, 69*(5), 440–446. doi:10.1108/00022669710367425.

Cherubini, A., Passama, R., Crosnier, A., Lasnier, A., & Fraisse, P. (2016). Collaborative manufacturing with physical human–robot interaction. *Robotics and Computer-Integrated Manufacturing, 40*, 1–13. doi:10.1016/j.rcim.2015.12.007.

Chong, L., Ramakrishna, S., & Singh, S. (2018). A review of digital manufacturing-based hybrid additive manufacturing processes. *International Journal of Advanced Manufacturing Technology, 95*(5–8), 2281–2300. doi:10.1007/s00170-017-1345-3.

Chung, C. A. (2004). *Simulation modelling handbook. A practical approach.* London: CRC Press/Taylor & Francis Group.

Dalenogare, L. S., Benitez, G. B., Ayala, N. F., & Frank, A. G. (2018). The expected contribution of Industry 4.0 technologies for industrial performance. *International Journal of Production Economics, 204* (July), 383–394. doi:10.1016/j.ijpe.2018.08.019.

Damiani, L., Demartini, M., Guizzi, G., Revetria, R., & Tonelli, F. (2018). Augmented and virtual reality applications in industrial systems: A qualitative review towards the industry 4.0 era. *IFAC-PapersOnLine, 51*(11), 624–630. doi:10.1016/j.ifacol.2018.08.388.

Day, C. P. (2018). Robotics in industry—Their role in intelligent manufacturing. *Engineering, 4*(4), 440–445. doi:10.1016/j.eng.2018.07.012.

Djuric, A. M., Urbanic, R. J., & Rickli, J. L. (2016). A framework for collaborative robot (CoBot) integration in advanced manufacturing systems. *SAE International Journal of Materials and Manufacturing, 9*(2), 457–464. doi:10.4271/2016-01-0337.

Elia, V., Gnoni, M. G., & Lanzilotto, A. (2016). Evaluating the application of augmented reality devices in manufacturing from a process point of view: An AHP based model. *Expert Systems with Applications, 63*, 187–197. doi:10.1016/j.eswa.2016.07.006.

Fantini, P., Pinzone, M., & Taisch, M. (2020). Placing the operator at the centre of Industry 4.0 design: Modelling and assessing human activities within cyber-physical systems. *Computers and Industrial Engineering, 139*. doi:10.1016/j.cie.2018.01.025.

Fatorachian, Hajar, & Kazemi, H. (2018). A critical investigation of Industry 4.0 in manufacturing: Theoretical operationalisation framework. *Production Planning and Control, 29*(8), 633–644. doi:10.1080/09537287.2018.1424960.

Frazzon, E. M., Hartmann, J., Makuschewitz, T., & Scholz-Reiter, B. (2013). Towards socio-cyber-physical systems in production networks. *Forty Sixth CIRP Conference on Manufacturing Systems 2013*, 49–54. doi:10.1016/j.procir.2013.05.009.

Ghobakhloo, M. (2018). The future of manufacturing industry: A strategic roadmap toward Industry 4.0. *Journal of Manufacturing Technology Management, 29*(6), 910–936. doi:10.1108/JMTM-02-2018-0057.

Ghobakhloo, M. (2020). Determinants of information and digital technology implementation for smart manufacturing. *International Journal of Production Research, 58*(8), 2384–2405. doi:10.1080/00207543.2019.1630775.

Gilchrist, A. (2016). *Industry 4.0 The Industrial Internet of Things*. Berkeley, CA: Apress. doi:10.1007/978-1-4842-2047-4.

Gu, F., Guo, J., Hall, P., & Gu, X. (2019). An integrated architecture for implementing extended producer responsibility in the context of Industry 4.0. *International Journal of Production Research, 57*(5), 1458–1477. doi:10.1080/00207543.2018.1489161.

Gubbi, J., Buyya, R., Marusic, S., & Palaniswami, M. (2013). Internet of Things (IoT): A vision, architectural elements, and future directions. *Future Generation Computer Systems, 29*(7), 1645–1660.

Gürdür, D., & Asplund, F. (2018). A systematic review to merge discourses: Interoperability, integration and cyber-physical systems. *Journal of Industrial Information Integration, 9*, 14–23. doi:10.1016/j.jii.2017.12.001.

Haag, S., & R. Anderl. (2018). Digital twin–Proof of concept. *Manufacturing Letters, 15* (Part B), 64–66. doi:10.1016/j.mfglet.2018.02.006.

Haverkort, B. R., & Zimmermann, A. (2017). Smart Industry: How ICT Will Change the Game! *IEEE Internet Computing, 21*(1), 8–10. doi:10.1109/MIC.2017.22.

Jimeno, A., & Puerta, A. (2007). State of the art of the virtual reality applied to design and manufacturing processes. *The International Journal of Advanced Manufacturing Technology, 33*(9–10), 866–874. doi:10.1007/s00170-006-0534-2.

Kagermann, H., Helbig, J., Hellinger, A., & Wahlster, W. (2013). *Recommendations for Implementing the Strategic Initiative INDUSTRIE 4.0: Securing the Future of German Manufacturing Industry*. Available at: https://www.din.de/blob/76902/e8cac883f42b-f28536e7e8165993f1fd/recommendations-for-implementing-industry-4-0-data.pdf

Kamble, S. S., Gunasekaran, A., & Gawankar, S. A. (2018a). Sustainable Industry 4.0 framework: A systematic literature review identifying the current trends and future perspectives. *Process Safety and Environmental Protection*, *117*, 408–425. doi:10.1016/j.psep.2018.05.009.

Kamble, S. S., Gunasekaran, A., & Sharma, R. (2018b). Analysis of the driving and dependence power of barriers to adopt industry 4.0 in Indian manufacturing industry. *Computers in Industry*, *101* (March), 107–119. doi:10.1016/j.compind.2018.06.004.

Karadayi-Usta, S. (2020). An interpretive structural analysis for Industry 4.0 adoption challenges. *IEEE Transactions on Engineering Management*, *67*(3), 973–978. doi:10.1109/TEM.2018.2890443.

Karaköse, M., & Yetiş, H. (2017). A cyberphysical system based mass-customization approach with integration of Industry 4.0 and smart city. *Wireless Communications and Mobile Computing*, *2017*, pp. 1–9. doi:10.1155/2017/1058081.

Kazancoglu, Y., & Ozkan-Ozen, Y. D. (2018). Analyzing Workforce 4.0 in the Fourth Industrial Revolution and proposing a road map from operations management perspective with fuzzy DEMATEL. *Journal of Enterprise Information Management*, *31*(6), 891–907. doi:10.1108/JEIM-01-2017-0015.

Khatib, O., Yokoi, K., Brock, O., Chang, K., & Casal, A. (1999). Robots in human environments: Basic autonomous capabilities. *The International Journal of Robotics Research*, *18*(7), 684–696. doi:10.1177/02783649922066501.

Kopacek, P. (1999). Intelligent manufacturing: Present state and future trends. *Journal of Intelligent and Robotic Systems*, *26*(3–4), 217–229.

Kusiak, Andrew. (2018). Smart manufacturing. *International Journal of Production Research*, *56*(1–2), 508–517. doi:10.1080/00207543.2017.1351644.

Lee, J, Bagheri, B., & Jin, C. (2016). Introduction to cyber manufacturing. *Manufacturing Letters*, *8*, 11–15. doi:10.1016/j.mfglet.2016.05.002.

Lee, J, Bagheri, B., & Kao, H. A. (2015). A Cyber-Physical Systems architecture for Industry 4.0-based manufacturing systems. *Manufacturing Letters*, *3*, 18–23. doi:10.1016/j.mfglet.2014.12.001.

Lee, Jay, Jin, C., & Bagheri, B. (2017). Cyber physical systems for predictive production systems. *Production Engineering*, *11*(2), 155–165. doi:10.1007/s11740-017-0729-4.

Letichevskyi, A. A., Letychevskyi, O. O., Skobelev, V. G., & Volkov, V. (2017). Cyber-physical systems. *Cybernetics and Systems Analysis*, *53*(6), 821–834.

Li, X., Li, D., Wan, J., Vasilakos, A. V., Lai, C. F., & Wang, S. (2017). A review of industrial wireless networks in the context of Industry 4.0. *Wireless Networks*, *23*(1), 23–41. doi:10.1007/s11276-015-1133-7.

Liao, Y., Deschamps, F., Loures, E., & Ramos, L. F. P. (2017). Past, present and future of Industry 4.0 – A systematic literature review and research agenda proposal. *International Journal of Production Research*, *55*(12), 3609–3629. doi:10.1080/00207543.2017.1308576.

Lidong, W., & Guanghui, W. (2016). Big data in cyber-physical systems, digital manufacturing and Industry 4.0. *International Journal of Engineering and Manufacturing*, *6*(4), 1–8. doi:10.5815/ijem.2016.04.01.

Liu, C., Jiang, P., & Zhang, C. (2018). A resource-oriented middleware in a prototype cyber-physical manufacturing system. *Proceedings of the Institution of Mechanical Engineers, Part B: Journal of Engineering Manufacture*, *232*(13), 2339–2352. doi:10.1177/0954405417716494.

Liu, Y., & Xu, X. (2017). Industry 4.0 and cloud manufacturing: A comparative analysis. *Journal of Manufacturing Science and Engineering, Transactions of the ASME*, *139*(3), 1–8. doi:10.1115/1.4034667.

Longo, F., Nicoletti, L., & Padovano, A. (2017). Smart operators in industry 4.0: A human-centered approach to enhance operators' capabilities and competencies within the new smart factory context. *Computers and Industrial Engineering, 113*, 144–159. doi:10.1016/j.cie.2017.09.016.

Lu, Y. (2017). Industry 4.0: A survey on technologies, applications and open research issues. *Journal of Industrial Information Integration, 6*, 1–10. doi:10.1016/j.jii.2017.04.005.

Lu, Yuqian, Liu, C., Wang, K. I. K., Huang, H., & Xu, X. (2020). Digital Twin-driven smart manufacturing: Connotation, reference model, applications and research issues. *Robotics and Computer-Integrated Manufacturing, 61* (July 2019), 101837. doi:10.1016/j.rcim.2019.101837.

Ma, H. D. (2011). Internet of Things: Objectives and scientific challenges. *Journal of Computer Science and Technology, 26*, 919–924. doi:10.1007/s11390-011-1189-5.

Mittal, S, Khan, M. A., Purohit, J. K., Menon, K., Romero, D., & Wuest, T. (2020). A smart manufacturing adoption framework for SMEs. *International Journal of Production Research, 58*(5), 1555–1573. doi:10.1080/00207543.2019.1661540.

Mittal, S, Khan, M. A., Romero, D., & Wuest, T. (2019). Smart manufacturing: Characteristics, technologies and enabling factors. *Proceedings of the Institution of Mechanical Engineers, Part B: Journal of Engineering Manufacture, 233*(5), 1342–1361. doi:10.1177/0954405417736547.

Mittal, Sameer, Khan, M. A., Romero, D., & Wuest, T. (2018). A critical review of smart manufacturing & Industry 4.0 maturity models: Implications for small and medium-sized enterprises (SMEs). *Journal of Manufacturing Systems, 49* (June), 194–214. doi:10.1016/j.jmsy.2018.10.005.

Monostori, L., Kádár, B., Bauernhansl, T., Kondoh, S., Kumara, S., Reinhart, G., Sauer, O., Schuh, G., Sihn, W., & Ueda, K. (2016). Cyber-physical systems in manufacturing. *CIRP Annals, 65*(2), 621–641. doi:10.1016/j.cirp.2016.06.005.

Pannirselvam, G. P., Ferguson, L. A., Ash, R. C., & Siferd, S. (1999). Operations management research: An update for the 1990s. *Journal of Operations Management, 18*(1), 95–112. doi:10.1016/S0272-6963(99)00009-1.

Park, H. S., & Tran, N. H. (2014). Development of a smart machining system using self-optimizing control. *International Journal of Advanced Manufacturing Technology, 74*(9–12), 1365–1380. doi:10.1007/s00170-014-6076-0.

Pedersen, M. R., Nalpantidis, L., Andersen, R. S., Schou, C., Bøgh, S., Krüger, V., & Madsen, O. (2016). Robot skills for manufacturing: From concept to industrial deployment. *Robotics and Computer-Integrated Manufacturing, 37*, 282–291. doi:10.1016/j.rcim.2015.04.002.

Rauch, E., Unterhofer, M., & Dallasega, P. (2018). Industry sector analysis for the application of additive manufacturing in smart and distributed manufacturing systems. *Manufacturing Letters, 15* (Part B), 126–131. doi:10.1016/j.mfglet.2017.12.011.

Reinhart, G., & Patron, C. (2003). Integrating augmented reality in the assembly domain – Fundamentals, benefits and applications. *CIRP Annals-Manufacturing Technology, 52*(1), 5–8. doi:10.1016/S0007-8506(07)60517-4.

Rüßmann, M., Lorenz, M., Gerbert, P., Waldner, M., Justus, J., Engel, P., & Harnisch, M. (2015). *Industry 4.0: The Future of Productivity and Growth in Manufacturing Industries.* Available at: https://image-src.bcg.com/Images/Industry_40_Future_of_Productivity_April_2015_tcm9-61694.pdf

Sanchez, M., Exposito, E., & Aguilar, J. (2020). Industry 4.0: Survey from a system integration perspective. *International Journal of Computer Integrated Manufacturing, 33*(10–11), 1017–1041. doi:10.1080/0951192X.2020.1775295.

Saridis, G. N., & Valavanis, K. P. (1988). Analytical design of intelligent machines. *Automatica, 24*(2), 123–133. doi:10.1016/0005-1098(88)90022-2.

Sung, T. K. (2018). Industry 4.0: A Korea perspective. *Technological Forecasting and Social Change, 132* (November 2017), 40–45. doi:10.1016/j.techfore.2017.11.005.

Tao, F., Qi, Q., Liu, A., & Kusiak, A. (2018). Data-driven smart manufacturing. *Journal of Manufacturing Systems, 48* (Part C), 157–169. doi:10.1016/j.jmsy.2018.01.006.

Tao, F., & Zhang, M. (2017). Digital twin shop-floor: A new shop-floor paradigm `towards smart manufacturing. *IEEE Access, 5,* 20418–20427. doi:10.1109/ACCESS.2017.2756069.

Tao, F., Zuo, Y., Da Xu, L., & Zhang, L. (2014). IoT-Based intelligent perception and access of manufacturing resource toward cloud manufacturing. *IEEE Transactions on Industrial Informatics, 10*(2), 1547–1557. doi:10.1109/TII.2014.2306397.

Uva, A. E., Gattullo, M., Manghisi, V. M., Spagnulo, D., Cascella, G. L., & Fiorentino, M. (2018). Evaluating the effectiveness of spatial augmented reality in smart manufacturing: A solution for manual working stations. *The International Journal of Advanced Manufacturing Technology, 94,* 509–521. doi:10.1007/s00170-017-0846-4.

Uygun, Y., & Ilie, M. (2018). Autonomous manufacturing-related procurement in the era of Industry 4.0. *Digitalisierung Im Einkauf,* 81–97. doi:10.1007/978-3-658-16909-1_6.

Vázquez-Bustelo, D., Avella, L., & Fernández, E. (2007). Agility drivers, enablers and outcomes: Empirical test of an integrated agile manufacturing model. *International Journal of Operations & Production Management, 27*(12), 1303–1332. doi:10.1108/01443570710835633.

Wan, J., Tang, S., Hua, Q., Li, D., Liu, C., & Lloret, J. (2018). Context-aware cloud robotics for material handling in cognitive industrial Internet of Things. *IEEE Internet of Things Journal, 5*(4), 2272–2281. doi:10.1109/JIOT.2017.2728722.

Wang, B. (2018). The future of manufacturing: A new perspective. *Engineering, 4*(5), 722–728. doi:10.1016/j.eng.2018.07.020.

Wang, J., Ma, Y., Zhang, L., Gao, R. X., & Wu, D. (2018). Deep learning for smart manufacturing: Methods and applications. *Journal of Manufacturing Systems, 48,* 144–156. doi:10.1016/j.jmsy.2018.01.003.

Woo, J., Shin, S. J., Seo, W., & Meilanitasari, P. (2018). Developing a big data analytics platform for manufacturing systems: Architecture, method, and implementation. *International Journal of Advanced Manufacturing Technology, 99*(9–12), 2193–2217. doi:10.1007/s00170-018-2416-9.

Wuest, T. (2019). Smart manufacturing builds opportunities for ISEs. *ISE Magazine,* pp. 40–44. www.iise.org/ISEmagazine.

Xu, L. D., & Duan, L. (2019). Big data for cyber physical systems in Industry 4.0: A survey. *Enterprise Information Systems, 13*(2), 148–169. doi:10.1080/17517575.2018.1442934.

Xu, L. D., Xu, E. L., & Li, L. (2018). Industry 4.0: State of the art and future trends. *International Journal of Production Research, 56*(8), 2941–2962. doi:10.1080/00207543.2018.1444806.

Xu, X. (2012). From cloud computing to cloud manufacturing. *Robotics and Computer-Integrated Manufacturing, 28*(1), 75–86. doi:10.1016/j.rcim.2011.07.002.

Xu, X. (2017). Machine Tool 4.0 for the new era of manufacturing. *International Journal of Advanced Manufacturing Technology, 92*(5–8), 1893–1900. doi:10.1007/s00170-017-0300-7.

Yang, C., Shen, W., & Wang, X. (2016). Applications of Internet of Things in manufacturing. In *Computer Supported Cooperative Work in Design (CSCWD), 2016 IEEE 20th International Conference On,* pp. 670–675.

Zhang, L., Luo, Y., Tao, F., Li, B. H., Ren, L., Zhang, X., Guo, H., Cheng, Y., Hu, A., & Liu, Y. (2014). Cloud manufacturing: A new manufacturing paradigm. *Enterprise Information Systems, 8*(2), 167–187. doi:10.1080/17517575.2012.683812.

Zhang, Y, & Tao, F. (2016). *Optimization of Manufacturing Systems Using the Internet of Thing.* Academic Press, Elsevier.

Zhang, Y., Zhang, G., Wang, J., Sun, S., Si, S., & Yang, T. (2015). Real-time information capturing and integration framework of the Internet of manufacturing things. *International Journal of Computer Integrated Manufacturing, 28*(8), 811–822. doi:10.1080/09511 92X.2014.900874.

Zheng, M., & Ming, X. (2017). Construction of cyber-physical system–integrated smart manufacturing workshops: A case study in automobile industry. *Advances in Mechanical Engineering, 9*(10), 1–17. doi:10.1177/1687814017733246.

Zhong, R. Y., Xu, X., Klotz, E., & Newman, S. T. (2017). Intelligent manufacturing in the context of Industry 4.0: A review. *Engineering, 3*(5), 616–630. doi:10.1016/J. ENG.2017.05.015.

Zhuang, C., Liu, J., & Xiong, H. (2018). Digital twin-based smart production management and control framework for the complex product assembly shop-floor. *The International Journal of Advanced Manufacturing Technology, 96*, 1149–1163. doi:10.1007/ s00170-018-1617-6.

8 Artificial Intelligence-Based Hiring in Data Science Driven Management Context

Prachi Bhatt

CONTENTS

8.1 INTRODUCTION

It is stunning to see what the businesses today are experiencing with regard to speed and rigor of change in the business rhetoric in management. Businesses have become more inclined and are evolving toward data science driven management. Technology is playing a significantly instrumental role in this evolution. Growth in business cases, in magnitude and type, dealing with big data to machine learning to artificial intelligence (AI) is quite impressive. Technology is both changing and challenging the ways businesses are run at global level (Erixon, 2018). The changes posed by the technological advancements are also reshaping the way HR functions are being performed. Development of technology-mediated practices has stimulated

DOI: 10.1201/9781003048862-8

the transformation of work practices, and change in focus of talent acquisition (Shufutinsky, Beach and Saraceno, 2020; Martinez, 2020). Embracing the technological interventions in the HR operations in organizations has taken different forms and challenges. One of the challenges is to compete at global level in terms of efficient and effective hiring process.

Globally, hiring decision-making is one of the emerging cases of business use of AI. In the Indian talent market context as well, the processes of recruitment and selection have been immensely affected by the latest technological trends, AI being one of them (Goyal, 2017; Sharma, 2018; Kharade, 2020). Attracting and hiring people using AI applications has gained quite a traction in the HR community and practitioners across businesses in general. Although to attract and hire top talent in talent market in India is competitive, the extent of AI application in hiring process varies across business sectors. According to the Human Resources Professionals Association (2017), approx. 43 percent of recruiters are applying AI in form or other in their recruitment processes. Baxter (2018) predicts the extensive use of AI in the recruitment process such as interviewing potential candidates. But, amid the AI excitement, some see AI as another overhyped proposition (Guszcza, Lewis, and Evans-Greenwood, 2017). AI in hiring processes have not seen a complete elimination of the human element. Currently, human recruiters support significant human involvement in each and every step in hiring process (O'Donovan, 2019; Paramita, 2020). This implies that with the perceived benefits associated with the use of AI in hiring processes, there are apprehensions associated with it as well.

Hence, it seems very relevant to explore how HR managers perceive AI-based hiring practices. There are no relevant research evidences to the best of the author's knowledge, which addresses what are the factors that would influence the choice of using AI application for hiring process in organizations. In the Indian context as well, there is no research that addresses this question. Another important question is – what HR managers think about AI application in hiring in terms of its perceived benefits and apprehensions. Thus, exploring the viewpoints of HR managers toward AI and its use in hiring in Indian workplaces is very pertinent, more so in the prevalent Covid-19 pandemic context of workplaces and practices at work.

8.2 ARTIFICIAL INTELLIGENCE (AI) AND HIRING

Recruitment and selection practices have evolved to be technology-linked (Ryan et al., 2015; O'Donovan, 2019; Galanaki, Lazazzara, and Parry, 2019; Johnson, Stone, and Lukaszewski, 2020). Technology has reshaped hiring in terms of tools, platforms, online reviewing systems. Use of multimedia applications like social networking websites (Kluemper, Davison, Cao, and Wu, 2015; Roth, Bobko, Van Iddekinge, and Thatcher, 2016), unproctored or mobile testing (Burke, Mahoney-Phillips, Bowler and Downey, 2011), and video resumes (Hiemstra and Derous, 2015) are few examples of technology intervention in hiring function.

One such emerging trend in technology-based hiring function is AI. According to Nilsson (2005), human-level AI is the ability of machines to do tasks that require human intelligence. AI is an intelligent system with the ability to think and learn. According to Salin and Winston (1992), AI can be explained as a group of techniques which allow machines to do jobs which call for human intelligence and human skills.

Application of AI in the recruitment function of HRM is emerging as one of the remarkable trends (Upadhyay and Khandelwal, 2018). However, restricting to traditional methods of hiring hinders the real usage of AI in hiring process (Pillai and Sivathanu, 2020). Upadhyay and Khandelwal (2018) highlight that AI is changing recruitment processes by replacing routine tasks that are performed by human recruiters. HR department generally conducts evaluation of the received job applications manually. But utilization of AI can make recruiters job of screening and evaluation much more efficient with help of AI-based ranking systems and algorithms (Faliagka, Ramantas, Tsakalidis, and Tzimas, 2012). Sourcing applicants' information from blogs, professional websites, etc., and treating the data using linguistic analysis can also help capturing more details about the potential candidates' personality, emotions, and the like (Faliagka et al., 2012). AI can be used, like HireVue employs, to interpret and analyze applicant's video interviews to uncover finer aspects of communication. HireVue widely uses AI-based applications in hiring functions. Hirevue's application of AI compares the applicants' interviews to that of highly talented employees and suggest the best applicants to recruiters (HireVue, 2017, 2018).

Recent trends and technological developments have impacted candidate assessments during the hiring processes of many firms. However, the understanding about the factors influencing the decisions of adopting AI-based applications in the hiring process is unclear. Largely, in the Indian context, wider application of AI is missing in the hiring processes of firms across various businesses and industries. Thus, it is pertinent to explore the key apprehensions and benefits perceived by Indian HR managers toward the AI-based hiring process, which is also missing in the literature. The ongoing COVID-19 pandemic further underlines the relevance of the present work. Hence the present study covers firstly, the factors influencing the decisions of HR managers in adopting AI-based hiring processes. And secondly, it deals with the identification of perceived benefits and apprehensions of HR managers toward adopting AI-based technology intervention in hiring processes of firms. Further it deals with allocation of relative weights to the identified benefits and apprehensions, respectively.

8.3   ABOUT THE STUDY

8.3.1   OBJECTIVES

The two key objectives of the present study are to:

1. Explore the factors influencing the decisions of HR managers in adopting AI-based hiring processes.
2. And secondly, it deals with the identification of the perceived benefits and apprehensions of HR managers toward adopting AI-based technology intervention in hiring processes of firms, and allocation of relative weights to the identified benefits and apprehensions, respectively.

8.3.2 METHODOLOGY

For the first objective, a review of relevant literature was conducted. And, for the second objective, domain experts were approached for their input, and the following two techniques were employed:

- The Delphi method for exploring the perceived benefits and perceived apprehensions associated with of AI-based hiring by the domain experts;
- The analytic hierarchy process (AHP) approach to obtain relative weights separately for each of the identified benefits and apprehensions.

8.3.2.1 Delphi Method to Identify the Benefits and Apprehensions

Delphi method is used to determine the key benefits and apprehensions associated with AI-based hiring, as perceived by the HR experts. As AI in the hiring process is a very specific area of work, hence it was necessary to involve HR professionals to be involved as an expert panel in identifying the benefits and apprehensions associated with the AI-based hiring. A total of six experts, five experts in the area of HR function, specifically working in hiring and strategic decisions belonging to different industries, and one expert from academia were approached for this study.

In the first stage, respondents were asked to respond to the open-ended question about what do you think are the benefits and apprehensions associated with adopting AI-based hiring in today's workplaces. After receiving responses from all the six experts approached, lists of relevant benefits and apprehensions items was generated. At this stage, data was analyzed by clustering basis similarity of the responses received and deleting the duplicate responses. This step yielded 7 benefits and 9 apprehensions items.

In the second stage, respondents were asked to respond to the two questionnaires which were distributed for step 1 analyses for the 7 benefits and 9 apprehensions, respectively. Respondents used the Likert scale to reveal the importance of the items as: "very important, 5"; "important, 4"; "general, 3"; "unimportant, 2"; and "Not at all important, 1." In step 2, the result analyzed in the step 1 were again presented to the experts for their response and possible revisions seeing the step 1 results. Responses were analyzed and the items in benefits and apprehensions with lower scores were deleted which finally yielded 6 benefits and 7 apprehensions items.

8.3.2.2 AHP Method: Benefits and Apprehensions

AHP was employed separately for both benefits and apprehension items to obtain their relative weights. Relative weights imply the importance of each of the benefits and apprehension through pair comparison analysis with the help of the same six-membered expert panel who were approached again at a later stage for seeking inputs for AHP.

According to Saaty (1980), AHP is a multi-criteria decision-making (MCDM) technique supportive in analyzing complex decision-making involving multiple criteria. AHP is an appropriate method especially in cases where decision-making is influenced by subjective judgments of experts (Dalalah, Hayajneh, and Batieha, 2011; Forman and Gass, 2001). AHP helps decision-makers to rationally, meaningfully analyze vastly different criteria, in a context-preserving manner (Saaty, 2001).

TABLE 8.1
Intensity of the Importance for Pair-Wise Comparison

Intensity of Importance	Definition	Explanation
1	Equal importance	Both 1 and 2 contribute equally to the objective
3	Moderate importance	Experience and judgment slightly favor 1 over 2
5	Strong importance	Experience and judgment strongly favor 1 over 2
7	Very strong	1 is favored very strongly over 2
9	Extreme importance	The evidence favoring 1 over 2 is of the highest possible order of affirmation
2, 4, 6, 8	Intermediate values	A compromise between the two
1/3, 1/5, 1/7, 1/8, etc.	Reciprocal values	For reciprocal comparison of the aforementioned

Steps of AHP followed were as per the widely used methodology of Zahedi (1986).

Step 1 is to decompose the decision problem and construct the hierarchy of inter-related decision elements. In the present study, the level of hierarchy used is one.

Step 2 is collecting the data for pair-wise to compare the criteria of decision-making. The intensity of the importance for pair-wise comparison by the experts is mentioned in Table 8.1. Matrix using pair-wise comparison matrix, i.e., [A] was obtained. The pair-wise comparison matrix can be formed as follows:

$$A = \begin{bmatrix} 1 & \cdots & a_{in} \\ \vdots & \ddots & \vdots \\ 1/a_{in} & \cdots & 1 \end{bmatrix}$$

Next, normalizing was done, i.e., normalizing the pair-wise comparison **An**. The matrix [An] is calculated using the following formula:

$$n_{jk} = \frac{a_{jk}}{\sum_{i=1}^{n} n_{jk}}$$

Step 3 estimates the relative weights of the decision elements using eigenvalue method. B is the vector with relative weights.

$$B = \begin{bmatrix} b1 \, b2 \ldots bi \, bn \end{bmatrix},$$

$$b_i = \frac{\sum_{j=1}^{n} n_{ij}}{n}$$

In step 4, the relative weights of decision elements are aggregated so as to get ranks for the decision items. The present study uses only one-level of hierarchy, i.e., the relative weights at the first level are treated as the relative ranking.

Step 5 quantifies the inconsistency in decision-making of the experts by calculating the consistency ratio (CR, formula CR = CI/RI). Following steps are involved:

Step 5.1 multiply the pair-wise comparison matrix [A] with the eigenvector [B] yielding vector [C].

$$\begin{pmatrix} c1 \\ \dots \\ cn \end{pmatrix} = \begin{pmatrix} 1 & \cdots & a_{in} \\ \vdots & 1 & \vdots \\ 1/a_{in} & \cdots & 1 \end{pmatrix} \begin{pmatrix} b1 \\ \dots \\ bn \end{pmatrix}$$

Step 5.2 Elements of [C] are divided by their corresponding elements [B], thus resulting into the vector [D].

$$D = \left[\frac{c1}{b1} \dots \frac{cn}{bn} \right] = \left[d1 \dots dn \right]$$

Step 5.3 Average of vector [D] elements of gives a value known as λ_{max}

$$\lambda_{max} = \frac{\sum_{k=1}^{n} d_k}{n}$$

Step 5.4 Calculation of Consistency Index (CI) is done using formula CI = $(\lambda_{max}-n)/(n-1)$ is where n is the size of the pair-wise comparison matrix.

Step 5.5 Random index (RI) is identified. Table 8.2 shows the random index number value for matrices of different sizes as provided by Saaty (2013). It is used for calculating CR, as in the next step.

Step 5.6 calculates consistency ratio (CR) using the following formula, CR = CI/RI. Value of CR = 0.1 is considered acceptable upper limit for CR (Saaty, 2000).

TABLE 8.2

Random Index Number (Saaty, 2000)

1	2	3	4	5	6	7	8	9
0.00	0.00	0.58	0.90	1.12	1.24	1.32	1.41	1.45

8.4 RESULTS AND DISCUSSION

8.4.1 FACTORS INFLUENCING THE AI-BASED HIRING ADOPTION DECISION

Firstly, the study highlights the important factors influencing the decisions of HR managers in adopting AI-based hiring processes. The review of available relevant literature in the area revealed mainly the following seven influencing factors (Table 8.3).

Best-fit decision-making is an important factor of AI-based hiring, as it is highly linked with positive job performance. Also, other crucial factors are valid assessments and choice of techniques being applied for best-fit decisions, and its link with use of valid assessments. AI-based hiring function is a high-impact decision involving huge investment; thus RoI makes complete sense as one of the key factors especially from an organization investment perspective. It is expected that the outcomes of AI application overall justify the investments made in terms of time and money. RoI factor also entails implications associated with reducing administrative costs and improving profitability. Also, AI-based hiring involves a great deal of data handling, both magnitude and types of information, about the candidates, the process, and the criteria of decision-making, etc. Hence, the efficacy in effectively handling data is an

TABLE 8.3
Important Factors Influencing the Decisions of HR Managers in Adopting AI-Based Hiring Processes

Factors	Literature Support
Best-fit hiring decisions	Ryan and Derous (2019), Stone, Stone-Romero, and Lukaszewski (2003), Johansson and Herranen (2019), Lam and Hawkes (2017), Bhaskar (2017), Forrester (2018), Burkhardt, Hohn and Wigley (2019), Upadhyay and Khandelwal (2018), Michailidis (2018)
Return on investment (RoI)	Stone, Stone-Romero, and Lukaszewski (2003), Okolie and Irabor (2017), Johansson and Herranen (2019), Lam and Hawkes (2017), Upadhyay and Khandelwal (2018), Johnson, Lukaszewski and Stone (2016)
Data handling	Ryan and Derous (2019), Burkhardt, Hohn, and Wigley (2019), Forrester (2018), Michailidis (2018), Beamery Report (2020), Forbes Report (2019)
Hiring turnaround time	Stone, Stone-Romero, and Lukaszewski (2003), Krishnakumar (2019), McGovern et al., 2018), Johansson and Herranen (2019), Lam and Hawkes (2017), Nawaz and Gomes (2019), Johnson, Lukaszewski and Stone, 2016), Faliagka et al. (2012), Bullhorn (2018)
User-friendliness	Heric (2018), Johansson and Herranen (2019), Lam and Hawkes (2017), Upadhyay and Khandelwal (2018), Johnson, Lukaszewski and Stone (2016), Michailidis (2018)
Candidate experience	Ryan and Derous (2019), Tambe, Cappelli, and Yakubovich (2019), Krishnakumar (2019), Burkhardt, Hohn, and Wigley (2019), Bullhorn (2018), May (2016), Bhaskar (2017), Upadhyay and Khandelwal (2018)
Diverse candidate pool	Tambe, Cappelli, and Yakubovich (2019), Forbes Report (2019), Johansson and Herranen (2019)

important factor. AI-based hiring also involves concerns ensuring security of huge data and thus calls for effective data handling practices. User-friendliness of AI-based technology along with the turnaround (reduced) time for hiring are considered important while taking a decision of AI application in hiring. User-friendliness may also encompass the practical implication of smooth streamlining of an AI-based interface with the existing or future HR processes of organizations. The traditional hiring process is a time-consuming process, but AI proposes to transform it with technological developments. Various capabilities need to be leveraged to streamline, standardize, and digitize high-volume tasks in the different phases of hiring processes surpassing limitations of time and geography. The access to capturing a diverse candidate pool is revealed in the literature as another factor considered important with regard to the decision of AI-based intervention in hiring functions. Candidates' experience is another factor derived from the literature that deals with the extent to which the AI-based hiring process provides a fair and transparent experience to the candidates.

8.4.2 BENEFITS AND APPREHENSIONS

The Delphi method yielded two lists of benefits and apprehensions of AI-based hiring as perceived by the HR experts. Table 8.4 presents the 6 items of benefits and 7 items of apprehensions, which were the input to the AHP method.

8.4.2.1 Weightage of the Benefits of AI-based Hiring

Tables 8.5–8.8 reveal the calculations, i.e., results, emerged from the AHP Method for the benefits of AI-based hiring. And Tables 8.9–8.12 reveal that of the apprehensions

---

TABLE 8.4

Benefits (B1–B6) and Apprehensions (Apprh1–Apprh7) List

Benefits

B1	Automating and accelerating high-volume tasks/processes
B2	Ensuring and improving quality of hire, i.e., best-fit decisions
B3	Get more time to focus on different HR aspects of business
B4	More proactive hiring approach instead of reactive hiring
B5	More effective sourcing and outreach
B6	Engaging candidates and improving the candidate experience

Apprehensions

Apprh1	Gaining clear understanding about AI-based practices. There exist not enough and clear understanding of the AI as a technology and its use in HR functions
Apprh2	Unclear industry standards – investing in technology platforms of AI following the industry standards
Apprh3	Handling potential candidates' skepticism and apprehension toward AI-based hiring practices
Apprh4	Unstructured hiring process and limited planning pre-hiring
Apprh5	Ensuring skill-set necessary to fully capitalize the benefits
Apprh6	Streamlining with existing digital platforms of HR operations
Apprh7	Cost is another critical factor-Justifying huge amount of financial investment in AI sourcing platforms

TABLE 8.5
Benefits – Aggregated Pair-Wise Comparison Matrix [A]

N	B1	B2	B3	B4	B5	B6
B1	1.000	0.907	3.455	0.619	0.469	0.875
B2	1.103	1.000	2.534	1.642	2.290	1.270
B3	0.221	0.274	1.000	0.387	0.801	0.539
B4	1.617	0.356	2.584	1.000	0.391	1.521
B5	2.131	0.364	1.249	2.559	1.000	2.999
B6	1.143	0.602	1.854	0.658	0.333	1.000

TABLE 8.6
Benefits – Normalized [An] Matrix

N	B1	B2	B3	B4	B5	B6
B1	0.139	0.259	0.273	0.090	0.089	0.107
B2	0.153	0.286	0.200	0.239	0.433	0.155
B3	0.031	0.078	0.079	0.056	0.152	0.066
B4	0.224	0.102	0.204	0.146	0.074	0.185
B5	0.295	0.104	0.099	0.373	0.189	0.366
B6	0.158	0.172	0.146	0.096	0.063	0.122

TABLE 8.7
Weightage of the Benefits Associated with AI-Based Hiring

	B1	B2	B3	B4	B5	B6
Weights	0.159	0.244	0.077	0.156	0.238	0.126

TABLE 8.8
Benefits – Matrix

	B1	B2	B3	B4	B5	B6
B	0.159	0.244	0.077	0.156	0.238	0.126
C	0.965	1.575	0.498	0.984	1.539	0.780
D	6.057	6.447	6.471	6.316	6.479	6.176

associated with AI-based hiring. The CI and CR calculated were 0.06 and 0.08, respectively, highlighting the appropriateness of the weights. CI measures the degree of logical consistency among pair-wise comparisons. Consistency ratio (CR) value, indicating that the pair-wise comparison is appropriate and consistent. The allowed CR value must be less than 0.10.

The AHP analysis revealed two of the benefits perceived as really important by the HR managers are best-fit decisions, i.e., ensuring and improving quality of hire, and more effective sourcing and outreach of the candidate. It is interesting to note

TABLE 8.9

Apprehensions – Aggregated Pair-Wise Comparison Matrix [A]

A	Apprh1	Apprh2	Apprh3	Apprh4	Apprh5	Apprh6	Apprh7
Apprh1	1.000	0.559	3.191	0.662	0.279	0.911	0.182
Apprh2	1.786	1.000	2.271	1.530	0.993	1.228	0.737
Apprh3	0.313	0.306	1.000	0.443	0.827	0.552	0.373
Apprh4	1.509	0.413	2.256	1.000	0.447	1.432	0.319
Apprh5	3.567	1.003	1.210	2.238	1.000	2.564	0.754
Apprh6	1.094	0.647	1.644	0.698	0.390	1.000	0.289
Apprh7	5.444	1.588	2.947	1.879	1.326	3.462	1.000

TABLE 8.10

Apprehensions – Normalized [An] Matrix

N	Apprh1	Apprh2	Apprh3	Apprh4	Apprh5	Apprh6	Apprh7
Apprh1	0.068	0.101	0.220	0.078	0.053	0.082	0.050
Apprh2	0.121	0.181	0.156	0.181	0.189	0.110	0.202
Apprh3	0.021	0.055	0.069	0.052	0.157	0.049	0.102
Apprh4	0.103	0.075	0.155	0.118	0.085	0.128	0.087
Apprh5	0.242	0.182	0.083	0.265	0.190	0.230	0.206
Apprh6	0.074	0.117	0.113	0.083	0.074	0.090	0.079
Apprh7	0.370	0.288	0.203	0.222	0.252	0.311	0.274

TABLE 8.11

Weightage of the Apprehensions Associated with AI-Based Hiring

	Apprh1	Apprh2	Apprh3	Apprh4	Apprh5	Apprh6	Apprh7
eights	0.093	0.163	0.072	0.107	0.200	0.090	0.274

TABLE 8.12

Apprehensions – Matrix

	Apprh1	Apprh2	Apprh3	Apprh4	Apprh5	Apprh6	Apprh7
B	0.093	0.163	0.072	0.107	0.200	0.090	0.274
C	0.674	1.169	0.516	0.785	1.461	0.649	2.032
D	7.237	7.175	7.130	7.303	7.312	7.202	7.411

that almost all the emerged benefits are mainly highlighting two dimensions of hiring in which AI is perceived to be adding value. Firstly, hiring process-related and, secondly hiring outcome-related. Automation, effective sourcing and outreach, proactive hiring approach can be clustered in the former. And candidate experience and quality of hiring can be clustered as outcome-related benefits. Also, another perspective is evident from one of the items under benefits is that AI could help HR managers in getting more time to focus on different HR aspects of business, underlining great amount of time and efforts that hiring functions require of HR managers today, consequently implying how critical the hiring function is.

8.4.2.2   Weightage of the Apprehensions Associated with AI-based Hiring

The CI and CR calculated were 0.04 and 0.03, respectively, highlighting the appropriateness and consistency of the pair-wise comparison and the weights.

Two of the most critical apprehensions associated with AI-based hiring are – cost involved in AI-based applications, and the required skill-set to be successful. In the process of identification of apprehensions (Delphi method) it was realized that HR managers strongly felt about the cost issue associated with AI-based intervention in hiring. AI intervention is a huge cost to a company, and justification of this cost if a huge challenge that HR managers are faced with. A wrong hiring decision can cause economical losses (Newell, 2005; Muir, 1988). A wrong decision owing to such human limitations can cost an organization in terms of losing right candidates as well as in economic terms (Baron and Agustina, 2018). Both the above aspects are causes of concern for HR managers. As firms have their existing digital platforms of HR operations, the above factors can hinder effective integration of AI-based hiring into the existing HR processes in organizations. Thus, required set of competencies emerges to be an important concern that needs to be addressed properly for effectively utilizing the technology in hiring and consistently reaping benefits of the same in future. Also, Shufutinsky, Beach, and Saraceno (2020) supported that it is important to fill the skill gap regarding necessary technical acumen for effective talent acquisition.

Although third in terms of the weight allocation, but an important perspective emerges, i.e., no clear industry standards related with the use of AI-based technology in hiring process. It is one of such dimensions which is not only important for AI-based hiring, but also applicable in case of overall AI-based HR functions, thus provides avenues for further research. Another point of concern for HR managers deals with handling the potential candidates' doubts regarding AI-based techniques and processes used during hiring. It would be another issue however not emerged as an important concern of all apprehensions, but needs attention of HR managers and careful address.

AI enabled phases of hiring processes is the latest addition to the technology driven change. Accuracy and effectiveness of employee assessment in the hiring processes has always been a point of concern for HR professionals. It impacts firms in more than one way. And certainly, technology plays a critical role in employee assessments, and the way is only going forward. AI-based hiring is one such intervention that has quickly gained traction in the corporate practices. It is very crucial for HR professionals to take informed decisions about AI-based intervention in the already existing hiring technology and processes of organizations.

The sources and processes of hiring is continuously changing owing to the need of firms to differentiate themselves from the competitors (Taylor and Collins, 2000). Today, AI is disrupting the hiring industry. AI is changing the very competition in the hiring industry. It is changing the priorities and the parameters on which hiring effectiveness is evaluated. In this context, the present study contributes to a great extent in terms of factors influencing HR managers' decisions of adopting AI-based hiring and how they perceive the benefits and apprehensions about it. Taking note of the present findings would help firms and HR managers understand different perspectives of AI-based hiring.

8.5   CONCLUSION AND FUTURE IMPLICATIONS

The results of the current study highlight important factors that influence decisions of using AI-based application for hiring process in firms. Out of the seven factors, best-fit decisions, RoI, and data handling emerged as the really critical factors influencing HR managers' decisions. Based on the results, practical implementation can be drawn toward the criteria that influence the decisions of HR managers (and organizations). These factors will enable HR managers to evaluate and take informed decisions while evaluating their respective requirements, feasibility, and desired outcomes expected from the decision of choosing AI for the hiring process of firms. Realizing the importance of a particular factor and its effectiveness for any business operation is important for both practitioners and academics. Factors influencing such decisions may vary with the type of business operations and industry, thus, it calls for further research in this direction.

Amid changing trends, the emerging benefits and threats consequently lead to perceived confidence and apprehensions of managers toward AI-based hiring at global workplaces. The findings also present a set of important benefits and apprehensions perceived by the HR practitioners involved in talent acquisition. Key benefits, i.e., best-fit decisions and more effective sourcing and outreach, highlight the perceived value that HR managers see in the AI-based hiring.

Some recent work such as McRobert, Hill, Smale, Hay, and Van der Windt (2018), Bondarouk and Brewster (2016), are of the viewpoint that the human touch in recruitment is becoming lessened, and thus this research is pushing the envelope toward the use of AI in hiring. However, effectiveness and efficiency of AI tools used in hiring processes can still be argued, i.e., whether any such AI-based application would be able to do justice to the purpose. The perceived apprehensions highlight that there are some perceived challenges associated with AI application in hiring, the most important being the huge cost involved and its associated challenge to justify such a financial investment in AI sourcing platforms. Followed by cost is the doubt in terms of the required competencies to handle AI-technology. Another point of concern is that there exists no clear industry standards related to AI use in hiring across businesses. This essentially poses an important research question to assess the industry standards required for AI-based application in hiring. Also, this research implication can be further extended to AI-based applications in other HR functions. Such research would add immense value to the effective planning, application, and monitoring of AI applications in hiring and other HR functions.

The present work sets the groundwork for future research in the domain of AI-based application in hiring, but there is a need of more research to be conducted across industries for better understanding the practical and complex managerial environment specific to different business sectors with regard to AI-based hiring. Developing a decision-making support framework could be considered as a critical issue for determination of hiring strategies in the future. Further, in context of different business capabilities, external or internal, considering firms' interpretations regarding both benefits and issues related to AI application is another avenue for extending this study.

The growing experience and research are contributing to the mixed understanding that AI has both benefits and stresses alike leading to the confidence in and apprehension related to the use of AI-based applications. Globally, AI-based discourse of hiring seems to have grown more complicated both conceptually and practically. Needless to say, the relevance of such a work grows manifolds for workplaces amid the context of the current COVID-19 pandemic. HR professionals are often bombarded with the latest trends feeding into the rapid adoption of AI tools in hiring. Many technological trends promise to make hiring tasks of the talent acquisition leaders' jobs easier, but at the same time there exists skepticism among them. Thus, the current study contributes by uncovering perceived benefits and apprehensions of HR managers in India toward AI-based application. The contribution of the present study also lies in improving the knowledge and awareness about the ambiguity around the AI applications in hiring. Thus, this study is an attempt to understand and uncover some of the concerns raised in the question of whether AI is either apocalypse or utopia?

ACKNOWLEDGMENTS

The author is thankful to the reviewers for their input. The author also gratefully acknowledges the infrastructural support provided by the FORE School of Management, New Delhi toward the preparation of this paper.

REFERENCES

Baron, Ihil S., and Hellya Agustina. "The challenges of recruitment and selection systems in Indonesia." *Journal of Management and Marketing Review* 3, no. 4 (2018): 185–192.

Baxter, M. (2018). "Information-age", accessed July 11, 2019, https://www.information-age.com/business-analytics-intelligence-123477004/.

Beamery Report (2020), "AI for recruiting: The good, the bad, and the unknown," accessed February 24, 2018, https://beamery.com/blog/ai-recruiting.

Bhaskar, M., "Machine learning and AI: How applicant tracking systems are empowering recruiters with AI talent acquisition excellence," November 18, 2017, https://www.hr.com/en/magazines/talent_acquisition/november_2017_talent_acquisition/machine-learning-and-ai-how-applicant-tracking-sys_ja51hti9.html.

Bondarouk, Tanya and Chris Brewster, "Conceptualising the future of HRM and technology research." *The International Journal of Human Resource Management* 27, no. 21 (2016): 2652–2671.

Bullhorn. (2018)."2018 UK recruitment trends report: The industry's outlook for 2018," accessed August 11, 2019, http://pages.bullhorn.com/rs/131-YQK-568/images/2018%20Trends%20Report_UK.pdf.

Burke, Eugene, John Mahoney-Phillips, Wendy Bowler, and Kate Downey, "Going online with assessment: Putting the science of assessment to the test of client need and 21st century technologies." In *Technology-enhanced assessment of talent* (pp. 355–379). San Francisco, CA: Jossey-Bass, 2011.

Burkhardt, Roger, Nicolas Hohn, and Chris Wigley. "Leading your organization to responsible AI." *McKinsey Analytics* (2019).

Dalalah, Doraid, Mohammed Hayajneh, and Farhan Batieha. "A fuzzy multi-criteria decision making model for supplier selection." *Expert Systems with Applications* 38, no. 7 (2011): 8384–8391.

Erixon, Fredrik. "The economic benefits of globalization for business and consumers." *European Centre for International Political Economy* (2018).

Faliagka, Evanthia, Kostas Ramantas, Athanasios Tsakalidis, and Giannis Tzimas. "Application of machine learning algorithms to an online recruitment system." In *Proc. International Conference on Internet and Web Applications and Services.* 2012.

Forbes Report. (2019). "Expert panel, Forbes Coaches Council, 10 downsides of using artificial intelligence in the hiring process," August 14, 2019, https://www.forbes.com/sites/forbescoachescouncil/2019/08/14/10-downsides-of-using-artificial-intelligence-in-the-hiring-process/?sh=608beeb8685e.

Forman, Ernest H., and Saul I. Gass. "The analytic hierarchy process—An exposition." *Operations Research* 49, no. 4 (2001): 469–486.

Forrester. (2018). "Forrester predicts IoT, AI, AR, and VR will change the tech world by 2021," September 12, 2016, https://www.forrester.com/Forrester+Predicts+IoT+AI+AR+And+VR+Will+Change+The+Tech+World+By+2021/-/E-PRE9464.

Galanaki, Eleanna, Alessandra Lazazzara, and Emma Parry. "A cross-national analysis of e-HRM configurations: Integrating the information technology and HRM perspectives." In *Organizing for digital innovation* (pp. 261–276). Cham: Springer, 2019.

Goyal, Malini, "How artificial intelligence is reshaping recruitment, and what it means for the future of jobs," *The Economic Times*, October 8, 2017, http://economictimes.indiatimes.com/articleshow/60985946.cms?from=mdr&utm_source=contentofinterest&utm_medium=text&utm_campaign=cppst.

Guszcza, Jim, Harvey Lewis, and Peter Evans-Greenwood. "Cognitive collaboration: Why humans and computers think better together." *Deloitte Review* 20 (2017): 8–29.

Heric, Michael, "HR new digital mandate," *Bain & Company*, October 10, 2018, https://www.bain.com/insights/hrs-new-digital-mandate.

Hiemstra, A., and Eva Derous. "Video résumés portrayed." In *Employee recruitment, selection, and assessment.* London: Psychology Press/Taylor & Francis Group (2015): 45–57.

Hirevue. (2017). "Hilton cuts time to hire nearly 90% with Hirevue assessment," August 20, https://cdn2.hubspot.net/hubfs/464889/Hilton%20Aug%202017/2017_12_SuccessStory_Hilton_CustomerMarketing3.pdf?__hstc=&__hssc=&hsCtaTracking=b76cefe9-cece-4631-bef5-53084aa900e5%7Ca26c5bca-5fbe-46e3-b0e4-c1f79894f72c.

Hirevue. (2018), "HireVue video interview software," accessed August 1, 2019, https://www.hirevue.com/platform/online-video-interviewing-software.

Human Resources Professionals Association. (2017), "A new age of opportunities: What does Artificial Intelligence mean for HR Professionals?," accessed August 1, 2019, https://www.benefitscanada.com/wp-content/uploads/2017/11/HRPA-Report-Artificial-Intelligence-20171031.pdf.

Johansson, Jennifer, and Senja Herranen. "The application of artificial intelligence (AI) in human resource management: Current state of AI and its impact on the traditional recruitment process." Thesis, Business administration, John Hopkins University (2019).

Johnson, Richard D., Kimberly M. Lukaszewski, and Dianna L. Stone. "The evolution of the field of human resource information systems: Co-evolution of technology and HR processes." *Communications of the Association for Information Systems* 38, no. 1 (2016): 533–553.

Johnson, Richard D., Dianna L. Stone, and Kimberly M. Lukaszewski. "The benefits of eHRM and AI for talent acquisition." *Journal of Tourism Futures* 7 no. 1 (2020): 40–52.

Kharade, Mahesh. "AI is transforming recruitment and hiring," February 8, 2020, https://www.peoplematters.in/article/hr-technology/how-ai-is-transforming-recruitment-and-hiring-24626.

Kluemper, Donald H., H. Kristl Davison, Xiaoyun Cao, and Bingqing Wu. "Social networking websites and personnel selection: A call for academic research." In *Employee recruitment, selection, and assessment* (pp. 73–91). Psychology Press, 2015.

Krishnakumar, Akhil. "Assessing the Fairness of AI Recruitment systems." Master Thesis, Management of Technology, Delft University of Technology, January 25 (2019).

Lam, Sue, and Ben Hawkes. "From analytics to action: How Shell digitized recruitment." *Strategic HR Review* 16, no. 2 (2017): 76–80.

Martinez, Alonso, "AI to data privacy: How hiring tools and trends will drive workplace changes in 2020," January 16, 2020, https://www.forbes.com/sites/alonzomartinez/2020/01/16/ai-to-data-privacy-how-hiring-tools-and-trends-will-drive-workplace-changes-in-2020/?sh=53d25e685698.

McGovern, S. L., Vinod Pandey, Steve Gill, Tim Aldrich, Chad Myers, Chirag Desai, Mayank Gera, and V. Balasubramanian. "The new age: Artificial intelligence for human resource opportunities and functions." *Ey. com* (2018).

McRobert, Cliona J., Jonathan C. Hill, Tim Smale, Elaine M. Hay, and Danielle A. van der Windt. "A multi-modal recruitment strategy using social media and internet-mediated methods to recruit a multidisciplinary, international sample of clinicians to an online research study." *PloS One* 13, no. 7 (2018): e0200184.

Michailidis, Maria P. "Hie challenges of AI and blockchain on HR recruiting practices." *Cyprus Review* 30, no. 2 (2018): 169–180.

Nawaz, Nishad, and Anjali Mary Gomes. "Artificial intelligence chatbots are new recruiters." *(IJACSA) International Journal of Advanced Computer Science and Applications* 10, no. 9 (2019): 263–264.

Nilsson, Nils J. "Human-level artificial intelligence? Be serious!." *AI Magazine* 26, no. 4 (2005): 68–68.

O'Donovan, Deirdre. "HRM in the organization: An overview." In *Management science*, (pp. 75–110). Cham: Springer, 2019.

Okolie, Ugo Chuks, and Ikechukwu Emmanuel Irabor. "E-recruitment: Practices, opportunities and challenges." *European Journal of Business and Management* 9, no. 11 (2017): 116–122.

Paramita, Dhyana. "Digitalization in talent acquisition: A case study of AI in recruitment." (2020). https://www.diva-portal.org/smash/get/diva2:1440107/FULLTEXT01.pdf (accessed September 10, 2020).

Pillai, Rajasshrie, and Brijesh Sivathanu "Adoption of artificial intelligence (AI) for talent acquisition in IT/ITeS organizations," *Benchmarking: An International Journal* 27, no. 9 (2020): 2599–2629.

Roth, Philip L., Philip Bobko, Chad H. Van Iddekinge, and Jason B. Thatcher. "Social media in employee-selection-related decisions: A research agenda for uncharted territory." *Journal of Management* 42, no. 1 (2016): 269–298.

Ryan, Ann Marie, and Eva Derous. "The unrealized potential of technology in selection assessment= El potencial de la tecnología no empleado en la evaluación de la selección." *Journal of Work and Organizational Psychology* 35, no. 2 (2019): 85–92.

Ryan, Ann Marie, Ilke Inceoglu, Dave Bartram, Juliya Golubovich, Matthew Reeder, Eva Derous, Ioannis Nikolaou, and Xiang Yao. "Trends in testing: Highlights of a global survey." In *Employee recruitment, selection, and assessment: Contemporary issues for theory and practice* (pp. 136–153). Psychology Press, 2015.

Saaty, Thomas L. *The analytic hierarchy process: Planning, priority setting, resources allocation.* New York: McGraw, 1980.

Saaty, Thomas L. *Fundamentals of decision making and priority theory with the analytic hierarchy process* (Vol. 6). RWS Publications, 2000.

Saaty, Thomas L. *Decision making for leaders: The analytical hierarchy process for decisions in a complex world* (Vol. 2). Pittsburgh, PA: RWS Pubs, 2001.

Saaty, Thomas L. *Decision making for leaders: The analytical hierarchy process for decisions in a complex world* (3rd ed.). Pittsburgh, PA: RWS Pubs, 2013.

Salin, E. D., and P. H. Winston. "Machine learning and artificial intelligence: An introduction." *Analytical Chemistry (Washington, DC)* 64, no. 1 (1992): 49A–60A.

Sharma, Anushree, "Can technology replace recruiters?," April 23, 2018, https://www.peoplematters.in/article/talent-acquisition/can-technology-replace-recruiters-18068.

Shufutinsky, Anton, Anselm A. Beach, and Anthony Saraceno. "OD for Robots? Implications of Industry 4.0 on talent acquisition and development." *Organization Development Journal* 38, no. 3 (2020): 59–76.

Stone, Dianna L., Eugene F. Stone-Romero, and Kimberly Lukaszewski. "The functional and dysfunctional consequences of human resource information technology for organizations and their employees." In *Advances in human performance and cognitive engineering research*. Emerald Group Publishing Limited, 2003.

Tambe, Prasanna, Peter Cappelli, and Valery Yakubovich. "Artificial intelligence in human resources management: Challenges and a path forward." *California Management Review* 61, no. 4 (2019): 15–42.

Upadhyay, A. K., and K. Khandelwal. "Applying artificial intelligence: Implications for recruitment." *Strategic HR Review* 17 no. 5 (2018): 255–258.

Zahedi, Fatemeh. "The analytic hierarchy process—A survey of the method and its applications." *Interfaces* 16 no. 4 (1986): 96–108.

9 New Patterns in Cyber Crime with the Confluence of IoT and Machine Learning

Benison Mugweni and Rose Mugweni

CONTENTS

DOI: 10.1201/9781003048862-9

9.1   INTRODUCTION

Web users must have a genuine degree of certainty that the internet and gadgets connected within it are sufficiently secure to do the sorts of activities they need to accomplish, according to threat toleration related to those activities. Moreover, according to [1], the Internet of Things (IoT) is something similar in such a manner with accordance to security in IoT which is an exceptionally fundamental level of connection to capacitate clients so that confide their current environment. Even more so, if people do not believe the connected computerized devices and their information is reasonable and secure from misuse, the emerging crumbling of trust creates hesitance to use the internet. Along these lines, ensuring security in IoT devices should be considered as the first sector concern. Thereupon interfacing gadgets to the internet, emerging examples of security misuse weaknesses broaden, where insecure gadgets enable cybercrimes, permitting vindictive individuals to reinvent IoT gadgets causing malfunction. Imperfect gadgets reveal information to hackers, leaving data insufficiently secured. Thus, malfunctioning or failing devices create security weaknesses. Henceforth, IoT gadgets must have the capabilities to withstand cybercrimes on their own, which means that they have to be programmed using machine learning (ML) algorithms that can enable IoT devices to block undesirable communication with accuracy. For instance, ML algorithms have enabled Google to block undesirable communication with 99% accuracy.

9.2   BACKGROUND

The IoT according to [2–4] is an extension of the web into the real world for collaboration with genuine substances the environmental surroundings [5]. Barnaghi [6] claim that gadgets and components are the keys inside the IoT environment, as depicted in Figure 9.1. Surely, a substance in IoT can be an electronic machine or a shut open environment [7]. This is the reason communication among components is made by hardware, for instance, cell phones, sensors, and actuators, which grant substances to interface with the computerized world as per [8].

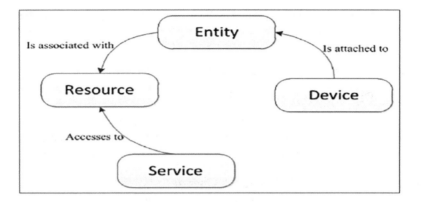

FIGURE 9.1 IoT model: key concepts and interaction.

So then apart from IoT benefits, several constraints can be identified [9]. Connected devices are amazingly significant to digital assailants for different reasons, which include:

- Several IoT gadgets work on their own without being monitored by individuals, so it is easy for a hacker to gain control over them.
- Secondly, IoT segments convey remote organizations where an unauthorized user could get secret information by sniffing or snooping around.
- Finally, IoT segments find it difficult to uphold security standards due to low force and handling resource limits.

In addition, digital dangers can be dispatched against any IoT assets, conceivably causing debilitating system activity, endangering the overall workforce, or causing unintentional financial harm to proprietors and clients [10, 11]. Until further notice, there needs to be a mechanization framework and an acceptance of accountability for warning systems. In essence, information accumulated from sensors implanted in warning systems can be utilized to determine whether somebody is home or out. In conclusion, it is perceived that embracing IoT innovation homes and business conditions pave for new security issues.

9.3 OBJECTIVES

- Protecting the physical parts and programming setup of IoT gadgets.
- Effectively install gadgets on a network so that undetermined components are unauthorized.
- Build a framework for efficient, continuous monitoring of vulnerability.
- Ensure reliable IoT activity and check the conduct of devices against security approaches.
- Increase resistance of IoT networks against DDoS attacks.
- Advancement of devices and strategies for ensuring delicate data and client security.

- Building of network safety stage that goes a long way past condition of workmanship.

9.4   CYBER CRIMES ASSOCIATED WITH IoT DEVICES

9.4.1   DENIAL OF SERVICE (DDoS) ATTACK

This refers to a malicious disruption of normal traffic of a server, service, or network by an overpowering encompassing foundation with an overflow of web traffic. Particularly, DDoS achieves adequacy using different computer systems as a traffic attack.

9.4.1.1   How Does a DDoS Attack Operate?

Typically, DDoS assaults are done within the network organization of interconnected gadgets (IoT). Truth be told, these organizations comprise computer frameworks and other gadgets – explicitly IoT gadgets – that would have been influenced by malware, permitting them to be controlled distantly by an aggressor. In this circumstance, these free gadgets are alluded to as bots. Furthermore, an assortment of bots is called *botnets*.

9.4.1.2   Forms of DDoS Attacks

- Volume-based assaults
- Protocol assaults
- Application phase attacks

9.4.2   BOTNETS

Botnets refer to a variety of virtual world-connected internet gadgets affected by malware which give hackers control over them. Hackers use botnets to incorporate malicious activities, for instance, DDoS attacks as shown in Figure 9.2.

9.4.2.1   How Does a Botnet Attack Work?

In like manner, a botnet proprietor can access an enormous number of personal computers (PCs) all at once and have the option to command them to do noxious activities. Essentially, criminals at first access IoT gadgets by utilizing unique Trojan infections to attack the gadgets security framework, before actualizing command and control software which at that point empowers them to do malignant activities for a huge scope. Once more, botnet attacks can be computerized to support whatever number of synchronous attacks as could reasonably be possible.

9.4.2.2   Types of Botnet Attacks

- Providing an assailant or attacker admittance to a gadget and its connection within a network organization.
- Web application attacks to steal information.
- Validating arrangements of certification stuffing attacks prompting account takeovers.
- DDoS attacks that cause impromptu application vacation.

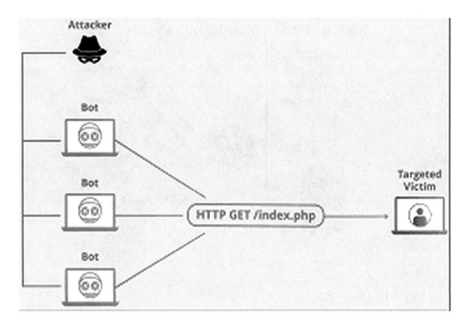

FIGURE 9.2   Botnet.

9.4.3   IDENTITY THEFT

Identity theft refers to the process of obtaining individual data, for example, passwords, ID numbers, MasterCard numbers, or government-managed retirement numbers, and abuse them to act falsely in the victim's name. Appropriately, these touchy subtleties can be utilized for different unlawful purposes – namely making online purchases, applying for loans, or accessing the victim's financial data as shown in Figure 9.3.

9.4.3.1   How Does Identity Theft Work?

Public profiles on interpersonal networks and other well-known online services can be utilized as the wellspring of information assisting criminals with mimicking their objectives. Moreover, when personality thieves have gathered such secret data, they can utilize it to buy great and assume control over the casualty's online records or make a lawful move in their name. Hence, influenced people can endure monetary misfortune because of unapproved withdrawals and purchases in their names.

9.4.3.2   Types of Identity Theft

- Synthetic identity theft
- Internet of Things (IoT) identity fraud
- Online shopping fraud
- Biometric ID theft

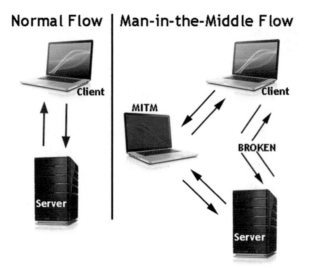

FIGURE 9.3 Identity theft.

9.4.4 SOCIAL ENGINEERING

First of all, this act deals with manipulating individuals so that they surrender classified data. Currently, the data that lawbreakers look for vary. They intend to trick the users so that they can attempt to gain access to IoT gadgets and introduce vindictive programming which provides admittance on individual information in IoT gadgets as mentioned in Figure 9.4

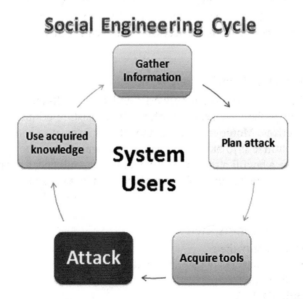

FIGURE 9.4 Social engineering.

9.4.4.1 How Does Social Engineering Work?

Meanwhile, social engineering is as yet the most well-known cyber-attack, since it is profoundly effective to criminals. Most of all, users are targeted either via telephone or online. Telephone scammers act as representatives of an organization or association, e.g., for a bank, and after some run-of-the-mill questions they will at that point request login credentials and passwords.

9.4.4.2 Types of Social Engineering

- Phishing
- Watering hole
- Whaling attack
- Pretexting

9.4.5 MAN-IN-THE-MIDDLE (MITM) CONCEPT

In contrast, this is where attackers intrude on break interchanges between two separate system frameworks. These attacks are incredibly risky and dangerous in IoT on account of gadgets hacking. IoT structure devices and apparatus connected things, for example, smart televisions (TVs) as shown in Figure 9.5.

9.4.5.1 How Does the MITM Attack Work?

On contrary suppose the user got an email that seemed, by all accounts, to be from his or her bank, requesting that the user should sign into the account to affirm their contact data. The user clicks on a connection in the email and is taken to what exactly has all the earmarks of being their bank's website, where the user will login and play out the mentioned task.

Unquestionably in this case, MITM sends an email to the user, appearing to be legitimate. Moreover, the attacker creates a website that is similar to the user's

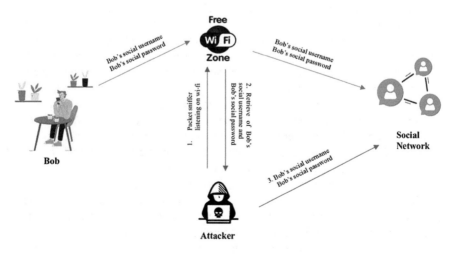

FIGURE 9.5 Man-in-the-middle.

electronic banking website. That user then enters their login credentials without hesitation by clicking the link on the email. Obviously when the user does that, he or she will be handing their credentials to the attacker.

9.4.5.2 Kinds of Man-in-the-Middle Attacks

* IP (internet protocol) spoofing
* DNS (domain name server) spoofing
* Wi-Fi eavesdropping

9.5 SECURITY CHALLENGES OF IoT DEVICES

Ordinarily, IoT gadgets are unique concerning customary computers and other computing gadgets in fundamental manners that challenge security [1]. Numerous IoT gadgets explicitly customer sent at an enormous scope of significant degrees past that of conventional web-connected gadgets. As a result, the expected nature of connections between gadgets is exceptional. It implies, existing techniques, apparatuses, and procedures related to IoT security thoughts.

Secondly, gadgets are deployed with foreseen administration life in this manner many years than is normal for connected hardware. Gadgets can be deployed in a condition that is difficult to redesign. This case illustrates security components satisfactory on organization probably won't last the life expectancy of the gadget as security dangers develop. Likewise, it creates weaknesses that persevere for a while. Similarly, as opposed to the worldview of conventional computer system frameworks that are typically redesigned with operating system software programming updates, the life duration of computers able to address new security threats is finite.

Various IoT deployments comprise assortments of indistinguishable gadgets. IoT gadgets are deliberately designed without the capacity to be upgraded. For instance, consider the 2015 Fiat Chrysler: 1.4 million vehicles reveal fixing weaknesses, which permitted attackers to remotely hack vehicles. These vehicles should be taken to a Fiat Chrysler vendor for a manual redesign. Thus, the truth is that a high number of these cars are likely not receiving software updates for their onboard computers due to the fact that enabling updates bothered proprietors, leaving their cars without online protection – particularly when the vehicle appears to be performing well.

Furthermore, numerous gadgets work where the user has next to no genuine perceivability of the inside operations of a gadget and the information produced. This weakens security when a user accepts gadgets to perform specific tasks, when as a general rule these gather more information than the users. Capacities likewise change without notice if the producer provides an update, leaving the client helpless against changes. Some IoT gadgets are probably deployed where actual security is difficult to improvise. Attacks direct actual admittance on gadgets.

Devices like numerous ecological sensors are intended to be implanted in the environment, where the user doesn't monitor operation status. Additionally, gadgets have no method to alarm the user when a security issue emerges, making it hard for a user to note security infiltration. Unauthorized access may only continue for a short time before security measures are made and breaches can be fixed if intervention is swift and pragmatic. Early models expect IoT will result in huge public innovation endeavors.

9.6   SECURITY THREATS, ATTACKS, AND WEAKNESSES

When dealing with security risks, the components that make up IoT must be recognized first, and making an inventory of assets that include IoT gadget parts. According to [12], the essential resources of IoT systems are system hardware, software, and administration information [13].

9.6.1   WEAKNESSES

There can be shortcomings within system design allowing an interloper to gain unauthorized access and gain control over confidential information, direct service attacks [14, 15]. Weaknesses are found in assortment regions in IoT systems, specifically, shortcomings in system hardware, software, strategies, and the methodology utilized in a system, and system users [16]. Moreover, IoT depends on primary segments (hardware and software) having regular scans for configuration imperfections. In the same manner, hardware weaknesses are difficult to recognize and difficult to fix regardless of whether weaknesses were identified due to hardware compatibilities with operating systems. However, various variables can lead to software configuration defects and unpredictability. Therefore, the consequences of not understanding necessities include beginning the project with poor communication among developers, users, resources, abilities, and information, and neglecting control over the system [16].

9.6.2   EXPOSURE

Specifically, exposure is an issue or slip-up of system configuration permitting the aggressor to lead data hacking exercises. Usually, IoT gadgets might be liable to be set in areas where attackers are available. More so, this likelihood that attackers may capture gadgets, separate privileged insights, alter programming, and supplant with their malicious gadget is heavily influenced by the proximity of the attacker [17].

9.6.3   THREATS

According to Brauch [18], threat refers to an activity that exploits security shortcomings in a system thus affecting it negatively. Also, threats start from individuals. Even though human threats are made by individuals, for example, malicious interior attacks [19], and external threats (an individual working externally to a network) to harm a system [20]. Since IoT has become reality, developing pervasive gadgets has raised the number of security threats – i.e., the most unfortunate aspect of this innovation is that IoT accompanies a new arrangement of security threats. This means that developing advanced cellphones, computers, and gadgets can be targeted by cybercriminals and hackers.

9.6.4 ATTACKS

Attacks refer to moves, procedures made to disturb operation with strategies that target instruments' weaknesses. The measurement of the attack on the resources and inspiration is called cost attack [14]. As indicated by [21], attack actors are a danger to the digital world. This case assault itself may emanate various networks to monitor delicate, latent assaults, checking network communications encoded.

Basic cybercrime attacks are:

Physical
- This tempers with hardware equipment because of unattended and circulated IoT nature. Moreover, gadgets ordinarily work on outside conditions, which are profoundly exposed to assaults.

Surveillance
- Deals with the disclosure mapping system, services, weaknesses. For instance, examining network [22], packet traffic analysis, sending inquiries concerning address data.

(DoS) Denial of Service Attack
- Particularly this attack actions to make the network inaccessible to the proposed user. As a result, restricted computation. However greater IoT gadgets are powerless toward enervation attacks.

Authorization
- This is an attack where an individual gains unapproved admittance to gadgets or networks upon which they have no access rights. Access assaults are classified into two which are physical authorization where interloper access physical gadgets and remote access to internet protocol-connected devices.

Privacy
- Certainly, security in IoT is challenging because large volumes of data are accessible through remote components.

Cybercrimes
- Since the web is used abuse users and information increase, that is theft, identity theft, and extortion [16, 21, 23].

9.7   SECURITY AND PRIVACY OBJECTIVES FOR IoT

To accomplish productive IoT, we must know about security objectives, which are:

9.7.1 CONFIDENTIALITY

This refers to a significant IoT security highlight. It applies in most situations where delicate information must not be revealed by unauthorized elements. For instance, confidential information and business information accreditations and emit keys should be stowed unauthorized elements.

9.7.2 INTEGRITY

Accordingly, integrity offers dependable support to IoT users, since it is obligatory security. Various IoT systems have different respectability necessities [24]. In this case, the remote patient observing system has high arbitrary respectability because of its data integrity. Therefore, this guards against dire misfortune (i.e., the risk of loss of life), so the protection of patient information is crucial.

9.7.3 AUTHENTICATION AND AUTHORIZATION

As the global network of IoT has created the need for validation on account of IoT conditions, conceivable communication happens between gadgets. Therefore, diverse confirmation necessities need various system arrangements. However, examples include validation systems. The property of approval permits just authorized elements to play out specific activities in the network.

9.7.4 AVAILABILITY

The IoT gadget must fit services at the required point. Disparate hardware, software components of IoT gadgets, must be robust to offer services within malicious elements circumstances, although different systems or gadgets have diverse accessibility prerequisites.

9.7.5 ACCOUNTABILITY

Moreover, when creating security techniques executed in a protected network, there are responsibilities and explicit obligations for activity usage network security approaches. In addition, it guarantees other security techniques.

9.7.6 AUDITING

Abomhara and Køien [25] describe how security is a precise assessment of service security, depending on how it adjusts to a criterial setup. Because of numerous bugs and weaknesses in systems, auditing assumes function deciding exploitable shortcomings which expose information at risk. Therefore, IoT systems need to inspect each application, the company's reliance on it, and thus its worth.

9.7.7 PRIVACY GOALS

Privacy is a component's entitlement to decide the degree to which it will connect with its current environment, and the extent to which it imparts information to other people.

9.7.7.1 IoT's Main Privacy Goals

Device Privacy

• Certainly, it relies upon physical and compensation privacy. This means that delicate data can leak from a gadget in instances of gadget theft, diminishing flexibility for dealing with attacks.

Communication

• Unquestionably, this turn on gadget accessibility, integrity dependability. In this case, IoT gadgets singularly diminish information security disclosure on communication.

Storage

• To secure information for a gadget, guidelines for the storage and safe removal of potentially sensitive information must be accessible in the gadget's user information for the disposal or recycling of such a gadget.

Privacy in Processing

• Again, it relies upon gadgets and communication integrity [26]. Therefore, information must also be unveiled and held by outsiders without information on proprietor information.

Location

• Furthermore, the geographical situation of applicable gadgets should only be discoverable to an authorized entity (gadget) [27].

9.8 IoT SECURITY SOLUTIONS BASED ON MACHINE LEARNING (ML)

The IoT that coordinates different gadgets to network offers astute services that need secure user privacy attacks, e.g., spoofing attacks, jamming, eavesdropping [28]. Therefore, since IoT is about independent devices communicating together and sharing information over the internet network, clearly shows that these devices are prone to attacks. Therefore, there must be security solutions dependent on ML methods or algorithms which incorporate supervised learning, unsupervised learning, and reinforced learning. Undeniably we need to focus on IoT ML validation, access control, and malware identification ensuring information protection.

ML is there to help these devices to be standalone and mimic human behavior by trying to resist and handle cybercrimes. This shows that ML gives IoT devices the ability to reason and make decisions based on the current occurring situation. Moreover, since IoT devices are increasing day by day, it means that if they cannot tackle crimes on their own, a lot of problems will be created since they lead to the rise of new patterns in cybercrimes. This leads to vulnerabilities and many weaknesses, allowing attacks to pave their way in targeting IoT devices.

However, to manage billions of IoT devices and save them from cybercrime or cyber-attacks, ML algorithms have to be put in place within IoT devices so that they will be able to resist and fight against cybercrimes smartly and efficiently without human intervention. Certainly, the use of ML in IoT devices is a great move, since some IoT devices operate in space and others in the outskirts of cities where humans barely monitor such devices, and are sometimes reluctant in updating and securing IoT devices – hence being left vulnerable. Unquestionably, ML algorithms are the best in securing IoT devices.

9.9 USED MACHINE LEARNING (ML) ALGORITHMS

Certainly, the most widely recognized ML algorithms that can be utilized for IoT security are as shown in Table 9.1.

- Random forest (RF)
- Deep learning (DL)
- Neural network (NW)
- Reinforcement learning (RL) algorithms

Moreover, the utilization of ML in IoT gadgets gives them space to choose protection strategy deciding critical security parameters protocols trade-off in the heterogeneous network (see Table 9.2).

TABLE 9.1
Used Machine Learning Algorithms

Reference	Used Machine Learning Algorithms
Nobakht et al. [29]	Support vector machine
Wang et al. [30]	Extreme learning machine (ELM)
Aminanto et al. [31]	Support vector machine (SVM) and artificial neural network (ANN)
Gao and Thamilarasu [32]	Decision tree learning
Cho et al. [33]	Naïve Bayes
Roux et al. [34]	Neural network
Diro and Chilamkurti [35]	Deep learning
Domb et al. [36]	Random forest
Outchakoucht et al. [37]	Reinforcement learning (RL) algorithms

TABLE 9.2
IoT Achievements

Measure	Use
Authentication	Helps IoT devices to distinguish the source and address the identity-based attacks such as spoofing and sybil attacks
Access control	Prevents unauthorized users to access IoT resources
Secure offloading	Enable IoT devices to use computation and storage resources
Malware detection	Protects IoT devices to use the computation and storage resources of the servers and edge devices for computational intense and latency sensitive task

9.10   MACHINE LEARNING TECHNIQUES

Firstly, since they are various ML algorithms to be used in IoT devices. These algorithms are derived from various ML techniques which are:

9.10.1   SUPERVISED LEARNING

Technically, random forest (RF) and naïve Bayes (NB) likewise are utilized names for the network traffic of IoT gadgets. More so, IoT devices can also use signal magnitude vector (SMV) to detect network interruption and spoofing attacks, malware detection, and use a neural network to uncover network interruption. Again, NB can likewise be utilized in IoT gadgets in the interruption identification along with RF classifier can be utilized to identify malware. However, IoT gadgets with enough computation and memory assets can utilize a deep neural network (DNN) to identify spoofing attacks.

9.10.2   UNSUPERVISED LEARNING

Additionally, this doesn't need information in supervised learning as it also researches closeness between information various gatherings. For instance, gadgets use multivariate relationship examination identifying attacks and validation privacy protection [38].

9.10.3   REINFORCEMENT LEARNING

Furthermore, this ML comprises techniques such as Q-learning. Its purpose is to enable IoT devices to pick the security protocols, just as the critical parameters against different attacks through experimentation Q-learning stereotype of RL procedure are utilized to improve verification. Certainly, IoT gadgets can actualize Dyna in the verification and malware recognition identifying changes.

9.10.4   ML-BASED IoT SECURITY METHODS

This section shows the types of attacks that are prone to IoT devices, security techniques that must implemented against IoT attacks, then ML techniques or algorithms that can be used to help in securing IoT devices, and lastly, the performance that is brought with the use of ML in securing IoT devices shown in Table 9.3.

9.11   CONCLUSION

IoT devices refer to an independent device that communicates and share data over the internet network. These devices are prone to various cybercrimes such as social engineering, DDoS attacks, and man-in-the-middle. More so, the cybercrimes are committed using different attacks which are access attacks, privacy attacks, physical attacks, and DoS. Since IoT devices are increasing, therefore, they bring forth new patterns in cybercrimes to violate IoT securities which are confidentiality, integrity, authorization and authentication, availability, accountability, and auditing. Certainly, IoT devices have to be in a position to learn the new patterns and bring upon better

TABLE 9.3
ML-Based IoT Security Methods

Attacks	Security Techniques	Machine Learning Techniques	Performance
DoS	Secure IoT offloading	Neural network (NN)	Detection accuracy
	Access control	Multivariate correlation analysis	Root mean error
		Q-learning	
Jamming	Secure IoT offloading	Q-learning	Energy consumption
		DQN	SINR
Spoofing	Authentication	Q-learning	Average error rate
		Dyna-Q	Detection accuracy
		SVM	Classification accuracy
		DNN	False alarm rate
		Incremental aggregated gradient	Miss detection rate
Intrusion	Access control	Support vector machine	Classification accuracy
		Naïve Bayes	False alarm rate
		K-NN	Detection rate
		Neural network (NN)	Root mean error
Malware	Malware detection	Dyna-Q	Classification accuracy
	Access control	PDS	False positive rate
		Random Forest	Ture positive rate
		K-nearest neighbors	Detection accuracy
			Detection latency
Eavesdropping	Authentication	Q-learning	Proximity passing rate
		Non-parametric Bayesian	Secrecy data rate

methods to fight against cybercrimes. Additionally, for IoT devices to be in a position to succeed, they must be programmed in ML so that they are able to standalone and mimic human behavior in implementing required security measures against imposed cyber-attacks, thus achieving new patterns in cybercrime confluence in IoT and Machine Learning (ML)

REFERENCES

1. Internet Society, "Values and principles," *Internet Society*, 2015. http://www.internetsociety.org/who-we-are/mission/values-and-principles.
2. S. Andreev and Y. Koucheryavy, "Internet of things, smart spaces, and next-generation networking," Springer, *LNCS*, vol. 7469, p. 464, 2012.
3. L. Atzori, A. Iera, and G. Morabito, "The internet of things: A survey," *Computer Networks*, vol. 54, no. 15, pp. 2787–2805, 2010.
4. J. S. Kumar and D. R. Patel, "A survey on internet of things: Security and privacy issues," *International Journal of Computer Applications*, vol. 90, no. 11, pp. 20–26, March 2014, published by Foundation of Computer Science, New York, USA.
5. G. Xiao, J. Guo, L. Xu, and Z. Gong, "User interoperability with heterogeneous IoT devices through transformation," 2014.
6. S. De, P. Barnaghi, M. Bauer, and S. Meissner, "Service modeling for the internet of things," in *Computer Science and Information Systems (FedCSIS), 2011 Federated Conference On*. IEEE, 2011, pp. 949–955.

7. J. Gubbi, R. Buyya, S. Marusic, and M. Palaniswami, "Internet of things (IoT): A vision, architectural elements, and future directions," *Future Generation Computer Systems*, vol. 29, no. 7, pp. 1645–1660, 2013.

8. M. Zorzi, A. Gluhak, S. Lange, and A. Bassi, "From today's intranet of things to a future internet of things: A wireless-and mobility-related view," *Wireless Communications, IEEE*, vol. 17, no. 6, pp. 44–51, 2010.

9. Cha, Y. Shah, A. U. Schmidt, A. Leicher, and M. V. Meyerstein, "Trust in m2m communication," *Vehicular Technology Magazine, IEEE*, vol. 4, no. 3, pp. 69–75, 2009.

10. Y. Cheng, M. Naslund, G. Selander, and E. Fogelstrom, "Privacy in machine-to-machine communications a state-of-the-art survey," in *Communication Systems (ICCS), 2012 IEEE International Conference On*. IEEE, 2012, pp. 75–79.

11. M. Rudner, "Cyber-threats to critical national infrastructure: An intelligence challenge," *International Journal of Intelligence and CounterIntelligence*, vol. 26, no. 3, pp. 453–481, 2013.

12. O. Vermesan, P. Friess, P. Guillemin, S. Gusmeroli, H. Sundmaeker, A. Bassi, I. S. Jubert, M. Mazura, M. Harrison, M. Eisenhauer, et al., "Internet of things strategic research roadmap," *Internet of Things-Global Technological and Societal Trends*, pp. 9–52, 2011.

13. D. Watts, "Security and vulnerability in electric power systems," in *35th North American power symposium*, vol. 2, 2003, pp. 559–566.

14. E. Bertino, L. D. Martino, F. Paci, and A. C. Squicciarini, "Web services threats, vulnerabilities, and countermeasures," in *Security for Web Services and Service-Oriented Architectures*. Springer, pp. 25–44, 2010.

15. D. L. Pipkin, *Information Security*. Prentice-Hall PTR, 2000.

16. J. M. Kizza, *Guide to Computer Network Security*. Springer, 2013.

17. D. G. Padmavathi, M. Shanmugapriya, et al., "A survey of attacks, security mechanisms and challenges in wireless sensor networks," *arXiv preprint arXiv:0909.0576*, 2009.

18. H. G. Brauch, "Concepts of security threats, challenges, vulnerabilities and risks," in *Coping with Global Environmental Change, Disasters and Security*. Springer, pp. 61–106, 2011.

19. A. J. Duncan, S. Creese, and M. Goldsmith, "Insider attacks in cloud computing," in *Trust, Security and Privacy in Computing and Communications (TrustCom), 2012 IEEE 11th International Conference On*. IEEE, pp. 857–862, 2012.

20. P. Baybutt, "Assessing risks from threats to process plants: Threat and vulnerability analysis," *Process Safety Progress*, vol. 21, no. 4, pp. 269–275, 2002.

21. B. Schneier, *Secrets and lies: Digital security in a networked world*. John Wiley & Sons, 2011.

22. S. Ansari, S. Rajeev, and H. Chandrashekar, "Packet sniffing: A brief introduction," *Potentials, IEEE*, vol. 21, no. 5, pp. 17–19, 2002.

23. C. Wilson, "Botnets, cybercrime, and cyberterrorism: Vulnerabilities and policy issues for congress." DTIC Document, 2008.

24. B. Jung, I. Han, and S. Lee, "Security threats to the internet: A Korean multi-industry investigation," *Information & Management*, vol. 38, no. 8, pp. 487–498, 2001.

25. Mohamed Abomhara and Geir M. Køien, "Department of Information and Communication Technology, University of Agder, Norway" Publication 22 May 2015.

26. C. P. Mayer, "Security and privacy challenges in the internet of things," *Electronic Communications of the EASST*, vol. 17, 2009.

27. A. R. Beresford, "Location privacy in ubiquitous computing," *Computer Laboratory, University of Cambridge, Tech. Rep*, vol. 612, 2005.

28. X. Li, R. Lu, X. Liang, and X. Shen, "Smart community: An Internet of Things application," *IEEE Commun. Magazine*, vol. 49, no. 11, pp. 68–75, November 2011.
29. M. Nobakht, V. Sivaraman, and R. Boreli, "A host-based intrusion detection and mitigation framework for smart home IoT using openflow," in *2016 11th International Conference on Availability, Reliability, and Security (ARES). Presented at the 2016 11th International Conference on Availability, Reliability, and Security (ARES)*, IEEE, Salzburg, Austria, pp. 147–156, 2016. doi:10.1109/ARES.2016.64.
30. L. Wang, ed., *Support Vector Machines: Theory and Applications, Studies in Fuzziness and Soft Computing*. Springer, Berlin, 2017.
31. M. E. Aminanto, H. C. Tanuwidjaja, P. D. Yoo, and K. Kim, "Wi-Fi intrusion detection using weighted feature selection for neural networks classifier," in *2017 International Workshop on Big Data and Information Security (IWBIS). Presented at the 2017 International Workshop on Big Data and Information Security (IWBIS), IEEE, Jakarta, Indonesia*, pp. 99–104, 2017. doi:10.1109/IWBIS.2017.8275109.
32. S. Gao and G. Thamilarasu, "Machine-learning classifiers for security in connected medical devices," in *2017 26th International Conference on Computer Communication and Networks (ICCCN). Presented at the 2017 26th International Conference on Computer Communication and Networks (ICCCN), IEEE, Vancouver, BC, Canada*, pp. 1–5, 2017. doi:10.1109/ICCCN.2017.8038507.
33. T. Cho, H. Kim, and J. H. Yi, "Security assessment of code obfuscation based on dynamic monitoring," *Android Things. IEEE Access*, vol. 5, pp. 6361–6371, 2010. doi:10.1109/ACCESS.2017.2693388.
34. J. Roux, E. Alata, G. Auriol, V. Nicomette, and M. Kaaniche, "Toward an intrusion detection approach for IoT based on radio communications profiling," in *2017 13th European Dependable Computing Conference (EDCC). Presented at the 2017 13th European Dependable Computing Conference (EDCC)*, IEEE, Geneva, Switzerland, pp. 147–150, 2005. doi:10.1109/EDCC.2017.11.
35. A. A. Diro and N. Chilamkurti, "Distributed attack detection scheme using deep learning approach for Internet of Things," *Future Generation ComputerSystems*, vol. 82, pp. 761–768, 2018. doi:10.1016/j.future.2017.08.043.
36. M. Domb, E. Bonchek-Dokow, and G. Leshem, "Lightweight adaptive Random-Forest for IoT rule generation and execution," *Journal of Information Security and Applications*, vol. 34, pp. 218–224, 2017. doi:10.1016/j.jisa.2017.03.001.
37. A. Outchakoucht, H. Es-Samaali, and J. Philippe, "Dynamic access control policy based on blockchain and machine learning for the Internet of Things," *International Journal of Advanced Computer Science and Applications*, vol. 8, 2017. doi:10.14569/IJACSA.2017.080757.
38. L. Xiao, Q. Yan, W. Lou, G. Chen, and Y. T. Hou, "Proximity-based security techniques for mobile users in wireless networks," *IEEE Trans. Information Forensics and Security*, vol. 8, no. 12, pp. 2089–2100, October 2013.

10 A Review for Cyber Security Challenges on Big Data Using Machine Learning Techniques

Savitri Mandal, A. Sai Sabitha, and
Deepti Mehrotra

CONTENTS

10.1 INTRODUCTION

The number of cyber-attacks are increasing with the increasing number of users daily within the cyber world. The scope of cyber security is vast and various security measures are taken to reduce the number of cyber-attacks. When the user faces any fraud using the internet, then cyber security is the only option that comes first in our mind (Aburrous et al., 2010). In spite of taking various security measures, the graph of cyber crime is increasing rapidly; therefore, this is the time to take effective security measures in order to secure the important data (Almeshekah & Spafford, 2016). Cyber crime can be anything like stealing user's important data (for e.g., bank-related information), attacks like Dos attack, Man in the middle attack and so on; these can also lead to financial loss to the users (Adams & Makramalla, 2015). Also, traditional security measures for handling the large volume of data over the network are not sufficient enough. Therefore, big data analyses are utilized by cyber experts (Staheli et al., 2014).

Various machine learning techniques can be used to deeply study the pattern of data used or created by users or any information on the internet. Techniques like logistical regression, SVM, deep learning, and K-means nearest neighbor are used that will boost the protective measures (Benzel et al., 2006). Basically, machine

DOI: 10.1201/9781003048862-10

135

learning is categorized into two groups – supervised learning and unsupervised learning. In the case of supervised learning, it is provided with the labeled training data and the machine training (Devakunchari et al., 2019). Meanwhile, in the case of unsupervised learning, labeled data is not provided and we do not need to supervise the model.

10.2 SYSTEMATIC REVIEW

Here are some research questions that were framed relating to the cyber security issues and machine learning techniques used to resolve them. The explanations to the questions are addressed by the reviews below. These research questions have been addressed in our studies:

RQ1: Security of personal as well any organizational data are highly essential for every user who is on the network or using the internet. *What are the important machine learning techniques to be aware of that have been involved in cyber security issues?*

RQ2: It should be clear whether our data is really secure or not – users should be aware about the security measures. *Does cyber hygiene improve security or just offset risk?*

RQ3: It is important to analyze the effect of each of the assets used while performing any machine learning technique. *Does detailed analysis of data improve security or just reduce the range of assets available in a successful attack?*

RQ4: *What are the effective machine learning techniques that can be used for designing accurate models?*

RQ5: *What challenges are faced regarding applying various security techniques using machine learning?*

RQ6: *What are the cyber security strategy motives that are followed?*

RQ7: *How does analysis of datasets play an important role in the field of cyber security?*

10.3 SEARCHING STRATEGIES FOR GROUNDWORK STUDIES

From different data sources, the relevant research papers are collected using certain search strategies.

10.3.1 INFORMATION COLLECTION

Using various search strategies as discussed above, a total of 120 research papers were selected. The papers not meeting the search requirements were excluded, leaving a total of 80 relevant papers and their references that could be selected for review in this study. Refer to Table 10.1 for details. So as to conduct the latest research on machine learning techniques with respect to cyber security issues, any papers since 2000 have not been taken for study due to limited findings of research work.

TABLE 10.1
Research Paper Collection from Research Database

S. No.	Source of Data Bases	No. of Search Results Retrieved	Number of Relevant Research Papers Found
1.	Google Scholar	25	12
2	Springer	20	9
3.	IEEE Xplore digital library	14	12
5.	ACM Digital Library	40	40
6.	Other journals	12	7
Total		**120**	**80**

10.4   RESULTS

> RQ1: *What are the important machine learning techniques that have been used for cyber security issues?*

Research question 1 of the SR (Systematic Review) was intended to find different machine learning techniques which have been used for resolving the cyber security issues. Some important and distinct techniques used for cyber security are mentioned in Tables 10.2 and 10.3.

TABLE 10.2
Research on Techniques of Machine Learning Used for Cyber Security Issues

Serial No.	Authors	Title	Year	Methodologies/Techniques
1.	Bland et al.	Machine learning cyber-attack and defense strategies	2020	Reinforcement learning, petri net
2.	Blowers and Williams	Machine learning applied to cyber operations in network science and cybersecurity	2014	False alarm, intrusion detection system, attack type, connection record, base intrusion detection system
3.	Czejdo et al.	Integration of external data sources with cyber security data warehouse	2014	Machine learning – supervised and unsupervised learning
4.	Goodall	Integration of external data Sources with cyber security	2014	Natural language processing
5.	Buczak and Guven	A survey of data mining and machine learning methods for cyber security intrusion detection	2015	Data mining and machine learning
6.	Cano	Cyber-attacks – the instability of security and control knowledge	2016	Cybersecurity, auditorium: cyber-attack, entities, evaluation, and measures risk
7.	Chmielarz & Szumski	Cyber security patterns of students' behavior and their participation in loyalty programs	2019	Cyber endeavor, cyber security patterns, loyalty programs

TABLE 10.3

Machine Learning Techniques Used for Cyber Security with Solutions

Serial No.	Authors	Title	Year	Methodologies/Techniques
1.	Das & Morris	Machine learning and cyber security	2017	Random forests, support vector machine, naïve Bayes, decision tree, artificial neural network, and deep belief network
2.	Ding & Zhai	Intrusion detection system for NSL-KDD dataset using convolutional neural networks	2018	Deep learning, convolution neural network
3.	El Kouari et al.	Using machine learning to deal with phishing and spam detection	2020	Machine learning to detect phishing and spam
4.	Ford & Siraj	Applications of machine learning in cyber security	2014	Machine learning for phishing detection
5.	Fraley & Cannady	The promise of machine learning in cybersecurity	2017	Artificial neural networks
6.	Ganesan et al.	Optimal scheduling of cybersecurity analysts for minimizing risk	2017	Optimization, recourse allocation. risk mitigation, simulation, schedule

Summary and comparative analysis of techniques of machine learning from Table 10.2 for cyber security issues: Difficulties such as being unable to perform scientific experiments due to lack of a properly labeled dataset makes it challenging to demonstrate adoptability approaches and operational limits (Czejdo et al., 2014). By providing the only relevant data, analysis can focus more on intrusion and threats, also allows anticipation and detection of the vulnerabilities before they present a problem (Czejdo et al., 2014). According to the literature survey of ML and DL for determining the effectiveness of methods, several criteria need to be taken into account (Buczak & Guven, 2015). For time management and better efficiency, the Dijkstra algorithm is used Abt, S., & Baier, H. (2014, November).

RQ2: *Do cyber crime preventive measures improve security or just negotiate the risk?*

Research question 2 of the SR was intended to find whether the security techniques used really improve the security of data in a system or it just ignore the risk details. Some important distinct techniques used for cyber security are mentioned below in Table 10.4.

Summary and comparative analysis of machine learning techniques from Table 10.5 for cyber security issues: The efficiency of hybrid neutral network and genetic algorithm is higher (Ahmad et al., 2019). The research has explored the dataset for malware attack and created a Fuzzy K-Means clustering algorithm. It also provides a model that can detect anomalies and provide higher accuracy with reduced human analysis time (Teoh et al., 2018)

TABLE 10.4

Machine Learning Techniques as a Preventive Measure Used for Cyber Security

Serial No.	Authors	Title	Year	Methodologies/Techniques
1.	Zhou Lu et al.	Cyber security in the smart grid survey and challenges	2013	Smart grid
2.	Teoh et al.	Analyst intuition inspired neural network-based cyber security anomaly detection	2018	Neural network, Big Data multilayer perceptron
3.	Lakhno et al.	Applying the functional effectiveness information index in cyber security adaptive expert system of information and communication transport systems	2017	Expert systems, sign clustering
5.	Geers et al.	Understanding nation-state motives behind today's advanced cyber-attacks	2014	This report sought to highlight the same phenomenon in regard to
6.	Ghani et al.	A contextual approach protecting online privacy, a crucial need	2019	privacy, security. protecting security, online security, internet privacy
7.	Guri et al.	Bridging the air gap between isolated networks and mobile phones in practical cyber-attack	2017	Air gap, data exfiltration

TABLE 10.5

Research on Machine Learning Techniques with Improved Accuracy

Serial No.	Authors	Title	Year	Methodologies/Techniques
1.	Hawrylak et al.	Practical cybersecurity solutions for science DMZ	2019	Science DMZ
2.	He et al.	An efficient phishing webpage detector	2011	Anti-phishing tools. E-commerce, black LIS-based
3.	Hill	Dealing with cyber security threats	2015	cyber warfare, ITRS, ITU, WCIT
4.	Hirschprung et al.	Analyzing and optimizing access control choice architectures in online social networks	2017	Access control, privacy, choice architecture, social networks
5.	Irfan et al.	A malware detection framework based on forensic and unsupervised machine learning methodologies	2020	Big Data, machine learning, threat hunting
6.	Jang-Jaccard & Nepal	A survey of emerging threats in cybersecurity	2014	Cybersecurity, malware, emerging technology trends, emerging cyber threats
7.	Kaloudi & Li	The AI-based cyber threat landscape: A survey	2020	Cyber threat prevention, cyber physical systems, smart grid, attack analysis

- The "min" and "max" operators are used for the fuzzy union and the fuzzy intersection. Machine learning algorithms can achieve recognition results of standard classes in range of 76.5–99.1% (Alhaidari et al., 2019).
- The multilayer perceptron classifier provides an accuracy of 90.18%, which is smaller as compared to the accuracy of hybrid neutral network and genetic algorithm (Killourhy & Maxion, 2011).

RQ3: *How are machine learning techniques used to predict future cyber security issues?*

Research question 3 of the SR was intended to find different machine learning techniques which have been used to predict effective cyber security techniques. Various machine learning techniques have been used for securing the data. Some distinct techniques have been mentioned in Table 10.6.

Summary and comparative analysis of machine learning techniques from Table 10.7 for prediction of cyber crimes

- Deep neural networks demonstrate that highly complicated data can be accurately modeled (Suryotrisongko & Musashi, 2019).
- Also, prototypes could demonstrate a very accurate model with low complexity data in a shallow network (Azmi et al., 2016).
- Deep neural networks are better than shallow networks.
- Detailed analysis is done using Big Data and machine learning (Peisert & Bishop, 2007).

RQ4: *What are the effective machine learning techniques that can be used for designing the accurate models?*

TABLE 10.6
Machine Learning Techniques for Prediction of Cybercrimes – Part 1

Serial No.	Authors	Title	Year	Methodologies/Techniques
1.	Barabde and Gaud	A survey of data mining techniques for cyber security	2019	Association rule, clustering, decision tree techniques
2.	Kleimnann and Wool	Automatic construction of state chart-based anomaly detection models for multi-threaded industrial control systems	2017	ICS, SCADA, network intrusion detection system, state char Siemen
3.	Kumar	Analyzing efficiency of pseudo-random number generators using machine learning	2016	Pseudo-random number generator, machine learning. supervised learning, random forest classifier
4.	Lakhno et al.	Applying the functional effectiveness information index in cybersecurity	2017	Cyber-attack recognition, expert system, sign clustering, functional learning effectiveness
5.	Leung et al.	Scalable security for peta scale parallel file systems	2007	Secure object-based storage, capabilities, high performance

TABLE 10.7
Research on Machine Learning Techniques for Prediction of Cybercrimes – Part 2

Serial No.	Authors	Title	Year	Methodologies/Techniques
1.	Liu et al.	Predicting cyber security incidents using feature-based characterization of network-level malicious activities	2015	Network security, prediction, network reputation, line series data
2.	Mahaini et al.	Building taxonomies based on human-machine teaming	2019	Natural language processing
3.	Majhi and Bera	A security enforcement framework for virtual machine migration auction	2015	Virtual machine, VM migration auction, cloud service provider
4.	Malin and Van Heule	Continuous monitoring and cyber security for high performance computing	2013	Continuous monitoring, supercomputer, cyber security
5.	Maltinsky et al.	ACM transactions on intelligent systems and technology	2017	Adversarial model
6.	Maxion et al.	Why is there no science in cyber science?	2010	Experimentation, research methodology, science of security
7.	Morel	Artificial intelligence and the future of cybersecurity	2011	Bayesian updating cross-site request forgery (CSRF), probabilities reasoning

TABLE 10.8
Major Algorithms for Cyber Security

Serial No.	Authors	Title	Year	Methodologies/Techniques
1.	Sathyadevan	Crime analysis and prediction using data mining	2014	Naïve Bayes, a priori algorithm, decision tree, MongoDB, GraphDB
3.	Barabde & Gaud	A survey of data mining techniques for cyber security	2019	Fuzzy logic, fuzzy rules, fuzzy-rule-based cyber expert systems
4.	Truong et al.	Artificial intelligence in the cyber domain: offense and defense	2020	Neural network, Big Data, multilayer perceptron

Research question 4 of the SR was intended to find the most effective *machine learning* techniques in optimization of data complexity. Various algorithms are compared to find the effective and accurate output. See Table 10.8.

Summary and comparative analysis of machine learning techniques from Table 10.5 for prediction of cyber crimes:

- The efficiency of linear regression is higher and provides accurate output for identifying the crime data based on the input given by the training set (Sathyadevan, 2014).

- A decision tree is not very effective in terms of performance and accuracy for crime data and its related features. It gives output only when the working of dataset matches with the model designed).
- Linear regression handles the degree of randomness very smoothly for testing dataset (Yampolskiy & Spellchecker, 2016).
- Analysis is done using Big Data for cyber security and to handle the missing data (Xin et al., 2018).

> RQ5: *What challenges are faced regarding applying various security techniques using machine learning?*

Research question 5 of the SR was intended to find the challenges that are faced when applying various machine learning techniques. The research that defines the challenges well are referred to below in Table 10.9.

Summary and comparative analysis of challenges from Table 10.6 in terms of cyber security:

- The challenge is how to represent the cyber security strategy for all parts of society, starting from the government sector to the private sector to civil society (Berman et al., 2019).
- Another challenge is to deal with changing environment. As it is a disruptive technology, that may call into a number of questions for military affairs, business, public policy, and civil society (Atoum et al., 2014).

TABLE 10.9
Research on Challenges in Terms of Cyber Security

Serial No.	Authors	Title	Year	Methodologies/Techniques
1.	Raiyu	A survey of cyber-attack detection strategies *International Journal of Security and its Applications*	2014	Homeland security, cyber attack
2.	Barabde & Gaud	A survey of data mining techniques for cyber security	2019	Fuzzy logic, fuzzy rules, fuzzy-rule-based cyber expert systems
3.	Sabillon et al.	A comprehensive cybersecurity audit model to improve cybersecurity assurance: the cybersecurity audit model (CSAM)	2017	Cybersecurity audit model, cybersecurity assurance, cyber security controls
4.	Sathyadevan	Cyber security in the smart grid	2014	Naïve Bayes, a priori algorithm, decision tree
5.	Truong et al.	Artificial intelligence in the cyber domain: offense and defense	2020	Neural network, Big Data, multilayer perception
6.	Savukynas	Security means in multilayered architecture of internet of things for secure communication and data transmission	2018	Internet of Things, data transmission, multilayered architecture

- Another challenge is creating a good strategy for the uncertainty of the technology change (Singh & Silakari, 2009).

RQ6: *What are the cyber security strategy motives that are followed?*

Research question 6 of the SR was intended to find the motive of strategies used. Various machine learning techniques have been used for securing the data. Refer to Table 10.10 below:

Summary and comparative analysis strategies and motives of cyber security:

- The motive of machine learning is to develop the patterns of data and use the algorithms to manipulate the patterns (Arnaldo & Veeramachaneni, 2019).
- So, to manipulate the patterns, we need more and more data from everywhere because it is important to represent data from as many as potential sources as possible (Oprea et al., 2018).
- The focus is not only on the quantity of data but also on its quality: it should be rich with context, it should be complete and relevant (Kleinmann & Wool, 2017). The focus should be on the cleaning of data, so that it makes sense of data that is selected (Jentzsch, 2015).

RQ7: *How does analysis of datasets play an important role in the field of cyber security?*

TABLE 10.10
Research on Strategies and Motives of Cyber Security

Serial No.	Authors	Title	Year	Methodologies/Techniques
1.	Sheng et al.	Context information-based cyber security defense of protection system	2007	Cyber security, probabilistic neural networks
2.	Sathyadevan	Crime analysis and prediction using data mining	2014	Naïve Bayes, Apriori algorithm, Decision Tree, Mongo DB, Graph DB
4.	Shrestha Chitrakar and Petrović	Efficient K-means using Triangle inequality on spark for cyber security analytics	2019	K-means clustering
5.	Ghate and Agrawal	A literature review on cyber security in the Indian context	2017	Cyber crime, information security, hacking, phishing, cyber prevention, and detection
6.	Singh et al.	Improved support vector machine for cyber-attack detection	2011	Support vector machine
7.	Zhong et al.	Applying Big Data-based deep learning systems to intrusion detection	2011	Big Data mining and analytics

TABLE 10.11

Parameters for UNSW-NB15

Parameters	UNSW-NB15
Year of creation	2015
Modern network traffic and attacks	Yes
Attack traffic generation	IXIA perfect storm tool
Duration of data collected	16 hours and 15 hours
Feature extraction tools	BroIDS, Argus
Features	47
Attack categories	9
Publicly available	Yes
Labeled dataset	Yes

- Various features of datasets like the KDD dataset, NSLKDDD, have been analyzed; it is found that about 75–78% of records are redundant in training and testing datasets, thus affecting the accuracy of the model and can be harmful to the network like U2R, R2L, etc. (AzzahKabbas & Munsh, 2020).
- After improving the features of KDD, the new dataset NSLKDD has been developed. It does not have duplicate records in the training and testing dataset (Ovelgönne et al., 2017). It can act as a benchmark for the researchers to compare various security models.
- The pattern of attacks and network data changes drastically in a regular period of time (Hollingsworth, 2016). To fill this gap, use the UNSW-NB-15 dataset that covers the variety of modern attacks (Arab Mohammed Shamiulla (2019).
- UNSW-NB-15 is the dataset that was developed by a group of cyber security members at the Australian center (Al Mazari et al., 2018). The dataset selection is an extremely important task, as the correct dataset decides the credibility of model evaluation (Wang et al., 2015).

Table 10.11 shows the various parameters of the UNSW-NB15 dataset.

10.5 CONCLUSION

Based on the above seven research questions, RQ5, RQ6, and RQ7 questions encouraged research in the field of cyber security using machine learning. This literature paper represents reviews of machine learning techniques for the cyber security domain. Recent research papers are included in the search that introduces the most commonly used techniques applied within the field of security. Techniques like deep learning, support vector machine, clustering, decision tree, artificial neural network, Bayesian network have been used widely in the research papers, while association rule, multilayer perceptron, a priori algorithm have been used rarely.

10.6 FUTURE SCOPE

From this review paper, I found that for determining new and modern attacks UNSW-NB15 dataset will be suitable as compared to KDDcup99, NSLKDD dataset. However, there are issues with the current dataset available publicly that restrict the action of analysis. For future work, more research can be done to improve the scope of rarely used machine learning techniques.

REFERENCES

Abt, S., & Baier, H. (2014, November). A plea for utilising synthetic data when performing machine learning based cyber-security experiments. In *Proceedings of the 2014 Workshop on Artificial Intelligent and Security Workshop* (pp. 37–45).

Aburrous, M., Hossain, M. A., Dahal, K., & Thabtah, F. (2010). Intelligent phishing detection system for e-banking using fuzzy data mining. Expert systems with applications, *37*(12), 7913–7921.

Adams, M., & Makramalla, M. (2015). Cybersecurity skills training: An attacker- centric gamified approach. Technology Innovation Management Review, *5*(1).

Ahmad, A., Shafiuddin, W., Kama, M. N., & Saudi, M. M. (2019, August). A New Cryptojacking Malware Classifier Model Based on Dendritic Cell Algorithm. In *Proceedings of the 3rd International Conference on Vision, Image and Signal Processing* (pp. 1–5).

Al Mazari, A., Anjariny, A. H., Habib, S. A., & Nyakwende, E. (2018). Cyber terrorism taxonomies: Definition, targets, patterns, risk factors, and mitigation strategies. In *Cyber Security and Threats: Concepts, Methodologies, Tools, and Applications* (pp. 608–621). IGI Global.

Alhaidari, S., Alharbi, A., Alshaikhsaleh, M., Zohdy, M., & Debnath, D. (2019, April). Network traffic anomaly detection based on Viterbi algorithm using SNMP MIB data. In *Proceedings of the 2019 3rd International Conference on Information System and Data Mining* (pp. 92–97).

Almeshekah, M. H., & Spafford, E. H. (2016). Cyber security deception. In Cyber deception (pp. 23–50). Springer, Cham.

Arab Mohammed Shamiulla (2019). Role of Artificial Intelligence in Cyber Security, International Journal of Innovative Technology and Exploring Engineering (IJITEE) ISSN: 2278-3075, 9(1).

Arnaldo, I., & Veeramachaneni, K. (2019). The Holy Grail of "Systems for Machine Learning" Teaming humans and machine learning for detecting cyber threats. ACM SIGKDD Explorations Newsletter, *21*(2), 39–47.

Atoum, I., Otoom, A., & Ali, A. A. (2014). A holistic cyber security implementation framework. Information Management & Computer Security.

Azmi, R., Tibben, W., & Win, K. T. (2016). Motives behind Cyber Security Strategy Development: A Literature Review of National Cyber Security Strategy.

AzzahKabbas, AtheerAlharthi, and Asmaa Munsh (2020). Artificial Intelligence Applications in Cybersecurity, IJCSNS International Journal of Computer Science and Network Security, 20(2).

Barabde, K. P. and Gaud, V. Y. (2019). A survey of data mining techniques for cyber security. *Jetir*, 6(5).

Benzel, T., Braden, R., Kim, D., Neuman, C., Joseph, A., Sklower, K., … Schwab, S. (2006, March). Experience with deter: A testbed for security research. In *2nd International Conference on Testbeds and Research Infrastructures for the Development of Networks and Communities, 2006. TRIDENTCOM 2006.* (p. 10). IEEE.

Berman, D. S., Buczak, A. L., Chavis, J. S., & Corbett, C. L. (2019). A survey of deep learning methods for cyber security. Information, *10*(4), 122.

Bland, J. A., Petty, M. D., Whitaker, T. S., Maxwell, K. P., & Cantrell, W. A. (2020). Machine learning cyberattack and defense strategies. Computers & security, 92, 101738.

Blowers, M., & Williams, J. (2014). Machine learning applied to cyber operations. In Network science and cybersecurity (pp. 155–175). Springer, New York, NY.

Czejdo, Bogdan D., Iannacone, Michael D., Bridges, Robert A., Ferragut, Erik M., & Goodall, John R. (2014). Integration of External Data Sources with Cyber Security Data Warehouse, *Proceedings of the 9th Annual Cyber and Information Security Research Conference.*

Buczak, A. L., & Guven, E. (2015). A survey of data mining and machine learning methods for cyber security intrusion detection. IEEE Communications surveys & tutorials, *18*(2), 1153–1176.

Cano, J. J. (2016). Cyberattacks—The Instability of Security and Control Knowledge.

Chmielarz, W., & Szumski, O. (2019). Cyber Security Patterns Students Behavior and Their Participation in Loyalty Programs. In *Cyber Law, Privacy, and Security: Concepts, Methodologies, Tools, and Applications* (pp. 1247–1263). IGI Global.

Das, R., & Morris, T. H. (2017, December). Machine Learning and Cyber Security. In *2017 International Conference on Computer, Electrical & Communication Engineering (ICCECE)* (pp. 1–7). IEEE.

Devakunchari, R. et al. (2019). A Study of Cyber Security using Machine Learning Techniques, International Journal of Innovative Technology and Exploring Engineering (IJITEE). ISSN: 2278-3075, Vol. 8, Issue 7C2.

Ding, Y., & Zhai, Y. (2018, December). Intrusion detection system for NSL-KDD dataset using convolutional neural networks. In *Proceedings of the 2018 2nd International Conference on Computer Science and Artificial Intelligence* (pp. 81–85).

El Kouari, O., Benaboud, H., & Lazaar, S. (2020, March). Using machine learning to deal with Phishing and Spam Detection: An overview. In *Proceedings of the 3rd International Conference on Networking, Information Systems & Security* (pp. 1–7).

Ford, V., & Siraj, A. (2014, October). Applications of machine learning in cyber security. In *Proceedings of the 27th International Conference on Computer Applications in Industry and Engineering.*

Fraley, J. B., & Cannady, J. (2017, March). The promise of machine learning in cybersecurity. In *SoutheastCon 2017* (pp. 1–6). IEEE.

Ganesan, R., Jajodia, S., & Cam, H. (2017). Optimal scheduling of cybersecurity analysts for minimizing risk. ACM Transactions on Intelligent Systems and Technology (TIST), *8*(4), 1–32.

Geers, K., Kindlund, D., Moran, N., & Rachwald, R. (2014). World War C: Understanding nation-state motives behind today's advanced cyber-attacks. FireEye, Milpitas, CA, USA, Tech. Rep., Sep.

Ghani, M. A. N. U., Farooq, E., & Asghar, K. (2019, November). A Contextual Approach Protecting Online Privacy, A Crucial Need. In *2019 International Conference on Innovative Computing (ICIC)* (pp. 1–10). IEEE.

Guri, M., Monitz, M., & Elovici, Y. (2017). Bridging the air gap between isolated networks and mobile phones in a practical cyber-attack. ACM Transactions on Intelligent Systems and Technology (TIST), *8*(4), 1–25.

Hawrylak, P. J., Louthan, G., Hale, J., & Papa, M. (2019). Practical Cyber- Security Solutions for the Science DMZ. In *Proceedings of the Practice and Experience in Advanced Research Computing on Rise of the Machines (learning)* (pp. 1–6).

He, M., Horng, S. J., Fan, P., Khan, M. K., Run, R. S., Lai, J. L., ... Sutanto, A. (2011). An efficient phishing webpage detector. Expert systems with applications, *38*(10), 12018–12027.

Hill, R. (2015, May). Dealing with cyber security threats: International cooperation, ITU, and WCIT. In *2015 7th International Conference on Cyber Conflict: Architectures in Cyberspace* (pp. 119–134). IEEE.

Hirschprung, R., Toch, E., Schwartz-Chassidim, H., Mendel, T., & Maimon, O. (2017). Analyzing and optimizing access control choice architectures in online social networks. ACM Transactions on Intelligent Systems and Technology (TIST), *8*(4), 1–22.

Hollingsworth, C. R. (2016). Auditing for FISMA and HIPAA: Lessons Learned Performing an In-house Cybersecurity Audit.

Irfan, A. N., Ariffin, A., Mahrin, M. N. R., & Anuar, S. (2020, February). A Malware Detection Framework Based on Forensic and Unsupervised Machine Learning Methodologies. In *Proceedings of the 2020 9th International Conference on Software and Computer Applications* (pp. 194–200).

Jang-Jaccard, J., & Nepal, S. (2014). A survey of emerging threats in cybersecurity. Journal of Computer and System Sciences, *80*(5), 973–993.

Jentzsch, N. (2015). Horizontal and Vertical Analysis of Privacy and Cyber- Security Markets. IPACSO White Paper Series.

Kaloudi, N., & Li, J. (2020). The AI-based cyber threat landscape: A survey. ACM Computing Surveys (CSUR), *53*(1), 1–34.

Killourhy, K. S., & Maxion, R. A. (2011, August). Should security researchers experiment more and draw more inferences? In CSET.

Kleinmann, A., & Wool, A. (2017). Automatic construction of statechart-based anomaly detection models for multi-threaded industrial control systems. ACM Transactions on Intelligent Systems and Technology (TIST), *8*(4), 1–21.

Kumar, S. (2016, December). Analyzing efficiency of Pseudo-Random Number Generators using Machine Learning. In *Proceedings of the 4th International Conference on Information and Network Security* (pp. 66–72).

Lakhno, V. A., Kravchuk, P. U., Pleskach, V. L., Stepanenko, O. P., Tishchenko, R. V., & Chernyshov, V. A. (2017). Applying the functional effectiveness information index in cybersecurity adaptive expert system of information and communication transport systems. Journal of Theoretical and Applied Information Technology, *95*(8), 1705–1714.

Leung, A. W., Miller, E. L., & Jones, S. (2007, November). Scalable security for petascale parallel file systems. In *Proceedings of the 2007 ACM/IEEE conference on Supercomputing* (pp. 1–12).

Liu, Y., Zhang, J., Sarabi, A., Liu, M., Karir, M., & Bailey, M. (2015, March). Predicting cyber security incidents using feature-based characterization of network-level malicious activities. In *Proceedings of the 2015 ACM International Workshop on International Workshop on Security and Privacy Analytics* (pp. 3–9).

Mahaini, M. I., Li, S., & Sağlam, R. B. (2019, August). Building Taxonomies based on Human-Machine Teaming: Cyber Security as an Example. In *Proceedings of the 14th International Conference on Availability, Reliability and Security* (pp. 1–9).

Majhi, S. K., & Bera, P. (2015, October). A Security Enforcement Framework for Virtual Machine Migration Auction. In *Proceedings of the 2015 Workshop on Automated Decision Making for Active Cyber Defense* (pp. 47–53).

Malin, A., & Van Heule, G. (2013, June). Continuous monitoring and cyber security for high performance computing. In *Proceedings of the first workshop on Changing landscapes in HPC security* (pp. 9–14).

Maltinsky, A., Giladi, R., & Shavitt, Y. (2017). On network neutrality measurements. ACM Transactions on Intelligent Systems and Technology (TIST), *8*(4), 1–22.

Maxion, R. A., Longstaff, T. A., & McHugh, J. (2010, September). Why is there no science in cyber science? a panel discussion at NSPW 2010. In *Proceedings of the 2010 New Security Paradigms Workshop* (pp. 1–6).

Morel, B. (2011, October). Artificial intelligence and the future of cybersecurity. In *Proceedings of the 4th ACM workshop on Security and artificial intelligence* (pp. 93–98).

Oprea, A., Li, Z., Norris, R., & Bowers, K. (2018, December). Made: Security analytics for enterprise threat detection. In *Proceedings of the 34th Annual Computer Security Applications Conference* (pp. 124–136).

Ovelgönne, M., Dumitras, T., Prakash, B. A., Subrahmanian, V. S., & Wang, B. (2017). Understanding the relationship between human behavior and susceptibility to cyber attacks: A data-driven approach. ACM Transactions on Intelligent Systems and Technology (TIST), 8(4), 1–25.

Peisert, S., & Bishop, M. (2007). How to design computer security experiments. In Fifth World Conference on Information Security Education (pp. 141–148). Springer, Boston, MA.

Sabillon, R., Serra-Ruiz, J., Cavaller, V., & Cano, J. (2017, November). A comprehensive cybersecurity audit model to improve cybersecurity assurance: The cybersecurity audit model (CSAM). In *2017 International Conference on Information Systems and Computer Science (INCISCOS)* (pp. 253–259). IEEE.

Sathyadevan, S. (2014, August). Crime analysis and prediction using data mining. In *2014 First International Conference on Networks & Soft Computing (ICNSC 2014)* (pp. 406–412). IEEE.

Savukynas, R. (2018). Security Means in Multilayered Architecture of Internet of Things for Secure Communication and Data Transmission. In Doctoral Consortium/Forum@ DB&IS (pp. 127–134).

Sheng, S., Chan, W. L., Li, K. K., Xianzhong, D., & Xiangjun, Z. (2007). Context information-based cyber security defense of protection system. IEEE Transactions on Power Delivery, 22(3), 1477–1481.

Shrestha Chitrakar, A., & Petrović, S. (2019, March). Efficient k-means using triangle inequality on spark for cyber security analytics. In *Proceedings of the ACM International Workshop on Security and Privacy Analytics* (pp. 37–45).

Shweta Ghate and Pragyesh Kumar Agrawal (2017). A Literature Review on Cyber Security in Indian Context. Journal of Computer Science Engineering & Information Technology.

Singh, S., & Silakari, S. (2009). A survey of cyber-attack detection systems. International Journal of Computer Science and Network Security, 9(5), 1–10.

Singh, S., Agrawal, S., Rizvi, M. A., & Thakur, R. S. (2011, October). Improved Support Vector Machine for Cyber Attack Detection. In *Proceedings of the World Congress on Engineering and Computer Science* (Vol. 1).

Staheli, D., Yu, T., Crouser, R. J., Damodaran, S., Nam, K., O'Gwynn, D., … Harrison, L. (2014, November). Visualization evaluation for cyber security: Trends and future directions. In *Proceedings of the Eleventh Workshop on Visualization for Cyber Security* (pp. 49–56).

Suryotrisongko, H., & Musashi, Y. (2019, November). Review of Cybersecurity Research Topics, Taxonomy and Challenges: Interdisciplinary Perspective. In *2019 IEEE 12th Conference on Service-Oriented Computing and Applications (SOCA)* (pp. 162–167). IEEE.

Teoh, T. T., Nguwi, Y. Y., Elovici, Y., Ng, W. L., & Thiang, S. Y. (2018). Analyst intuition inspired neural network based cyber security anomaly detection. International Journal of Innovative Computing Information and Control, 14(1), 379–386.

Wang, J., Xue, Y., Liu, Y., & Tan, T. H. (2015, April). JSDC: A hybrid approach for javascript malware detection and classification. In *Proceedings of the 10th ACM Symposium on Information, Computer and Communications Security* (pp. 109–120).

Xin, Y., Kong, L., Liu, Z., Chen, Y., Li, Y., Zhu, H., … Wang, C. (2018). Machine learning and deep learning methods for cybersecurity. IEEE Access, 6, 35365–35381.

Yampolskiy, R. V., & Spellchecker, M. S. (2016). Artificial intelligence safety and cybersecurity: A timeline of AI failures. arXiv preprint arXiv:1610.07997.

11 Research Agenda for Use of Machine Learning and Internet of Things in "People Analytics"

Rosemary Guvhu, Terence Tachiona,
Munyaradzi Zhou, and Tinashe Gwendolyn Zhou

CONTENTS

DOI: 10.1201/9781003048862-11

11.1 INTRODUCTION

Production of Big Data through increased usage of IoT applications (OECD, 2016) has prompted public and private sectors across the globe to migrate from traditional human judgment techniques refereed as biased and flawed than the use of machine learning (ML) and Internet of Things (IoT) (Zantalis et al., 2019) for key decision-making and improvement of staff performance and productivity (Fecheyr-Lippens, Schaninger, and Tanner, 2015). Prioritizing ML and IoT application in people analytics (PA) centers on the understanding that such digital technologies offer cherished visions anticipated by peoples' managers in executing their functions, from talent acquisition to retirement or retrenchment of employees. The use of ML and IoT in PA has gained recognition as it empowers managers to make sound decisions that improve staff performance and productivity (Tomar and Gaur, 2020).

Studies undertaken in the field of IoT reveal that the area is gaining momentum with anticipated projections of billions of connected IoT devices and a soaring of the economic activity in trillions by 2025 (Rose, Eldridge, and Chapin, 2015). Contrary to the above projections, some researchers suggest that the pros usage of IoT in PA might be outweighed by the cons especially when some news headlines publicly report issues of privacy fears, hacking of internet-connected devices and surveillance concerns (Chen, 2012; Rose et al., 2015; Nižetić et al., 2020). However, the debate among researchers, professionals and policymakers about the effects and concerns of ML and IoT application in PA appears to be inconclusive.

Therefore, this chapter is important in bringing awareness among human resources managers, business leaders, academics, and policymakers with evidence concerning the effects and concerns of ML and IoT application in PA. If implementers of ML and IoT technologies lack clear understanding of the influence and key concerns of

ML and IoT application in PA they might fail to deal with factors militating against appropriate usage, security and privacy issues associated with successful implementation of ML and IoT visions.

The chapter is unique and important in terms of its focus, breadth, and scope more specifically because it focuses on the little researched opportunities and challenges of ML and IoT application in PA by:

i.   Outlining the history of PA and highlighting the major challenges of using traditional techniques in people analytics.
ii. Discussing PA highlighting its opportunities and challenges.
iii. Describing the process of PA.
iv. Exploring the use of IoT, Big Data, and ML in PA highlighting the opportunities and challenges faced when using these technologies.
v.   Proposing alternative policies and practices to address challenges of IoT and ML usage optimizing organizational performance.

The chapter is therefore significant since it contributes to a new body of literature by discussing the use of ML and IoT in PA and proposes a research agenda on how ML and IoT might be used in PA by organizations to improve organizational effectiveness and efficiency.

11.2 LITERATURE REVIEW

The literature review is mainly confined in the following areas, namely, the history of PA (traditional techniques in people analytics and modern-technology-based PA); ML and IoTs data-driven technologies for people analytics (application, opportunities, and challenges); and frameworks relating to the concepts of ML, IoT, and people analytics.

11.2.1 DEFINITION OF TERMS (PEOPLE ANALYTICS, ML, AND IoT)

The terms people analytics (PA), human resource analytics, talent analytics, and PA are used interchangeably. PA focuses on the process of data collection and analysis before hiring, during hiring and the entire lifetime of an employee within an organization. This gives the lifeblood to an organization in terms of decision-making. However, for this research PA is being used and is related to talent analytics even though the term talent analytics is not adopted. Human resource analytics is related to workforce analytics. The two concepts are not discussed even though its elements interlink with the aforementioned.

11.2.1.1 People Analytics

People analytics is a new term in the technology era which focuses on exploiting Big Data for the best business outcomes through managing human resource talent (Momin and Momin, 2015). The concept helps to eliminate human flaws based on gut feeling and intuition during decision-making processes. The processes start from the time of hiring up to when an employee will leave placement (West, 2019). Furthermore, PA can be defined as the application of big-data analytics using technological tools to redefine and disrupt the processes of human resource talent management to achieve sustainable business success (Isson and Harriot, 2016). According to Gal, Jensen, and Stein (2017) PA enables organizations to be more effectual, objective, and logical in their decision-making about people. With PA, organizations are able to understand their employees holistically, as individuals, and in different team environments by making the data about employee characteristics, conduct and performance more accessible, interpretable, and actionable (Pape, 2016).

In general, PA is not a new phenomenon, since organizations have been using human resources metrics to evaluate or track how effective human resources are or how it contributes to organizations at large for years. A number of organizations are enjoying the value of PA irrespective that only 16% of the institutions have actually implemented PA. This has resulted in various academic discussions on opportunities and challenges that PA presents to organizations (Minbaeva, 2017; Peeters, Paauwe, and Van De Voorde, 2020). Pillaring from the mushrooming interest in this area of PA, this chapter is critical as it will provide an insight into what it is that organizations should do to incorporate people analytics into their everyday operations.

11.2.1.2 Workforce Analytics

Workforce analytics is the use of data-based tools and metrics including Big Data silos, software tools like Python, SPSS, and Excel to improve and enhance decision-making and predictions (data value-addition). It includes the use of information communication techniques which are endowed with data visualization and analytics tools which is applied on employees' profiles and performance data (Tursunbayeva, Di Lauro, and Pagliari, 2018). Software tools result in seamless data collection, aggregation, optimization, transformation, and analytics. Decision-making capabilities include managing and hiring top talent, aligning compensation with performance, training and so on, enhancing this data by integrating it, organizing the data, and transforming it for decision-making (Momin and Momin, 2015; Gaur, Shukla, and Verma, 2019). During the process, data is collected within the organization and externally.

11.2.1.3 Internet of Things (IoT)

Various scholars have used different definitions to describe or promote a specific understanding of IoT and its features. IoT is viewed as an integration of computing capability and network connectivity of devices, sensors, objects, and "things" not typically regarded as computers (Halevi et al., 2016; Rose et al., 2015).

Devices and non-computer items such as tablets, cameras, smart microwaves, self-driving cars, smart TVs, smartwatches, are referred to as "things." Hence, the interconnection of two to millions of the billions of "things"/devices is referred to IoT. IoT data flow to and from IoT devices, thus they collect (e.g., sensors) and share data usually in real-time (mainly via the cloud, Bluetooth, and integrated software) with a given platform. The software then analyses and transmits the data to users via mobile applications and or websites. Sensor-based devices IoT environment integrates data from various systems and applies analytics to share important information with other applications. Using ML, the "things" can screen useful information and redirect other to appropriate "things." The information is integrated, cleansed, and processed for decision-making. Internet-of-Things devices are all around us; constantly transmitting data and "talking" with other IoT devices (Pathak and Bhandari, 2018; CISCO, 2020).

IoT includes monitoring "things" that are connected via the internet for seamless communication among people, processes, and things with minimal human intervention. In this internetworked globe, digital systems can record, monitor, and adjust each interaction among connected devices. The physical world and the digital world are synced (Pathak and Bhandari, 2018; CISCO, 2020). IoT-ML and analytics, along with access to varied and vast amounts of data stored in the cloud, organizations seamlessly add value to their data, improves operational efficiency, improves worker productivity (Pathak and Bhandari, 2018; CISCO, 2020).

11.2.1.4 Big Data

Big data is the vast quantity of both qualitative and quantitative data that is now available both online and offline (Oussous, Benjelloun, Lahcen, and Belfkih, 2018). According to Furht and Villanustre, 2016; Karthiban and Raj (2019), and Lee (2017), Big Data is defined by three major characteristics namely volume, velocity, and variety.

Due to an increase in technological innovations, new insights can be discovered, and is becoming the backbone of organizational performance and economic growth (Chase, 2016). IoT and Big Data technologies are emerging technologies which have the power to support critical decision-making (Ge, Bangui, and Buhnova, 2018).

11.2.1.5 Machine Learning (ML)

ML is a key concept of artificial intelligence (AI) that mimic human intelligence and explores the field and application of algorithms that have learning and prediction capabilities to improve performance. ML is a subset of AI (Pathak and Bhandari, 2018; ML CISCO, 2021a, 2021b).

ML empowers knowledge discovery and aids intelligent decision-making (Oussous et al., 2018). Supervised machine learning (SML) and unsupervised machine learning (UML) constitute the two basic ML algorithms. SML involves guidance from the supervisor who gives guidance to reach a known conclusion., who (predefined output). Examples of SML are support vector machines, multiclass classification, linear and logistic regression algorithms, and. UML employs an independent method whereby a computer learns to identify complex processes and patterns without human "involvement" and does not have predefined output. UML algorithms include principal and independent component analysis, k-means, association rules and clustering rules. The structure, use case and volume of data determines the type to ML algorithm to adopt. SML algorithms are the most commonly used (CISCO, 2021a, 2021b).

11.2.2 History of Peoples Analytics

Operational and strategic human resources management has been used for decades before technology-based PA was adopted. The former has traditionally revolved around personal relationships or decision-making based on experience, which mainly results in misinformed decisions, bias, and so on, which is usually costly to an organization. The hiring process has been made easier through Big Data analytics tools for example through web-scraping on profiles like GitHub, LinkedIn, and Facebook. The aggregated results from these sites might help in choosing the best candidate, to identify flaws in the processes like variant compensation of employees which results in high level of attrition (Fecheyr-Lippens, Schaninger, and Tanner, 2015; Isson and Harriot, 2016).

11.2.2.1   People Analytics – Human-Driven Human Resources (HR) (Solely Human-based Analysis)

Traditional PA is based on solely human intervention, it is the cornerstone for technology-based PA hence it cannot substitute direct engagement of employees to understand their mindsets, challenges, and needs. Employee data analysis has been generally manual with little or no use of technology. Advancement of technology has called for technology-centered PA (Fecheyr-Lippens, Schaninger, and Tanner, 2015; Momin and Momin, 2015).

11.2.2.2   People Analytics – Data-Driven HR (Technology-based Analysis)

Generally, analytics in HR has been mainly focused on tracking basic HR metrics or providing reports to managers. Conversely, PA focuses mainly on aggregation and analysis of historical and real-time data from disparity locations like wearable devices, stress monitors, voice detectors, alarms, smart watches and so on, hence Big Data. Big Data allows application of Dmachine-learning algorithms and tools to create new insights on employees such as loyalty, retention, attrition, and satisfaction and so on (Fallucchi et al., 2020).

11.2.3   TYPES OF PEOPLE ANALYTICS

There are different types of PA, namely, descriptive, predictive, prescriptive, and diagnostic analytics (Tomar and Gaur, 2020).

11.2.3.1   Descriptive Analytics

Descriptive analytics is used to gather and analyze data from dashboards that describes the real-time and historical data (Tomar and Gaur, 2020). It includes the groups of ML-based algorithms that process and summarize high volumes of unprocessed data and produce actionable insights (Adi, Anwar, Baig, and Zeadally, 2020). Descriptive analytics results in data silos (Big Data) which later informs decision-making by HR personnel.

11.2.3.2   Predictive Analytics

Predictive analytics also makes use of real-time and historical data. It applies statistical techniques like data mining and ML in an attempt to optimize operations and improve the employee experience (Tomar and Gaur, 2020). Unlike descriptive analytics, predictive analytics is all about data-driven insights and the approach uses statistical methods, ML techniques, and data mining models that analyze and extract existing and historical facts to make predictions (Mishra, Lama, and Pal, 2016). Ultimately, predictive analytics results in improvement and efficiency in the work processes.

11.2.3.3   Prescriptive Analytics

Prescriptive analytics is historically based; it gives suggestions on what to do based on predictions on existing data (Tomar and Gaur, 2020). It is a more sophisticated predictive analytics concept that integrates optimization techniques with statistical analysis (Kapoor and Kabra, 2014). It can be used to inform future hiring decisions.

11.2.3.4   Diagnostic Analytics

Diagnostic analytics show the causes of the results exhibited descriptive analytics. It explains the underlying cause, which helps us to focus our efforts to decrease the problem (Tomar and Gaur, 2020). It uses information from descriptive analytics to reach a conclusion about the situation. Inefficiencies in recruitment processes, production lines and so on can be easily identified.

11.2.4   PEOPLE ANALYTICS CASE STUDIES, OPPORTUNITIES AND CHALLENGES OF PEOPLE ANALYTICS

Many organizations including retail, healthcare, fast foods, IT, oil, automotive industries, and government departments have used PA (power of data analytics in talent management) and have achieved different advantages. These include saving money by predicting who will quit; relating store income with engagement; cutting costs with natural attrition; doubling customer satisfaction; getting ahead of employee attrition; testing employee training effectiveness; tackling employee absence; employee engagement; reducing regrettable attrition; and identifying, attracting, developing, and retaining talent. In general, PA returns competent employees and results in better business decisions (Isson and Harriot, 2016; AIHR Analytics, 2018; Fallucchi et al., 2020).

11.2.4.1   Advantages of People Analytics

The widespread emergency of cloud computing has resulted in its tapping within HR systems to get more insights from the PA-related data (data about employees and possible employees). This results in improving business performance through competent personnel, while at the same time it boosts employee experience and well-being. PA generally, results in reduced attrition rates. Competent employees are mushroomed during the process of hiring and after hiring. The hiring process can be done seamlessly and usually the best-diversified qualified candidates will be pulled out (Arellano, DiLeonardo, and Felix, 2017; West, 2019).

11.2.4.2   Disadvantages of People Analytics

A team of experienced IT personnel is required which might be costly to hire and are in high demand during this period of data analytics. The lack of such analytical acumen skills results in incorrect, unreliable, or hard-to-access data. HR IT-centered personnel are responsible for integrating appropriate hardware and software tools to achieve PA. HR personnel buy-in might be a challenge since they might feel technology-based decisions are biased and undermine their expertise (Lanwehr and Mayer, 2018; West, 2019).

11.2.5   THE PROCESS OF PEOPLE ANALYTICS

The strategy and processes involved during PA need to be identified. Employees must be ready to use and be part of the PA projects. In general, the process includes the readiness of the organization, stakeholders' buy-in, and defining the roadmap.

11.2.5.1   Readiness of the Organization

Technology solutions will not help organizations unless they have been adopted and are in use to find deeper insights to grow and improve employees. PA and the employees' planning is centered on change management which can be supported by tools, technology, statistics, and ML. An in-house solution or a customized solution might be chosen (Isson and Harriot, 2016; Dearborn and Swanson, 2018).

11.2.5.2   Stakeholders Buy-In

A data-driven culture entails a complete organizational transformation and change-management plan. From senior management to work floor employees, all must support the investment and use of PA technologies. Involvement of all stakeholders results in them as agents of change. Employers must overcome resistance and persuade employees to willingly become quantified employees. It is essential to ensure legal compliance during the process of data collection, transformation, and up-to-date analysis to avoid legal battles (Isson and Harriot, 2016).

11.2.5.3   Defining the Roadmap

There is a need for defining a business-goal-oriented roadmap while implementing PA for benchmarking attainments and the impact and related organizational changes. Understanding areas of focus results in the application of the correct statistical, data mining, ML, survey management, and strategic workforce management tools. Ultimately, an action plan must be availed and benchmarked for success using data solutions explored (Isson and Harriot, 2016; Dearborn and Swanson, 2018).

11.2.6   USE OF IoT, BIG DATA, AND MACHINE LEARNING IN PEOPLE ANALYTICS

IoT technology can be used to solve problems and improve work processes, since the systems integrations result in Big Data which can be analyzed. IoT devices connected to the cloud, sensors, and other information communication technologies applications and devices inter-connected provides a great analytic power after application of ML algorithms for making business decisions (providing new insights). PA has been initiated by an increase in employees' data and being more available; an increase in analytical capabilities (increase in processing power of information communication devices and availability of data analysis tools and skills); and the popularity of Big Data analysis and its seamless application, and its financial impact on increasing return on investment on data analytics.

11.2.6.1 IoT in People Analytics, Opportunities, and Challenges

The use of IoT devices and "things" in PA and in general has posed a number of opportunities and challenges. Leveraging on IoT, PA has been used to improve organizational decisions that are associated with hiring, motivation, efficacy, and retention of competent employees in the organization (Gaur, Shukla and Verma, 2019). The automated analysis of data collected through IoTs can provide insights into previously unknown relationships between things, their environment, and their users facilitating an optimization of people's behavior (Stople, 2016).

Internet connectivity and network monitoring is a major concern as they can pose unavailability and security concerns, hence there is need for experts to continually support the systems; for example, by fixing software bugs, conducting penetration testing, and monitoring the network in general. Experts in IoT are in demand and the costs of hiring might be expensive and matching the ever-changing IT landscape might be a mammoth task. Smartphones and other "things" are ever-evolving and applications and user demands to support these are ever increasing. The battery lifespan of most sensors calls for replacement or upgrade and or regular charging which can be a challenge. A good and available internet connection is always essential for systems' uptime. Africa and Latin America might face challenges in implementation of IoT-supported systems (connecting sensors/"things") due to unreliable Wi-Fi speeds (Chen, 2012; Nižetić et al., 2020). This adversely affects the process of data generation and transmission. System downtime might ultimately result in unavailability of data and uninformed decision-making (compromised reliability and availability of data) using ML, irrespective of the power of "things" in sending and receiving data in well integrated systems.

11.2.6.2 Big Data in People Analytics, Opportunities, and Challenges

From a HR viewpoint, Big Data from variety of sources, integrated from organizational processes which involve high transactional data can be analyzed in relation to data relating individual actions or team environments (Fairhurst, 2014). This ultimately, results in informed decision-making.

In today's fast-paced world, analyzing large quantities of different information is an uphill task, but it is doable. Kumar (2018) notes that when HR functions within organizations tap into the power of Big Data, it increases their ability to decrease the cost of bad hires, increase retention rates, predict candidate or employee performance, and improve their remuneration packages. This outlines the opportunities that are created by Big Data for PA. Putting high value on people data to underpin good decision-making has derived positive results for data-driven institutions. According to a Forbes 2020 report, PEMCO, an insurance company in the USA which has adopted Big Data analytics in HR, attested that organized and cleaned data supports organizational throughput, research development and innovation. Insightful dashboards integrating key processes from hiring to last day of employment (Forbes Human Resources Council, 2020).

Studies show that there are both technical and human barriers, traditional HR processes, archaic information systems and poor data quality are impeding improved PA implementation. This, coupled with a lack of business analysis and understanding skills, poses additional challenges to the ability of Big Data roles in PA as organizations fail to transcend the traditional compliance-driven HR culture mainly because of misconceptions about Big Data (Dahlbom, Siikanen, Sajasalo, and Jarvenpaa, 2019). In addition, incorrect data management, lack of analytical skills and lack of organizational agility hinders PA implementation within the organization (Gaur, 2020).

According to Dahlbom et al. (2019), most organizations' top management do not expect any significant value from people's analytics, but HR and business professionals see the potential value of the spare. This indicates the need for greater collaboration among top management, data analysts, business, and HR professionals to provide and understand people's data in business-related decision-making. In addition, the impact of HR practices, along with the technical barriers to comics, may require a change in culture and a corporate overhaul. The use of PA and the transformation of HR roles seem to be closely linked, and this transformation reinforces each other.

11.2.6.3 Machine Learning in People Analytics, Opportunities, and Challenges

HR technocrats use numerous techniques to monitor and track employees for decision-making. This includes verifying if email and internet are productively utilized. This can reflect on employee productivity, dependability, interaction, location, and health. ML techniques can be applied to analyze the data gathered from an individual from the start of their hiring process right until their last day of employment. The concepts feed into the organizational processes such as the hiring process to get better applicants, increase employee performance, improve retention, and make smarter hiring decisions (Gaur, Shukla and Verma, 2019).

ML has the capability to enhance the speed to make decisions, and providing new insights. However, solely depending on auto-generated decisions without human intervention might mislead decision makers and might lead to legal issues. Employees' privacy is essential and must not be infringed upon. Authority must be sought if there is a justifiable cause if an employer must invade one's privacy. A good example arose in the context of the European Human Rights Convention and data protection legislation where excessive, unnecessary, or unjustified monitoring of employees is unethical (McKay, 2020). An employer should be mindful of the data protection principles set out in the organizational policies, national policies and international policies such as the EU General Data Protection Regulation (the 'GDPR'). ICT bodies, governments, and organizations must come up with their own policy documents regarding the use of ML in PA (McKay, 2020).

Implementation of monitoring must be done after a policy document is enacted and has been endorsed by all stakeholders and legal and related risks have been addressed including new technologies. The policy document must include elements like what the goal of monitoring; data analysis and use purposes; the pros and cons of a technology and security issues concerning the collected data. Computer-based automated decisions need to be certified by humans before their application. In addition, human input conducted ethically results in more insights identification (McKay, 2020).

11.2.7   Theoretical and Conceptual Frameworks on People Analytics

This section presents a review of frameworks proposed for using ML and IoT in PA. These frameworks may be utilized to deal with issues of ML and IoT usage, security risks and breach of privacy to optimize future opportunities of ML and IoT in PA.

11.2.7.1   Frameworks for Use of ML and IoT

Adi, Anwar, Baig, and Zeadally (2020) proposed a framework that enables IoT applications to interchange knowledge, generate new knowledge and adaptively learn from the knowledge so that they can become appropriate across different domains or case studies. The framework was adopted from verificationism theory and it employs natural language processing (NLP) techniques to understand human language. Secondly the framework exchanges ontologies with other smart objects and the ontologies are structured in such a way that the inference rules are understandable by humans. The framework might help in coming up with organizational policies to implement PA (technology-based).

Gaur (2020) proposed an HR framework for improving employee engagement in an organization. The framework proposes the use of ML and AI to transform PA processes Gaur (2020)'s study endeavors to show how organizations can exploit ICT tools to radically change the use of people data. The study undertaken by Mohanty and Mishra (2020) proposed a framework for PA. Using the Delphi method, the researchers analyzed the effects of IoT applications on HR activities. They concluded that IoT sensors on employees can be used to access information of employees on their behavioral outcomes in various situations. These frameworks help in developing a customized PA architecture for an organization.

The Big Data which is both structured and unstructured with varied timestamps, collected using the IoTs results in challenges associated with real-time data collection, processing and decision-making (Saqlain, Piao, Shim, and Lee, 2019). For analytics to be truly useful, it must be embedded into user workflows and real-time analytics employed to help organizations improve the gathering, correlation and analysis of the key data. Gaur, Shukla and Verma (2019) proposed a framework through the implementation of wearable IoT devices for real-time data analytics. The device is enabled with different sensors for real-time data collection and the data collected can give unknown trends and patterns about an individual employee or teams.

11.2.7.2   Security Risks and Breach of Privacy to Optimize Future Opportunities of ML and IoT in People Analytics

The primary role of using dependable, reliable, and secured data in PA is to make confident, informed decision-making within an entity. The use of unreliable and unsecure data during PA processes is detrimental to organizations hence these challenges need to be alleviated. More than 70% of organizations exploit real-time employee data in services-oriented processes (Feravich, 2011). Unfortunately, at least 50% of the organizations lack skills to verify the reliability and secureness of the data they use for analytics of which consequently data breaches can be experienced (McKendrick, 2012). The concept of Big Data in PA has increased complexities including the domain of information governance (data access, sharing), on individual, corporate, national, and international levels and among these.

According to Tonidandel, King, and Cortina (2015), data governance practices frameworks or models provide a universal approach to management, improvement, and use of data in PA. Data governance models need to be customized according to organizational, national, regional and international standards in terms of controlling the quality of data, managing how it is stored, transmitted, processed, and used, and the security and privacy parameters implemented. Tonidandel et al. (2015) also concurs that data governance frameworks need to be developed as they're key in Big Data hence it supports PA.

Data ethics and security practices compliance becomes critical in this ever-advancing technological world and the implementation of PA (Josh Bersin Academy, 2020). The PA models implemented must be employee-centric as they support data ethics and security practices compliance. The concepts to be dovetailed include privacy, security, mitigating bias and assessing the impact of PA to employees and at organizational level. Stakeholders' involvement is critical in synergizing ICT processes with PA processes and all systems at the organization to attain security and privacy compliance. A two-way communication loop will be essential to attain results (Josh Bersin Academy, 2020; Chen, 2012; Nižetić et al., 2020). In summary, models concerning security and privacy issues in PA need to be developed, implemented and continuous improvements are essential since technological advancements are on the rise.

11.3 METHODOLOGY

The authors used multiple data sources including surveys conducted through semi-structured and open-ended interviews with four participants, each conveniently and purposively sampled from the four organizational sectors. In addition, a thorough literature review was conducted. All research ethics were adhered to and consent forms were completed by participants prior to interviews. Issues of privacy, confidentiality, and anonymity of information were addressed, and real names of participants and institutions were masked. Respondents indicated their views on a 3-Likert scale coded with 1 (Unsure) being the lowest, followed by 2 (No) and (3) Yes being the highest. As shown in Table 11.1, participants' demographic features (items 1–4) were sourced including their gender, organizational sector, country status whether developed or developing, and their primary functional roles. The 300 participants randomly sampled from the industry, business, education, and healthcare sectors, deemed to be information rich sites since it is focusing on the key concerns of IoT and ML application in PA as noted in the literature review. Data was collected within 4 months between October 2020 and February 2021. Qualitative data was analyzed thematically while quantitative data was analyzed using descriptive statistics computed through SPSS version 20.0.

Review of related literature, analyzing, and discussing case studies at both international and local levels provided the larger portion of our results. The search criteria and selection of material to include in the research was based on the value the work informs PA. For instance, HR Analytics/Workforce Analytics concepts are a domain

TABLE 11.1
Respondents' Demographic Data

Item	Variable	Category (N = 300)	Frequency	%Percent
1	Gender	Male	192	64.0%
		Female	108	36.0%
2	Organization	Industry	88	29.3%
		Business	109	36.3%
		Education	46	15.3%
		Healthcare	57	19.0%
3	Country status	Developed	100	33.3%
		Developing	200	66.7%
4	Primary role	Leaders/Manager	79	26.3%
		Human Resource Personnel	96	32.0%
		IT Director	74	24.7%
		Other	51	17.0%

of PA. The major databases that were used to inform the research included Google Scholar, Elsevier, SAGE, and Emerald Insight. The key words that guided the research were PA, ML, IoT, and Big Data.

11.4   RESULTS AND ANALYSIS

In this section, results obtained from multiple data sources which included survey questionnaire and interviews conducted for 4 months from October 2020 to February 2021 with institutional leaders, managers, human resource personnel, IT Directors and other participants which involves in the implementation of IoT and ML technologies within their organizations are presented and analyzed. Literature review and analysis of case studies on IoT and ML systems in PA from selected organization sectors such as industry, business, education, and healthcare were included in this chapter. Table 11.1 displays the demographic data of 300 respondents, (192) 64.0% are males and (108) 36.0% are females. The respondents answered a randomly distributed closed-ended survey questionnaire to provide their views on IoT and ML application in PA within the purposively selected organizations namely: industry, business, education, and healthcare, which researchers believed would be information rich sites as shown by trends in existing and previous literature both locally and internationally.

The results show that more males than females responded to the questionnaire while the business sector topped the list of participants with (109) 36.3%, followed by industry (88) 29.3%, healthcare (57) 19.0%, and lastly education (46) 15.3% participants. More respondents (200) 66.7% had their organizations based in developing countries while (100) 33.3% were based in developed nations. This might be due to the fact that researchers had better access to developing nations in the Southern African Development Community (SADC) where their country, Zimbabwe is located. In terms of their primary job functions, (79) 26.3% were either organizational leaders or managers, (96) 32% constituted the human resource personnel, (74)

24.7% were IT Directors while other respondents totaled (51)17% of the sample. It was important to source the demographics of the participants since these would help the researchers in understanding the context in which the emerging technologies were being used by different participants.

11.4.1 IoT and ML Uses, Challenges and Strategies to Enhance People Analytics

Table 11.2 shows descriptive statistics including the minimum, maximum, mean, and standard deviation, depicting the views of the 300 respondents concerning the use and effects of IoT and ML technologies in PA. Results for items 5, show that organizations represented by these participants moderately applied IoT tools such as surveillance cameras and tracking systems with mean (1.9133) and a standard deviation (0.80912). The same applies to their views on whether or not these technologies offered more benefits than risks to participants' organizations (item 9) with slightly above average mean of 1.9133 and standard deviation 0.80081. Almost similar responses (1.9400) mean and low standard deviation of (0.76048) were provided in item 10 concerning availability of participants' strategies to use in protecting employees' privacy and security while at the same time enhancing innovative usage

TABLE 11.2
Descriptive Statistics Showing Views of Respondents on IoT and ML Usage and Impacts in People Analytics

No	Survey items	N	Minimum	Maximum	Mean	Std. Deviation
1	Does your company use IoT monitoring tools (e.g., surveillance cameras, tracking system)?	300	1.00	3.00	1.9133	.80912
2	Does your company analyze employees' data using ML tools?	300	1.00	3.00	2.1500	.76340
3	Do your employees possess skills in using IoT and ML for workforce analytics?	300	1.00	3.00	2.1533	.72450
4	Is it true that IoT creates challenges to privacy beyond existing data privacy issues?	300	1.00	3.00	2.0233	.82769
5	Do you think IoT &ML tools bring more benefits than risks to your organization	300	1.00	3.00	1.9133	.80081
6	Are there any strategies that your company use to protect employee's privacy and security while enhancing innovative use of IoT?	300	1.00	3.00	1.9400	.76048
7	Does your organization integrate privacy-by-design principles into its co values?	300	1.00	3.00	2.0133	.82183
8	Do you perceive the quick change in IoT and ML systems as overtaking capacity of policy, legal, and regulatory structures to adapt?	300	1.00	3.00	2.2300	.79952
9	Do you think IoT and ML applications hold impressive promises in achieving your organizational goals?	300	1.00	3.00	2.1233	.77683
	Valid N (listwise)	300				

Source: Survey data.

of IoT tools. The low standard deviations below 1.000 indicate consensus among respondents on the aspects of IoT and ML being explored.

Similarly, responses from items 6, 7, 8, 11, 12, and 13 have above average means 2.0 plus, and low standard deviations below 1, illustrating agreement among participants that the organizations use ML tools to analyze employee's data (2.1500) mean; 0.76340 standard deviations. They also agree that IoT creates challenges to privacy beyond existing data privacy issues as previously argued by Rose et al. (2015) and Gaur et al. (2019). From both items 10 and 11, participants in the studied sectors hoped to successfully integrate privacy-by-design principles into their core values (2.0133; mean) and (0.82183; standard deviation) while the majority of them perceived the quick changes in IoT and ML systems as being overtaking the capacity of security and privacy policies as well as legal and regulatory structures in terms of copying with such emerging technology use in PA (2.2300; mean) and 0.79952; standard deviation). A close analysis of these quantitative results shows that meanwhile IoTs and ML application in PA seem to be bringing very impressive opportunities for optimizing organization productivity, there are security and privacy policies, legal and regulatory organizational structures which need to be considered and applied to obtain full benefits from both IoT and ML application in PA. It is, however, apparent from the responses of participants shown in Figure 11.1, that although the new technologies are likely to bring more opportunities to different sectors, if more (136) 45.3% employees lacked such skills than (105) 35% who possessed needed skills in

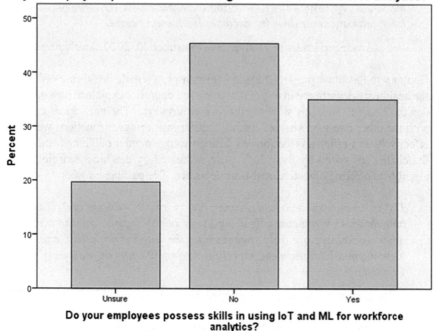

Do your employees possess skills in using IoT and ML for workforce analytics?

FIGURE 11.1   Employees' skills in using IoT and ML in PA. (*Source*: Survey data).

conducting PA through IoT and ML. It is unlikely that smart devices may not adequately benefit organizations in improving decision-making skills through PA. These results suggest a dire need for continuous professional and technical training in the usage of emerging technologies by employees for increasing business performance.

To better understand the usage and influence of IoT and ML digital technologies in PA, in-depth open-ended and semi-structured interviews were conducted with four participants, two males and two females, each purposively and conveniently selected from the four chosen sectors, industry, business, education, and healthcare.

11.4.2 Specific IoT and ML Technologies Implemented in People Analytics

When asked about specific IoT devices which they applied in PA, three out four (75%) of the participants confirmed that they used specific smart devices which included smart phones, wrist bands, watches, surveillance cameras, tracking systems in PA starting from talent sourcing up to relieving but were still to be adequately oriented toward proper usage of the smart devices which at times posed particular challenges whenever they tend to apply them in workforce analytics. One male academic leader from the education sector reiterated that:

These things you are talking about are rarely seen in our schools and universities. I can confirm that it's only during examinations we see CCTVs meant to monitor students, guarding against copying from each other or bringing information to copy. Applicants still bring the expected six sets of applications and interviews are never done by machines but human beings.

(Academic leader at a university November 20, 2020, developing country)

Contrary to the above academic leader's responses, a female healthcare officer from the healthcare department in one of the developed countries explained how new smart devices and ML systems were useful to their contexts. The participant concurred with the other two who stressed that all their human resource functions were being effectively and efficiently performed through using Internet of Things and most of the challenges posed by these IoTs were addressed by machines learning and AI algorithms offering objective, real-time decisions. The participant said:

The smart phones, smart cities, smart homes, smart buildings and all the wearable devices we are currently using in our health sectors, transport and many other workplaces are truly strengthening the way we work, live, and manage human capital development, especially during difficulty these times of COVID-19 pandemic.

(Healthcare officer from a developed nation, interviewed December 30, 2020)

A careful analysis of views of these participants suggests that the new technologies are beneficial in PA for both developing and developed nations. However, in some developing countries, it appeared that the implementation of those smart devices is still in its infancy which concurs with literature. This implies that such developing economies have a greater obligation to provide ICTs infrastructure and access booths and tools to users for implementation across sectors. This tallies with Gaur (2020) and Mohanty and Mishra (2020)' studies that proposed application of sophisticated tools such as IoTs, ML, and AI which promote real-time decision-making and employee engagement for high business productivity.

11.4.3   Benefits and Risks Associated with IoT and ML Application in PA

The question on whether or not IoT and ML tools bring more benefits than risks was approached with mixed views by all the four participants. Some argued that the technologies were a key panacea to the handling of Big Data challenges especially with its high velocity, volume, veracity, variety among other features when dealing with human side of the organization coupled with the need to achieve organizational effectiveness and efficiency. The IT Director who was interviewed from an industrial company asserted that the use of IoT monitoring devices and ML algorithm is like two sides of the coin, it brings both benefits and risks. He argued:

> *Those surveillance cameras, ID badges, geolocation trackers and other wearables are useful in talent sourcing, resume scanning, recruitment, employee assessment, engagement and development but can cause real havoc through invading workers' privacy at the workplace and even at home.*

(IT Director, 4 January 2021, Industrial Sector-Developed country)

On the other side, to address security and privacy concerns arising from usage of IoT and ML techniques, one Executive Managing Director from a big multinational company suggested that:

> *There is need for security, protection and proper governance of private people data at any place whether home, transport, workplace or health centers' policies are needed for transparent tracking, monitoring and maintaining employees' wellness, fitness for high organizational outcomes.*

(February 25, 2021 interview with Executive Managing Director)

When probed about the best strategies that might be used to secure and protect both employees and organizational data while promoting innovative use of sophisticated technology ecosystems, three out of for participants (75%) proposed that users should be guided and controlled by best privacy practices and policies which need to be presented and clearly articulated to these users for them to understand. This might be crucial since most of the users lack technological content knowledge to apply advanced smart devices without breaching employees' privacy at the workplaces as asserted by Josh Bersin Academy (2020) and Kongnso (2015).

Furthermore, a human resource officer operating from a smart campus in the developed country was asked about which specific policies she thought might be applied to address challenges of IoT and ML in analyzing people data, and she responded that IoT and ML designers need to infuse the so-called privacy-by-design policies when framing their visions, strategic plans and core values focusing on user privacy rights and ethics. As opposed to the above suggestions, the other two participants who were interviewed in February 2021, IT Director and the Executive Managing Director held different perceptions on the idea of designing policies which the human resource person had proposed. The two directors argued that software developers and most of the IoT systems have complex technical issues, time limitations, financial costs, inadequate resources, high power utilization, and low memory issues that hinder developers from trying new alternatives of resolving existing technology challenges. Rose et al. (2015) suggested that companies need conduct cost benefits analysis and establish if the proposed technology innovations have more benefits than costs to avoid loss and wastages.

11.4.4 Discussion of Findings

Based on the key results for literature review, analysis of case studies from international and local settings, quantitative and qualitative results done with reference to industry, business, education and healthcare, the chapter found that there is a significant paradigm shift in people's functions due to the inception of more data-driven technologies such as ML and IoT application for effective and efficient PA at workplaces. ML and IoT application both positively and negatively influence PA, presenting dire need for remarkable reforms in people's functions, digital technologies, skills development, and qualifications of personnel. Managers should consider improving staff performance and productivity across sectors.

Funding and support for establishment of relevant digital technology infrastructure enabling effective and efficient usage of ML and IoT smart devices like smart camera, CCTV; smart buildings and other wearables promote a digital culture and ecosystem among government, business and industrial sectors. Case studies analyzed suggested that most managers lack digital technology expertise and ICT infrastructural resources needed for them to effectively and efficiently track applicants, make transparent assessments, attract top talent, and predict workforce engagement, performance, and attrition through ML and IoT systems.

The results demonstrate some of the specific security challenges and breach of privacy issues dominant in integrating ML and IoT digital technologies in PA to enhance staff performance and productivity. Little understanding of the best practices and approaches in addressing issues of appropriate ML and IoT usage, security risks and breach of privacy hinders effectiveness and efficiency of digital technology utilization in PA. Each type of PA; namely, descriptive, predictive, prescriptive, and diagnostic are unique for specific PA within an organization. The opportunities of using modern PA outweigh the challenges and more so the world is becoming more and more digitalized. The challenges can be easily addressed by employing IT personnel in HR sections who have an appreciation of HR management. All stakeholders' involvement is essential as the experts are engaged. Defining well the process of PA is essential for its successful implementation.

11.5   CONCLUSION

The use of ML, IoT, and Big Data in PA undoubtedly results in improvements and efficiencies in management of employees. The processes and types involved in PA have been discussed. Traditional PA without being complemented with ML, IoT, and Big Data results in misinformed decision-making hence there is a need to complement human-based decisions with technology. IoT, ML, Big Data application in PA has been discussed including opportunities and challenges. The challenges identified can be alleviated through well informed IT-based systems. Drawing from existing frameworks results in seamless integration of IoT, ML and Big Data in PA. Further research includes coming up with a model to mitigate IoT security risks and concerns so that organizations will adopt IoT-based technologies. In addition, a qualitative data collection and analysis using interviews and expert reviews can be done at national and international levels. This involves different sectors including telecommunications industry, retail, mining industry, Higher and Tertiary education institutions to come up with holistic frameworks.

The authors received no financial aid for this study.

The researchers declare that the do not have any conflict of interest

REFERENCES

Adi, E., Anwar, A., Baig, Z., & Zeadally, S. (2020). "Machine learning and data analytics for the IoT". *Neural Computing and Applications*, *32*, 16205–16233.

AIHR Analytics. (2018). "15 HR analytics case studies with business impact". Retrieved from https://www.analyticsinhr.com/blog/hr-analytics-case-studies/ (accessed March 18, 2021).

Arellano, C., DiLeonardo, A., & Felix, I. (2017). "Using people analytics to drive business performance: A case study". *McKinsey Quarterly*, *2017*(3), pp. 114–119.

Chase, C. W. (2016). *Next Generation Demand Management: People, Process, Analytics, and Technology*. 1st edn. New Jersey: John Wiley & Sons, Inc.

Chen, Y. K. (2012). Challenges and opportunities of internet of things. *Proceedings of the Asia and South Pacific Design Automation Conference, ASP-DAC*, January 2012, 383–388. https://doi.org/10.1109/ASPDAC.2012.6164978

CISCO (2020). Internet of Things. https://www.oracle.com/internet-of-things/what-is-iot/

CISCO (2021a). Emerging-Technologies. https://www.oracle.com/emerging-technologies/

CISCO (2021b). Machine-Learning. https://www.oracle.com/data-science/machine-learning/what-is-machine-learning/

Dahlbom, P., Siikanen, N., Sajasalo, P., & Jarvenpaa, M. (2019). "Big data and HR analytics in the digital era". *Baltic Journal of Management*, *15*(1), 120–138.

Dearborn, J., & Swanson, D. (2018). *The Data Driven Leader: A Powerful Approach to Delivering Measurable Business Impact Through People Analytics*. 1st edn. New Jersey: John Wiley and Sons Inc.

Fairhurst, P. (2014). "IES Perspectives on HR" (IES Report 504, 2014). ISBN: 978-1-85184-452-4-I.

Fallucchi, F., et al. (2020). "Predicting employee attrition using machine learning techniques". *Computers*, *9*, 1–17. doi:10.3390/computers9040086.

Fecheyr-Lippens, B., Schaninger, B., & Tanner, K. (2015). "Power to the new people analytics". *McKinsey Quarterly* (1).

Feravich, S. (2011). "Ensuring protection for sensitive test data". Retrieved from https://www.dbta.com/Editorial/Think-About-It/Ensuring-Protection-for-Sensitive-Test-Data-79145.aspx.

Forbes Human Resources Council. (2020). "Nine benefits of embracing Big Data in human resources". *Forbes*, January 2. Retrieved from https://www.forbes.com/sites/forbeshumanresourcescouncil/2020/01/02/nine-benefits-of-embracing-big-data-in-human-resources/?sh=15b266536582 (accessed March 14, 2020).

Furht, B., & Villanustre, F. (2016). "Introduction to Big Data". In *Big Data Technologies and Applications* (pp. 3–11).

Gal, U., Jensen, T. B., & Stein, M.-K. (2017). "People analytics in the age of Big Data: An agenda for information systems research". In *Proceedings of the International Conference on Information Systems*. Retrieved from http://aisel.aisnet.org/cgi/viewcontent.cgi?article=1000&context=icis2017

Gaur, B. (2020). "HR4.0: An analytics framework to redefine employee engagement in the fourth industrial revolution". In *11th International Conference on Computing, Communication and Networking Technologies (ICCCNT)*, Kharagpur, India, pp. 1–6. doi:10.1109/ICCCNT49239.2020.9225456.

Gaur, B., Shukla, V. K., & Verma, A. (2019). "Strengthening people analytics through wearable IOT device for real-time data collection". In *2019 International Conference on Automation, Computational and Technology Management, ICACTM 2019*. IEEE (April), pp. 555–560. doi:10.1109/ICACTM.2019.8776776.

Ge, M., Bangui, H., & Buhnova, B. (2018). Big data for internet of things: a survey. *Future Generation Computer Systems*, 87, 601–614.

Halevi, T., Memon, N., Lewis, J., Kumaraguru, P., Arora, S., Dagar, N., … Chen, J. (2016, November). Cultural and psychological factors in cyber-security. In *Proceedings of the 18th International Conference on Information Integration and Web-based Applications and Services* (pp. 318–324).

Isson, J. P., & Harriot, J. S. (2016). *People Analytics in the Era of Big Data: Changing the Way You Attract, Acquire, Develop, and Retain Talent*. 1st edn. New Jersey: John Wiley & Sons, Inc.

Josh Bersin Academy. (2020). "Privacy in people analytics". 20 July. Retrieved from https://bersinacademy.com/blog/2020/07/privacy-in-people-analytics (accessed March 3, 2021).

Kapoor, B., & Kabra, Y. (2014). "Current and future trends in human resources analytics adoption". *Journal of Cases on Information Technology*, 16, 50–59.

Karthiban, K., & Raj, J. S. (2019). "Big Data analytics for developing secure Internet of everything". *Journal of ISMAC*, *1*(2), 129–136.

Kongnso, F. J. (2015). "Best practices to minimize data security breaches for increased business performance". Doctoral dissertation, Walden University, Walden University ScholarWorks.

Kumar, V. (2018). "The role of Big Data in human resource management". *AIIM*, December 20. Retrieved from https://info.aiim.org/aiim-blog/role-of-big-data-in-human-resource-management (accessed March 7, 2020).

Lanwehr, R., & Mayer, J. (2018). *People Analytics im Profifußball: Implikationen für die Wirtschaft*.

Lee, I. (2017). "Big data: Dimensions, evolution, impacts and challenges". *Business Horizons*, *60*(3), 293–303.

McKay, F. (2020). *Artificial Intelligence-Monitoring employee behaviour through AI*. Edinburgh.

McKendrick, J. (2012). "Cost of big data breach $194 per record". Retrieved from https://www.zdnet.com/article/cost-of-a-data-breach-194-per-record/

Minbaeva, M. (2017). "Human capital analytics: Why are not we there?" *Journal of Organizational Effectiveness People and Performance*, 4(2), 110–118.

Mishra, S. N., Lama, D. R., & Pal, Y. (2016). "Human resource predictive analytics (HRPA) for HR management in organizations". *International Journal of Scientific and Technology Research*, 5(5), 33–35.

Mohanty, S., & Mishra, P. C. (2020). "Framework for understanding Internet of Things in human resource management". *Revista ESPACIOS*, 41(12), 3–15.

Momin, W. Y. M., & Momin, T. M. d Abdu. (2015). "HR analytics Transforming Human Resource Management". *International Journal of Applied Research*, 1(9), 688–692. doi:10.13140/RG.2.2.35461.70884.

Nižetić, S., Šolić, P., González-de-Artaza, D. L. D. I., & Patrono, L. (2020). Internet of Things (IoT): Opportunities, issues and challenges towards a smart and sustainable future. *Journal of Cleaner Production*, 274, 122877.

OECD. (2016). "The Internet of Things – Seizing the benefits and addressing the challenges". *OECD Digital Economy Papers* (252), pp. 4–11. Retrieved from http://search.proquest. com/docview/1797548811?accountid=8144%5Cnhttp://sfx.aub.aau.dk/sfxaub?url_ ver=Z39.88-2004&rft_val_fmt=info:ofi/fmt:kev:mtx:book&genre=unknown&sid=Pro Q:ABI%2FINFORM+Global&atitle=&title=THE+INTERNET+OF+THINGS+SEIZI NG+THE+BENEFITS+AND.

Oussous, A., Benjelloun, F.-Z., Lahcen, A. A., & Belfkih, S. (2018). "Big Data technologies: A survey". *Journal of King Saud University – Computer and Information Sciences*, 30, 431–448.

Pape, T. (2016). "Prioritising data items for business analytics: Framework and application to human resources". *European Journal of Operational Research*, 252, 687–698.

Pathak, N., & Bhandari, A. (2018). *IoT, AI, and Blockchain for .NET. Building a Next-Generation Application from the Ground Up*. Apress.

Peeters, T., Paauwe, J., & Van De Voorde, K. (2020). "People analytics effectiveness: Developing a framework". *Journal of Organizational Effectiveness People and Performance*, 7(2), 203–219.

Rose, K., Eldridge, S., & Chapin, L. (2015). The internet of things: An overview. *The Internet Society (ISOC)*, 80, 1–50.

Saqlain, M., Piao, M., Shim, Y., & Lee, J. Y. (2019). "Framework of an IoT-based industrial data management for smart manufacturing". *Journal of Sensor and Actuator Networks*, 8(25), 1–21. doi:10.3390/jsan8020025.

Stople, M. (2016). "The Internet of Things: Opportunities and challenges for distributed data analytics". *ACM SIGKDD Explorations Newsletter*, 18(1), 15–34.

Tomar, S., & Gaur, M. (2020). "HR analytics in business: Role, opportunities, and challenges of using it". *Journal of Xi'an University of Architecture & Technology*, XII (VII), 1299–1306. doi:10.37896/JXAT12.07/2441.

Tonidandel, S., King, E. B., & Cortina, J. M. (2015). *Big Data at Work: The Data Science Revolution and Organizational Psychology*. New York: Taylor & Francis.

Tursunbayeva, A., Di Lauro, S., & Pagliari, C. (2018). "People analytics – A scoping review of conceptual boundaries and value propositions". *International Journal of Information Management*, 43, 224–247.

West, M. (2019). *People Analytics for Dummies*. 1st edn. New Jersey: John Wiley & Sons, Inc.

Zantalis, F., et al. (2019). "A review of machine learning and IoT in smart transportation". *Future Internet*, 11(4), 1–23. doi:10.3390/FI11040094.

12 IoT-Integrated Photovoltaic System for Improved System Performance

Apurv Yadav

CONTENTS

12.1 INTRODUCTION

The global energy-intensive nature and expanse of industrialization have led to the gradual depletion of fossil fuels, which are the predominant source for the production of energy [1]. Hence, in order to reduce dependence on fossil fuels, it is incredibly crucial to pursue alternative resources [2]. Renewable energy has become an indispensable component of the global energy mix and solar, especially, is playing a significant role [3]. The root of all forms of renewable energy is light from the sun. It can be transformed directly to electricity by the use of photovoltaic (PV) systems [4]. The potentials of these PV systems could vary based on location, types of systems, weather conditions, and some other parameters. The return on investments on these systems depends upon the electric potential of the systems, cost of per unit electricity in the region and payback period [5].

Hence, sufficient measures are required for the installation of every PV system to ensure higher energy potentials can be achieved. However, these systems

DOI: 10.1201/9781003048862-12

occasionally face maintenance problems, e.g., system failures, especially in remote areas, which could result in a significant loss of energy if not checked in time. Human involvement in the monitoring of these systems has limitations of accuracy, judgment, and constant attention.

The most suitable approach to cater to this problem is the adoption of a remote smart monitoring system. Internet of Things (IoT) is an emerging technology using the internet to quickly connect, interact with, and regulate most electronic and electrical devices. IoT uses network and information protocols, digital communication tools, microcontrollers, and transceivers to take feedback from the systems and then guide them accordingly. This technology provides detailed information about the devices and opens the arena for new scopes of development. PV systems comprise a number of components with different operational behavior. The dependence of solar irradiance on weather and time of the day does not guarantee constant power generation throughout the PV system operation. It also indirectly affects the performance of system parameters like battery state of charge, the voltage level of charge inverter, demand-supply to loads etc. Dust accumulation on panels, rain, wind, cloud, or shadows also causes a decline in system performance.

12.2   IoT-BASED STRUCTURE FOR PHOTOVOLTAIC SYSTEMS

There are three layers in the IoT-based structure of photovoltaic systems; PV system design environment, gateway linkage, and the remote monitoring and control layer. In the first layer, i.e., PV system design environment, all the connections for the components are as per the user-defined layout. These system components and the Arduino server are interlinked. This Arduino server is a part of the second layer. The second layer or gateway linkage layer functions as an interconnection between the web server and the hardware layout of the PV system. The web server connection is made with the help of a router with an internet firewall option. The web server integration through wireless router module or Ethernet is done by Arduino server. This Arduino server contains a microcontroller that can monitor, manage, and control the hardware components in the PV system. Finally, this information is forwarded to the third layer, i.e., the remote monitoring and control layer. From here, the server provides all the information from the PV system into storage. This storage is used to generate periodical reports of various parameters of the PV system.

IoT in PV systems enables a few new features in the current trend of the solar market. These features comprise a quick response to fault detection, effective operational efficiencies, continuous monitoring, increased revenue, emerging business analytics from historic data generation, etc. Sahana et al. proposed the construction of an energy management system in the home that is scalable, interoperable, and reusable with an IoT-based PV system to achieve energy efficiency [6]. Adhya et al. also studied an IoT-based smart PV system that used wireless devices and a "web console-based interface" for remote plant supervision and data transmission [7]. Shrihariprasath et al. proposed monitoring of power conditioning system in a PV plant by IoT [8]. This method provided satisfactory results in monitoring report generation, parameters, energy outputs and cloud data storage. Nadpurohit et al. used IoT to make a smart hybrid system with a unified power supply unit, battery storage and primary energy sources [9]. This system helps to charge and operate the battery during the presence of an energy source and also storage shifting option during the absence of an energy source.

12.3 IoT-BASED PHOTOVOLTAIC SYSTEMS WITH ARTIFICIAL INTELLIGENCE

IoT for PV systems uses various artificial intelligence (AI) algorithms for regulating aspects such as PV system sizing, PV system modeling and simulation, and system control. Its application can basically be classified into the following main categories.

12.3.1 PARAMETERS IDENTIFICATION OF SOLAR CELLS MODEL

It is critical to do the accurate modeling of solar cells for efficient estimation of a PV system performance. A PV system is first modeled mathematically, and then its parameters are extracted. A solar cell has two equivalent circuit models: the single diode and the two diode models [10]. There are five parameters in a single diode model, namely diode ideally factor, series resistance, shunt resistance, diode saturation current, and photo-generated current [11]. On the other hand, the double diode model consists of seven parameters where the second diode ideally factors and its diode saturation current are the extra two factors [12]. The sizing and modeling of PV systems depend critically on the accurate estimation of these parameters. Conventional parameter identification methods of solar cells are reported in much literature.

Xu and Wang used a flower pollination algorithm for parameter identification in PV cells and found it to be superior to most of the reported algorithms [13]. Oliva et al. used a modified chaotic whale algorithm to estimate PV cell parameters and found that even complex functions can be optimized [14]. Abbassi et al. compared the salp swarm algorithm to many established algorithms in PV parameter identification and found positive results [15]. Guo et al. used a cat swarm algorithm in solar cell parameter identification and found that it has the advantages of flexibility, consistency, and accuracy [16]. Cotfas et al. obtained high accuracy results by the use of successive discretization algorithm [17]. Gao et al. reported better accuracy and robustness by the use of improved shuffle complex evolution algorithm [18]. Karatpe et al. presented a single diode model of solar cells using artificial neural network (ANN) methods [19]. The dependency of circuit parameters on environmental factors was investigated and found to be very random. Askarzadeh et al. proposed the application of a harmony search algorithm (HAS) for parameter identification [20]. The results exhibited the superiority of HAS over other algorithms. Oliva et al. used the artificial bee colony (ABC) algorithm for parameter identification and found that even with noise, this algorithm is capable of designing solar cells [21]. Jacob et al. compared artificial immune system (AIS) to particle swarm optimization and genetic algorithm (GA) for solar cell parameter identification [22]. AIS was found to be more accurate using various measurement indices as compared to PSO and GA. Table 12.1 summarizes some AI-based algorithms used for solar cells in recent years.

TABLE 12.1
Artificial-Intelligence-Based Algorithm for Parameter Identification of Solar Cells

S. No.	Algorithm	Diode Model	Root Mean Square Error	Reference
1	Hybrid Pollination	SD, DD	1.086296E–03	13
2	Improved Chaotic Whale algorithm	SD	9.8602E–04	14
3	Salp swarm-inspired algorithm	DD	3.6935e–04	15
4	Cat swarm optimization	SD, DD	9.8602E–04	16
5	Successive discretization algorithm	SD	9.8598E–04	17
6	Improved shuffled complex evolution algorithm	SD, DD	9.860219E–04	18
7	Neural network	SD	moderate	19
8	Harmony search	SD	9.9510e–4	20
9	Artificial bee colony	SD, DD	9.8E–4	21
10	Artificial immune system	SD, DD	3.415e–5	22

12.3.2 PV SYSTEM SIZING

AI can be very helpful in the determination of the most suitable number of PV panels, their tilt angle, and the size of inverter and batteries. Khalil and Asheibi used gray wolf optimization for PV sizing and found promising results [23]. Bhatti et al. implemented particle swarm optimization for the PV sizing system and found a 16% reduction in cost [24]. Heydari and Varjani applied perturb and observe algorithm and found optimization in size and cost of the PV system [25]. Rosselan et al. used a dolphin echolocation algorithm and found a reduction in computational time [26]. Othman et al. compared a bat-inspired algorithm for an on-grid PV system sizing to PSO and found it better than the former [27]. Millet used GA and NN in a remote area to determine the optimum size of the plant [28]. Khatib et al. used the PSO algorithm for the determination of the number of PV modules, tilt angle, and array arrangement [29]. Table 12.2 presents IoT-based algorithms used in PV system sizing.

TABLE 12.2
IoT-Based Algorithms in PV System Sizing

S. No.	Algorithm	Parameter	Reference
1	Gray wolf optimization	Temperature, radiation, load data	23
2	Particle swarm optimization	Electric vehicle capacity, solar radiation	24
3	Perturb and observe	Solar irradiation	25
4	Dolphin ecolocation algorithm	Solar irradiance, temperature	26
5	Bat-inspired algorithm	–	27
6	Genetic algorithm and neural networks		28
7	Regression neural networks		29

12.3.3 PV System Control

AI algorithms can also be used to exercise control over the functioning of PV systems. It helps in the performance enhancement of the system. Mainly sun tracking, inverter, and maximum power point tracking is controlled by the use of AI systems

12.3.3.1 Sun Tracking

As per Lambert cosine's law, the maximum intensity of light is received when the angular deviation between the source and the receiver is 0 degrees. Therefore, if a solar panel continuously tracks the sun, it will absorb more amount of sunlight. A control system is needed for this function to happen. Single-axis tracking sun tracking guides the panel on the east to west movement of the sun. Double-axis sun-tracking controller uses upward and downward movement also to track the sun. Ali et al. compared the firefly algorithm with other popular algorithms for sun tracking of the PV system and found it to be superior [30]. Batayneh et al. proposed the use of AI in dual-axis sun tracking [31]. Dubey et al. developed two control algorithms to track the sun [32]. Chen et al. used a field-programmable gate array to make a smart sun-tracking system [33]. Sabir et al. used multiple algorithms to track the sun [34]. Table 12.3 depicts some AI-based algorithms used in sun-tracking systems.

12.3.3.2 Inverter Control

The inverter in a PV system converts DC voltage from the solar panels and converts it to AC before sending it to grid. There are two switches in a half-bridge inverter and four switches in a full-bridge inverter that perform the function of DC to AC conversion. AI can be used to optimally control the operation of these switches. Cecati et al. used a fuzzy-logic-based controller to govern a multilevel half-bridge inverter [35]. Letting et al. used PSO in a fuzzy controller to regulate the inverter function [36]. Demirtas et al. simulated inverter control using ANN [37]. Ling-Zhi et al. proposed the use of ANN based on radial basis function (RBF) to control a three-phase inverter [38]. Sefa et al. designed an inverter control system using fuzzy-proportional integral (PI) [39].

TABLE 12.3
IoT-Based Algorithms in Sun-Tracking Systems

S. No.	Algorithm	Type of Tracking	Reference
1	Firefly algorithm	Dual axis	30
2	Fuzzy logic	Dual axis	31
3	Neural network	Dual axis	32
4	Field-programmable gate array	Dual axis	33
5	Particle swarm algorithm	Dual axis	34

TABLE 12.4

IoT-Based Algorithms in Maximum Power Point Tracking of PV Systems

S. No.	Algorithm	Type	Efficiency	Reference
1	Particle swarm optimization	AI		40
2	Moth-flame optimization algorithm (MFO)	AI	99.91	41
3	Sine cosine optimization	AI	98.4	42
4	Perturb and observe	AI	92.6	43
5	Adaptive-neuro-fuzzy inference	AI	–	44

12.3.4 MAXIMUM POWER POINT TRACKING (MPPT)

It is very necessary for a solar PV system to continuously track the maximum power point and guide the system to match those values. An AI-based algorithm helps in optimal tracking of maximum power. Li et al. used particle swarm algorithm in MPPT systems with improved results [40]. Aouchiche et al. implemented moth-flame optimization and obtained over 99% efficiency in MPPT systems [41]. Padmanaban et al. optimized MPPT systems by using a novel sine cosine optimization algorithm [42]. Salman et al. applied perturb and observe algorithm in a 200W PV system and obtained improved efficiency [43]. Amar et al. improved the performance of a PV system by using an adaptive-neuro-fuzzy inference system [44].

Miyatake et al. used PSO in multiple PV modules for MPPT [45]. Subiyanto et al. did MPPT using fuzzy logic controller optimized by the Hopfield neural network [46]. Jiang et al. proposed ant colony optimization (ACO) for the MPPT problems [47]. Algazar et al. did MPPT at different irradiation and temperature using fuzzy logic controller [48]. Table 12.4 summarizes some AI-based algorithms used for MPPT of PV systems.

12.3.5 IRRADIANCE FORECASTING AND PV OUTPUT POWER ESTIMATION

The output of a PV plant relies on many factors such as irradiance of the sun, the tilt angle of panels, the temperature of the location, wind speed, cloud formation and rain. The proper prediction of the intensity of these parameters gives the benefit of efficient planning in the design and architecture of PV systems. AI helps in the prediction of these parameters in PV systems. The prediction of solar irradiance is of primary importance to predict the power output of a PV plant – hence many research evaluated the application of numerous algorithms for this purpose [49]. Messai et al. forecasted solar irradiance using the multiple parameter neural network [50]. Sivaneasan applied fuzzy logic and ANN for the forecasting of solar power [51]. Chen et al. proposed a new algorithm that can work on varying parameters of irradiance in real time [52]. Baharin et al. forecasted hourly irradiance using a support vector machine [53]. Yadav and Chandel reviewed power-forecasting techniques of PV plants using AI [54]. Mandal et al. used a wavelet transform technique for PV output power forecasting [55]. Yazdanbaksh et al. predicted PV output power using a dynamic neural network

TABLE 12.5
IoT-Based Algorithms in PV System Fault Detection

S. No.	AI Technique	Fault Detection	Reference
1	ANN	Shading effect	[61]
2	Fuzzy logic	Series losses	[62]
3	Deep conventional neural network	Line-to line current and voltage	[63]
4	Image processing and machine learning	Hot spot fault	[64]
5	Radial basis function	Shading effect	[65]

[56]. Jiang et al. used a back propagation algorithm in a neural network to forecast PV power [57].

12.3.6 FAULT DIAGNOSIS OF PHOTOVOLTAIC SYSTEMS

Most solar power plants are prone to harsh outdoor environments. Due to this reason, they suffer from various kinds of faults, which could lead to critical obstruction in the functioning of a power plant. Fault detection by only human interaction may not be sufficient to notice all areas of rectification. Zhao et al. proposed a decision tree algorithm for fault detection [58]. Lin et al. used a back propagation algorithm in ANN for fault detection [59]. Li et al. compared the performance of the back propagation algorithm and wavelet neural network algorithm in PV plant fault detection and found the latter to be superior [60]. Table 12.5 presents the summary of IoT-based algorithms in system fault detection of PV systems.

12.4 CONCLUSIONS

The use of IoT ensures a proper record of performance data, fault monitoring, and also reduces the need for frequent site visits. Also, it can predict and forecast a future failure and scope for improvement by using system analytics. It can pinpoint the reasons and areas for low system performance effectively without any significant efforts. IoT enables the reduction of the tedious jobs of frequent plant visits, monitoring faults, and recording performance data. The human-to-machine interaction for the monitoring of the system can be reduced, as well as the maintenance frequency. IoT will play an important role in effectively controlling remotely located PV systems, as well as others. IoT helps in the identification of PV system faults and causes for substandard performance in an effective way without the input of much effort. IoT can record the performance and failure data uninterrupted, so that it can be used for analytics for forecasting and predicting the future power generation possibilities, income generation, etc. Frequent maintenance of PV systems is also prevented. As day by day there is more integration of renewable energy sources into the utility grid, IoT for monitoring and control of PV systems is important. This intellectualization and automation will lead to better decision-making in the design process of future large-scale PV plants.

REFERENCES

1. Yadav, A., Pal, N., Patra, J., & Yadav, M. (2020). Strategic planning and challenges to the deployment of renewable energy technologies in the world scenario: Its impact on global sustainable development. *Environment, Development and Sustainability, 22*(1), 297–315.
2. Da Cunha, J. P., & Eames, P. (2016). Thermal energy storage for low and medium temperature applications using phase change materials–a review. *Applied Energy, 177*, 227–238.
3. Hussain, A., Arif, S. M., & Aslam, M. (2017). Emerging renewable and sustainable energy technologies: State of the art. *Renewable and Sustainable Energy Reviews, 71*, 12–28.
4. Satish, M., Santhosh, S., Yadav, A., Kalluri, S., & Madhavan, A. A. (2020). Optimization and thermal analysis of Fe_2O_3 nanoparticles embedded myristic acid-lauric acid phase change material. *Journal of Electronic Materials*, 1–7.
5. Anisur, M. R., Mahfuz, M. H., Kibria, M. A., Saidur, R., Metselaar, I. H. S. C., & Mahlia, T. M. I. (2013). Curbing global warming with phase change materials for energy storage. *Renewable and Sustainable Energy Reviews, 18*, 23–30.
6. Sahana, M. N., Anjana, S., Ankith, S., Natarajan, K., Shobha, K. R., & Paventhan, A. (2015, December). Home energy management leveraging open IoT protocol stack. In *2015 IEEE Recent Advances in Intelligent Computational Systems (RAICS)* (pp. 370–375). IEEE.
7. Adhya, S., Saha, D., Das, A., Jana, J., & Saha, H. (2016, January). An IoT based smart solar photovoltaic remote monitoring and control unit. In *2016 2nd International Conference on Control, Instrumentation, Energy & Communication (CIEC)* (pp. 432–436). IEEE.
8. Shrihariprasath, B., & Rathinasabapathy, V. (2016, March). A smart IoT system for monitoring solar PV power conditioning unit. In *2016 World Conference on Futuristic Trends in Research and Innovation for Social Welfare (Startup Conclave)* (pp. 1–5). IEEE.
9. Nadpurohit, B., Kulkarni, R., Matager, K., Devar, N., Karnawadi, R., & Carvalho, E. (2017). Iot enabled smart solar pv system. *International Journal of Innovative Research in Computer and Communication Engineering, 5*(6), 11324–11328.
10. Chaibi, Y., Allouhi, A., Malvoni, M., Salhi, M., & Saadani, R. (2019). Solar irradiance and temperature influence on the photovoltaic cell equivalent-circuit models. *Solar Energy, 188*, 1102–1110.
11. Bana, S., & Saini, R. P. (2016). A mathematical modeling framework to evaluate the performance of single diode and double diode based SPV systems. *Energy Reports, 2*, 171–187.
12. Sandrolini, L., Artioli, M., & Reggiani, U. (2010). Numerical method for the extraction of photovoltaic module double-diode model parameters through cluster analysis. *Applied Energy, 87*(2), 442–451.
13. Xu, S., & Wang, Y. (2017). Parameter estimation of photovoltaic modules using a hybrid flower pollination algorithm. *Energy Conversion and Management, 144*, 53–68.
14. Oliva, D., Abd El Aziz, M., & Hassanien, A. E. (2017). Parameter estimation of photovoltaic cells using an improved chaotic whale optimization algorithm. *Applied Energy, 200*, 141–154.
15. Abbassi, R., Abbassi, A., Heidari, A. A., & Mirjalili, S. (2019). An efficient salp swarm-inspired algorithm for parameters identification of photovoltaic cell models. *Energy Conversion and Management, 179*, 362–372.

16. Guo, L., Meng, Z., Sun, Y., & Wang, L. (2016). Parameter identification and sensitivity analysis of solar cell models with cat swarm optimization algorithm. *Energy Conversion and Management, 108*, 520–528.
17. Cotfas, D. T., Deaconu, A. M., & Cotfas, P. A. (2019). Application of successive discretization algorithm for determining photovoltaic cells parameters. *Energy Conversion and Management, 196*, 545–556.
18. Gao, X., Cui, Y., Hu, J., Xu, G., Wang, Z., Qu, J., & Wang, H. (2018). Parameter extraction of solar cell models using improved shuffled complex evolution algorithm. *Energy Conversion and Management, 157*, 460–479.
19. Karatepe, E., Boztepe, M., & Colak, M. (2006). Neural network based solar cell model. *Energy Conversion and Management, 47*(9–10), 1159–1178.
20. Askarzadeh, A., & Rezazadeh, A. (2012). Parameter identification for solar cell models using harmony search-based algorithms. *Solar Energy, 86*(11), 3241–3249.
21. Oliva, D., Cuevas, E., & Pajares, G. (2014). Parameter identification of solar cells using artificial bee colony optimization. *Energy, 72*, 93–102.
22. Jacob, B., Balasubramanian, K., Azharuddin, S. M., & Rajasekar, N. (2015). Solar PV modelling and parameter extraction using artificial immune system. *Energy Procedia, 75*, 331–336.
23. Khalil, A., & Asheibi, A. (2019, November). Optimal sizing of stand-alone PV system using grey wolf optimization. In *2019 International Conference on Electrical Engineering Research & Practice (ICEERP)* (pp. 1–6). IEEE.
24. Bhatti, A. R., Salam, Z., Sultana, B., Rasheed, N., Awan, A. B., Sultana, U., & Younas, M. (2019). Optimized sizing of photovoltaic grid-connected electric vehicle charging system using particle swarm optimization. *International Journal of Energy Research, 43*(1), 500–522.
25. Heydari, E., & Varjani, A. Y. (2019, February). A new variable step-size P&O algorithm with power output and sensorless DPC method for grid-connected PV system. In *2019 10th International Power Electronics, Drive Systems and Technologies Conference (PEDSTC)* (pp. 545–550). IEEE.
26. Rosselan, M. Z., Sulaiman, S. I., & Othman, N. (2017, February). Sizing optimization of large-scale grid-connected photovoltaic system using dolphin echolocation algorithm. In *Proceedings of the 9th International Conference on Computer and Automation Engineering* (pp. 336–340).
27. Othman, Z., Sulaiman, S. I., Musirin, I., & Mohamad, K. (2015, November). Bat inspired algorithm for sizing optimization of grid-connected photovoltaic system. In *2015 SAI Intelligent Systems Conference (IntelliSys)* (pp. 195–200). IEEE.
28. Mellit, A. (2007). Sizing of a stand-alone photovoltaic system based on neural networks and genetic algorithms: Application for remote areas. *Istanbul University-Journal of Electrical & Electronics Engineering, 7*(2), 459–469.
29. Khatib, T., & Elmenreich, W. (2014). An improved method for sizing standalone photovoltaic systems using generalized regression neural network. *International Journal of Photoenergy, 2014*.
30. Ali, M., Nurohmah, H., Suharsono, J., Suyono, H., & Muslim, M. A. (2019, October). Optimization on PID and ANFIS controller on dual axis tracking for photovoltaic based on firefly algorithm. In *2019 International Conference on Electrical, Electronics and Information Engineering (ICEEIE)* (Vol. 6, pp. 1–5). IEEE.
31. Batayneh, W., Owais, A., & Nairoukh, M. (2013). An intelligent fuzzy based tracking controller for a dual-axis solar PV system. *Automation in Construction, 29*, 100–106.

32. Dubey, R., & Joshi, D. (2012, December). Optimization of solar power by azimuthal angle and neural network control of a PV module. In *2012 IEEE 5th India International Conference on Power Electronics (IICPE)* (pp. 1–6). IEEE.

33. Chen, J. H., Yau, H. T., & Hung, T. H. (2015). Design and implementation of FPGA-based Taguchi-chaos-PSO sun tracking systems. *Mechatronics, 25*, 55–64.

34. Sabir, M. M., & Ali, T. (2016). Optimal PID controller design through swarm intelligence algorithms for sun tracking system. *Applied Mathematics and Computation, 274*, 690–699.

35. Cecati, C., Ciancetta, F., & Siano, P. (2010). A multilevel inverter for photovoltaic systems with fuzzy logic control. *IEEE Transactions on Industrial Electronics, 57*(12), 4115–4125.

36. Letting, L. K., Munda, J. L., & Hamam, Y. (2012). Optimization of a fuzzy logic controller for PV grid inverter control using S-function based PSO. *Solar Energy, 86*(6), 1689–1700.

37. Demirtaş, M., Cetinbas, I., Serefoğlu, S., & Kaplan, O. (2014, September). ANN controlled single phase inverter for solar energy systems. In *2014 16th International Power Electronics and Motion Control Conference and Exposition* (pp. 768–772). IEEE.

38. Su-Fen, H., Ling-Zhi, Y., Ju-Cheng, L., Zhe-Zhi, Y., & Han-Mei, P. (2009, April). Design of three-phase photovoltaic grid connected inverter based on RBF neural network. In *2009 International Conference on Sustainable Power Generation and Supply* (pp. 1–5). IEEE.

39. Sefa, I., Altin, N., Ozdemir, S., & Kaplan, O. R. H. A. N. (2015). Fuzzy PI controlled inverter for grid interactive renewable energy systems. *IET Renewable Power Generation, 9*(7), 729–738.

40. Li, H., Yang, D., Su, W., Lü, J., & Yu, X. (2018). An overall distribution particle swarm optimization MPPT algorithm for photovoltaic system under partial shading. *IEEE Transactions on Industrial Electronics, 66*(1), 265–275.

41. Aouchiche, N., Aitcheikh, M. S., Becherif, M., & Ebrahim, M. A. (2018). AI-based global MPPT for partial shaded grid connected PV plant via MFO approach. *Solar Energy, 171*, 593–603.

42. Padmanaban, S., Priyadarshi, N., Holm-Nielsen, J. B., Bhaskar, M. S., Azam, F., Sharma, A. K., & Hossain, E. (2019). A novel modified sine-cosine optimized MPPT algorithm for grid integrated PV system under real operating conditions. *IEEE Access, 7*, 10467–10477.

43. Salman, S., Xin, A. I., & Zhouyang, W. U. (2018). Design of a P-&-O algorithm based MPPT charge controller for a stand-alone 200W PV system. *Protection and Control of Modern Power Systems, 3*(1), 1–8.

44. Amara, K., Fekik, A., Hocine, D., Bakir, M. L., Bourennane, E. B., Malek, T. A., & Malek, A. (2018, October). Improved performance of a PV solar panel with adaptive neuro fuzzy inference system ANFIS based MPPT. In *2018 7th International Conference on Renewable Energy Research and Applications (ICRERA)* (pp. 1098–1101). IEEE.

45. Miyatake, M., Veerachary, M., Toriumi, F., Fujii, N., & Ko, H. (2011). Maximum power point tracking of multiple photovoltaic arrays: A PSO approach. *IEEE Transactions on Aerospace and Electronic Systems, 47*(1), 367–380.

46. Subiyanto, S., Mohamed, A., & Hannan, M. A. (2012). Intelligent maximum power point tracking for PV system using Hopfield neural network optimized fuzzy logic controller. *Energy and Buildings, 51*, 29–38.

47. Jiang, L. L., Maskell, D. L., & Patra, J. C. (2013). A novel ant colony optimization-based maximum power point tracking for photovoltaic systems under partially shaded conditions. *Energy and Buildings, 58*, 227–236.

48. Algazar, M. M., Abd El-Halim, H., & Salem, M. E. E. K. (2012). Maximum power point tracking using fuzzy logic control. *International Journal of Electrical Power & Energy Systems, 39*(1), 21–28.

49. Mellit, A., & Pavan, A. M. (2010). A 24–h forecast of solar irradiance using artificial neural network: Application for performance prediction of a grid-connected PV plant at Trieste, Italy. *Solar Energy, 84*(5), 807–821.
50. Messai, A., Mellit, A., Pavan, A. M., Guessoum, A., & Mekki, H. (2011). FPGA-based implementation of a fuzzy controller (MPPT) for photovoltaic module. *Energy Conversion and Management, 52*(7), 2695–2704.
51. Sivaneasan, B., Yu, C. Y., & Goh, K. P. (2017). Solar forecasting using ANN with fuzzy logic pre-processing. *Energy Procedia, 143*, 727–732.
52. Chen, S. X., Gooi, H. B., & Wang, M. Q. (2013). Solar radiation forecast based on fuzzy logic and neural networks. *Renewable Energy, 60*, 195–201.
53. Baharin, K. A., Abd Rahman, H., Hassan, M. Y., & Gan, C. K. (2014, October). Hourly irradiance forecasting in Malaysia using support vector machine. In *2014 IEEE Conference on Energy Conversion (CENCON)* (pp. 185–190). IEEE.
54. Yadav, A. K., & Chandel, S. S. (2014). Solar radiation prediction using Artificial Neural Network techniques: A review. *Renewable and Sustainable Energy Reviews, 33*, 772–781.
55. Mandal, P., Madhira, S. T. S., Meng, J., & Pineda, R. L. (2012). Forecasting power output of solar photovoltaic system using wavelet transform and artificial intelligence techniques. *Procedia Computer Science, 12*, 332–337.
56. Yazdanbaksh, O., Krahn, A., & Dick, S. (2013, June). Predicting solar power output using complex fuzzy logic. In *2013 Joint IFSA World Congress and NAFIPS Annual Meeting (IFSA/NAFIPS)* (pp. 1243–1248). IEEE.
57. Jiang, H., & Hong, L. (2013). Application of BP neural network to short-term-ahead generating power forecasting for PV system. In *Advanced Materials Research* (Vol. 608, pp. 128–131). Trans Tech Publications Ltd.
58. Zhao, Y., Yang, L., Lehman, B., de Palma, J. F., Mosesian, J., & Lyons, R. (2012, February). Decision tree-based fault detection and classification in solar photovoltaic arrays. In *2012 Twenty-Seventh Annual IEEE Applied Power Electronics Conference and Exposition (APEC)* (pp. 93–99). IEEE.
59. Lin, H., Chen, Z., Wu, L., Lin, P., & Cheng, S. (2015, November). On-line monitoring and fault diagnosis of PV array based on BP neural network optimized by genetic algorithm. In *International Workshop on Multi-disciplinary Trends in Artificial Intelligence* (pp. 102–112). Springer, Cham.
60. Li, X., Yang, P., Ni, J., & Zhao, J. (2014, June). Fault diagnostic method for PV array based on improved wavelet neural network algorithm. In *Proceeding of the 11th World Congress on Intelligent Control and Automation* (pp. 1171–1175). IEEE.
61. Mekki, H., Mellit, A., & Salhi, H. (2016). Artificial neural network-based modelling and fault detection of partial shaded photovoltaic modules. *Simulation Modelling Practice and Theory, 67*, 1–13.
62. Belaout, A., Krim, F., & Mellit, A. (2016, November). Neuro-fuzzy classifier for fault detection and classification in photovoltaic module. In *2016 8th International Conference on Modelling, Identification and Control (ICMIC)* (pp. 144–149). IEEE.
63. Lu, X., Lin, P., Cheng, S., Lin, Y., Chen, Z., Wu, L., & Zheng, Q. (2019). Fault diagnosis for photovoltaic array based on convolutional neural network and electrical time series graph. *Energy Conversion and Management, 196*, 950–965.
64. Kurukuru, V. B., Haque, A., Khan, M. A., & Tripathy, A. K. (2019, April). Fault classification for photovoltaic modules using thermography and machine learning techniques. In *2019 International Conference on Computer and Information Sciences (ICCIS)* (pp. 1–6). IEEE.
65. Hussain, M., Dhimish, M., Holmes, V., & Mather, P. (2019). Deployment of AI-based RBF network for photovoltaics fault detection procedure. *AIMS Electronics and Electrical Engineering, 4*(1), 1–18.

13 Metaheuristic Optimization in Routing Protocol for Cluster-Based Wireless Sensor Networks and Wireless Ad-Hoc Networks

Subhrapratim Nath, Rana Majumdar, Jmuna Kanta Singh, and Subir Kumar Sarkar

CONTENTS

DOI: 10.1201/9781003048862-13

13.1 INTRODUCTION

Metaheuristic is a heuristic algorithm depicted to locate, produce, or choose a heuristic search process that can offer a satisfactorily precise way to an optimization problem, specifically with inadequate or deficient data or confined computation capacity. Metaheuristics sample a set or solutions which is too enormous to be absolutely sampled. Metaheuristic approach is unable to solve certain problems due to its frequent assumptions about a problem being solved. As likened with optimization algorithms and iterative means, metaheuristics do not assure a global optimal solution is achievable for specific problem classes. In few cases metaheuristics implements stochastic optimization, where solution space usually be contingent with a set of random variables, but for combinatorial optimization, metaheuristics can often find suitable optimized solutions. As such, they are beneficial procedures for optimization problems. The domain of metaheuristics is indeed vast and interesting. All-important algorithms that are instrumental contribute to the routing like PSO, firefly algorithm (FA); the ant colony optimization (ACO) algorithm owes great contribution to metaheuristic technology. The chapter is metaheuristics application on wireless sensor network (WSN). WSN system on large-scale environment gains its popularity and mass-acceptability over a number of issues. WSN is a collection of distributed nodes which can gather information with others' nodes near to it. WSN finds implementation in varied fields because of their provision for protocols which are scalable and adaptive. Protocols used to maintain a constant data flow. First of all, the application of protocols helps in energy conservation, the second prime factor is to maintain a stable connection among the other set of nodes. This can be achieved by clustering technique in WSN which provides reliability for the node connectivity and also enhances the system efficiency.

Clustering indicates formation of groups of nodes in a certain topographical distribution. This phenomenon is mainly used in highly scalable networks and regions having limited power supplies. While forming a cluster, it has head node(s) and the sensor nodes. Head nodes are responsible for the creation of linkages and to make the intercommunication link between the other sensor nodes. With the recent advances in technology, clustering can be fruitful in data transmission between nodes. In infrastructure topology, the Base Station(s) can receive the data, or in case of ad-hoc topologies, the data can be prevented by cluster neighbor or by another cluster. The 802.11 standards used have three primary divisions. The 802.11n is a fast protocol, but a lot of power and bandwidth are required and the 801.11a is relatively old, hence not suitable for WSN. In WSN 802.11b is the only optic WANET and MANET both are infrastructure-less networks which have self-configurable property. To establish transmission between nodes, wireless technologies use 802.11 standards. In quick development of sensor nodes, MANETs find importance in systems where it can be used to extract the data from the sensor or disaster management. MANET supports routers which are specialized routers determining optimal routing. The dynamic natures in network topology of MANET can concise complexities in the routing environment. Ad-hoc on-demand distance vector (AODV) is a robust procedure which depends on the dynamic nature of the MANET system the routing table changes dynamically. The periodic broadcasting of the request messages as received by the neighboring nodes among present work can easily detect if there is any sort of breakage present in the link. The recently modified technique in like route discovery technique and some work on ad-hoc routing (MANET) and wireless sensor technology are based on this technique only which includes work on WSN by ACO and PSO. Now, it's the implementation efficiency of the ACO upon which the efficiency of ad-hoc routing in MANET and routing efficiency in WSN depends upon. These technologies are almost at the peak of their performance by a dint of metaheuristic approach. The rest of the discussions proceed with the development and working of these technologies and algorithms, and their sound impact in the field of industrial automation. The rest part of the chapter is arranged as detailed next. Section 13.2 describes the elementary theory of metaheuristics followed by Section 13.3, where WSN and MANET basics are given. Section 13.4 illustrates metaheuristics used in WSN, whereas Section 13.5 explains metaheuristics used in MANET. Lastly, the chapter concludes with Section 13.6.

13.2 METAHEURISTIC ALGORITHMS

13.2.1 ANT COLONY OPTIMIZATION (ACO)

The ACO algorithm [1] represents a probabilistic approach which provides an optimistic solution competent for different computational problems, the miniaturized version of which shows significant achievement to reflect upon good paths through graphs. ACO by nature is a probabilistic swarming algorithm inspired by the supportive actions of ant. In the real world, the search processes for foods in the case of ants involve a convergence from different paths toward the ultimate destination. Describing the biological process detail, one may mention pheromones, a chemical substance, to act as precedents and the chief deciding factor at every point of the search space so as to advance to the next right path. To be more vivid – it's the higher levels of pheromone concentration that acts a pioneer. The ultimate goal is to march via the shortest path toward final mission. The probability of selection of a node j from node i, presented by Eq. (13.1),

$$p_{ij} = \frac{\tau_{ij}^{\alpha}, \eta_{ij}^{\beta}}{\sum \tau_{ij}^{\alpha}, \eta_{ij}^{\beta}} \tag{13.1}$$

where, p_{ij} represents the prospect of choosing a node i from node j, τ_{ij} is the pheromone of joining node i and node j and $\eta_{ij} = (1/d_{ij})$, where d_{ij} represents the space between the nodes i and j. α and β stands for control factors. Every iteration is followed by updating of the pheromone value as represented in Eq. (13.2).

$$\tau_{ij} = \left(1-\rho\right).\tau_{ij} + \sum_{i=1}^{m}\Delta\tau_{ij}^{d}\tau_{ij} = \left(1-\rho\right).\tau_{ij} + \sum_{i=1}^{m}\Delta\tau_{ij}^{d} \tag{13.2}$$

where ρ stands for the evaporation constraint, m denotes the total number of effective ants and $\Delta\tau_{ij}^{d}$ is the pheromone capacity laid on path (i, j) by packet k. ACO algorithm, is in need of multiple iterations to emerge as flying colors in context of performance measurement.

13.2.2 PARTICLE SWARM OPTIMIZATION (PSO)

PSO bears the feature of genetic algorithms and evaluates mainly upon the fitness of the function. The concept is to select the best suitable set depending upon the higher order of the function. It is a pure case of artificial Intelligence where we apply heuristics concept for optimization and re-optimization of the set involving repeated analysis so as to obtain a set that can be used to harp upon any real-time problem, so as to enhance the dynamicity of the back-end program. The PSO model comprises a swarm of n particles following an iterative approach in a D-dimensional problem space encouraging search for better solution. The mathematical approach involves considering the particles representing the position vector $x_l = (x_1, x_2, x_3, ..., x_n)$ and velocities represented by the velocity vector $v_l = (v_1, v_2, v_3, ..., v_n)$. During the ongoing search process, an individual's particle positional change is based on the position of neighboring particles and its own previous experience. Each iteration time t leads to the update of position and velocity by implementing equations:

$$V^{\rightarrow t+1}{}_i = WV^{\rightarrow t}{}_i + \varphi_1 U^{\rightarrow t}{}_1\left(b^{\rightarrow}\Big|_i^t - x^{\rightarrow}ti\right) + \varphi_2 U^{\rightarrow t}{}_2\left(1^{\rightarrow t}{}_i - x^{\rightarrow t}{}_i\right) \tag{13.3}$$

$$x^{\rightarrow t+1} = x^{\rightarrow t}{}_i + v^{\rightarrow t+1}{}_i \tag{13.4}$$

where positive constants φ_1 and φ_2 are acceleration coefficients both usually initialized to 2. r_1 and r_2 are two random variables with the values appearing between 0 and 1. The maximum velocity is secured to a value of vmax, used to provide assistance to the effectiveness of a particle in search space. p_i and p_g are the particles' previous best and group's previous best position. The convergence to the optimal solution by PSO is achieved by updating velocity and positions vector in the above equation.

13.2.3 FIREFLY ALGORITHM

In mathematical optimization, the FA [2, 3] represents a metaheuristic approach proposed by Xin-She Yang. The key idea is to implement the swarming nature of the fireflies. The ultimate goal is to converge toward an optimal solution, as we have discussed the case of ACO. However, here the behavior of the algorithm completely resembles that of the firefly utilizing their flashing nature as a clue to decide the next approach. Initial development of algorithm owes much too little to the biological facts of fireflies. Notifiable features among them are as follows:

- Attraction toward partner of opposite sex is one of the key-determining factors as the path is determined mainly based on luminous intensity (i.e., moving from a less bright firefly to a firefly which is brighter).
- The main constraint is the brightness of each firefly which is proportional to the attractiveness of each firefly.
- Minimum visibility represents that no firefly is brighter than the present firefly.

The attractiveness for each firefly is created using the firefly attractiveness function, defined in Eq. (13.5):

$$B = \beta^0 e^{-yr^2} \tag{13.5}$$

Where the attractiveness atr_0 is β^0 and the light absorption constant is γ and the distance between any two fireflies at x_i and x_j is r_{ij} given in Eq. (13.6):

$$r_{ij} = |x_i - x_j| = \sqrt{\sum_{k=1}^{d} (x_{i,k} - x_{j,k})^2} \sqrt{\sum_{k=1}^{d} (x_{i,k} - x_{j,k})} \tag{13.6}$$

and the attractiveness of the firefly is defined by Eq. (13.7):

$$x_i = x_i + \beta_o e^{\gamma r_{ij}^2} (x_j - x_i) + a\left(rand - \frac{1}{2}\right). \tag{13.7}$$

The x_i is the current position and $\beta_o e^{\gamma r_{ij}^2} (x_j - x_i) e^{\gamma r_{ij}^2} x (x_j - x_i)$ is the brightness of the firefly.

13.3 BASICS OF WIRELESS SENSOR NETWORKS (WSN) AND WIRELESS AD-HOC NETWORKS

13.3.1 WIRELESS SENSOR NETWORK

Interestingly ARPANET had been influential for over a constant period of time, collaborating with 200 hosts at academia and research institutes [4]. The initial assumptions about data source name (DSNs) was that it has multiple cost effecting sensing nodes, collaborating with each other but the mode of operation bears autonomous character, with information being routed by selecting the best node. The concept of DSN was dormant at that point of time due to technological setback. To be more vivid, the culprit was the size of the sensor and the limited number of potential applications added fuel to fire. Last but not the least; it's the fault of compactness that accounts for loose association of the earliest DSN with wireless connectivity. The development started at its fullest extent after advancement in computing, communication, and micro-electromechanical technology. Basically, the work has gained pace around 1998 and to present day has become the center of attention and interest among the researchers and individuals. However, the center of focus is on networking information processing and also its technology which is competent for highly dynamic ad-hoc environments and resource-constrained sensor nodes. Furthermore, the microlevel sizes of sensor nodes have made it applicable for all and sundry. But the pioneer in this work was DARPA and the initiative transformed into reality by implementing a research agenda called SensIT [5] equipped with new competences such as ad-hoc networking, dynamic querying, and tasking, reprogramming, and multitasking [6]. Industrial automation is considered to be one of the crucial fields of WSN applications. The central subject behind the development of industrial communication technology is its immensely high-cost budget. The improvement of the product quality and reduction in energy consumption are the main objectives for the implementation of optimal control based on the important parameters. In today's market, the picture is quite encouraging as three-fourths of the industrial WSN income owes its origin from the process industry. The application area is prevalent in the power industry also which, according to the current report is now undergoing the power grid upgradation, WSN technology is also performing a lead role in the context of security monitoring over power transmission and transformation equipment accompanied by the reconstruction of billions of smart meters. But at the core of the development of WSN lies the application of metaheuristic whose decisional factors contribute for the routing efficiencies of the overall routing phase making WSN competent and user-friendly. WSN represents a group of spatially dispersed and dedicated sensors, environmental parameters such as temperature, sound, pollution levels, humidity, wind, etc. are measured by WSN. This is just the general overview of the concept. To explore in more detail, we focus on the metaheuristics part, whose utilization is maximum in WSN with the sole objective to provide best possible solution to the problem generated owing to the varied and mobile nature of WSN. The concept bears marked resemblance with the wireless ad-hoc networks (MANET) in terms of reliability on wireless connectivity and spontaneous formation of networks to ease the wireless transmission of sensor data efficiently. From a structural perspective, the WSN is built of thousands of "nodes" with individual connectivity to one or multiple sensors. Individual sensor network node typically has several parts namely a radio transceiver in collaboration with an internal antenna or connection to an external antenna, a microcontroller, an electronic circuit acting as an interface in between the sensors and an energy source, usually a battery or an embedded form of energy model. Variation is observed in terms of sensor nodes from micro level to ultramini level, directly influencing the cost parameter because they influence the corresponding constraints on resources such as energy, memory, computational speed, and communications bandwidth. The topology domain perspective of WSNs ranges from a simple star network, at the bottom level and finally broadens to form the upper layer accumulating an advanced multi-hop wireless mesh network. The propagation through hops of the network consists of an alternative of either routing or flooding. Application areas incorporate area monitoring, health monitoring,

Environmental/Earth sensing, air pollution monitoring, industrial monitoring natural calamities detection, etc. Now as previously mentioned a clear investigation of AODV routing protocol will confirm us about the efficiency and vitality of the said WSN.

13.3.2   MOBILE AD-HOC NETWORK

Wireless mobile *ad-hoc* networks (MANET) are auto-configured dynamic networks in which nodes have the freedom to roam and there lies the competencies of using the technology as devices can be connected irrespective of the geographical location. To be more vivid in the description, relay of unrelated packets through a router is one of the prime working features of the said ad-hoc network. However, the present challenge includes maintaining a stable connection among the devices. Network performance depends on the connectivity, mobility of devices within the network. Now, MANET can be classified into groups based on certain applications, which are as follows:

- An internet-based mobile ad-hoc network (iMANETs) integrates TCP/UDP and IP. The network-layer routing protocol is associated with the mobile nodes and it establishes routes distributed and automatically.
- Hub-spoke MANET – Multiple sub-MANETs are linked in a classic hub-spoke VPN to make a geographically dispersed MANET. Ad-hoc routing algorithms don't really work in these networks. One implementation of these networks is persistent systems cloud relay.

13.3.3   AD-HOC ON-DEMAND DISTANCE VECTOR ROUTING PROTOCOL

AODV routing [7] is a significant routing algorithm used in WSN, MANETs, etc. The network contributes actively in routing by communicating data dynamically based on network connectivity and the routing algorithm in use. Periodic broadcasting of the request messages is the symbol of Active Networks, and any failure in receiving the message will hint toward failure of the link. Data transmission for anonymous sites establishes new routes joining the intermediate nodes as route reply (RREP) packet that eventually discovers its source after the receipt of Route Request (RREQ) packets from neighbor nodes. Based on their shortest hop counts, numerous RREPs are sorted. This process cannot be utilized as optimization process that uses metaheuristics to ensure a possible ion solution for packet transmission. AODV was then introduced and tested and implemented in 2005.

13.3.4   CLUSTERING IN WSN

This course of picking one node to act as a servicing node for several neighbor nodes is known as "clustering." In most WSN applications the complete network must have the power to do operate by oneself in hard conditions. In WSN applications the sensor nodes are often deployed randomly in the area of interest and they associate with each other to form a network in an ad-hoc manner. Due to stringent constraints and very nature of radio communications it is impossible that every node will reach the gateway directly. Hop by hop data-transfer is one kind of solution but not a good solution. But the drawback is "overhead," diminishing lifetime of those node, which are very near to gateway and henceforth, they will be used as relay node. This makes the network virtually non-existent. Though there exist many algorithms to resolve the issue, clustering shows exemplary competency among many.

13.4 METAHEURISTIC ALGORITHMS IN WIRELESS SENSOR NETWORKS

13.4.1 ACO BASED CLUSTERING IN WSN

The idea of ACO-based approach centers around mass-feedback about a particular way to reach the optimum solution and act accordingly. While formulating the problem mathematically [8], initially we consider a set of m artificial ants' agents, constructs solutions from identities of a finite set of available search space components, $C = \{c_{ij}\}$, $I = 1, ..., n, j = 1, ..., |D_i|$. The construction processes make it first set mark with an empty solution. The process of developing the solution resumes with construction of graph GC (V, E). These allowed paths in GC are implicitly defined by the solution construction mechanism that defines the set N (sp) with respect to a partial solution sp. The choice of a solution component from N (sp) is made by applying probability at the individual formation step where the rule given in (i).

$$p\left(s^p\right) = \frac{\tau_{ij}^\alpha, \eta_{ij}^\beta}{\sum \tau_{ij}^\alpha, \eta_{ij}^\beta}, \forall c_{ij} \in N\left(s^p\right) \qquad (13.8)$$

where τ_{ij} and η_{ij} are pheromone value and the heuristic value associated with the component c_{ij} α and β are positive real parameters

$$\tau_{ij} \leftarrow \left(1-\rho\right).\tau_{ij} + \rho\sum_{i=1}^{m}F\left(s\right), s \in S_{upd} \mid c_{ij} \in s\tau_{ij} = \left(1-\rho\right).\tau_{ij} + \sum_{i=1}^{m}\Delta\tau_{ij}^d, \qquad (13.9)$$

where S_{pud} is the set of solutions that are used for the update, $\rho \in [0,1]$ is a parameter called evaporation rate, and $F: S \to R + 0$ is a function such that $f(s) < f(s') \Rightarrow F(s) \geq F(s')$, $\forall s \neq s' \in S$.

$F(\cdot)$ commonly referred to as the fitness function. Eventually it can be said without hesitation that ACO [9] is iteration based, providing the best route or solution. This implies, with increasing number of iterations, the provided solution will converge toward an optimal one. But the drawback accounts for the given limited power supply and the mobile nature of the clustered nodes, resulting in delay in output.

13.4.2 PSO-BASED CLUSTERING IN WSN

PSO is a swarming algorithm based on population, which is the solution for both continuous as well as discrete problems. PSO [9] makes use of agents to scour the search space to reach an optimal solution. The position of these agents, or particles, represents the solution for the said optimization problem, of the given search space of the traversal path. However, alteration of the particle's velocity with respect to present position is performed to achieve the better velocities over the previous one. The logic initiates by spawning particles at random positions, accompanied by an initialization region $\Theta' \subseteq \Theta$. Attempts are made to limit velocities within Θ' but as an alternative way to the former approach initialization can be made to zero or by minute random values with the sole objective to resist the dangerous situation where particles generally abandon the search space during the first iterations. Apart from this, if we discuss the functionalities of the main loop of the algorithm, then we experience an iterative re-initialization of velocities and positions using (3) and (4) until the termination condition is successfully achieved.

The core oblique elements are random integers evenly dispersed within the interval [0,1] in two n × n diagonal matrices. At each iteration, these matrices are again generated. The vector $l^{\to t}$, is denoted as the neighborhood best, and is the best position achieved by any particle within the neighborhood of the particle p_i, that being, $f(l^{\to t}) \leq f(b^{\to t}) \; \forall p \in N$. Here we assume our control over the values of w, φz and φ in an efficient manner; we basically achieve victory on two things simultaneously. Firstly, by virtue of this approach the particle's velocity doesn't reach the infinity level and secondly the most crucial issue is that the best fitness solution is successfully reached. The updating scheme discussed so far in PSO [10, 11] speaks off its vast application domain in context of the inter cluster communications. The velocity updating is instrumental to resemble the WSNs dynamic movements along with choosing an optimized path to ease the data flow at a competent rate. However, the PSO algorithm concept does not hold its actual relevance or in vagueness when it comes to the multicluster optimizations. The initialization phase of the PSO [12], particles make use of completely random positions, but then it doesn't have a lot of significance value as it is without any guidance. Despite the varied nature, and distances between the clusters of WSNs, mere updating of position vector for nearing optimization may not succeed to achieve the target cluster at all, and there lies the requirement of a more comprehensive and guided approach during the entire process of multinode optimizations.

13.5 METAHEURISTIC ALGORITHMS IN WIRELESS AD-HOC NETWORKS

Constriction based PSO (PSO-C) for cluster formation in the learning phase, is deployed marking an improvement in the densities. Considering the dynamic nature of the typologies of WSNs, accompanied by a decrement in power supply, fast routing conditions are indispensable which leads us in using ACO with Lévy flight ACO-LF, which follows random walk tendencies and aim to converge toward the ultimate mission faster effectively and in a more comprehensive manner.

13.5.1 CONSTRICTED PSO FOR CLUSTER FORMATION IN WSN

Constricted PSO [13] has been set to music during the optimizations of a more random behavior. The introduction of the constriction factor diminishes the expansion distance of the cluster formations resulting a decrement to the overall distance of the nodes in a cluster, eventually assisting accommodation of multiple nodes in a cluster, enhancing a comprehensive performance in channel network communications. The constriction is whimsical to provide assistance in diminishing the swarm explosion by introducing conditions, which bears positive proportional relationship to the search results of the previous iteration. X representing the constriction factor,

$$X = \frac{2}{\left[2 - \varphi - \left(\varphi^2 - 4\varphi\right)^{\frac{1}{2}}\right]}, \varphi = \varphi_1 + \varphi_1 > 4; \qquad (13.10)$$

After the substitution in the velocity equation with the constriction factor,

$$\vec{V}^{t+1}_{i} = X\left[\vec{V}^{t}_{i} + \varphi_1 \vec{U}^{t}_{1}\left(\vec{b}^{t}_{i} - \vec{x}^{t}ti\right) + \varphi_2 \vec{U}^{t}_{2}\right],$$

modified to Eq. (13.11)

$$\vec{V}^{t+1}_{i} = X\left[\vec{V}^{t}_{i} + \varphi_1 \vec{U}^{t}_{1}\left(\vec{b}^{t}_{i} - \vec{x}^{t}ti\right) + \varphi_2 \vec{U}^{t}_{2}\right] \qquad (13.11)$$

Generally, the value of φ is around 4.1, generating the value of X at 7.29 [11]. The previous velocities are multiplied by 0.729. To deal with stability cases, these values are only considered only during implementing constriction in PSO. The values of the searches are stored in a knowledge base and are used for updating the fitness of the agents.

13.5.2 Lévy-Flight-Based ACO Routing Optimization in WSN

The Lévy-flight-based ACO (ACO-LF) resembles each other in terms of working principle of ACO, however marking significant contrast in case of varied movement characteristics of the ants. The working principle is based upon the random walk to achieve optimizations functionally instrumental for topographies resembling those of WSNs. In lieu of decomposition of ρ, the constant property holds relevance in ACO [14], this is a clash in behavioral pattern with the agents, i.e., the ants preferring the levy distribution to achieve search results. In the random walk, the velocities, i.e., u, v follow the normal distribution, and are defined by N (0, σ^2), and combine to give the Lévy flight equation as $L(s) \sim \dfrac{u}{|v|^{\frac{1}{\beta}}}$. By substituting it in Eq. (13.2) the pheromone equation is modified as in Eq. (13.7).

$$(t+1) = (1 - \rho_{i,}) * (t) + \Delta\tau_{ij}(t), \rho_{i,j} \sim levy(\beta) \qquad (13.12)$$

where $\quad levy(\beta) \sim \dfrac{u}{|v|^{\frac{1}{\beta}}}\left(\tau_{ij}(t+1)-\tau_{ij}(t)\right)\quad$ and $\quad u \sim N(0,\ \sigma^2),\quad v \sim N(0,\ 1),$

$$\sigma_u = \frac{\tau\left(1+\beta\right)\sin\left(\beta\pi/2\right)^{1/\beta}}{\tau\left(\dfrac{1+\beta}{2}\right)\beta 2^{(\beta-1)/2}}$$

13.5.3 ALGORITHM LÉVY FLIGHT ACO FOR ROUTING

Step 1: *Initialization of Hello Packets*
Step 2: *Set the initial path of the traversal, to any of Cluster Heads, and set it as the start node*
Step 3: *Initialize the traversal paths. Step 4: If (current node = destination node)*
Step 4: *Add node to the path*
Step 5: *Else if, the node contains a routing table:*
Step 6: *Check whether the routing table contains destination node Step 7: Set the current node to the destination node; go to Step 4*
Step 7: *Sort the node distribution w.r.t the pheromone concentration, defined by (β), u and σ_u as in (7).*
Step 8: *Select the node based on the pheromone concentration Step 10: Initiate the random walk; go to Step 4.*

13.5.4 EXPERIMENTAL SETUP

The simulation is implemented using the INET Framework in OMNET++ 5.0. Some changes have been performed to the.ini file to encourage simulation in the real-time situations. Implementation of minor tweaks is crucial to instigate a more natural phenomenon and conditions. The urgent attributes for the effective implementation of the WSN networks are highlighted in the simulation area in Table 13.1 For proper setting up of a simulation environment for the iterative procedures to harp, it is trail

TABLE 13.1
Simulation Features

Topology Size	**1200 m × 1200 m**
No. of Nodes	600
Size of Data Packet	4 bytes
Size of Control Packet	100 bits
Initial Energy Per Node	2.1 J
Mobility Model	Random walk
Channel Power (max)	2 mW
Radio Bitrate	1000 kbps
Simulation Time	3400 s
Simulation Style	Cmdenv-fast-mode

blazed for duration of 3400s. Given below are representations of the WSN and clustering highlighted in the Cmdenv of the OMNET++ 5.0?

The simulation results procured for pre-clustering and the post clustering scenarios are depicted in Figures 13.1 and 13.2 respectively. Figure 13.2. Represents the simulation proximate to the terminating point of the simulation in totality on introduction of PSO-C. The nature of the data being continuous, it is impractical to be portrayed in the charts. Hence the continuous data banks are purposely plotted against possible parameters.

In Figure 13.3 a comparison is made between the number of non-functional nodes against time for the unguided clustering and the guided PSO-constricted clustering. However due to its constrictively to a specified search domain, with a knowledge base to surf through, the production of non-functional nodes due to PSO-C diminishes appreciably. This has a two-fold effect or rather the former leads to second. Firstly, by virtue of the mentioned facility helping a better density to the cluster is obtained, this causes betterment in the relay properties, for which they are deployed

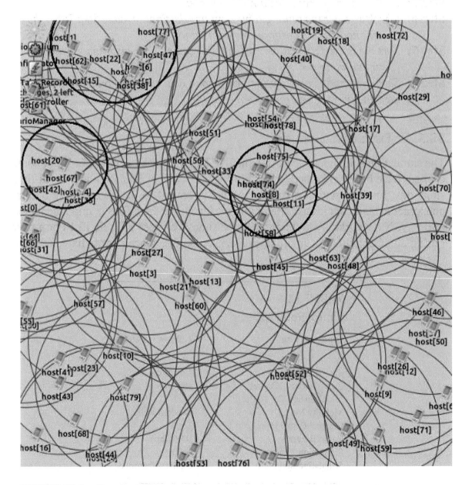

FIGURE 13.1 Pre-clustering scenario.

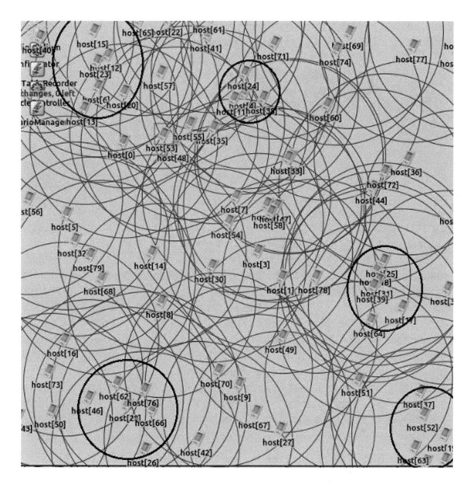

FIGURE 13.2 Clustering using PSO-C algorithm.

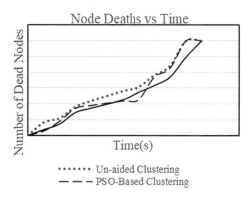

FIGURE 13.3 Comparison cluster formation.

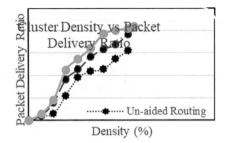

FIGURE 13.4   Comparison of node cluster connectivity.

in the first place. Although the ultimate fate is convergence toward the end of the simulation, the PSO-C algorithm acts as betterment over unguided clustering, in the given amount for the simulation, resulting in a better data collection.

Figure 13.4 represents the packet-delivery ratio when pitted against the unguided routing, the ACO based routing and the ACO-LF based data routing. It can be inferred without hesitation that the unguided routing, is a failure in its performance perform and cannot touch the 85% dense cluster structures for data routing. The ACO and ACO-LF crosses 80% barrier, but ACO loses it actual relevance or losses it's importance on the basis of its iterative drawback. ACO is in urgent need of multiple iterations to output an effective result, but in the context of a decomposed power supply, it loses its relevance to the random-walk-inspired ACO-LF. The performance is appreciably better than the ACO in terms of scouring the entire search space (the topography), for its ultimate mission, providing the best possible result, superior and comprehensive in comparison to its basic counterpart.

13.6   HYBRIDIZATION USING METAHEURISTIC IN A WIRELESS AD-HOC NETWORK

13.6.1   ACO AND FA HYBRID-BASED AODV ROUTING PROTOCOLS IN MANET

Before proceeding with AODV with ACO and FA in MANET there is sufficient reason to discuss the modified route discovering methodology as it forms the building block or the root cause where the later phase of our discussion includes the methodology or one kind of technical approach to fulfill the cause to achieve the desired end. Now, modified route discovery methodology includes initial stages of simulated diagramming of the AODV topology achieved by broadcasting of the HELLO packets. The RREQ packets share a similar broadcasting nature thus achieving throughout for the entire topology. The issue of multicasting RREP packets via specific nodes depends upon the condition that node intercepting the RREQ bears the path to the source. We commence our journey with the initial deployment of FA to control flooding of the RREQ packets, with the sole objective to plot a route to the neighbor nodes. This plan assumes realistic nature by dint of the intensity values which by default is introduced in every node with the designation of constraint. This intensity constraint is computed by taking assistance of the native expression of FA in (vii) newly selected nodes. The timestamp is purposely deployed to make determination about the nearest and the 'brightest' node. The closest neighbor node to the sending node in course of traversals is determined by the least difference in timestamps. Hence this node will get priority for selection. In a completely mobile set of nodes, traversing only to the nearest node does not hold significant relevance in the context of elimination of specific node from the entire topology in a lapse of time. Hence, with the objective to randomize the RREQ packets further among the nodes in the topology, lies the role of ACO. After the successful mapping of the neighbor table in totally is executed promptly by FA, ACO is deployed with the sole motive to trace the suitable paths to the goal where virtual ant stands for RREQ packet. The initial objective of the modified hybrid approach is storage of behavior of the node to the pheromone tables. The said 2D matrix of pheromone table possess the τ_i, j^k, symbolical of the pheromone value from node i to destination k over the neighbor j given in (ii). The working principle of conventional AODV protocol in route discovery phase is not free from limitation when applied in MANET. In fact, serious drawbacks like overheads hampering the node-function to a large extent resulting into network delays are some of the serious issues posing serious threat in terms of competency and efficiency. To be in detail it deploys the joint application of blind flooding of the neighboring nodes with RREQ requests, facilitating hopping to the best neighboring node. Here the culprit behind the existing limitation is nothing but limited resources of MANET. The problem may assume further complication with non-utilization of routing table high path drop rate when added with the former issue then it is like adding fuel to fire, which affects the whole routing phase by ignoring better under the circumstances when

$$\Theta = \arctan\left(QUOTE \frac{(y_2 - y_1)}{(x_2 - x_1)} \cdot \frac{180}{\pi} \right)\frac{(y_2 - y_1)}{(x_2 - x_1)} \cdot \frac{180}{\pi} \right) \tag{13.13}$$

The LZA basically acts like a determining factor when there is a question to explore the best possible nodes with a mission to transfer in the HELLO packets. Updating is performed for the pheromone coefficient in accordance with the equation

$$\tau_{ij} = (1-\rho).\tau_{ij} + \sum_{i=1}^{m} \Delta\tau_{ij}^d \tau_{ij} = (1-\rho).\tau_{ij} + \sum_{i=1}^{m} \Delta\tau_{ij}^d$$

which are eventually mapped to time-to-live (TTL) field of IP header of RREQ packet with the sole objective of computing the hop counts of a singular packet along with two significant phenomenon which accounts for the evaporation of pheromone, after a certain number of hops, followed by dropping of packets in accordance with TTL phenomenon? However, the modified hybrid algorithm aims to emerge as a single solution to combat with the existing limitation of the conventional AODV and

ACO-based AODV successfully thereby enhancing optimization result of routing protocol in MANET, competently compared to traditional approach.

13.6.2 ALGORITHM FOR ACO AND FA HYBRID-BASED AODV

RREQ format:

01. *If TTL = 0 drop packets*
02. *Else return RREP (for all other conditions) 03.*
04. *Otherwise perform sort operations on routing table based on the node fitness*
05. *Fitness value = current TTL*
06. *Y the best nodes*
07. *Select the most intense node*
08. *Perform TTL = TTL-1*
09. *Sort the neighbors based on the intensity values*
10. *Fitness value = TTL timestamp*
11. *TTL = TTl-1*
12. *Select X = total number of nodes/factor of spread*
13. *Select the most intense node*
14. *Start this for all the nodes individually*

13.6.3 EXPERIMENT SET UP AND RESULT FOR ACO AND FA-HYBRID-BASED AODV

13.6.3.1 Experimental Setup

The operation is performed considering OMNET++ 5.0 simulator with Ubuntu 14.04 LTS; INET framework as realized from Table 13.2.

Based on the given nature of the simulation, a considerable amount of stress is generated on the entire subsystem of nodes. Now, in collaboration with the random walk mobility model of the simulation, along with the imposed stress conditions (indispensable while implementing a sparse distribution) near realistic scenario has been set to action.

TABLE 13.2
Simulation Attributes

Topology Dimensions (m)	600 × 600	1200 × 1200	1800 × 1800	2000 × 2000
No. of wireless hosts:	20	40	60	80
Mobility model:	Random walk			
Channel power (max):	2 mW			
Radio bitrate:	100 kbps			
Simulation time (s):	3400			
Total packets sent:	3397			
Simulation style:	Cmdenv-fast-mode			

TABLE 13.3
Comparative Studies on the Algorithms

		Loss Percentage		
Nodes	**Topology (m)**	**Regular AODV**	**ACO_AODV**	**Hybridized_AODV**
20	600 × 600	78.261	72.14	69.129
40	1200 × 1200	88.61	87.57	83.2733
60	1800 × 1800	97.64	93.36	89.2174
80	2000 × 2000	98	96.07	92.1169
		Packets Received		
Nodes	**Topology (m)**	**Regular AODV**	**ACO_AODV**	**Hybridized_AODV**
20	600 × 600	740	946	1049
40	1200 × 1200	374	422	569
60	1800 × 1800	99	254	367
80	2000 × 2000	68	133	266
		Packet-Delivery Ratio (%)		
Nodes	**Topology (m)**	**Regular AODV**	**ACO_AODV**	**Hybridized_AODV**
20	600 × 600	.2178	.2748	.309
40	1200 × 1200	.1101	.124	.168
60	1800 × 1800	.0292	.072	.108
80	2000 × 2000	.02	.0392	.078

Individual conditions were executed for duration of 3400 seconds to achieve a near actual environment with each simulation individually accounting for the transmission of 3397 packets as realized from Table 13.2. The simulations were performed with special care taken over two issues. First and foremost is that the regular AODV should be kept as the standard, and secondly the ACO-based AODV for comparison purposes. The results of all the algorithms are recorded in Table 13.3.

The table draws a mark comparison between traditional AODV and ACO based AODV experimented with same hybridized AODV and the end result shows the victory of second approach over the former in terms of loss percentage of packets, where our second routing approach emerges as a successful approach in minimizing loss percentage with an increment in the number of nodes in the network. Another inference is about the negative relationship between increases in topology with the efficiency of the previous algorithms which exhibits a steady decrease although our approach still possesses the power to nullify this condition, at a much-improved rate in comparison to packet-delivery ratio. However, it is the mobile nature of all the previous algorithms in the MANET system which should be held responsible for such ill-performance.

Figure 13.5 depicts the successful application of the hybridized AODV algorithm in terms of number of packets arrives when compared against its orthodox equivalents. This reflects the proportionate relationship between the increasing number of topology, with an increase in packet transfer out of 3397 to the destination number of nodes (prevalent for all algorithms), as now the hybridized AODV possess the

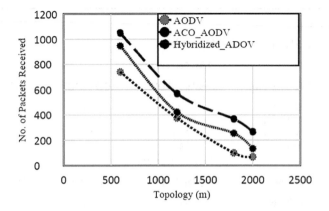

FIGURE 13.5 Packets received vs. MANET topology.

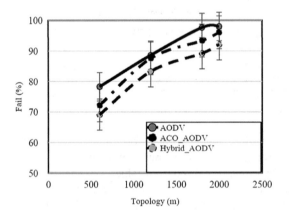

FIGURE 13.6 Packet fail % received vs. MANET topology.

capability to receive more packets out of the 3397 ones sent to the destination in a simulation time of mere 3400s. This is the solution of all the rising iterative issues that the ACO based MANET faces, and thereby improves the result further which is reflected on Figure 13.6.

13.7 CONCLUSION

The application of metaheuristics has opened a totally new chapter in the research field, spreading its branches and sub-branches all over the modern systems and applications. There are many systems and applications which are totally non-functional without the application of metaheuristics acting as a base for all modern algorithms. For example, in our case, we have discussed WSN. A WSN system on a large-scale environment gains its popularity and mass-acceptability over a number of issues. First of all, it helps in energy conservation the second prime factor is to maintain a stable connection among the other set of nodes. This can be achieved by clustering technique in WSN which provides reliability for the node connectivity and also enhances the system efficiency. The introduction of the constricted factor of PSO is a step ahead in establishing clustering concept as one of the best concept in routing, by proclaiming it's unique property of faster and a denser cluster formation in high scalable WSN environment adding to the former extension it finds its application where there is requirement of smooth convergence. The ACO-LF on the other part follows the random walk to establish better connectivity within the topographies, in a more enhanced way because of its Lévy flight characteristics, which elevates the results as compared to the original ACO. The concept proves its establishment in providing an efficient and robust means for creation and data routing for cluster-based wireless sensor networks. Again, considering the varied topologies, the stability of network is largely questioned in MANET systems to ease data transfers. Though AODV resolute those concerns, by making a steady procedure for MANET. Even in huge MANET topologies, the hybridization is instrumental, for transmission of data within the network. So, summing up all the details, in this chapter we basically dealt with two issues firstly the approach, to make the AODV more efficient, for betterment of result, which is proved by simulation results. Last but not the main aim of this chapter is to highlight the effectiveness of metaheuristics via its applications thereby acknowledging its vast domain in research purpose as well as projecting it's comprehensiveness and vitality in both normal and special application to enhance the efficiency of the back-end logic instrumental for the total functionalities of an electronic machine to perform at its best. However, there are future scopes of improvement, based on some unresolved issues, for example mere simulation cannot cope up with real-life a scenario which is indeed dynamic in nature. Fine-tuning is one of the solutions to the said problem, in accordance with the variation in topology. Thus, resolving these issues will result in better packet-delivery ratio further confirming a greater reliability and scalability.

Many proven metaheuristic algorithms employed in wireless sensor networks are fruitful although come with limitations. The introduction of the constricted factor of PSO is a step ahead in establishing c Mustering concept as one of the best concept in routing, by proclaiming its unique property of faster and a denser cluster formation in high scalable WSN environment adding to the former extension it fix s its application where there is requirement of smooth convergence. The ACO-LF on the other part, follows the random walk to establish better connectivity within the topographies, in enhanced way because of its Lévy flight characteristics, which elevates the results as compared to the original ACO. The concept proves its establishment in providing an efficient and robust means for creation and data routing for cluster-based wireless sensor networks. Again, considering the varied topologies, the stability of network is largely sectioned in a wireless ad-hoc network, a system to ease data transfers. Finally, the main aim of this chapter is to highlight the effectiveness of metaheuristics via its applications thereby acknowledging the vast domain in research purchase as well as projecting the comprehensions and vitality in both normal and special application to enhance the efficient y of the back-end logic in for the total functionalities of an electronic machine to perform at its best.

REFERENCES

1. K. Romer and F. Mattern, "The design space of wireless sensor networks," *Wirel. Commun. IEEE*, Vol. 11, No. 6, 2004, pp. 54–61.
2. Sh. M. Farahani, A. A. Abshouri, B. Nasiri, and M. R. Meybodi, "A Gaussian firefly algorithm," *International Journal of Machine Learningand Computing*, Vol. 1, 2011 December.
3. X.-S. Yang, "Chaos-enhanced firefly algorithm with automatic parameter tuning," *International Journal of Swarm Intelligence Research*, 2011 December.
4. C.-Y. Chong and S. P. Kumar, "Sensor networks: Evolution, opportunities, and challenges," *Proceedings of the IEEE*, Vol. 91, No. 8, 2003, pp. 1247–1256.
5. S. Kumar and D. Sensit Shepherd, "Sensor information technology for the warfighter," in *Proceedings of the 4th International Conference on Information Fusion (FUSION'01)*, 2001, pp. 3–9.
6. P. Coy and N. Gross, et al. "21 ideas for the 21st century," *Business Week Online*, 1999, pp. 78–167. Available at: http://www.businessweek.com/1999/99_35/2121_content. htm.
7. B. Mamalis, D. Gavalas, C. Konstantopoulos, and G. Pantziou, "Clustering in wireless sensor networks." In: Theoretical Frameworks and Practical Applications (2012): n. pag. Print.
8. T. Karthikeyan and J. M. Sundaram, "A study on ant colony optimization with association rule," *IJARCSSE*, Vol. 2, Issue 5, 2005 May.
9. D. P. Rini, S. M. Shamsuddin, and S. S. Yuhaniz, "Particle swarm optimization: Technique, system and challenges," *IJCA*, Vol. 14, 2011 January.
10. J. ReginaParvin and C. Vasanthanayaki, "Particle swarm optimization-based clustering by preventing residual nodes in wireless sensor networks," *IEEE Sensors Journal*, Vol. 15, Issue 8, 2015.
11. R. K. Yadav, Varun Kumar, and R. Kumar, "A discrete particle swarm optimization based clustering algorithm for wireless sensor networks," Vol. 338: *Advances in Intelligent Systems and Computing*, Springer International Publications, Cham, 2015.
12. V. Selvi and R. Umarani, "Comparative analysis of ant colony and particle swarm optimizaton techniques," *IJCA*, Vol. 5, 2005 August.
13. Y. Marinakis, M. Marinaki, and N. Matsatsinis, "A hybrid clustering algorithm based on multi-swarm constriction PSO and GRASP," in *Data Warehousing and Knowledge Discovery*, Springer, Berlin/Heidelberg.
14. H. Wang and C. Liang, "An improved ant colony algorithm for continuous optimization based on levy flight," *Chemical Engineering Transactions*, Vol. 51, 2016.

14 Artificial Intelligence
A Threat to Human Dignity

Archit Mallik

CONTENTS

14.1   INTRODUCTION

John McCarthy of the Davis United Nations agency is known as the father of computer science. The definition of computer science is an intelligent machine that may possess human-like capabilities to resolve issues generically instead of resolving it within a boundary. He did the primary demonstration of associate AI rule at Carnegie Melon University. Later, in 1929, he discovered the data processing program (LISP). There are several alternative definitions of AI, just like the definition by the aforementioned Davis United Nations agency, that their area unit bound tasks that we tend to treat decipherment like a verbal language, translating into information, and speaking – however, these tasks area units are difficult to program on a laptop. Hence, the artificial intelligence (AI) in keeping with him is to perform these tasks. More specifically, the conception of AI analysis was based in a workplace from the Dartmouth area during 1956. At that point, it had been foretold that machines could be as smart as a human being; immense amounts of money were invested into this vision to make it a reality. In Figure 14.1, an AI-powered robot can be seen [1]. Investment and curiosity in AI grew within the first years of the twenty-first century. After that point, machine learning was with success practical to several issues in the academe and trade because of existence of a strong machine [2].

FIGURE 14.1   An AI-powered robot. (*Source:* https://i2.wp.com/d3njjcbhbojbot.cloudfront. net/api/utilities/v1/imageproxy/https://coursera-course-photos.s3.amazonaws.com/f7/9812f9 78144ce8ac721727bc516cb0/Intro-to-AI-Naimo.jpg?resize=300%2C300&ssl=1)

14.2   RESEARCH METHODOLOGY

The heuristic that we adopt to conduct a detailed study on the threats of AI toward human dignity comprises researching, analyzing, and gathering secondary data from various data sources such as newspaper, books, articles, radio, television, and other viable sources. Statistical tools such as primary data storage methods such as quantitative data storage as well as qualitative data storage are also used.

14.3   BACKGROUND

It was the 1880s once a good person suggested this term and from then tons of uprisings came within the field that aided the corporate and also the budget to success [3] the basic patent for the discovery of the telephone occurred in 1876 and AI came later. In right relations, the world of AI analysis was built at a work area that persevered in the field of Dartmouth during the seasonal of 1956. At that time, it was absolutely expected that a machine could be as smart as a person; thus, over the years, time, research, and money have been invested to realize this vision [4].

1. **1974 – Computers flaunted**
   Generally, with period the trend of computers began. With the period, they developed quicker, cheaper, and were ready to store more and more information.

The simplest half was like they may assume theoretically but be able to self-realize and attained verbal process [5].

2. **1980 – The time of AI**

   In the 1980, AI study discharged after with an increase in supplies and algebraic machines. Having wide educational methods, the computer read with the user involvement.

3. **2000 – Landed to the landmark**

   After completely of the failing of tries, the industrial science was with success recognized however, till it had been within the year of 2000 the basic goals were also achieved. Till that point, AI succeeded notwithstanding a scarcity of the presidency of assets and communal devotion [6].

14.4   ADVANTAGES OF AI

AI is complicated. It uses a difficult mixture of computing, arithmetic, and different complicated sciences. Difficult programming helps these machines replicate the psychological feature skills of individuals. Figure 14.2 shows the numerous amounts of advantages of AI.

(i) **Decreases human error**

The expression "human error" stood produced by way of an outcome of the people creating errors from a time. The computers, nevertheless, do not create failures if they're programmed and automated accurately. Including AI, the varieties remain chosen after the earlier assumed data implementing a specific stack of processes. Since errors are decreased and therefore the chance of reaching exactitude with a greater point of precision may be a gamble.

(ii) **Can do risky things that pose a risk to human life**

This is one in every of the most important benefits of computing. We can overcome several risky limitations of humans by developing Associate in Nursing AI automaton that successively can do the risky things for US. Whether it involves planning to drop a bomb, explore the deepest elements of oceans, or mining for coal and oil, it may be used effectively in any quite natural or artificial disasters.

(iii) **It is available 24/7 and can work anytime**

An average person can do about 6–8 hours work without any break and for more hours; a person requires refreshment and breaks to reduce pressure and, further, an AI machine does not require any breaks and can work for a whole day without stopping and without getting bored. Figure 14.3 shows an ideation prototype of an AI assistant.

(iv) **Faster and resourceful results are made with the use of AI**

Humans do take time and space to make a decision or to give an output but while using the AI it is nothing like that. AI machines can give a faster output and within a small time it provides us the result as the machine is made for the work to do.

FIGURE 14.2   Advantages of AI. (*Source:* Source site is not available.)

(v) **It has daily applications like use of voice assistant like Siri, Bixby, Catana**

In our day-to-day life we are getting our small tasks done by these voice assistants. Without touching the phone, we can simply ask them to make a call or to text someone.

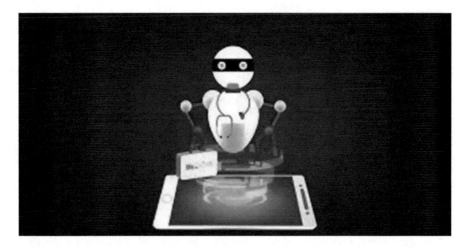

FIGURE 14.3   AI assistant helping to work faster. (*Source:* https://www.canstockphoto.com/robot-doctor-concept-vector-67950603.html)

14.5   DRAWBACKS OF AI

- **Cost of creation is very high**
  As AI is modernizing day-to-day the machinery system ought to be modernized with while to satisfy recent necessities. Machineries would like to repair and upkeep which require huge prices. Its construction needs tremendous prices like the complicated machines.
- **People become lazy**
  AI is creating individuals slow and lethargic with credentials systematizing the bulk of the tasks. Persons lean toward to make dependent on the discoveries which may cause burden to forthcoming peers. In Figure 14.4 we can see the

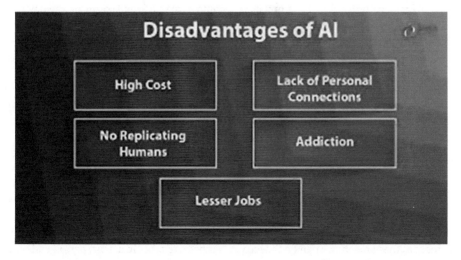

FIGURE 14.4   Disadvantages of AI. (*Source:* https://encrypted-tbn0.gstatic.com/images?q=tbn:ANd9GcQtr6uZ91rESfh-3WXmLU09zCxRLjD8zW3JBw&usqp=CAU)

disadvantages of AI with high managing cost. It also leads to lack of personal touch among the community.

- **Lack of out-of-box thinking**
  Gadgets will complete solely those works for what they are made or automated to try and do, something besides that they favor to clash or offer impertinent productions that can be a substantial scene or a major backdrop.
- **No connection and feelings**
  As we know that AI machines can do work faster and better than the humans, but they can't replace the humans from having emotions and making a group while working. These machines can't develop feelings and the bond with the humans as they are programmed to do a certain work.

14.6   THREAT TO HUMAN DIGNITY

One of the biggest problems of AI is that it has become a threat to human dignity in today's time and will become a major problem in the future. Now we are going to discuss about this major problem.

As AI is substituting the bulk of the monotonous works and different tasks with machines, human intrusion is varying into a smaller amount which can cause a significant downside within the job standards. Each party is wanting to exchange the least skilled people with AI machines or computers which could do alike work with added potency.

The tools that we've created are getting smarter, faster, and superior at interacting for the USA. This shift has the potential to enhance our lives by permitting the USA to specialize in a lot of advanced tasks, however, this shift is a lot of dangerous than several may think. The expansion of AI-powered gadgets like Google Duplex is kind of the danger to human dignity that to derive back in the period. It provides in the favored perception that one's self-esteem and value are only obsessed with our quality to society instead of conferred on the USA in creation by God.

AI may be utilized in ways in which devalue human life and therefore the deterioration of human flourishing as a result of they'll operate as a substitute for countries. It's already being enforced in several sectors of personal and free life, as well as medication, producing, finance, and warfare. Yet, for all the potential edges, real dangers exist, and that we should bear in mind of how it'll influence our society.

14.7   IMPACT ON JOBS

Can AI effect in job forfeiture and financial imbalance?

Despite its commercial growth and the PC uprising, the AI rebellion isn't replacing the jobs and careers of people like writers, artisans, human resource managers, and personal assistants. Instead, it's poised to cause wide devastation of low-skilled employment – principally lower-paying employment, however there are higher paying jobs too. These changes can end in grand earnings for the businesses that advance AI, likewise as the companies that adopt it. AI machines has caused the unemployment as these machines can do the easy and repetitive tasks in a short period and with an accuracy. Due to their fast results and impeccable record many big firms and industries are removing the lowest qualified humans with these AI-powered machines which is causing the unemployment.

For illustration – think the amount of money bike collectors make if they advance their commercial to use robots as an operator. Thus, the people are suffering from two developments that cannot be set together: those with tremendous accumulating wealth, and the high numbers with no employment.

These were a few benefits and drawbacks of AI. Every discovery will have both pros and cons, it's us who have to take its positive side and construct a more reliable world. AI has great potential profits. It's in the hand of humans that need to take care that the rise of robots should not take place and enslave humanity or the reduction in the human dignity.

14.8 PROPOSED SOLUTION

Solutions to defeat the hazards and the risks correlated with AI and improving the human dignity. The most noticeable things, which combine privacy crimes, unfairness, and changing of social practices, are additionally extra than more to aid hazard. Besides regarding there are the outcomes that are not understood or else encountered. Unfavorable effects – with the cost of human life, if AI medically code goes opposite or wrong, or the settlement of general safety, if a foe transmits wrong info to an army of AI machine – is desirable, and are so notable dares for the companies, from status loss and income loss to supervisory reaction, criminal enquiry, and decreases public belief.

AI machines has not taken all the industrial work as there are some works that requires a perfection and can be done only by the humans. Sometimes these machines may do the work with an error and may do the malfunctioning with the system, but humans may take time and do that with the perfection.

Now for increasing human dignity with the AI people should work with the help of AI for more faster results, and a part lies in educating people in the field where AI machines and tools are not good at. Example: AI machines are not suited for the jobs like planning, cross domain thinking and in creativity. We can create a lower-income jobs that requires the human skills which lacks in the use of AI, like bartenders, artifact collecting, and many more. These jobs require more human cooperation.

14.9 PROBABLE FUTURE

The specialists found that AI will give a boost to humans working but it will also be a threat to them. They even said that AI may exceed the human intelligence and some other capabilities to do the work like learning, decision making, etc. But for a better future for human development, AI and humans need to work together. So, for a better future of AI and humans together the AI technology should be used wisely by the humans for the future time and for development of the world. As we can see in Figure 14.5 the AI-enabled future can be bright and it can enhance the human experience and can easily change the way of living but on the other side it is autonomous to everything.

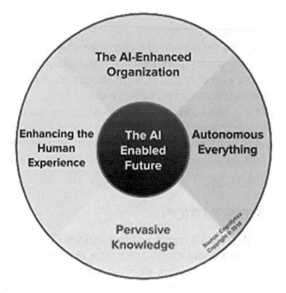

FIGURE 14.5 Future of AI and humans. (*Source:* https://thumbor.forbes.com/thumbor/960x 0/https%3A%2F%2Fspecials-images.forbesimg.com%2Fimageserve%2F5da92992cd594c00 06215c82%2FThe-AI-Enabled-Future%2F960x0.jpg%3Ffit%3Dscale)

14.10   CONCLUSION

Notwithstanding the benefits of AI, some scientist and leading scholar like Elon musk, Stephan Hawking, cautions us about the hazards of the AI and future technological similarities. It is concluded that genuinely brilliant creations whether it is machines or humans are bad for the humanity which causes many loses to humanity. On opposite side, AI does not seem to destroy humanity or the human dignity. Humans must take care of AI so that in future it would be easy to work together for a better output and for a developing world. But no matter how bad and worse AI can be to humans and to the humanity there is rapidity progress of expansion of AI. Despite what percentage deponents initiate against AI, there is no gratitude to stop its advancement. Forthcoming studies can help in guiding AI forever instead of threatening, however, despite what happens, there's positively no holding the wheels of momentum as they gradually crush ahead.

14.10.1   FUTURE SCOPE

Through this work we try to present a conclusive study of the probable threats of AI toward human dignity. But this work still has scope for future enhancement. Some recent advancements in AI and there impacts on our solidarity can be studied. Some surveys can be conducted so as to better gain a general idea of the notion of general populace toward AI can be investigated.

REFERENCES

1. "If You're So Smart, Why Aren't You Rich?" MIT Technology Review. Available at: https://www.technologyreview.com/2018/03.
2. "Artificiality." Wikipedia. Available at: https://en.wikipedia.org/wiki/Artificial.
3. "Kasra." Available at: http://www.kasra.com/history.html.
4. "Insights." Forbes.com. Available at: https://www.forbes.com/sites/insights.
5. "Hacker News." Available at: https://news.ycombinator.com/item?id=121.
6. "Which World Problems Are the Most Pressing to Solve?" 80,000 Hours. Available at: https://80000hours.org/career-guide/world-problems/.

15 Device Programming for IoT

In Defense of Python as the Beginner's Language of Choice for IoT Programming

Gift Mugweni and Rose Mugweni

CONTENTS

15.1 INTRODUCTION

The introduction gives the background and driving forces on the issues discussed in this chapter. As the fourth industrial revolution grows steadily closer and more devices become increasingly interconnected, the rise in popularity of internet-enabled devices has allowed for a whole new market sector to open up. With this new market, an important question for developers wishing to join the bandwagon is – what language should be used? In this chapter, the merits of Python are proposed as the language of choice for institutes and individuals seeking to introduce people to the Internet of Things (IoT) and start the ball running in this modern fast-paced landscape.

15.2 LITERATURE REVIEW

In the study of languages for IoT discussion, much has been learnt regarding the performance characteristics of languages such as C, C++, Java, or Python. In Choroszucho et al. (2019), the performance of C, C++, and Python were assessed, with the latter two having significantly better runtimes. However, as Fabio, Longo, and Santoro (2019) have shown, performance optimization is not the only important thing in future IoT devices. As our devices get more and more powerful, our demands on devices will further increase, which in turn means our devices need to get smarter and smarter. Though this is possible in C and C++, it must be acknowledged that the creation of such programs is inherently more difficult than in more friendly languages like Python or Java.

15.3 PROBLEM/GAP/ISSUE

Next, the problem, gap, and issue are unpacked and discussed. The devices most influenced by the rising popularity of the IoT are those in the embedded systems sector. More and more, we are seeing household devices with internet connectivity, such as smart fridges, watches, toasters, televisions, and others. At the core of this growth is the increasing computing power on smaller and smaller chips (Karl Rupp, 2018). As such, when the question of which language would be best to teach for embedded systems, a few come to mind such as C, C++, Python.

Regarding C/C++, these languages have traditionally been the language of choice due to their great optimization features that allow for great operation on resource-constricted devices that sometimes only have a few kilobytes of main memory to work on. Aside from this, due to them being close to the machine code, once compiled their runtimes are significantly superior to that of Python without much debate, since they are compiled programs while Python is interpreted.

However, though C/C++ programs are indeed highly optimizable, the languages themselves are significantly more difficult to learn as opposed to Python. With C being difficult in creating complex programs and C++'s steep learning curve, Python offers a nice middle ground for those seeking to sink their feet initially.

Aside from its ease of use, Python also has numerous libraries for varying functions that allow for easier implementation of other technologies popular in the IoT space, such as machine learning, image processing, and Big Data processing – to name a few. As such, the challenge at hand is how best to introduce Python as the entry language for less resource-constricted devices to allow beginners to grasp the core concepts of IoT programming and eventually go deeper into the medium.

15.4   APPROACH

In assessing Python's viability as the language of choice, the following questions were asked and subsequently answered by collecting the relevant information:

- How likely are beginner developers in the IoT sector likely to know C, C++, or Python beforehand?
- Which aspects does each language excel at?
- How does library support across languages compare regarding IoT use cases?
- What are the limitations of each language in the IoT stack?

15.5   PROGRAMMING LANGUAGE POPULARITY FOR IoT DEVELOPMENT

According to a recent survey (Eclipse IoT, 2020), the popularity of the programming languages varies according to the nature of the IoT device being developed on, as shown in Table 15.1.

Upon obtaining the results, the suspected three languages were noted to have a strong foothold in the IoT sector, however, a new language, i.e., Java, was noted to also have a firm footing across all tiers like Python. This revelation prompted further investigation into the popularity of Java vs. Python as the beginner's candidate language, from which the below information was obtained.

A broader survey (Stack Overflow, 2020), which focused less on IoT developers in general, found that while Python and Java are both similarly popular, Python was the third most-loved and most-wanted language, while Java was the seventeenth most-loved and ninth most-dreaded. These facts naturally led to the conclusion that it is significantly easier to introduce IoT programming concepts in Python, as developers feel more comfortable with it and hence are less likely to be dissuaded during the learning stage.

TABLE 15.1
Top Four Programming Languages by Tier

IoT-Constrained Device	IoT Gateway/Edge Node	IoT Cloud
1. C	1. Java	1. Java
2. Java	2. Python	2. Python
3. C++	3. C	3. JavaScript
4. Python	4. C++	4. C++

15.6 COMPETITIVE ADVANTAGES OF C, C++, AND PYTHON FOR IoT DEVELOPMENT

15.6.1 LANGUAGE OVERVIEW

Before diving deeper into the pros and cons of the language of choice, it is important to have a brief overview of each language and expected environment of use.

15.6.1.1 C Overview

The C language is quite an old language, dating back as far as the 1970s, and has consistantly stood the test of time. Like most languages, C is a procedural language but what makes it unique is its numerous powerful optimization options and barebone access to your system memory. Owing to this, the language has found great popularity in resource-constricted devices as programmers can pay careful attention to how they wish to manage their memory.

15.6.1.2 C++ Overview

Following from the above, the C++ language was a language that sought to add more features to the original C language. Of note, was the divergence of the language to allow for object-oriented programming, which was a feature not inherently supported in C. This development has allowed for C++ to be much more useful in creating more complicated software where performance is still important and as such, it once again found popularity in use for resource-constrained devices.

15.6.1.3 Python Overview

Different from the first two, Python is an interpreted language whose design philosophy focused on readability as opposed to performance. This in turn has led to the language being at a higher level of abstraction than C/C++ and hence reducing the optimization methods available. However, for what it sacrificed in freedom, the language made up for in convenience as it is well known for being easy to understand and learn for many beginners while still offering great depth the further in you go. All these facts combined have thus seen the continual increase in popularity of the language as time goes on.

15.6.2 PROS OF C/C++

A quick or deep dive into the literature will show that, at its core, the key advantage brought by C/C++ is performance. Both languages are very low-level languages allowing for incredibly elegant optimizations to occur that can squeeze out all the potential in your devices. The ability to manipulate memory directly though is potentially dangerous, but can also enable a developer to have fine control over how they access information and potentially allow for even faster executions than if all decisions had been left to the compiler. These simple, yet powerful facts have justly earned C/C++ a throne for development on resource-constrained devices where every bit of extra performance leads to a better experience overall, allowing for programs with significantly faster runtimes.

15.6.3 Pros of Python

Python's call to fame once again lies in the seemingly simple and mundane. To begin with, Python's popularity guarantees that there more developers proficient in it than either C/C++. Aside from this, the language is known for its "writability, error reduction and readability" (Radcliffe, 2016), which are all important factors that lead to significantly faster development cycles than would be possible if creating a program in C/C++. These simple facts mean that – provided the IoT device has enough resources – a potential IoT developer can make very intricate systems with only an introductory-level knowledge in programming concepts.

15.7 LIMITATIONS OF C, C++, AND PYTHON FOR IOT DEVELOPMENT

15.7.1 Cons of C/C++

Due to the inherently freer nature of C/C++, these two languages are quite well known to be "slow to write, error-prone, and frequently unreadable" (Radcliffe, 2016). More often than not, in the bid to get the most optimal solutions, final code base can end up being incredibly cryptic and difficult to maintain and, hence, care must be taken when developing with these two languages as there are few safety nets. As such, it follows that the development times of C/C++ programs are longer. Aside from this, though not an issue for C++, C has no support for object-oriented programming leading to significant difficulty in implementing more complex algorithms.

15.7.2 Cons of Python

Ironically, Python's greatest weakness lies in its significantly slower runtimes when compared to C/C++. Although there are optimization strategies that can make some features in Python modules as fast as C/C++ programs, in general they are slower and as such, this language is not ideal for use cases where speed is an important factor.

15.8 COMMUNITY SUPPORT OF C, C++, AND PYTHON FOR IOT DEVELOPMENT

Though all three languages have strong community support providing many libraries which greatly enhance the core language functionality, it must be noted that Python dominates this category regarding the variety of functionality offered. Many frameworks exist (for example, Flask, Django, and others) that can help developers better manage their code bases. Aside from this, the popularity of the Raspberry Pi, which works extensively with Python, also means that the language has many libraries interfacing with the hardware. These two facts combine to enable Python to be a powerful middleman between the cloud servers and the sensors at the edge.

15.9 CONCLUSION

In conclusion, with its numerous libraries, frameworks, and ease of use, the Python language is a great candidate for a developer looking for a place to dive into the IoT development space. Provided that timing constraints allow, Python slowly chips away at the seemingly monolithic task of creating devices and programs for an increasingly interconnected world. Any developer seeking to join the bandwagon need not fear being left behind.

REFERENCES

Choroszucho, Agnieszka, Piotr Golonko, Jakub Bednarek, Mateusz Sumorek, and Jakub Żukowski. 2019. "Comparison of high-level programming languages efficiency in embedded systems". In *Photonics Applications in Astronomy, Communications, Industry, and High-Energy Physics Experiments* 1117661.

Eclipse IoT. 2020. *IoT Developer Survey 2020 Results*. https://outreach.eclipse.foundation/eclipse-iot-developer-survey-2020.

Fabio, D'Urso, Carmelo Fabio Longo, and C. Santoro. 2019. "Programming intelligent IoT systems with a Python-based declarative tool". In *AI&IoT@AI*IA*.

Radcliffe, Tom. 2016. *DZone*. 5 September. https://dzone.com/articles/python-vs-cc-in-embedded-systems (accessed October 27, 2020).

Karl Rupp. 2018. *42 Years of Microprocessor Trend Data*. 15 February. https://www.karlrupp.net/2018/02/42-years-of-microprocessor-trend-data/ (accessed April 21, 2021).

Stack Overflow. 2020. *2020 Developer Survey*. https://insights.stackoverflow.com/survey/2020#technology (accessed October 28, 2021).

16 Enhancing Real-Time Learning Experiences through Information Communication Technology, Augmented Reality, and Virtual Reality

Bakari Juma, Vinod Kumar Shukla,
Gagandeep Kaur, and Ashok Chopra

CONTENTS

DOI: 10.1201/9781003048862-16

16.1 INTRODUCTION

We are living in an age of rapid change. Digital media seem to open up extraordinary possibilities for encouragement and learning to be strengthened across various subject areas, levels of student growth, and educational environments. People can now experience immersive training in schools and homes, libraries, and community centers with significant advancement of realistic and accessible virtual reality tech and mixed reality [1]. Virtual reality is a simulated world that is perceived through tangible stimuli generated by a machine (such as sights and sounds) and in which one's behaviors partly decide what occurs in the environment [2].

The use of ICT technology creates an atmosphere that is simulated, particularly for teaching and learning. The most often used part of virtual reality is the head-mounted display (HMD). In virtual reality, audio-visual knowledge is most easily reproduced, but research and development are being carried out concerning the other senses. Tactile inputs allow users to feel as if, rather than sitting in a chair, they are walking through a simulation. Haptic innovations, too known as input innovation, have progressed from straightforward spinning-weight engines to ultrasound innovation of tall quality. Together with visual virtual reality (VR) encounters, it is presently conceivable to listen and feel true-to-life sensations. Many educational technology firms use VR tech to introduce real-life experiences to the schools when showcasing the potential of technology to encourage and draw students' interest. Completely immersive virtual laboratory simulations are intended to engage and enhance a student's natural curiosity while they study in the field of science, technology, engineering, and mathematics (STEM) education [3].

However, there are unquestionable risks too. Virtuoso is also trying to grasp VR's effect on the learning of children. Research conducted at their Stanford lab in 2008 by Bailenson and his team [4] looked at the possible psychological impact on young children using VR. Children who have encountered swimming with whales in a VR setting have in some cases developed false memories of visiting SeaWorld in real life [4, 5]. Bailenson suggests it is possible to resolve questions regarding VR use in two ways: moderation and supervision.

Despite the fact that VR gives the reenactment of a totally computer-generated perceptual encounter, expanded reality employs the normal world, not at all like VR, which produces a completely manufactured environment, then overlays new information on top of it. With physical objects, AR points to progress the computerized domain, empowering a real-world client to communicate consistently with advanced components. The point does not comprise exclusively of quantitative information enhancement [6]. AR is presently changing human forms by speeding up the development of abilities and spurring direction.

AR gives a specific collection of affordances from the distinctive specialized mediations. Consequently, since it is associated with learning circumstances, AR can be utilized in a startling way from other developments. We need to describe AR before checking AR apps Azuma [7] portrays AR to be when "3-D virtual objects are embedded in genuine time into a 3-D genuine environment." To begin with, the combination of virtual components and a genuine environment is required. Talking of AR as a portion of a continuum of virtuality conceptualized by Milgram and Kishino [8] is advantageous. The entirely genuine world is on one side of the range of virtuality, and the simply virtual environment is on the other side. Between these two extremes lies AR. Three-dimensional enrollment is the moment AR measures, so that the virtual components are congruous with the genuine world. The third AR prerequisite is interactivity with virtual components in genuine time. Hence within the genuine world, the virtual components must act as a real component. This indicates, but is not limited to, the AR system that refers to changes in the viewpoint of the user, improvements in lighting situations, impediments, and other physical laws.

16.2   MOTIVATION AND CHALLENGES

Related to, AR innovation clients may confront convenience issues and specialized issues, and this innovation may be complicated for a few understudies. Ease of use is one of the critical challenges of AR applications. There is no substantial evidence demonstrating that ease-of-use issues are mainly connected to AR innovation and may stem from deficient proficiency with creation, ruins with interface plan, mechanical troubles, or negative demeanors. As understudies may confront inconvenience exploring daydream and reality, there may be perplexity due to the blend of real and virtual objects.

To perform complex errands, utilizing AR innovation inside a learning environment requires multitasking, as understudies ought to bargain with vast amounts of information and various specialized gadgets. This could lead to cognitive over-burden and an overpowered or befuddled feeling. The misconception appears that an AR framework is accurate, but in a learning environment, this could be useless as understudies can lose track of the real world. A few consider report that cognitive stack is diminished by AR, whereas others report cognitive over-burden. Schools may force confinements on the utilization of AR innovation, and teachers may be reluctant to utilize AR, as this innovation also includes the presentation of imaginative educating approaches. The substance accessible through AR applications is regularly resolute, limiting the impact of the educator over the meaning and avoiding adjustment to meet understudy needs. By permitting clients to rework and construct AR applications, the accessibility of the writing program will overcome this issue. Another deterrent may be that the steadiness of versatile AR innovation isn't ensured. On the off chance that the innovation needs well-designed interfacing and informational, issues may emerge as this may cause the invention to be complicated. To get to be familiar with and comfortable with AR innovation, clients may require time.

VR is additionally known as a diversion that's not taken exceptionally seriously – it is agreeable to play but not usually perceived as a genuine learning tool. Understudies may show behaviors that offer assistance to win the pursuit but don't lock in their minds to memorize current information and essential considering. VR requires extraordinary design capabilities that are not doable at all times with standard computer hardware and may make impressive endeavors to realize smooth execution and inundation and interaction beneficial. VR is additionally provided as restrictive arrangements that other designers may not adjust with comparable environments. Many businesses give their devices to construct VR situations that are not congruent with the rest in terms of equipment and computer programs. For substance creation, add up to drenching, interaction, programming, and sending, VR will require specialized abilities.

16.3   RESEARCH OBJECTIVES

1. To understand computer-assisted learning (CAL) and the role of ICT.
2. To analyze the pros and cons of CAL.
3. To know the aim and scope of CAL.

16.3.1   RESEARCH GAP

1. Interviewers rejected the idea of substituting humanistic teachers with machine instructors, and they believed that the maximum of their learning happened in tutorials and established these as the most critical component of the module.
2. The solution is that rather than human tutors being replaced with machine tutors, they could use the machine tutors to produce them with totally different data. Additionally, what if the machine tutors would be there simply if the tutor isn't well.

16.4   COMPUTER-ASSISTED LEARNING

16.4.1   COMPUTER-ASSISTED LEARNING TECHNIQUES

CAL has regularly been acclimated to depicting the work and application of educational innovation for extended circumstances. From the mid-1980s to the beginning of the 1990s, the term CAL was typically usual to put through with the occasion of either one noxious program or an arrangement of programs that supplanted the extra old instructing procedures of direction, particularly the address. "Computer-assisted learning or innovation helped learning is laid out as learning through computers with subject shrewd learning bundles or materials." A CAL or technology-assisted learning may be laid out as learning or educating subjects like Math, Science, Topography, etc., through software programs or e-books with subject shrewd learning bundles or materials. CAL can be understood as:

1. It should embody all kinds of tech-enhanced learning (TEL), wherever technology is utilized to bolster the instructive strategy.
2. It's thought to become: "Pedagogy authorized by digital technology."
3. In a broader sense, it ought to be thought about as a locale of E-learning. Technologies that help learning may be sketched out as a noxious program or record created particularly for scholastic capacities. The method is utilized all over the planet in many kinds of setting, from primary school to schools and universities. Part of the CAL is to optimize the learner's course through a substance field on the preface of his disposition, mental highlight characteristics, and analyzed state of preparation [9].

16.4.2 Techniques Related to Computer-Assisted Learning (CAL) [10]

16.4.2.1 Visual Learning

Numerous students may be visual learners and benefit immensely from seeing a picture or an illustration of the terms being said in school. Additionally, you can use YouTube videos, or your individual comes to explain any extent further. It enables far more accuracy for the learner to see something really interesting or being used in a video to bring it to mind for much longer learning retention.

16.4.2.2 Hearing Practice

Tuning in the home might be an imperative portion of learning any dialect. By encouraging you to play music or record conversations, CAL makes a difference because your studies can be based on listening to the dialect really being used and in real situations. At that point, they can mimic the speakers or vocalists and understand in their modern language that they have a voice.

16.4.2.3 Tests

Computers are a fantastic way for exams to be supplied. You will either build an argument exam or make them sit at the computers in the schoolroom; pre-written assessments and elective test materials can be given via the internet and included in your classes. Taking exams on the screen may help studies to feel less daunting and enable the learner to feel more relaxed than being in a more pressurized situation like a schoolroom.

16.4.2.4 Games

Games could be one of the better ways to make use of CAL within the room. Dialect understudies (exceptionally youthful ones) love to participate in portable workstation diversions or do astonishments in their target dialect.

For those who don't want to learn, it feels like fun. Indeed, they would not care that they are being more brilliant as they strive to initiate a good level or illuminate a disturbing dilemma until, inevitably, they are studying and retaining information to accomplish future challenges.

16.4.2.5   Internet Browsers

Another fun way to use the target dialect inside a room is by making learners ask about it in spoken dialect online. Exercises such as WebQuest occur with the coach offering a secret to see up with a motor look to understudies. At that point, the understudies need to be required to explore the arrangement using their target dialect, which could be a real (but fun!) challenge.

16.4.2.6   Online Courses

CAL will provide sessions online. These sessions can be performed at home at one's time, either as a part of a complete stack of college programs, or they can be practiced as an extension of a dialect curriculum they are learning in person as of now. Online, hundreds of free or paying dialect courses can be found, and numerous of them can be remarkably viable.

16.5   CHALLENGES OF COMPUTER-ASSISTED LEARNING (CAL)

16.5.1   Aim and Scope of CAL

The scope of this chapter is to provide a platform for university learners to use computers to alter them for mainly network-based teaching and learning – the computer area unit's rapid developments resulting in the creation of primarily society-based associated information. With the technique we learn and comprehend, these modifications have produced pleasant effects on our life. If computers are correctly used, the cooperation of learners will be accelerated, and the construction of information will be enhanced. Academics' and students' preponderance would be likely to use new technology for teaching and learning. The combination of computers in education is gaining value as a powerful medium for magnifying teaching and learning strategies. Computers' role in education is generally associated with the educational innovation technique. Much technologically innovative provides the learners with information, the greater their level of acceptance and attention will be. Using computers in the learning technique can take a severe change to the educational standard that ensures blessings over the conventional learning scheme wherever computers in education slowly assume such old teaching aids as overhead projectors, picture slides, charts, and many others.

The benefits of computers over the opposite teaching aids include:

A. Computers' flexibility to store and manipulate an excessive amount of data within a matter of seconds.
B. Computers can also "communicate" using an application package with users/students.
C. In addition, a laptop is versatile and will act as a projector associate, graphs, tables, slides all rolled in one.
D. With the increased availability of fabric and package education, computers can be used in a variety of college data.

The aim of bringing pcs to education is:

A. To view every instructional system at the forefront of technological development and the professions of learners with those required in the workforce up to this stage.
B. To increase teaching and learning efficiency and productivity with the use of ICT.
C. It is transforming a lot of autonomous learning with students as active learners to build their knowledge, assisted by scholars. Model and animation area unit sometimes excellent educational instruments. The visual power of simulation offered in an excessively pc will generate images that can make it easier for students to know "why the area of things unites the approach they are." When using computers in training, information can be presented efficiently to allow learners to understand thoughts simply, especially thoughts about the abstract unit region that can be produced easier with transmission impacts through graphics and PC animation [11].

16.5.2 PROS OF COMPUTER-ASSISTED LEARNING (CAL)

CAL is individualized, which means that any student is free to function in his private accommodation, totally unconcerned with every other student's results. In a standardized way, knowledge is presented. CAL uses a broadcasting system that gives a cloudless representation of its development to the learner. Learners can also classify the content areas on which they have modified and require correction. It reduces the time needed to perceive abstract ideas by enabling learners to quickly form concepts and analyze the results of such administration. CAL makes a wide variety of interactions that are not otherwise available to learners. It includes audio as well as visual inputs for multimedia applications. This allows the learner to openly understand thoughts by using calming tools such as animation, blinking, graphical screens, etc. [9].

16.5.3 CONS OF COMPUTER-ASSISTED LEARNING (CAL)

16.5.3.1 It Can Be Costly

Price is perhaps the most significant hurdle to using CAL in the classroom. There are expensive computers, mobile gadgets, and applications. In addition, it's just not a fundamental objective for certain schools to get a laptop for every learner.

16.5.3.2 It Can Be Challenging for Teachers to Perform

Each when electronics are used with something, at least initially, it becomes more complicated. Before they can make their learners use it, teachers have to figure out how to use the tech themselves, and even the best teaching can take a lot of precious time. We've all had that one teacher who missed a lot of time during the class when they didn't discern how to use the overhead projector or computer, and nobody wants to be that instructor!

16.5.3.3 CAL Activities Don't Always Fit the Teacher's Goals

It's also hard to find one that perfectly fits the criteria or teaching approach using third-party apps, videos, or tutorials. There will be times where an online quiz does not have the exact details you need to ask for, or where the video you are watching contains a part of the speech you need to show. Instructors have to find a way to combine CAL into their teachings without letting it determine the information to be studied, and it can be challenging to achieve the scale often.

16.5.3.4 It Can Lead to Isolation Among Students

While an entity is a traditional thing, the tailored training adventure is not the solitude it may point to. Just imagine a classroom full of learners, each with their own computer, not looking at each other and just communicating with the computer in front of them. Socializing is an essential aspect of using words and verbalization because we learn new knowledge about language by communicating with each other. To help them understand, students need other classmates, and CAL will avoid this. Even when mixed in the classroom, CAL can be an excellent teaching resource. CAL will rebuild the ways students study languages or find something, for that matter, by using it to improve your program rather than dictate it [10].

16.6 AUGMENTED AND VIRTUAL REALITY

AR frameworks are digital advances that can provide both actual and simulated immersive circumstances. These technologies can be accomplished by technological devices such as mobile phones, head-mounted equipment, or a CAVE-programmed simulated reality (CAVE). Numerous firms render AR and VR equipment phases and various computer software companies that build computer programs to be used on different phases of equipment. A CAVE may be a dim space that allows people to wear AR glasses and be completely inundated with the dim room inside the virtual universe, including an additional effect on this virtual environment [12]. Increased Reality (AR) is the use of portable technologies used to superimpose and link an existing image of simulated objects externally to cover a real-world environment [9, 10].

The utilization of versatile technologies to provide a digital image of a carefully wet area devoid of the natural world environment can be portrayed as VR. The universal gadget buyer is incapable of seeing the outside world in a VR setting, in this manner communicating as it were with virtual substances that can be gotten to using versatile equipment, such as head-mounted equip. Whereas AR and VR give situations that can permit understudies to be inundated in their learning handle, challenges are moreover posed. The taken toll of various portable head-mounted units and CAVE rooms is frequently expensive [10]. In this case, instructive learning doesn't have a crucial viewpoint to encourage learning utilizing AR and VR situations; CAVEs are regularly exorbitant and permitted for a small number of individuals within the room.

16.7   EXPERIENTIAL LEARNING IN HIGHER EDUCATION DEFINING

The hypothesis of learning can assist the experiential learning handle with AR and VR use. It isn't conceivable to realize the part of innovation in instruction without identifying its reason. In instructive teaching, innovation is also actualized to make strides in educating and learning forms and guaranteeing understudy assets [13]. In expansion, mobile and electronic learning innovation can be an enabler to supply advanced substance on understudy portable phones in under-resourced settings [14]. The part of increased and VR in making difference learners realize experiential learning objectives through intuitive innovation is discussed in this chapter. The hypothesis of experiential learning can be portrayed as the method by which data is created by changing encounters." "The blend of getting a handle on and changing discernment benefits from data." The recommended four organized experiential learning cycles are explained in [14].

Experiential learning in Figure 16.1 permits learners to conceptualize, deliberately involve, reflect, and reinterpret their encounters. The central part that encounters play in accomplishing the learning result can encourage experiential learning. There are a few educational offerings in instructive education requiring understudies to total an encounter parcel to realize their evaluation. This chapter examines the potential part of expanded and virtual reality in promoting experiential learning in numerous areas. Understudies may, in this way, be submerged in learning situations

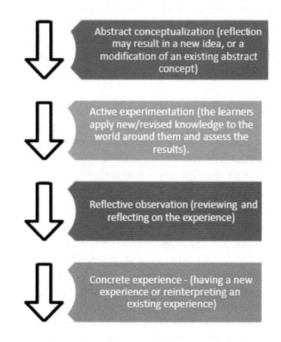

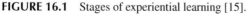

FIGURE 16.1   Stages of experiential learning [15].

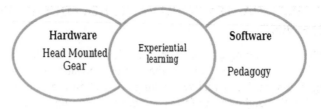

FIGURE 16.2   Usage of virtual and AR to assist the process of experiential learning.

whereas making the related VR innovations, which empowers them to get learning encounters as well.

16.7.1 Toward Virtual Reality Experiential Learning

We look at the crossing point between experiential learning, instructional methods, and potential advancements for expanded and virtual reality in this segment. Figure 16.2 is outlined within the taking after area:

16.7.1.1 Head-Mounted Equip (Hardware)

With the presentation of progressed head-mounted provide comprising of spinners and additive-enabling innovation, learning has gotten to be less complex with businesses propelling items such as the HTC Vive, the Oculus fracture, and the helpfully available VR case that empowers you to utilize versatile phone gadgets inside the adaptive case. In expansion, using sensors permitting comparing intuitive joystick permits for the plausibility of using a program that allows most excellent understudy engagement with the assignment postured to them.

16.7.1.2 Mobile Phones

As contradicted to other advances, such as tablets, creating nations have a few of the most noteworthy utilize of versatile telephones. Numerous open-source and exclusive computer programs are now being made to back instructing and learning on adaptable phones using expanded and virtual reality.

16.7.1.3 Software

There's an opportunity to empower adaptive learning encounters within the creation of applications enacted by versatile innovation whereas advancing the academic results set out in experiential learning assignments for understudies. The Visual, Aural, Perusing and Kinesthetic (VARK) model [1] traces that learning can take place in visual, aural, perusing, and composing and kinesthetic frames when considering academic approaches. These highlights characterized by the VARK show permit for educational comes about that can advantage from the characteristics of AR, and VR advances as they permit the creation and introduction of the program in this form.

16.7.1.4   Experiential Learning

As understudies can lock in with their assignments, their intelligence within the learning preparation is individual. Unique, active, and intelligent involvement helps form their positive learning encounters. Applications may moreover be built to allow concrete intuition to be connected to decide the degree of client comprehension. With each interaction, real-time interaction and real-time criticism permit understudies to create, reflect, and apply their obtained knowledge.

16.8   EVALUATION

The relationship between expanded reality and STEM instruction and its potential has been the subject of some later considerations. One of the foremost critical issues [6] is the instructive methods carried out by expanded reality. This kind of program was unused for the school, and one of the teachers' destinations was to survey the efficiency of the strategy. That's why three basic components were included within the demonstration that was utilized (Figure 16.3):

1. Well-defined priorities for learning objectives.
2. Practical learning experiences.
3. Evaluation-the outcomes of students and their learning experiences.

Conducting comparative tests is one approach to deciding the significance of making a proficient recreation. The knowledge picked up over one school year has appeared that recreated ponders have driven too much more progressed learning than in a conventional classroom would ever be done. They have these introductory comes about. It has appeared that recreations are a promising way to make strides in the learning results of understudies, particularly in STEM subjects. Assist investigations were performed in arrange to affirm this. Assessing whether learning objectives are being met, mainly when an awesome bargain of gear speculation has been made, is pivotal for utilizing this hardware. This incorporates an assessment arrange, the collection of assessment information, and suggestions for advance changes.

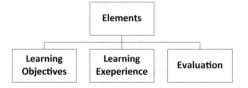

FIGURE 16.3   Elements to assess the efficiency of the framework.

16.9   CONCLUSION

The chapter is based on various articles, research papers, interviews, and information about CAL, and we can use or inject it into different learning institutes. This study also includes an initial observation of the awareness of computer-assisted education. The study was based on three study objectives, which research methodology was entitled to collect data evidence and analysis has been done. The conclusions are summarized in this section:

Objective 1: To understand computer-assisted learning (CAL): This research assumes the prospect of computer-assisted knowledge and timely possibilities. As a technique and scheme, education is primarily concerned with enabling education, learning methods, and providing/securing a conductive history of schooling instead of informal education and other socialization media. As the name suggests, CAL uses electronic instruments and computers to accomplish and explore instructional monitoring. CAL can be performed in nearly all fields of education, ranging from television/DVD play-learn programs for kindergarten youth to quadruple bypass procedures in medicine. CAL is indicated by connecting understanding from all areas of teaching and learning, communication between humans and computers (HCI), and cognition.

Objective 2: To analyze the pros and cons of CAL: This study concludes that each teacher decides whether computer-assisted learning is accurate for their teaching techniques. As extended as the pros and cons are somewhat accountable, using computers within the classroom can be an excellent way to utilize new technology and expand the language learning background. Furthermore, this research concludes that computer adoption among learners and educators should be encouraged, and practical computer skill courses should be suggested in the curriculum. The post-nursery and primary computer should be made mandatory to promote computer understanding among all learners, depending on the accessible sources.

Objective 3: Knowing CAL's purpose and scope: This study assumes that this research's aim and expansion is to highlight the importance and point of the CAL programs tradition in various topics. The content of this job is to deposit an internet-based teaching and learning program for learners to hire computer support that could empower them. Computers' fast progression is starting to develop an information-based civilization. These innovations have had excellent effects on our life, including our manner of learning and thinking. If computers are used appropriately, they can accelerate the cooperation of learners and increase the construction of understanding. In teaching and learning, almost every teacher and student would be able to use new technology. Computer mixing into education is gaining popularity as an effective platform to magnify teaching and learning.

REFERENCES

1. Liu, Dejian eds., et al., *Virtual, Augmented, and Mixed Realities in Education*. Singapore: Springer, 2017.
2. Virtual Reality (VR). "Merriam-Webster.com dictionary." *Merriam-Webster*. Available at: https://www.merriam-webster.com/dictionary/VR (accessed June 1, 2021).
3. Nersesian, Eric, Adam Spryszynski, and Michael J. Lee. "Integration of virtual reality in secondary STEM education." *2019 IEEE Integrated STEM Education Conference (ISEC)*. IEEE, 2019.
4. Oh, S. Y. and Bailenson, J. "Virtual and augmented reality." In *The International Encyclopaedia of Media Effects*. Hoboken, NY: John Wiley & Sons, Inc, 2017, pp. 1–16.
5. Kennedy, E. "Can virtual reality revolutionize education?" *CNN*, November 1, 2018. Available at: https://edition.cnn.com/2018/11/01/health/virtual-reality-education/index.html (accessed June 1, 2021).
6. Panciroli, Chiara, Anita Macauda, and Veronica Russo. "Educating about art by augmented reality: New didactic mediation perspectives at school and in museums." *Multidisciplinary Digital Publishing Institute Proceedings* 1.9 (2018).
7. Azuma, Ronald T. "A survey of augmented reality." *Presence: Teleoperators & Virtual Environments* 6.4 (1997): 355–385.
8. Milgram, Paul and Fumio Kishino. "A taxonomy of mixed reality visual displays." *IEICE Transactions on Information and Systems* 77.12 (1994): 1321–1329.
9. Sharma, Rishu. "Computer assisted learning – A study." *Computer* 4.2 (2017).
10. Schittek, Martin, et al. "Computer assisted learning. A review." *European Journal of Dental Education: Review Article* 5.3 (2001): 93–100.
11. Bharathy, Jesuraja Bosco. "Importance of computer assisted teaching & learning methods for chemistry." *Science Journal of Education* 3.4 (2015): 11.
12. Freina, Laura and Michela Ott. "A literature review on immersive virtual reality in education: State of the art and perspectives." *The International Scientific Conference Elearning and Software for Education* 1.133 (2015).
13. Kaliisa, Rogers and Michelle Picard. "A systematic review on mobile learning in higher education: The African perspective." *TOJET: The Turkish Online Journal of Educational Technology* 16.1 (2017).
14. Chaka, John Gyang and Irene Govender. "Students' perceptions and readiness towards mobile learning in colleges of education: A Nigerian perspective." *South African Journal of Education* 37.1 (2017).
15. Kolb, Alice Y. and David A. Kolb. "Experiential learning theory." *Encyclopedia of the Sciences of Learning* 978.1 (2012): 1215–1219.

17 Topic-Based Classification for Aggression Detection in a Social Network

Karanjot Singh, Sonia Saini, Ruchika Bathla,
Vinod Kumar Shukla, Ritu Punhani, and
Divi Anand

CONTENTS

17.1 INTRODUCTION

Cyberbullying can be defined as making fun of or sharing aggressive comments on people's posts on a social media platform. Indian teens stand first when it comes to being cyberbullied on the internet, and some of them commit suicide. With the help of machine learning, we could detect the aggressive comments and filter out those comments, and in turn, reporting those people who are guilty of committing such deeds. There are several methods by which the aggression comments could be detected using machine learning and are mentioned in this chapter select so that further actions could be taken against them.

In today's world of technology, every 8 out of 10 people on social media are cyberbullying someone or are being cyberbullied, which is a huge amount of people in the statistics. Especially the young kids, they are most vulnerable when it comes to being cyberbullied on social media. India stands third in the list in the crime of cyberbullying after China and Singapore, which is not a good score. The worst three social media platforms on which cyberbullying happens are Facebook, Instagram, and ask.fm. Here machine learning comes into the picture, it could detect those aggressive comments and report or block the guilty party's respective account just by

DOI: 10.1201/9781003048862-17

extracting the filtered comments from the database. Cyberbullying is a profoundly serious problem in this world of technology because it's happening to do every other person on social media. Most teenagers are vulnerable people when it comes to being cyberbullied.

17.2   RELATED WORK DONE FOR AGGRESSION DETECTION CLASSIFICATION IN A SOCIAL NETWORK

This chapter aims to analyze the methods proposed by several researchers to detect aggressive messages or comments on social networking sites such as Twitter, Facebook, MySpace, YouTube, etc.

By using several methodologies, we can apply them to the database of the data set and then extract the aggressive comments or messages from that database and come to a conclusion of whether the specific message or comment is negative, positive or neutral concerning the algorithms and methodologies that various researchers have used in their research papers.

Aggression detection in a social network is where the users communicate through aggressive comments or messages when felt offended by something or someone. There has been a continuous effort to stop them and introduce methodologies that would extract the aggressive comments and detect them from the database using machine learning concepts.

There are several directions to detect aggression comments in a social network, which are as follows:

- Semantic-enhanced marginalized stacked de-noising auto-encoder
- Pre-handling and The SMOTE strategy
- MyPageKeeper
- Paragraph2vec
- Random Forest

The researchers' methods are semantic-enhanced marginalized stacked de-noising auto-encoder, pre-handling, and the SMOKE strategy, ground truth, MyPageKeeper, Paragraph2vec, random forest, and pre-processing. Shruthi and Mangala (2017) used the methodology called semantic-enhanced marginalized stacked de-noising auto-encoder, which would classify the words into positive, negative, and neutral. The author has taken the data from two of the most common social media platforms Facebook and Myspace. Its algorithm starts like this; when an individual enters a remark or post in internet-based life, it goes into content pre-preparing for dissecting conclusion in a later step. Utilizing estimation examination, the extremity level of the content can be resolved. The extremity from assumption examination is recognized in five different ways as Very-Positive (VP), Positive (P), Neutral (NU), Negative (N), and Very Negative (VN). This calculation helps separate the content from the typical and harassing content, thus shielding a person from cyberbullying. As stated, this calculation assumes a significant job in arranging the content. The calculation with info and yield is referenced underneath as stepwise (Table 17.1).

TABLE 17.1
Result can be Either of the Three Conditions

Negative Polarity	Action to be Taken
< 50	Post the text as defined by the person.
>= 50 &&<= 80	Report to the person, whether the text can be posted or it cannot be. As per the person's detection, cither of the first or second result is carried forward.
>= 80	Block the comment from posting, to avoid bullying comment.

The "extremity esteem" goes into the extremity check calculation. As per the calculation, the after effect of the procedure is characterized. The outcome can be either of the following three:

This paper concludes that, from the proposed thought, it is unmistakably known 60–70% of content cyberbullying can be maintained a strategic distance from posting. This aids in keeping an individual from getting tormented and shield the web from cyberbullying wrongdoings. Utilizing assumption investigation extremity of the content has been characterized, and examining the corpus content helps recognize the most utilized cyberbullying content. Likewise, word embeddings have been used to naturally expand and refine torturing word records presented by the area information. Exhibition of our methodologies has been tentatively affirmed through mainly two cyberbullying corpora from social media: Myspace and Twitter. In the following stage, we intend to further improve the educated portrayal's vigor by considering word request in messages.

Tommasel et al. (n.d.) deal with detecting aggression in social media is 'Features for Detecting Aggression in Social Media: An Exploratory Study.' This paper centers on discovering forceful substance with regards to numerous social media destinations by investigating various kinds of highlights. Kumar et al. It involves 15,000 posts obtained from Twitter and Facebook. Posts were gathered from Hindi pages identified with news, gatherings, political parties, understudy's associations, and gatherings in help and resistance gatherings of ongoing episodes. Human annotators allocated the presents on one of three classes (clearly forceful, secretively forceful, and nonforceful). It contains roughly 3000 questions and replies removed from FormSpring. me10. In such a site, clients straightforwardly welcome others to inquire, and what is more, answer inquiries with the choice of anonymity. Posts were physically marked into three classifications (unequivocally forceful, feebly forceful, and non-forceful). As indicated by the creators, the best characterization accomplished a general precision of 81% when taking into consideration highlights identified with number of revile words as well as their force.

The experimental results of this methodology in this paper are as follows:

The exploratory assessment considered a few mixes of the highlights depicted in Section 17.3, presents the acquired results for both datasets. Each stacked bar reports the most exceedingly terrible and best outcomes for the comparing highlight set, for each of the chosen datasets. Even though outcomes were marginally higher (with contrasts up to 2%) when performing highlight choice by holding 75% of the most significant highlights indicated by Information Gain, such distinction was factually

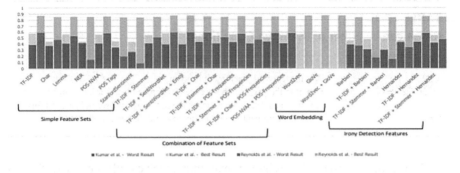

FIGURE 17.1   Aggression detection results.

inconsequential. In most cases, the most exceedingly awful outcomes were acquired for naïve Bayes, trailed by support vector machine (SVM) with a polynomial bit, paying little mind to the broke down the dataset. Then again, the best outcomes were, for the most part, to get with either SVM with a radial basis function (RBF) portion or a neural system with 0 shrouded layers as shown in Figure 17.1. Curiously, despite being the most computationally complex methods, neural networks with concealed layers did not accomplish the best outcomes.

This paper concludes that cyberbullying and cyber aggression are not trivial and are far-reaching issues progressively influencing internet clients. With the "help" of the far-reaching of web-based social networking systems, harassing once constrained to specific places or times (for example, schools) would now be able to happen whenever and anyplace. Cyber aggression can be characterized as forceful online conduct that plans to hurt someone else, including inconsiderate, annoying, hostile, prodding, or crippling remarks through online social media that target instructive capabilities, sex, family, or individual propensities. This paper concentrated on the difficulties presented by social media content's qualities and examined different capabilities for recognizing hostility. Capabilities included scorch, word, and enthusiastic based highlights, highlights utilized for identifying incongruity and word embeddings. Test assessment led on two certifiable internet-based life datasets demonstrated the challenges for precisely identifying animosity in web-based life posts. Besides, results uncovered the confinements of the chose include comparable to the attributes of the web-based life destinations, just as the qualities of the locales' clients. Taking everything into account, results prove the need to investigate the marvel, what is more, grow new, and progressively productive methodologies for cyber aggression location.

Ifrim et al. (n.d.) explain event detection on Twitter. Its objective is to portray the methods that have been utilized for the SNOW Information Challenge 2014. They show that forceful separating of tweets because of the length, structure joined with various labeled grouping of tweets and positioning of subsequent bunches achieves empowering outcomes.

The proposed methodology in this paper depends on two parameters:

1. Removal of abusive tweets
2. Various labeled grouping of tweets.

TABLE 17.2

Example Ground Truth Topics for the 2012 US Election Twitter Stream

Time	Topic Headline	Topic Keywords	Tweets Ids
07-11-12 00:00	Obama wins Vermont	Obama, Vermont, wins, projects, VT	265966881926688768,265 966897793740800
07-11-12 00:00	Romney wins Kentucky	Romney, wins, Kentucky, projects, KY	265966833524424704,265 966921537695744
07-11-12 00:00	Benue Sanders wins Senate seat in Vermont	Sanders, wins, Senate, Vermont, independent, VT	265967450074513108,265 967599123316736
07-11-12 00:00	Romney wins Indiana	Romney, wins, Indiana, IN	265966811449810945,265 966944522481665
07-11-12 00:30	Romney wins West Virginia	Romney, wins, West Virginia, WV	265974256159039488,265 974324148723712
07-11-12 00:30	Romney wins South Carolina	Romney, wins, South Carolina, SC	265975742649729024,265 975879736.373248
07-11-12 01:00	Obama wins Illinois	Obama, wins, Illinois.IL	265982157355376640,265 982400880861184
07-11-12 01:00	Obama wins Connecticut	Obama, wins, Connecticut, CT	265982401157689345,265 982401795215360
07-11-12 01:00	Obama wins Maine	Obama, wins, Maine, ME	265982400880861184,265 982412897529857

In this area, they research the impact of different parameters on the subsequent set of themes. For setting parameters, we utilize the subset of ground truth subjects given by the test coordinators to the 2012 stream, an example of which is appeared in Table 17.2. For correlation, in Table 17.3, they have shown the top 10 subjects recognized by our strategy (with parameters set as portrayed in the past segment) for the equivalent stream, for the scheduled opening beginning at 07-11-2012 00:00.

This paper can be finished up on the note that they present a point identification technique in Twitter streams. In light of forceful tweet/term sifting and two-phase various leveled bunching, first of tweets and second of coming about title texts from the primary grouping step. Their point features are genuine tweets so that the client can follow the news back to its unique tweet. Its weakness lies within the aspect of topic-fragmentation. And its strengths are that it's a simple technique and its efficiency.

G'omez-Adorno et al. (2018) focus on detecting aggressive tweets in Spanish in their study "A Machine Learning Approach for Detecting Aggressive Tweets in Spanish." Its main objective is to present their approach to the aggressive detection track at MEX-A3T 2018. The track consists of identifying whether a tweet is aggressive or not.

The methodology that they have adopted is called pre-processing. Before the extraction of features, they apply the following pre-processing steps to enhance n-grams representation and reduce part-of-speech (POS) tagging errors:1. Lowercase: This permitted us to improve the POS labeling process.

- Lowercase: This permitted us to improve the POS labeling process.
- Digits: Since the numbers do not convey semantic data, replace them with a solitary image (e.g., $1,599 \rightarrow 0,000$).

TABLE 17.3

Detected Top 10 Topics Using the Method for the 2012 US Election Twitter Stream

Time	Topic Headline	Topic Keywords	Tweets Ids
07-11-2021 00:00	WASHINGTON (AP) - Obama wins Vermont; Romney wins Kentucky. # Election2012	#election2012, @ap, ap, begins, breaking, calls, carolina, close, cnn, fox, georgia, indiana, kentucky, news, obama, presidential, projects, race, romney, south, vermont, washington, wins	265967355648167397, 265967692161363969, 265967306985844736, 265967261297295361, 265967261297295361, 268967255815340032
07-11-2021 00:00	Not a shocker NBC reporting #Romney wins Indiana & Kentucky #Obama wins Vermont	#obama, #romney, indiana, kentucky, nbc, reporting, vermont, wins	265967338992570368
07-11-2021 00:00	RT @SkyNewsBreak: Sky News projection: Romney wins Kentucky. #election2012	#election2012, @ skynewsbreak, indiana, kentucky, news, Obama	265967389974343680, 268967700734533633
07-11-2012 00:00	AP RACE CALL: Democrat Peter Shumlin wins governor race in Vermont. #Election2012	#election2012, ap, bernie, call, democrat, governor, peter, race, sanders, seat, senate, shumlin, vermont, wins	265968208291438592, 265967599123316736
07-11-2012 00:00	CNN Virginia exit poll: Obama 49%, Romney 49% #election2012	#election2012, cnn, exit, obama, poll, romney, Virginia	265967764815110146
07-11-2012 00:00	Mitt Romney Losing in Massachusetts a state that he governed. Why vote for him when his own people don't want him?	#Obama2012 #obama20012, governed, losing, massachusetts, mitt, people, romney. state, vote, want	265966841686544385
07-11-2012 00:00	Twitter is gonna be live and popping when Obama wins! #Obama2012	#obama2012, gonna, live, Obama, popping, Twitter, wins	265968524072218624
07-11-2012 00:00	INDINA RESULTS: Romney projected winner (via @NBC) #election2012	#dumbasses, #election2012, @huffingtonpost, @nbc, indiana, projected, results, romney, winner	265968527289249792, 265968527289249792
07-11-2012 00:00	If Obama wins I'm going to celebrate... If Romney wins I'm going to watch Sesame Street one last time #Obama2012	#obama2012, celebrate, going, last, obama, one, romney, sesame, street, time, watch, wins	265966816730435584
07-11-2012 00:00	#election2012 important that Romney won Independents in Virginia by 11 pts. With parties about even, winning Inds is key	#election2012, even, important, independents, inds, key, parties, pts, romney, virginia, winning, won	265968665915191296

- Notices: We just expel the @ image from the @USUARIO mark since keeping the notice (without the @) improves the highlights of the POS labels.
- Pics: The image joins are likewise supplanted by a solitary image (connect → 1).
- Slangs: Following the procedure introduced in, replaced slang words with their normalized variant from the Spanish online life vocabulary.

Another method that they used is the synthetic minority oversampling technique (SMOTE).

In this method, the minority class is over-tested by making engineered models. These new examples are made by taking every minority class test also, highlighting recent examples that happen along the line portions between the k closest information purposes of the minority class. The new examples are made by distinguishing the highlight vector of the genuine example and its nearest neighbor. This distinction is then duplicated by an irregular number somewhere in the range of 0 and 1. The consequence of this activity is then added to the component vector of the genuine example. This makes another information point between the two thought-about examples.

The result of the performed methodology was something like this. The exhibition proportion of the forceful identification track is the F1-score on forceful class. Table 17.1 showcases the 10-overlap cross-approval outcomes on preparing corpus, just like the testing corpus's official outcomes. Likewise, Table 17.4 shows a standard when every occasion anticipated as forceful class and the general consequences of the best performing groups in common errands. We achieved the fifth. The most outstanding outcome with run 2. It might be seen that run 2 (without SMOTE) demonstrated better outcomes on the test corpus, 42.85%. Be that as it may, during preparation corpus, run 1 accomplished outcome around 10% higher than run 2. Aftereffects of the two runs are way more than the pattern. Results below 10-overlap cross-approval on preparation corpus (Train) and testing corpus's official outcomes (Test). Both as far as F1-score %).

This paper concludes that their best run accomplished a 42.85% F1-score on the forceful class. They utilized an oversampling method (SMOTE) to defeat uneven information, which permitted them to accomplish better outcomes in the preparation corpus. Yet, it did not sum up well on the testing corpus. They accomplished fifth place out of 12, taking an exciting framework.

TABLE 17.4
Results under 10-fold Cross-Validation on the Training Corpus

Run	Train	Test
Shared task 1st. (INGEOTEC)	–	48.83
Shared task 2nd. (CGP$_{Team}$)	–	45.00
Shared task 3rd (GeoInt-b4msa)	–	13.10
Shared task 4th. (aragon-lopez)	–	43.12
run 1 (with SMOTE)	**85.53**	40.20
run 2 (without SMOTE)	74.32	**42.85**
baseline (aggressive class)	52.31	01.38

Holt (2016) deals with news outlets on social media. Its main objective is to analyze Facebooks news feeds from 1st to 7th October 2015.

The proposed methodology starts with exploring the most reliable news authorities, unbiased, reliable news authorities, and minimum reliable news authorities. The investigation chose each article posted on Facebook by the news sources between October 1 and October 7 2015, what is more, October 2, 2015 (Holt, 2016). Each remark was analyzed, marked, also, doled out a code dependent on the operational meanings of various kinds of hostility: "badgering," "provocative animosity," and "uninvolved hostility." The examination at that point looked at the methods for the absolute degrees of hostility over each of the three news source classes (generally dependable, nonpartisan, and least reliable) just as the methods for each kind of hostility for every one of the three news source classifications.

Four hypotheses were made So that they could go with the correct assumption, which shows the most accurate answer and code distinguish between the aggressive and non-aggressive comments. Following are the four-hypothesis made:

Hypothesis 1 says that news sources with the most reliability will have the least all-out forceful remarks. News sources with the least dependability will have the most all-out forceful remarks. In contrast, hypothesis 2 implies that the news authorities with the most reliability will have the highest all-out forceful comments. The news authorities with the minimum reliability will have the list all-out forceful comments. Hypothesis 3 says that the least dependable news sources would have the most provocative remarks, and the most reliable news sources would have the least provocative remarks. Hypothesis 4 says that the least reliable news sources would have the most aloof forceful remarks, and the most reliable news sources would have the least aloof forceful remarks.

Results of the hypothesis mentioned above are given as follows:

Table 17.5 shows that the prediction of hypothesis 1 did not support its theory, as there is a mean difference of 0.0132 between the least reliable and the most reliable news authorities.

Table 17.6 shows a mean difference of 0.0129 between the unbiased and the most reliable news authorities.

Table 17.7 shows a mean difference in the total offensive aggression of 0.0223 between the unbiased and the most reliable news authorities.

Table 17.8 shows a mean difference in the total passive-aggression of 0.2093 between the unbiased and the most reliable news authorities.

TABLE 17.5
One-Way between-Group ANOVA of Total Aggression

	Sum of Squares	df	Mean Square	F	Sig.
Between Groups	4.378	2	2.189	9.872	0.000
Within Groups	927.009	4181	0.222		
Total	931.387	4183			

TABLE 17.6

One-Way between-Group ANOVA of Harassment Aggression

	Sum of Squares	df	Mean Square	F	Sig.
Between Groups	.884	2	0.442	10.285	0.000
Within Groups	179.579	4181	0.043		
Total	180.462	4183			

TABLE 17.7

One-Way between-Group ANOVA of Provocative Aggression

	Sum of Squares	df	Mean Square	F	Sig.
Between Groups	10.903	2	5.451	45.124	0.000
Within Groups	505.213	4182	0.121		
Total	516.116	4184			

TABLE 17.8

One-Way between-Group ANOVA of Passive-Aggression

	Sum of Squares	df	Mean Square	F	Sig.
Between Groups	32.882	2	16.441	86.413	0.000
Within Groups	795.669	4182	0.190		
Total	828.551	4184			

Chatzakou et al. (2017) focus on the detection of aggressive comments on Twitter. Its main objective is to observe and analyze the user's activities on Twitter to identify whether they are part of cyberbullying or not.

They have collected the data during June–August 2016 from Twitter Streaming API two arrangements of the tweets: (i) a gauge of 1M irregular tweets, as well as (ii) a despise in regard to arrangement of 650,000 tweets dependent on 309 hashtags related to harassing and derisive discourse (Chatzakou et al., n.d.). The methodology section has used 'ground truth,' which differentiates the comments into bullies, aggressors, or normal ones. Altogether, 1,500 arrangements of tweets were utilized in the comment procedure keeping up a similar number of sets for both detest-related as well as arbitrary tweets. Each set was commented on by five extraordinary laborers. At the same time, at long last, the larger part vote was utilized to make the previous comment names barring the arrangements of tweets where the greater part could not be resolved. Generally, we finished up to 1,307 sets (containing 9,484 tweets altogether) wherein, 3.4% to aggressors, 4.5% compared to menace clients, 31.8% to the spammers, and about 60.3% to typical the ones. Over 15 machine learning

TABLE 17.9
Classification with Random Forest

	(a) Results			(b) Confusion Matrix			
	Prec.	Rec.	ROC	Bully	Aggres.	Normal	
bully	0.464	0.448	0.918	26	7	25	bully (GT)
aggressive	0.286	0.093	0.868	16	4	23	aggres. (GT)
normal	0.941	0.978	0.925	14	3	770	normal (GT)
Avg.	0.878	0.901	0.922				

algorithms were used in this research, such as probabilistic, tree-based, or ensemble classifiers, with an end goal to recognize menace also, forceful clients from the ordinary ones.

In this section, the results of the performed algorithms are displayed:

Table 17.9 shows the outcomes got with a 10-overlap cross-approval process. Generally speaking, the standard exactness and review 90.1% and is 87.8%, separately. In comparison, the weighted area under curve (AUC) of 92.2% depicts that the highlights as well as order method has the ability to perform very well at recognizing menaces, aggressors and recognizing them from run of the mill Twitter clients. Because of the disarray network (Table 17.9b), the misclassifications in the domineering jerk case, for the most part, dip in the ordinary class. In concern to the forceful case, we watch rising "disarray," which shows what the three classes' limits don't turn out to be satisfactory, and more amount of work is required along the line.

Therefore, this paper would conclude that it is a strategy that expands upon various sorts of highlights that were tried to recognize among menaces, aggressors, and run of the mill Twitter clients. The outcomes show this technique is promising in identifying forceful and menacing clients with high exactness.

Chatzakou et al. (2017) also focused on identifying bullies on the social media platform Twitter in their study called 'Mean Birds: Detecting Aggression and Bullying on Twitter' (Chatzakou et al., 2017). Its main objective is to introduce a reliable and flexible technique to detect cyberbullying easily on Twitter.

There is a total of seven steps in the methodology that the researcher has used in this paper:

(a) information gathering, (b) pre-processing of tweets, (c) sessionization, (d) ground truth, (e) extracting person-, textual content-, and structure-level attributes, (f) end-user base and classification, and (g) division.

In this section, all the steps will be discussed in detail, starting with the first step, i.e., 'information gathering' gathered by Twitter's application program interface (API). The second step involves entailing the elimination of unsolicited mail content material, that can get finished using a variety of techniques counting on the tweeting conduct. The third step is called "sessionization," which means combining the user's tweets into sessions based on their time-intervals. The Fourth step is called "ground truth." In this step, trained workers are recruited and are asked to classify the tweets/ comments into different labels. The next step is called "extracting person-, textual content-, and structure-level attributes," selecting the attributes from tweets and end-user profiles. The final step is called "division," and its task is to carry out the classification of the usage of the extracted characteristics and floor fact. Normally, various gadget studying techniques are utilized in this mission, consisting of probabilistic classifiers, decision trees, ensembles, or neural networks.

After performing the above seven steps on the tweets during June–August 2016, the results showed 9,484 total tweets. It received 1,303 annotated clusters. The classification results show that the cyberbullies are 4.5%, spammers are 31.8%, the normal users are 60.3%, and the aggressors are 3.4% of the total users, around 8% of the people are the abusive customers. Thus, we accept that the ground reality data compilation carries some consultant sample of the aggressive/offensive content.

The classification results after successfully performing the methodologies are given below:

It's seen that the random forest (RF) classifier prevails to recognize 43.2% of the authoritative jerk cases. In the forceful case, the review is incredibly low, 11.8% (STD = 0.078). In view of the disarray grid, the unorganized cases generally fall in either one of two cases, i.e., the typical or harassing classes, which lines up with the end-user comments assembled during the supporting stage. In general, the normal exactness is 71.6%, and the review is 73.32%, while the exactness is 73.45%, with 0.4717 kappa and 0.3086 RMSE.

In Table 17.10b, the classifiers work without the "spammers" and the results, in this case, are that as expected, for menace cases, there is a significant increment in both the exactness (14.4%) and review (17.7%). For aggressors, the accuracy and review esteems are nearly the equivalents, demonstrating that further assessment of this conduct is justified in what is to come. In general, the normal exactness and the review of RF model turns out to be 89.9% and 91.7%, individually, although, 91.08% is the precision with 0.5284 kappa esteem as well as 0.2117 RMSE.

Djuric et al. (2018) focus on detecting hate speech and the comments, and it's called 'Hate Speech Detection with Comment Embeddings.' Its objective is to understand accurately low-dimensional portrayals of remarks that use neural language

TABLE 17.10
Results on Four and Three Classes Classification

	(a) 4-Classcs Classification				(b) 3-Classcs Classification			
	Prec.	Rec.	AUC		Prec.	Rec.	AUC
bully (STD)	0.411 0.027	0.432 0.042	0.893 0.009	bully (STD)	0.555 0.018	0.609 0.029	0.912 0.009
aggressive (STD)	0.295 0.054	0.118 0.078	0.793 0.036	aggressive (STD)	0.304 0.039	0.114 0.012	0.812 0.015
spammer (STD)	0.686 0.008	0.561 0.010	0.808 0.002				
normal (STD)	0.782 0.004	0.883 0.005	0.831 0.003	normal (STD)	0.951 0.018	0.976 0.029	0.911 0.009
overall (avg.) (STD)	0.718 0.005	0.733 0.004	0.815 0.031	overall (avg.) (STD)	0.899 0.016	0.917 0.019	0.907 0.005

models which are late proposed and would then be taken care of as contributions to a characterization calculation.

They have proposed a two-advance method for detest discourse recognition. Firstly, they use paragraph2vec for joint displaying of words and remarks also, in which we gain proficiency with their disseminated displays in a joint space using the ceaseless BOW (CBOW) neural language model. The outcome in low-dimensional content installing, where semantically comparative words and remarks live in a resembling piece of the space. At this point, we use embeddings to come up with a parallel classifier to distinguish clean and derisive remarks. We surmise portrayal during deduction for recently watched remark by "collapsing in" using effectively learned word embeddings, as point by point.

The data was taken from the Yahoo finance website on a large scale, and as a result, 56,280 comments contained aggressive comments and 895,456 non-aggressive comments. This data was retrieved from a total of 209,776 users. Method used in this paper, called paragraph2vec, was put into comparison with the BOW representations, using tf and tf-idf so that after finding that result, we could conclude which method is better.

This paper can be concluded by looking at the above Table 17.11, that we can see that paragraph2vec has a higher area under the curve AUC than that of BOW (tf) and BOW (tf-tdf), and the outcomes plainly show the advantages of the proposed approach and establish a stage toward the arrangement of the issue of loathing discourse location in online client remarks.

Rahman et al. (n.d.) deal with the socware detection in a social network called 'Efficient and Scalable Socware Detection in Online Social Networks' (Rahman et al., n.d.). A socware can be defined as when a hacker tries to break into your system and find new ways to expand spams as well as malwares on the online social networks (OSNs) to your email or Facebook. This paper focuses on making a Facebook application called MyPageKeeper that would protect Facebook users from socware.

Now let's find out how a socware can affect your system in terms of Facebook. Firstly, it appears on your Facebook news feed, and it generally comes in the form of a URL that is connected to spam or malware to another end of the URL. Secondly, it could contain an attractive text message (such as *answer this quiz and win prizes*).

MyPageKeeper contains six functional units:

- User authorization module
- Crawling module
- Feature extraction module

TABLE 17.11
AUC of Various Methods

Algorithm	AUC
BOW (*tf*)	0.7889
BOW (*tf-idf*)	0.6933
paragraph2vec	**0.8007**

- Classification module
- Notification module
- User feedback module

MyPageKeeper would be tested on three different aspects of evaluation, and the first aspect would define its accuracy with which it classifies socware. The second aspect is that MyPageKeeper's contribution will be determined compared to URL blacklists, and lastly, its efficiency would be compared with alternative algorithms as shown in Figures 17.2 and 17.3.

Singh et al. (2018) pay attention on detecting aggressive comments utilizing neural networks, and it's called "Aggression Detection on Social Media Text Using Deep Neural Networks." Its objective is to present a profound learning-based arrangement framework for the Facebook posts and remarks of Hindi-English code-mixed content for distinguishing the forceful conduct toward clients (Singh et al., 2018). To make this happen, the information crept from open Facebook Pages and Twitter. The data was principally gathered from the pages/gives that are required to be talked about additional among the Indians (also, in Hindi) to explain the nearness of code-mixed content.

After applying and comparing the methodology with all other algorithms like multimodal NB, Decision Tree, SVM, MLP, LSTM, etc., we found out that CNN was the best methodology to go with and showed the best results after applying it.

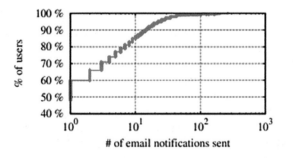

FIGURE 17.2   Forty-nine percent of MyPageKeeper's 12,456 users were notified.

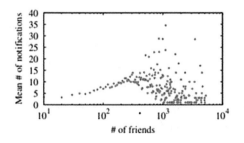

FIGURE 17.3   Correlation between vulnerability and social degree.

This paper concludes that they tried different things, Indi-English code-mixed sentences, as forceful or not. They cannot generally depend on neural systems to perform better than straightforward artificial intelligence (AI) calculations (e.g., SVM performs better than MLP). CNN worked best with an accuracy of 73.2% as well as the best F1-score of 0.58.

Now, below are some of the research papers that did their work on a similar topic and were successful in detecting aggressive comments/messages. Their name, along with their objectives, is mentioned below:

"Benchmarking Aggression Identification in Social Media" by Kumar et al. (2018) is a research paper that focuses on presenting report and discoveries of the Shared Task about Aggression Identification composed like a major aspect of the first Workshop of Trolling, Aggression, and cyberbullying (TRAC – 1).

"Aggression Detection in Social Media: Using Deep Neural Networks, Data Augmentation, and Pseudo Labeling" by Segun Taofeek Aroyehun and Alexander Gelbukh is a research paper that examines the viability of profound neural system models of differing intricacy (Aroyehun and Gelbukh, 2018). Our outcomes uncover that profound neural system models require more information to improve a naive Bayes and support vector machine (NBSVM) straight gauge dependent on character n-grams.

"Aggression-annotated Corpus of Hindi-English Code-mixed Data" by Kumar et al. (n.d.) is a paper that explains the advancement of an animosity sets and a clarified corpus of Hindi-English code-blended information from two of the most well-known social organizing/online life stages in India – Twitter and Facebook (Kumar et al., 2018).

Locate the Hate: Detecting Tweets against Blacks given by Kwok and Wang (2013) is a research paper that talks about a regulated AI approach, utilizing economically obtained named information from different Twitter records to get familiar with a parallel classifier for the names "bigot" and "nonracist."

The article "Aggression Detection in Social Media using Deep Neural Networks" by Madisetty and Desarkar (2018) focuses on an outfit-based framework to order a data post into one of three classes, to be specific, Covertly Aggressive, Overtly Forceful and Non-forceful (Kwok and Wang, 2013). Their methodology utilizes three profound learning techniques, to be precise, CNN, LSTM, and Bi-LSTM.

17.3 PREVENTION OF CYBER BULLYING

Today we are in a dilemma that whether the invention of internet and web is actually correct or not. As it is said that each and every thing in this world has a positive as well as a negative end to it, so is the case with the internet too. Today internet has become a huge part of our lives, bringing an ease in associating individuals around the world and making data accessible to the general public in just one click. The growth of the internet has made human life more comfortable and it gave plenty of favorable circumstances to individuals from varying backgrounds, however, it isn't without some level of risk. While it allows individuals to connect to the world and to democratize their information and data, however at the same time it allows people to take cover behind a veil of namelessness. With advancement came unexpected aspects of cyber offenses like cyberbullying. With the growing accessibility of social media as well as data services, cyber bullying in India has observed a disturbing rise. Cyberbullying whether it is done online or over a phone can have serious impact on the individual and can also haunt them for their entire lifetime. It is something which is open for business 24/7. Nowadays in this digital era, kids are exposed to all the technologies from a very young age making cyberbullying a household occurrence. With a limited knowledge of good or bad, teenagers are the most vulnerable to cyberbullying. In order to prevent such situations, parents should strictly keep a check on their child's internet usage. They must make sure that their kids are engaged more into outdoor activities than internet. Cyberbullying can shock families and if your children are sharing the pictures, texting, and posting remarks then it's important to have a discussion with them about what to do if they become a target of cyber bullying or even online harassment. Quite possibly the main advance now isn't to react and fight back, as reprisal just draws out the issue and doesn't tackle it. Blocking the phone numbers, screen names as well as email address and removing the person from your connections or friends list. Take screenshots and printouts of abusive and disturbing texts and keep them for proof. Most online sites have a set of rules against cyberbullying. Generally, we can find information on ways to report any form of abuse on website's community guidelines. Almost every social media platform today has a clear set of rules in order to report cyberbullying. They help the user to report and remove the offensive post. In India we can report cyberbullying by filing a complaint to complaint-mwcd@gov.in. Reporting a case of cyberbullying is the most important step for its prevention in the future. Don't keep it to yourself and talk to somebody about it. Telling a trusted adult is the most important of all. These days cyberbullying has become very common in schools and colleges. In case any student shows some indications of being bullied then the faculty must inform the higher authorities and the parents of that student. They must delicately handle the case. It should be made necessary for all schools and colleges to have counselors who can assist the student in overcoming such hard situations. However, we wish for a society where we actually have no need to prevent ourselves from online bullying. Parents should teach their children compassion and talk to them regarding their social media/online activities. On the other hand, teachers or guardians should also aid children to understand the difference between cruelty and funny. At the same point it is important that kids report the harassment and cyberbullying if they come across and offer the support. At the end of the day, we cannot deny the fact that, social media bullying is (unfortunately) all around us but we must take preventive measures for it.

17.4   CONCLUSION

From analyzing and learning from all of the above research papers featuring the detection of aggressive and abusive comments in a social network subnet, we have concluded that there should be a sort of warning sign to those users who are aggressive in terms of replying to certain comments or pictures or messages so that they think before they write another abusive or aggressive comment on somebody and hence giving them a chance to improve themselves in terms of talking to people.

We came across the methodologies while analyzing these papers were semantic-enhanced marginalized stacked de-noising auto-encoder, pre-handling and The SMOTE strategy, Ground Truth, MyPageKeeper, Paragraph2vec, Random Forest, and Pre-Processing.

The methodologies that were accurate and efficient were semantic-enhanced marginalized stacked de-noising auto-encoder and MyPageKeeper as both mentioned methodologies are easy to handle and give >90% accuracy rate.

REFERENCES

Aroyehun, S. T., Gelbukh, A. (2018). *Aggression Detection in Social Media: Using Deep Neural Networks, Data Augmentation, and Pseudo Labeling*, pages 90–97. Available at: https://aclanthology.org/W18-4411.pdf

Chatzakou, D., Kourtellis, N., Blackburn, J., Cristofaro, E. D., Stringhini, G., Vakali, A. (2017). *Mean Birds: Detecting Aggression and Bullying on Twitter* pages 13–22, Association for Computing Machinery, New York, NY, USA.

Chatzakou, D., Kourtellis, N., Blackburn, J., Cristofaro, E. D., Stringhini, G., Vakali, A. (n.d.). *Detecting Aggressors and Bullies on Twitter*. Available at: https://arxiv.org/abs/1702.06877

Djuric, N., Zhou, J., Morris, M. (2018). *Hate Speech Detection with Comment Embeddings*, pages 29–30. Available at: http://dx.doi.org/10.1145/2740908.2742760

G'omez-Adorno, H., Bel-Enguix, G., Sierra, G., S'Anchez, O., Quezada, D. (2018). *A Machine Learning Approach for Detecting Aggressive Tweets in Spanish*, pages 13–22. In: *Proceedings of the 3rd Workshop on Evaluation of Human Language Technologies for Iberian Languages (IberEval 2018), CEUR WS Proceedings.*

Holt, L. G. (2016). *News Outlets in Social Media: Aggression in Comments.*

Ifrim, G., Shi, B., Brigadir, I. (n.d.). *Event Detection in Twitter using Aggressive Filtering and Hierarchical Tweet Clustering*. Available at: http://ceur-ws.org/Vol-1150/ifrim.pdf

Kumar, R., Ojha, A. K., Malmasi, S., Zampieri, M. (2018). *Benchmarking Aggression Identification in Social Media*. Available at: https://aclanthology.org/W18-4401/

Kumar, R., Reganti, A. N., Bhatia, A., Maheshwari, T. (n.d.). *Aggression-annotated Corpus of Hindi-English Code-mixed Data*. European Language Resources Association (ELRA). Available at: https://aclanthology.org/L18-1226.pdf

Kwok, I., Wang, Y. (2013). *Locate the Hate: Detecting Tweets against Blacks*, pages 1621–1622. Available at: https://dl.acm.org/doi/10.5555/2891460.2891697

Madisetty, S., Desarkar, M. S. (2018). *Aggression Detection in Social Media using Deep Neural Networks*, pages 120–127. Available at: https://aclanthology.org/W18-4415.pdf

Rahman, M. S., Huang, T., Madhyastha, H. V., Faloutsos, M. (n.d.). *Efficient and Scalable Socware Detection in Online Social Networks*. Available at: https://web.eecs.umich.edu/~harshavm/papers/usenixsec12.pdf

Shruthi, G., Mangala, C. N. (2017). *A Framework for Automatic Detection and Prevention of Cyberbullying in Social Media. International Journal of Innovative Research in Computer and Communication Engineering (IJIRCCE)*, Vol. 5, Issue 6.

Singh, V., Varshney, A., Akhtar, S. S., Vijay, D., Shrivastava, M. (2018). *Aggression Detection on Social Media Text Using Deep Neural Networks*. Available at: https://aclanthology.org/W18-5106.pdf

Tommasel, A., Rodriguez, J. M., Godoy, D. (n.d.). *Features for Detecting Aggression in Social Media: An Exploratory Study*. Available at: https://47jaiio.sadio.org.ar/sites/default/files/ASAI-17.pdf

18 Role of ICT in Online Education during COVID-19 Pandemic and beyond
Issues, Challenges, and Infrastructure

Steffy Sebastian, Albert Thomson,
Vinod Kumar Shukla, and Iman Ajaj Naje

CONTENTS

DOI: 10.1201/9781003048862-18

18.1 INTRODUCTION

Pandemics are states of disease, with infections taking place more or less concurrently in communities around the world that are sharply growing. While it typically applies to infectious diseases, such as plague or influenza, other health problems, including cancer, obesity, and even addiction, are often referred to [1].

In 2009, an epidemic in the United States produced a new form of influenza, a virus known as H1N1. It spread rapidly and was identified as a pandemic by the World Health Organization (WHO) based on a structured process that took into account the precise nature of the countries in which infection was diagnosed [2]. The WHO reported that they no longer use a standardized classification to determine when an outbreak becomes a pandemic because infections from the 2019-coV coronavirus began to spread in early 2020 [3].

COVID-19: Coronavirus disease (COVID-19) is caused by a recently discovered coronavirus, an infectious disease. The first case in Wuhan, China, was found in December 2019. Common symptoms of COVID-19 include fever, cough, weakness, trouble breathing, and loss of smell and taste. Most people infected with the COVID-19 virus will develop mild to moderate respiratory disease and recover without needing special care.

COVID-19 passes from person to person after an affected person coughs, sneezes, and talks or breathes, primarily through the respiratory pathway. A new infection develops when other persons who are in direct contact with the infected person come into the mouth, nose, or eyes with virus-containing particles exhaled by an infected person, like respiratory droplets or aerosols [4].

Covid-19 and Education Domain: Educational structures worldwide have been affected by the COVID-19 pandemic, contributing to the almost complete closing of schools, universities, and colleges. In an effort to minimize the spread of COVID-19, most governments around the world have agreed to have educational institutions temporarily closed. As of September 30, 2020, in response to the pandemic, about 1,077 billion students are actually affected due to school closures. Currently, 53 countries are introducing national closures, and 27 are implementing local closures, according to United Nations Children's Fund (UNICEF) monitoring, affecting about 61.6 percent of the world's student population. Schools in 72 nations are open now.

School closures not only affect teachers, educators, and families. United Nations Educational, Scientific and Cultural Organization (UNESCO) suggested, in response to school closures, the use of distance learning services and open educational software and networks that can be used by schools and teachers to access learners remotely and reduce education disruption.

18.2   GLOBAL EDUCATION TRENDS

During the COVID-19 pandemic, higher education has gone through a considerable transition. It is clear, in the face of volatility, that organizations with previous investments in emerging technology are becoming more flexible and resilient. Online forums, for instance, have helped 30 percent of students feel more connected during this period with other students.

1. Learning will become more data-driven.
2. Soft skills training: a major trend in higher education.
3. Communication makes students feel connected.
4. Juggling questions about well-being.
5. Students are attracted to studying online.
6. Uncertainties around future plans exist.
7. Growing parent-university-community links [5].

18.3   DIGITAL TRANSFORMATION IN EDUCATION DOMAIN

Digital transformation is a physical and conceptual transition designed to meet students, faculty and campus' ever-rising demands and create a learning atmosphere where everything connects. In order to create efficient and personalized learning experiences, this ecosystem integrates technology, services, and security to bridge the digital gap.

Digitization is a significant force that is transforming industries and shaping the way companies and organizations function. Digital transformation refers to digital technology being used innovatively to change conventional ways of doing things. The filing of taxes or submission of customs documents for imports/exports via online workflow processes may be a perfect example of this. Technology-facilitated learning, which gives students some element of control over time, location, direction and/or speed.

Time: The school day or the school year is no longer limited to studying. The internet and the internet access devices have enabled the opportunity for students to learn at any time and anywhere.

Place: Learning is not limited to the classroom. Students have been able to learn anywhere across the world using technologies.

Path: Learning is no longer confined to the pedagogy of the instructor. Interactive and adaptive software encourages learners to learn, make learning personal and participate in their own style. New learning technologies deliver data in real time that provides teachers with the details they need to change instruction to suit each student's specific needs.

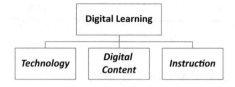

FIGURE 18.1 Components of digital learning.

Pace: Learning is no longer limited to the speed of a whole classroom of students. In order to achieve the same degree of learning, interactive and adaptive software enables students to learn at their own pace, spending more or less time on lessons or topics.

A combination of technology, digital content, and teaching includes digital learning. Figure 18.1 represents the main components of digital learning.

Technology: Technology is the tool that distributes content. It supports how content is received by learners. It requires internet connectivity and hardware, from a desktop to a laptop to an iPad to a smartphone, which can be any internet access computer. Technology is the tool, not the instruction.

Digital Content: The high-quality academic material that is distributed by technology is digital content. It ranges from advanced materials that are entertaining, interactive, and adaptive, to classical literature, to games and video lectures. It is not always a text PDF or a presentation in PowerPoint.

Instruction: For digital learning, educators are critical. The position of the teacher may be changed by technology, but it will never replace the need for a teacher. Teachers will be able to offer tailored instruction and assistance through digital learning to ensure students learn and remain on track to graduate from high school during the year and year after year.

18.3.1 DIGITAL TRANSFORMATION AND UNIVERSITY/SCHOOL CAMPUS

- Develop a powerful IT base
- Elevating good students
- Generate a stable campus
- Provide state-of-the-art cyber security
- Deploy organizational efficiency [6].

There are many tools and services that are developed in-house and purchased by IT teams for enhancing the quality of learning. The usage of technological tools or services is increased during a pandemic. For example: according to Microsoft, the number of active users of Microsoft Teams on a regular basis has doubled in recent months, from 32 million users on March 12 to 75 million on April 30, 2019 (Figure 18.2). Due to the pandemic introduction of social distancing and working from home, Microsoft has seen drastic rises in the everyday usage of its networking and collaboration platform over a short period of time.

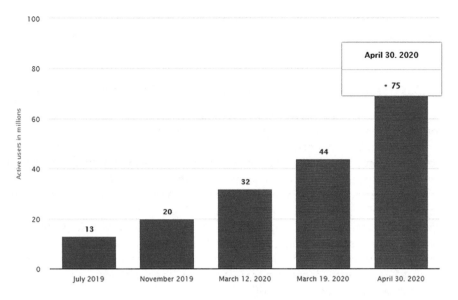

FIGURE 18.2 Number of users of MS-TEAMS-continuous growth.

18.3.2 UNDERSTANDING TECHNOLOGY'S IMPACT ON EDUCATION DURING THE CORONAVIRUS PANDEMIC

The COVID-19 pandemic has caused the biggest crisis in the history of education systems, affecting almost 1.6 billion learners in more than 190 countries on all continents. School and other learning room closures have affected 94% of the world's student population, up to 99% in low-and lower-middle-income countries [7].

During the time of school closures, maintaining the quality of learning became a priority for authorities around the world, many of whom switched to Information and Communication Technology (ICT), forcing teachers to switch to online lesson delivery. Countries state that based on education level, certain modalities have been used more than others have with variability across regions. Governments have used more approaches in areas with minimal access and have gained a lot of attention. With cell phone surveys, monitoring use and performance statistics from learning channels and applications, and incorporating rapid learning tests to recognize learning differences, student progress can be tracked. Each solution, particularly in terms of equity, has its own challenge [8].

The need to further equip schools with facilities and technology and to provide teachers and students with the skills required to adapt to the digital world was also highlighted in the pandemic. The need to further equip schools with facilities and technology and to provide teachers and students with the skills required to adapt to the digital world was also highlighted in the pandemic. Any of these technologies use Closed-circuit television (CCTV), drone camera imagery, electronic payment location data, and wristbands to monitor and evaluate the movement of people who might be positive for COVID-19 or have been ordered to quarantine for other proactive or reactive purposes. With this abrupt move away from the study hall in numerous pieces of the globe, some are contemplating whether the selection of internet learning will keep on persevering post-pandemic, and how such a move would affect the overall schooling market.

18.3.3 Tech Leverages Devices and Data for a Connected Experience

A smart campus is a digitally linked space in which devices and knowledge come together to provide students with a more intuitive learning experience.

Devices such as smartphones, laptops and tablets, smartwatches, and fitness trackers have become an integral part of people's lives. Technological solutions have been crucial in keeping our cities functional during the COVID-19 pandemic, and the long-lasting impacts of engaging technologies on urban areas can actually occur beyond COVID-19. Robots, drones, and contactless payments assist with food and pharmacy shopping online, especially for the elderly and vulnerable populations. IoT-enabled systems for control and automation assist producers and companies in providing services to remote employees. Thanks to the high-speed, accessible internet that 5G cells provide for urban areas, online health appointments, online learning and cultural services are possible [9].

18.4 IoT TECHNOLOGIES IN SMART CAMPUS

18.4.1 In-House Management System (IHMS)

An in-house web application for operational efficiencies. It is an integrated collection of interactive online services to provide safety information, tools, and resources to teachers, learners and those interested in education to support and enhance educational support. IT (Information Technology) being a key department during a pandemic, it was very important to respond quickly with some quality solutions to resolve these unseen situations. It varies from developing modules for capturing contactless student/staff attendance, tracing contacts of each and every student and staff present on campus, to creating tools for analyzing and generating different reports for measuring productivity and quality of these digital services in a secured way.

IT departments play an extended role as universities explore various tactics and technologies to protect student and faculty health on-campus by identifying and eliminating COVID-19 exposure. IT departments in universities are using/developing a web-based/mobile-based application which assists with COVID-19 screening and contact tracing. It needs to be efficient in monitoring the students on a regular basis inside the university and track students from entry to exit. To follow are the main areas covered, also represented in Figure 18.3.

1. Emergency and mass notification systems
2. Building sensors to control heating, ventilation, and air conditioning systems
3. Internet protocol (IP)-based video surveillance/security cameras
4. Smart ID Badges for student/staff

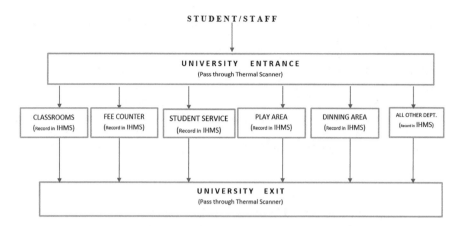

FIGURE 18.3   In-house management system.

5. Smart building access controls
6. Smart outdoor lighting
7. Automated retail/vending systems [10].

How it works:

o A thermal scanner has been installed in entry and exit gates to detect the temperature of whoever enters the university. An IHMS application is integrated with this thermal scanner, and authorities can retrieve real-time data at any time from this application.
o Student records are captured in each and every classroom, laboratories, play area, gym, and library, etc.
o If any person is found to be exceeding a recommended normal temperature, an alert is sent to the university's health and safety team.
o At the same time, the contact list of that person can be generated from the application for monitoring purposes.

18.4.2   TAKE A BREAK (TAB)

There has been an increase in awareness of the importance of mental and emotional well-being in society, especially in schools, in recent years. In many aspects of their lives, students/teachers nowadays face complex stressors and pressures, particularly with an increase in online activity.

As most of the students prefer attending class from home during this pandemic situation and teachers conducting class remotely, some are unaware of how important it is to step away from the computer and take a break. It's not just for physical health – it's for mental health as well. Breaks for some people come naturally. A bit of a heads-up is important for others.

TaB is an effective break timer application concept that will help users to relax and unwind while at online class/work. One gets instant updates and reminders over the course of the class or work to stay active and healthy. From easy eye exercises and short walks to simple and effective stretches, TaB aims to help users to develop healthy habits that will positively influence users' current and future well-being.

How it works: The TaB application will run in the background from the time system boot, and it will ask the user to do some effective stretches and simple exercises every 10 minutes. It has a good user interface that demonstrates a suggested exercise with the help of attractive GIF images in the notification window.

Advantages include:

1. Improved focus among students
2. Higher output levels and improved efficiency of faculties
3. Less absence among staff and students from illness
4. Physically healthier and improved general well-being
5. Reduce stress among students and teachers [11].

18.5   ONLINE EDUCATION: ISSUES AND CHALLENGES

In the last decade, technology and the internet have come a long way. The internet is now home to millions of databases that connect people across the globe. Online education is a form of education where students reside in their respective homes and are connected to the classroom through apps such as Microsoft Teams, Google Classroom, Zoom, etc.

It is also known as computer-based training, web-based training, e-learning, etc. But at its core, it means education that relies majorly upon technological devices and their auxiliaries. It helps students across the globe to log into their classes conveniently and not fall back on crucial learnings. It is a flexible delivery system in which educators can help students scattered across the world to learn and connect at their own pace.

Online education helps students learn efficiently, submit work at their own pace, refer to pre-recorded classes as many times as they want. Some students enjoy the convenience of online education, while others choose online education to cut on time wasted on traveling. This way online education is suitable for students as they learn to become responsible and persistent.

Using resources like the following makes online education effective:

- E-books
- Journals
- Recorded lectures
- Online quizzes
- Live questions and answers
- Online discussion forums

Online learning does not necessarily mean easier education. This form of education needs to adhere to and provide the same level and standards of excellence as traditional institutes.

However, every method has its pros and cons. Students go on to miss face-to-face interactions and are kept back from forming bonds with their classmates and educators. It requires immense self-discipline and punctuality. Online education does not allow any kind of procrastination on the part of students. Just because students have the comfort of being at home does not mean they can delay or avoid assignments and scheduled classes.

The need for online education has also increased immensely due to the widespread diseases that have caused a pandemic. In crucial situations like the current 2020 pandemic, the education of millions of students across the world cannot be put on hold. With the rapid rate of growth in technology, applications, and internet access, more and more options are viable for online education. As online learning techniques have developed, artificial intelligence (AI), plagiarism detectors, and software for exam integrity have advanced.

As more and more students of different ages and interests are coming up, the future of online education will continue to grow. We have all been part of the standard ways of education for a long time. It's a tedious routine, waking up daily, making an effort to commute to schools and other private institutions for both the students and the teachers/professors. A standard requirement for the traditional education system is the physical presence of both the learner and the teacher and the physical presence of learning materials such as books and writing tools to note down information for later learning. Overall, the whole process is such a hassle. That's where the modern style of learning comes in, which is better known as:

E-Learning: The benefit of e-learning is that it saves us a lot of resources and time and also allows for a more manageable and gratifying learning experience as it does not entail unreasonable waking hours and travel. Online education nullifies the need for the physical presence of the student, teacher and learning materials, instead allowing everyone to interact with facetime and take notes on their laptops. This also facilitates faster sharing of notes and documents as they are shared as files on the chatbox of facetime and do not require multiple copies for all the students.

A standard facetime app called Zoom, which is used to conduct online classes. As we see from this, students and teachers talk on video call and discuss their lessons and other activities over the call. The plus point to this is that there is no high cost to maintain a class like this.

History: Online education brings together innovations of several historical events like computers, telecommunication, internet, and even electricity.

- **1960**: The University of Illinois created an entrance for its students to access course materials and listen to pre-recorded lectures.
- **1986**: Electronic University Network (EUN) was set up to help universities establish distance learning.
- **1994**: The computer-assisted learning center offered its first online course that offered real-time instruction and interaction over the internet.

- **2002**: MIT begins offering lectures through its open courseware project over the internet.
- **2009**: The end of the first decade of the new century, but about 5.5 million students worldwide are taking at least one class online [12].
- **2013**: 30% of the void students are very enjoyed in some kind of distance education course.
- **2020**: The global coronavirus pandemic forced many schools and universities of the world to adopt an online form of education.

It is evident from the above that as generations have passed, online education has come a long way. Internet and technology have immensely helped backup this form. The progress that has been made today of just clicking a button and joining a call, connecting millions of students across the globe has been a hefty process.

The Need: Online education is an effective system that helps students across the globe to receive education from any educational institution. Online education is more useful and prominent in the following ways:

Natural calamities: Situation of a natural calamity like snowfall, rainfall, and other calamities that require being at home, students do not have to miss out on crucial topics and can get their education through an online system

Determination: For students with determination and other disabilities that cannot attend school, an online form of education is a very useful method. For example, students with walking disabilities do not have to strain themselves and do not have to miss education.

Accessible: The online form of education is very easily accessible for any kind of student irrespective of their age or geographical location. Older students that wish to complete their education can do so using an online form.

Cost-effective: The online form of education reduces transportation costs and saves time wasted in traveling. Students that wish to do a course with a university that is in another part of the world can do so without having to travel there.

Pandemic: In a situation of a pandemic where quarantine and physical distancing is advised by the WHO, an online form of education helps in meeting the educational needs of students. The 2020 coronavirus pandemic has forced almost all schools, universities, and other educational institutions to use online education for communication.

18.6   CHALLENGES IN ONLINE EDUCATION

While online education for all its modern style and benefits is very resourceful, it also has its own share of challenges and difficulties. These issues have to do with the technology used to conduct the learning. These include the following:

Internet: The internet is the backbone of e-learning. Without a suitable internet connection, speed and bandwidth, online learning becomes difficult and even impossible.

SOLUTION: *Make sure that your internet connection along with bandwidth is fairly good and to ensure that the connection is stable, especially during class and exam times.*

Outdated Technology: Similarly to the internet problem, if the technology we use isn't up to date, we hamper our learning experience as outdated technology would be slower and not have all the specifications required to enable e-learning or the new features that could improve it.

SOLUTION: *Make sure that courses are compatible on various devices, so students do not have to worry about the device compatibility of the app and that all the devices are updated so as to facilitate online learning.*

Lack of personal help: While it is true that the purpose of online education is to reduce the hassle of traveling, students sometimes need help from their professors and fellow students, which is a bit difficult in the online learning world. The lack of personal interaction can cause students to be fed up and even procrastinate, which is not exactly doing wonders for their already poor mental health caused by the excess workload.

SOLUTION: *The professors have to make sure that they pay attention to all the students and know which student is falling behind and arrange private meetings with them to tackle their issues and give them the extra help that they need. The students having problems also need to speak out about their troubles and ask for help either from their professors or their friends and fellow students. This can save time for both the students and professors and allow for smooth interaction.*

Lack of practice: E-learning is a relatively new style, so it's understandable that not everyone is capable of making very good use of it, and this includes the faculty. Often professors just read out the material in the slides and explain it. While this could work for the basic theory-based subjects, subjects that involve numerical problems cannot be simply explained and read out. They require practice which isn't one of e-learning's fortes. It proves difficult to solve problems on a video call, so it is either forgotten or less prioritized.

SOLUTION: *The professors have to set time aside for solving numerical problems and making sure students understand them. Online learning doesn't have to be just that. It can be a combination of both the traditional and modern style of learning, which would require the students to still occasionally need the use of books and pen to write down and solve problems for subjects that require it. Additionally, the professors can give the students home assignments to do to improve upon themselves but not so much so that it stresses them.*

The course material is lackluster: Students often find the learning material to be vague or hard to understand. This is because the material isn't researched well and sorted but instead simply taken from textbooks or guides and pasted as online documents. Students are greatly demotivated by such material, and they find it easier to learn from outside sources on their own.

SOLUTION: *The institutions need to ensure the availability of comprehensible and informative learning material, which will enable the students to not only prepare themselves for their exams but also understand and retain the useful information rather than just having them mug it all up and forget about it when they no longer have to write it down somewhere for marks.*

Time management: E-learning allows the students to manage time so they don't lap their personal and educational life, but so much freedom has its own drawbacks. If the students end up making too much time for their personal life and very little for their education, they will find it hard to cope with the syllabus and perform poorly during exam times and will have trouble completing their assignments on time. Conversely, if a student pays too much time to their studies as hard as it is to imagine, they leave no time for their personal lives and aren't able to spend time with their families and friends, which is critical to their mental health.

SOLUTION: *Students have to make sure they manage their time. They need to make sure that they allocate a reasonable amount of time toward their education as they will not be as lucky as to have their exams canceled a second time. Professors can also assign work to the students with a deadline to submit it to keep them engaged in their studies as well. Incentives can go along a long way. Professors can promise the students a set number of marks for the completion of their homework or for class participation, which will increase their overall GPA.*

Difficulty in concentrating: Concentration is necessary for education in general and online education can make an environment too relaxing – not to mention the added distraction of being online with social media and Netflix being a few clicks away. All of this does not bode well for the learning part of e-learning.

SOLUTION: *Students have to understand that e-learning is just more convenient than traditional learning and not easier. They have to make the same effort study-wise as they made before and not do things that they would not have done before. As stated above, marks for participation can be a good incentive – if the students are not paying attention in class, they can lose marks that they could have gotten had they not been playing e-hooky.*

Difficulty in adapting: As mentioned above, e-learning is a new and under-practiced method of learning. Students who have only known the traditional style of learning would have a difficult time adapting to the loss of the whole institution and instead learning through their handheld devices. Professors would also face the same difficulty in adapting as they are used to interacting with students on a personal level (those that do anyways), so the lack of interaction and participation from students would be discouraging to them.

SOLUTION: *It is the duty of the professors to assure the students that this new experience isn't as scary as it seems and that they will be beside the student every step of the way. The professors can also ease up on the students when trying e-learning for the first time by not giving them a huge pile of work and assignments and stressing them out even more than they already are, and be lenient in checking their initial exams so as to not completely crush them. Doing so will allow the students to adapt quickly, as they will gain* *confidence from the fact that e-learning isn't more difficult or pressurizing at all but less.*

Computer Literacy: While many students are well accustomed to technology and can easily use the channels provided to them for doing their work and submitting it, some students are not used to operating basic programs like Microsoft Word or PowerPoint and therefore are not able to do and submit their work. Some of them are even less tech-savvy as they have a hard time fixing problems that would be easy generally. E-learning requires a certain amount of proficiency in handling technology, so it will most certainly be helpful for the students to know more about the same.

SOLUTION*: It would be a good idea for the professors to acquaint the students with all the options and features of the new application that they are dealing with by sharing their screens and giving them a little tour of the features of the application. This will at least not hamper their education. Students can also look up how to manage and use such apps as the internet is a plethora of information just waiting to be seen. Students could also develop an interest in technology as they can't go wrong with knowing their technology in a world where it is a huge part of.*

The credibility of the course: Perhaps the biggest disadvantage of online education. The worth of this style of learning is not given the respect it deserves nor the trust. It is believed to be inferior to the traditional methods of learning because it is new, and the student's progress is not overseen in books or report cards. This problem is the same as superstition, fear of the unknown, or distrust in certain activities, which is basically the concept of e-learning.

SOLUTION*: As far as the trust in online courses goes, succeeding online enables a person to develop qualities such as discipline, initiative and time management skills, something many firms look for in their employees. Plus, many well-renowned universities offer online courses, which speak for itself, and the level or quality of education cannot be questioned just because some people don't understand it. There is also the added benefit of online courses that allows the students to manage their time so they can end up with more free time than when they are on campus if they finish their work and assignments early on, giving them more time to socialize.*

18.6.1 ISSUES FACED BY TEACHERS AND STUDENTS

18.6.1.1 Issues Faced by Teachers

During this pandemic, the role of teachers has been very critical. All of a sudden, approximately all schools and universities have taken the decision of going online so that the education of all students can be continued, but delivering this education via online medium has been very challenging for many teachers.

Alter course design and teaching strategies: The online form of education is very different from the traditional one. Teachers have to completely change the course design and their teaching techniques to ensure that students grasp the topic.

Traditional instructors: Traditional or older instructors that have been teaching in a physical atmosphere classroom all their lives have a difficult time adjusting to an online atmosphere. Learning to present and teach a course over a network while also maintaining the curiosity of students is an added burden for educators.

Student feedback: In an online system, where students are not always visible to the professors, getting feedback is a difficult task. In a traditional setting, instructors can effortlessly draw out student feedback and understanding by visually monitoring the expressions of students. This is a hiccup in an online setting. Students are sometimes shy or restrained from giving truthful feedback. Usually, educators can adjust their plans to better accommodate the need at that time. Facial expressions aren't as noticeable through a video call and make altering the schedule difficult.

Cannot ensure 100% participation: Attendance and participation can be easily supervised in a traditional setting. In an online class, students can just log in to their accounts and "attend the class" when actually doing some other work or even sleeping. There are no measures that instructors can take to avoid this as it is impossible to focus on each and every student, especially when the video cameras have been turned off.

Pranks of students: Online education has made pulling pranks on teachers easier for students. It has also made mass-bunking trouble-free. From muting the instructor in the meeting, removing fellow students from the meeting, faking a bad internet connection, and playing games during class, there seems to be an increase in pranks. These pranks may be harmless at times, but they disrupt the ongoing class. Instructors therefore now also have to ensure that students do not do these activities. This has only increased the burden and responsibilities of instructors.

Copy pasted answers: Ensuring the authenticity of answers when the students cannot be seen is a challenge many instructors face. Instructors can smoothly supervise the integrity of work done by students that are sitting in front of their eyes. When not overlooked, students can easily copy answers from the internet or other sources and turn them in as original work as they are in their own environment and while using their personal computer. Inspecting each student's work every day for plagiarism multiple times becomes a waste of time and effort for instructors.

Sense of isolation: Online teaching creates a monologue for instructors. There is no sentiment or attachment involved. The instructors never get to meet the students face-to-face. Social isolation backed with a lack of communication leads to mental health issues such as stress, anxiety, and negative thoughts of not having done enough. Not being able to mutually discuss topics and manners with colleagues also increases self-doubt.

18.6.1.2   Issues Faced by Students

As teachers were facing various challenges to deliver the session online, at the same time, it was not easy for the students too, as the online environment was very new for many of the students for learning and regular classes.

Adaptability struggle: Switching from a traditional routine classroom to a completely online format makes the learning experience completely different for students. This switch often causes resistance from students. The change in the environment makes them feel uncomfortable, and students need extra time to get familiar with the online environment.

Motivation and ease of procrastinating: Self-motivation is a very crucial requirement of online education. Being at home, in-comfortable attire in bedrooms and kitchen tables where distractions are many leads to an increase in procrastination. Students get demotivated and lose focus as they do not have defined study space, and their respective homes can be distractive.

Sense of isolation: Not being able to connect with classmates and educators in real life and without the buzz of the classroom setting creates a sense of isolation for the students. They feel disconnected and disjoined from their peers. This causes an additional burden of loneliness and a sense of solitude; this has an adverse effect on students as they are unable to clear their doubts or ask for additional help.

Computer literacy: Having enough technological language is essential for online education. Being able to successfully log into class, present screens, and submit work is a necessity for students. Nowadays, most students are proficient in computing, but there still exist some students that find it challenging to use online apps and their features. These students, therefore, lag behind their classmates, as they need extra time to perform tasks.

Technical issues: Online education relies mainly on internet connectivity, and often students do not have a stable internet connection or the proper devices required. Thus, students fail to catch up with the virtual course.

Time management: Online education requires students to adopt efficient time management skills as they need to balance family time, social life, and complete the scheduled classes all while being home. It's easier for students to get distracted and invest all their time in other activities as they are not in a binding environment where they have to focus on schoolwork only.

Cyber bullying: The online classroom has drastically increased the rate of cyber bullying between classmates. Online pranks like muting mics, removing classmates from meetings, and hacking creates a hurdle in education.

Impaired connectivity: Students are already an issue being distant from their peers. but online education has made group projects and connecting with group members to create innovative works even more difficult. Relying just upon online apps and texts do not create a creative and interactive environment.

Increased screen time -> increased eye problems: The online form of education requires students to be glued to a screen at all times. Students need to stare at screens during classes while completing assignments and during online extra-curriculum activities. An increase in exposure to screens has a negative effect on the eyesight of students, especially younger students. If online education continues for a long time, all students will be forced to get prescriptions.

18.7   CHALLENGES OF CONDUCTING ONLINE EXAMS

An online exam may be difficult to conduct as the whole concept of online learning and online exams is a new one. Some problems are bound to arise. Some problems that the examiner and examinee may face are listed below:

Internet connection: Internet connection may be a problem for students living in rural and remote areas. For many exams that have been conducted, internet connection has seemed to be a recurring problem.

Preparation of question paper: The quality of an online exam depends upon the quality of the questions on it. The institution should ensure that the questions on the exam match what is taught in the course material and that they are understandable to maintain a good quality of examination with no room for doubt and that parameters such as time allotted, total marks, total questions, total questions in every section, negative marking and marking scheme are all well-defined.

Communicating with the attendees: The professors or examiners need to make sure that they can communicate with each individual attending the exam in order to inform them of the exam or reach out to them in case they face difficulties in attending the exam or for any other inquiries.

Security: The biggest threat to the integrity of exams in general but made much worse. Security is a difficult thing to ensure during online exams as the examiner is unable to keep tabs on the students as they would normally. Nevertheless, the examiner has to make sure that the security of the exam is not compromised and that the right individuals are present for the exam and ensure that no malpractices take place. The system should be able to identify cheating or security lapses during the duration of the examination.

18.7.1   Recommendations/Solutions to Better the Examination Process

Conducting the exams through offline networks: Managing exams in the offline environment has many advantages such as:
- Exams can be managed without the need for worry of internet connectivity or speed.
- A large number of students can appear for the exam from remote locations by accessing different offline networks.
- The entire exam log audit log is maintained to identify manipulations or errors.
- It is a more efficient means to conduct such a large-scale examination.

Having reliable methods for keeping tabs on the candidates during the exam: Ensuring security is difficult in an online exam but it must still be ensured to prevent malpractice which can be done by the following:

Remote proctoring: This allows for the facility of live streaming the video off candidates in remote locations. It also allows for taking a snapshot of the candidate to verify their identity. Also allows for live chat with the candidates during the exam to authorize their attendance.

Secure browsers: Ensures that the candidate cannot open any other window during the exam process as this prevents them from opening other windows during exam activity.

Ensuring a credible test creation: Conducting an online exam is much easier than conducting an on-campus one, and so is creating it. By using certain software and researching online, tests can be conducted with more clarity than what would normally be possible and with a higher range of questions to choose from. Also, tests can be created with a single section or multiple ones with common marks for all questions or differing marking schemes for each section or question. Different questions can be set for each individual, or the same test can be given to all of them. Specifics can be added like dates, total marks, negative marking, and a section to write your name and roll number.

Reports: The exam results can be presented in a summary or detailed format after the exam Is over. It is possible to display the test results of the examinee when they submit their tests. This solves the problem of the absence of a physical report, and since tests are pre-made with answers to each of them already factored in, it is possible to have the exams corrected on the spot, which saves a lot of time for the examiners who would have to manually go through each of them afterward.

Using a user-friendly interface: As mentioned earlier, some students have a hard time managing technology, so it is crucial that exams be conducted on an interface, which is simple to use. This ensures that the examinee does not have trouble navigating and attending the exam. It can also be used for the examination as it can present a timer on top of the screen and provides easy navigation to flag or unflag questions but also makes sure that only the required amount of time is given to the examinee.

Statistical Report: To support our approach and get a better insight into the issues, we conducted a survey targeting students that are currently enrolled in online learning due to the pandemic. The following questions were asked in the survey:

- Do you have a strong and reliable internet connection?
- Do you stay motivated throughout the scheduled classes?
- Do you prefer online or traditional learning?
- Do you have the technical abilities to fulfill online learning requirements?
- Do you miss face-to-face interactions?

In addition, the options given to display their responses were:

- All the time
- Most of the time
- Rarely

The survey was taken by 1300 students from various universities and programs. The following results have been concluded:

Do you have a strong and reliable internet connection?

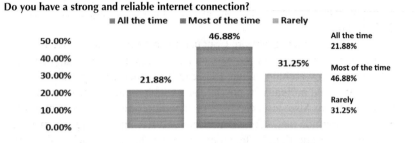

A strong and reliable internet connection is essential for online learning. It remains to be a hindrance for many students, as seen above. Out of 1300 students, approximately 30% do not have a proper internet connection, while 46% do not have a high bandwidth dependable one. Service providers need to work toward ensuring better connectivity to all students to avoid any disruption.

Do you stay motivated throughout the scheduled classes?

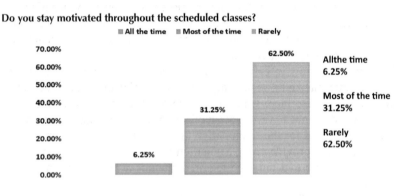

Self-motivation and being productive during online classes have been a challenge for most of the students. When classmates and educators in a physical setting do not surround students, it may be tempting to procrastinate, as evident from the results. A positive attitude is the only way through which students can power through and get all the necessary work done. A regular schedule and proper timetable can help students tackle this issue.

Do you prefer online education or traditional classes?

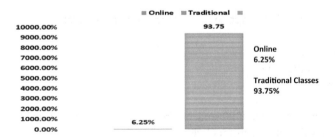

The majority of the students are extremely attached to traditional learning. Since childhood, they have been in a physical setting creating bonds with their peers and professors. It is therefore difficult for them to get used to and adapt to online education. Students need to accept the new learning situation with an open mind and heart. Understanding the benefits of e-learning and its requirement during these times with an open mindset better prepares students for online classes.

Do you have the technical abilities to fulfill the online learning requirements?

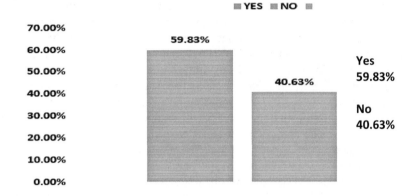

Technical knowledge and skills are of utmost importance in an online learning system. Knowing how to log into class and access data is key. Most of today's tech-savvy students know how to do this. However, some students do not have the skills. According to the results, almost 40% of the students do not possess the required skills. This could create a hindrance in their studies. The only way this can be resolved is for instructors to exercise extra patience with these students and provide them with additional help. The instructor has to also make sure these students do not feel left out or made fun of due to a lack of technical skills.

Do you miss face-to-face interactions?

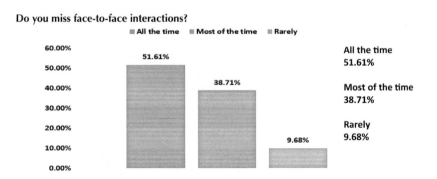

The buzz of a classroom, the faces of peers, and the voice of instructors without technical disturbances are longed for by most students. The above graphs [13, 14] tables make it evident that 90% of the students miss traditional schools and prefer it to online learning. This stops them from accepting and adopting the routine of online classes. There is no definite solution to this. Students need to understand the need of the hour and live in the situation. They need to be more involved. Students should log in daily to see course updates and class discussions, connect with other students, and communicate with faculty whenever required.

18.8   CYBER SECURITY

The COVID-19 pandemic has caused new practices like social distancing and remote working to be embraced by organizations and individuals. By designing and implementing new economic policies, policymakers are reconsidering ways to ensure that their countries are prosperous. Nevertheless, as the world focuses on the health and economic challenges presented by COVID-19, this crisis is inevitably being capitalized on by cyber criminals around the world.

As a lot of staff employed from home and students use virtual learning, virtual private network enterprise (VPN) servers have now become a lifeline for businesses/schools, and their security and accessibility will continue to be a major focus. There is a risk that the unpreparedness of an organization could lead to a security misconfiguration of VPNs in an effort to achieve this. The education domain is also targeted by phishing, ransomware/malware, lack of awareness, and other types of known attacks.

Exposing confidential internet information and even exposing the computers to attacks against Denial of Service (DoS). In addition to this, some users can use personal details, Computers for the execution of official duties, which may also be institutions face a great deal of danger. Organizations can guarantee that VPN services are safe and stable.

An organization's post-COVID-19 procedure might include cutting back by cutting off trade lines considered as non-critical, which may incorporate cyber security operations. It is advisable for organizations to update their business continuity plans (BCPs) and remote policies/practices for working while prioritizing during post-COVID-19 cyber security re-strategizing Phase [15].

The challenges education is facing include:

1. A lack of funding and budget, possibly leading to the lack of funds, whether software or personnel, to invest in cybersecurity.
2. In educational institutions, students using their own computer/devices culture is prevalent and can present difficulties in securing the wider network, particularly with IT staff already facing strained resources.
3. In large organizations with a diverse user base, it can be difficult to set rules for the use of the network and to ensure that they are adhered to [15].

18.9   EDUCATIONAL APPLICATIONS AND SECURITY

E-learning apps support a bundle of tools, including videoconferencing, voice-over protocols, share-screen, whiteboards and more. Some apps can include unlimited members. There are definitely some security vulnerabilities that come up, but the companies have tried their best to fix them. Most of it is because anyone can easily access all data; thus, it is important to divide the users into roles to ensure the best safety. Data theft, DoS attacks, and spoofing are some major concerns of IT companies when implementing security to their applications. This guide will look into the features of some of the digital applications serving educational purposes and discuss their security issues. Different educational platforms used for e-learning across the globe during the COVID-19 pandemic crisis, we have made an effort to make a list of their features and mainly their security issues.

Digital learning has been at the forefront for a long time; it provides adaptive learning and helps students to personalize their lessons with features of recordings, activities and helps them go at their own pace. E-learning has seen a massive rise globally ever since the beginning of the COVID-19 crisis, which demands social distancing, and teaching now is undertaken on digital platforms. This technology has enabled people all around the world to interact and hold meetings with something as simple as an internet connection and a device.

This has been an unprecedented challenge for IT and security professionals who are in search of collaboration apps, with the best security as one of their priorities. Platforms like Zoom, Skype, Microsoft Teams, Adobe Connect, WizIQ are serving this purpose. They all include a variety of virtual classroom tools which involve learner engagement. The participation and collaboration of the participants ensure an engaging atmosphere, and all concerns about learning in a new platform disappear. However, guarding against the potential pitfalls; data breaches, identity theft, unauthorized student access can be hectic. These apps include details about students. Their names, birth dates, profile photos, chats, recordings, academic details, etc. Thus, it is a priority to ensure security. Cybercriminals usually aim to attack collaboration apps. Most of these applications are linked to different third-party apps for data backup. They have messaging components that can be used for phishing attacks and to deliver malware through links and attachments. Information security can be obtained using methods of cryptography and network protocols. In this chapter, we will look into each of these above five mentioned digital applications, which are now used throughout the globe serving for educational purposes, and discuss their security issues and vulnerabilities.

18.9.1 Zoom

Zoom is the most popular application being used for educational purposes ever since the lockdown began. Its user count went up from 10 million in 2019, to 300 million daily meetings as of April 2020. Zoom is likely to give students the best educational experience with its unique and powerful features like webinars, whiteboard, and breakout rooms accessible in Windows, Mac, iOS, Android, Blackberry. It is laid out intuitively and is very well designed. Zoom also enables users to rename themselves and include other additional information, which empowers the learners and ensures their presence in the virtual classroom.

However, there are a number of security and privacy issues linked with the popular videoconferencing app. Professionals claim that Zoom's security has a lot of loose ends.

- The most notable issue is the presence of unwanted guests, i.e., hijacking over the meeting or "Zoom bombing." The easy use of the app makes it vulnerable to bombs. Zoom meetings could be both password-protected or not. The 9-to-11-digit meeting codes can easily be identified and research also prove how easy 6-digit passwords are to crack [16].
- Researchers had found a feature of the installer which could provide access to the user's personal data. One such case was reported in July 2019, in an iOS device where a bug was able to install programs without the user's knowledge and opened up webcams and microphones. The bug stayed even after the software was uninstalled due to a leftover local web server. Apple, however, silently pushed out an update to disable the bug. More issues were reported, including security flaws in the Windows 10 build of the platform's software, data being shared with social media platform Facebook, etc.
- There has also been a lot of scrutiny in the app's encryption policies: Zoom does not use "end-to-end encryption," which is considered as a standard for ensuring privacy. It uses the AES-256 ECB method of encryption in which the key for encryption of the audio and video data are public throughout the globe. This implies a chance of the servers (acting as middlemen) to store the data and ensures no confidentiality. However, on May 7, 2020, **Zoom announced that it had acquired Keybase**, which ensures end-to-end encryption and would be implemented soon [17].
- In mid-April there was widespread news about half a million Zoom accounts being sold on the dark web. Zoom, however, confirmed to their defense that it was not due to any kind of breach.

The company has been sued amid accusations, and people are skeptical about its privacy policies. Zoom has been banned for 1 month in the New York City Department of Education due to its security issues.

18.9.2 Microsoft Teams

Microsoft Teams is another application widely used for educational purposes. It is integrated with other Microsoft applications and is owned by Microsoft 365. The rise in working from home due to the pandemic spread across has contributed to the major success of the app with 75 daily million users for both business and educational purposes. As the name suggests, this platform is chat-based and provides classes or groups referred to as a team where users collaborate. It supports videoconferencing, share-screening, recording and whatnot, making it perfect for e-learning. Each Team has different channels where they can have conversations with the rest of the team. It supports videoconferencing, share-screening, recording and whatnot, making it perfect for e-learning.

Security analytic company Varonis monitors Teams, SharePoint, and OneDrive, which are synced applications of Office 365, to **prevent** data breaches. However, the security is complicated and can be compromised by attackers.

- Guest access is a new feature that enables cross-organizational visits. The team owner can invite users from outside the organization to the team. These guests get full access to team channels, chats, shared files, and meetings. The requirement for being a guest is having a business mail ID, but there are no other restrictions to govern who can or cannot receive guest access privileges. Thus, it could lead to identity theft and raises concerns on how proprietary data can be exposed to outsiders.
- Teams is a software as a service (SaaS) model application and receives and sends packets of data through the cloud. It could be malicious as it is vulnerable to malware and bugs, which can intercept the files during transmission and corrupt the data and even lead to data theft and DoS attacks.
- Microsoft Teams does not support end-to-end encryption. Data encryption on Teams is done in transit or at rest. Microsoft uses TLS (transport layer security) and SRTP (Secure Real-Time Transport Protocol) to encrypt data between users' devices and server ends. Thus, intermediate services can access and decrypt the data, which is a man-in-the-middle attack. Office 365 is backed by tools like content search and eDiscovery, which preserves the original data and provides search and display options. It serves as evidence in case of spoofing and tampering and ensures non-repudiation of the data. But these tools compromise security, as third-party apps can access this information through it [18].
- According to Techgenix, Microsoft Teams stores data in Exchange, Stream, Groups, SharePoint, and OneDrive. With all this data sharing, it is hard to believe that the data is 100% secure.

It is easy to create a new team, but this is leading to a waste of resources as multiple teams are created and then get abandoned after some time. This has contributed to the lack of oversight and puts information at risk due to wrong sharing settings. A data-centric approach must be implemented to avoid accidental sharing in Microsoft Teams.

18.9.3 SLACK

Slack is another platform used for educational operations. It started in 2013 and was better seen as an alternative to Microsoft's Teams and was used for business purposes. However, the emergence of a global health crisis, where schools and universities shifted to digital learning, backed the app to be used for e-learning across many states in the US and the world. Around 3000 institutions have already implemented the use of this application. It supports group chats, videoconferencing and other tools, which makes it very likely for a virtual classroom. However, this app has had a history of security issues, posing threats to businesses considering confidentiality. Similar could be the security risks when the application is used for learning.

— In Slack, bots and commands are all integrated, which shows its visibility making it prone to attacks. When a user shares a file on Slack, it is a public link and is accessible without any sort of credentials like a password or log-in usernames. The documents can thus be accessible to anyone easily without much security.

— It is easy for members outside the organization to join channels as a username is all required for verification. Thus, it is quite an open communication and data must be handled carefully. Members must be aware of other participants and share data accordingly.

— Slack is capable of syncing with outside applications with its feature add-ons. This is actually a weakness in its system as an attacker can design an add-on that may look useful but actually gives him unauthorized access to the data and exposes the Slack channels [19]. These apps (popular ones include Google Drive, Salesforce, etc.) increase the chance of risk and could compromise the security of the app itself.

— Slack is a platform vulnerable to phishing attacks and spam messages because of its invite-only feature, which allows open communication.

— Slack has a "bottom-up" approach, which means the app could be used to its full potential even without ensuring security. The users are not aware of the risks, nor the security tools, thus making the application more vulnerable to hackers.

18.9.4 ADOBE CONNECT

Adobe Connect is a web conferencing software that offers immersive online meeting experiences from small groups to large webinars. Adobe has no limit on the number of users in the meeting. Its features, including video chat, desktop and document sharing, and customizing new apps in sync, have made it a large base for educators to conduct remote digital learning. Adobe Connect Meetings is synced with Adobe Connect Webinars and Adobe Connect Learning, making it even more impressive and the best platform a true virtual classroom [20].

18.9.5 SKYPE

Skype is a multi-channel communications software owned by Microsoft. and has been in the market for a long time as the leading voice-over-internet protocol (VoIP) and videoconferencing platform but now has been even paved the way in the educational sector. Skype in the classroom is a tool that Skype has set up on its website, which provides a classic atmosphere for a virtual classroom. Many students can access it at a time, and the app promotes an engaging environment. Mystery Skype is another in-built feature that brings different classes together, making it more interactive and school-like.

However, over the years, Skype has had many risk factors, which questions its integrity and whether the app is best suited for digital learning. Cases of personal security leaks, downloads of viruses, and malware have been reported in the past.

This app has proved to be flexible and secure; security is in-built into the platform. Adobe has delivered the best of security with secure code designs, configuration settings, connections, and user interfaces. Adobe Connect works on the concept where only the host has control over the meeting, but roles can also be assigned to co-presenters and participants. However, a system with 100% security could only be a dream. Adobe Connect has been linked with security vulnerabilities in the past.

- Skype shares a privacy policy with Microsoft ever since it was purchased in 2011. Unfortunately, this makes Skype's security mechanisms very opaque. There is no legal knowledge of what information is collected in Skype as its policies aren't even mentioned explicitly in Microsoft's privacy statement. Further, in 2006 it was reported in an article that Skype gives away personal details when requested by governmental organizations, which puts forth a doubt toward its privacy policies.
- As Skype is open communication, its websites and software are not very child friendly for users under the age of 13; thus, parent supervision is important, which can be implemented by the parental control feature, Skypito. It is recommended to never post home address, phone number and other optional personal details on Skype.
- Skype is not considered to be a secure VoIP system as the calls are made over the network are not end-to-end encrypted, which means all data is sent from the users directly to the Microsoft servers, making it 100% accessible for monitoring.
- Cases where Skype callers' IP addresses have been found have been reported in the past. This can be done easily in the command prompt by listing all the transmission control protocol (TCP) connections to the device.
- Skype is vulnerable to transmitting viruses. The files shared could act as transmitters as viruses and malware can easily be embedded in them. The most serious piece of malware which affected this platform was in 2012, known as the "Dorkbot" worm, which had migrated from Twitter and Facebook. This worm made users inadvertently install the infection on their computers. The infected machine would be connected to a botnet, and the data remained inaccessible until a demand was paid [21].
- In February 2016, a malware T9000, which could record video and audio clippings, chats, and all media saved into a server, targeted Skype users.

18.10   ADDRESSING SECURITY VULNERABILITIES

Principe of zero-trust must always be applied because it makes one aware in case of security issues. Firewall and internet security must always be activated when using platforms for communications online by the users.

Strict policies must be followed with the installation of add-ons and their implementation. Roles must be split and not everyone must have access to major activities in the group. However, minimal privileges must be ensured to all users where they have access to perform legitimate activities

Apps synced with these platforms (including G-suite and SharePoint) must also have the best security policies as they also have whole access to the data shared. Security and compliance policies must be extended to all these apps to ensure that all data is consistent with the internal policies (FINRA, PII and data loss). Security hygiene must be maintained at all times and organizations should ensure that collaboration platforms are held to the same standards as other services.

Secure and complex passwords must be set, ensuring multi-factor authentication preserving the confidentiality of the data.

Training and workshops: Similarly, on the user behavior front, users should be trained to understand what phishing lures could look like within a Slack channel or a Teams chat [22]. Also, creating awareness around what is and is not okay to share on a platform is a foundational security tool too, according to researchers – and can vastly reduce the "jackpot" attractiveness for criminals in compromising an app like Slack.

– The encryption method must be changed to end-to-end encryption for the best security and privacy policies.

IT teams all across the world are engaged in trying to give us the best services in these hard times. The sudden emergence and mass use of platforms for e-learning can sometimes create chaos in security and lead to delayed feedback from the companies, so we are responsible for our cyber safety and must be ready for any kind of digital threat.

18.11 CONCLUSION

Online education is a new concept, and it's still being tested out. If used effectively, it can easily surpass the traditional style of education. However, if used carelessly or without effort, it can without a doubt backfire. We need to understand that in order to handle e-learning we have to first acknowledge its worth and not to think of it as inferior and/or easier than on-campus education. Students, teachers, institutions, and everyone else need to show the same amount of devotion to e-learning as they show to regular learning because if they don't, they will find it very hard to cope with it. It is also mandatory for all institutions to experiment with online education and not just use it as a means to an end during pandemics. Institutions also need to make sure that students are not burdened with so much more work, especially when they are new to this style of education. Students need to make sure they don't just idly laze around because they feel they can manage their time easily or maybe cheat the system. Overall, it is imperative for all the parties involved to co-operate with each other to ensure smooth sailing.

Hundreds and thousands of students have joined cyberspace academics for the first time this year due to the current pandemic. This move has hoped to maintain educational requirements and drift away from the resistance of online education.

The current crisis has majorly altered the teaching and learning mechanism of education. Dated technology has taken over classrooms and campuses. This has been a very drastic change for both students and educators. Online learning has come a long way since the 1900s. It has its pros and cons. On the one hand, it has allowed students to get access to education during a crisis, but on the other hand, it has demotivated and affected many students negatively.

This system is tremendously dependent on network connection which is very uncertain. Lack of network can lead to major hindrances for both parties. Educators are also facing a lot of challenges in adapting and adjusting not only themselves but also the students in this new system. Ensuring the integrity and authenticity of submitted work has been a major struggle. Educators also have to also certify 100% participation by students, which is difficult to do over a network. The United Arab Emirates (UAE) has immensely helped the education sector by launching courses and providing any kind of help required. Their approach is simple: All you have to do is ask. Although online education has a lot of disadvantages, its main advantages of providing access and connectivity outweigh them all. As a temporary approach, this system is effective and efficient, but for students that use this system in their everyday life, a lot of alterations are to be made.

REFERENCES

1. "What Is a Pandemic?" [Online], https://www.sciencealert.com/pandemic.
2. Centers for Disease Control and Prevention, "Origin of 2009 H1N1 Flu (Swine Flu): Questions and Answers" [Online], https://www.cdc.gov/h1n1flu/information_h1n1_virus_qa.htm.
3. Nicole Wetsman, "WHO Declares the Outbreak of the New Coronavirus Pandemic Is a Pandemic" [Online], https://www.theverge.com/2020/3/11/21156325/coronavirus-pandemic-who-declares-covid-19-outbreak-global-h1n1.
4. "Coronavirus" [Online], https://www.who.int/health-topics/coronavirus#tab=tab_1.
5. "The Evolution of Global Education and 5 Trends Emerging Amidst COVID-19" [Online], https://www.weforum.org/agenda/2020/11/evolution-higher-education-covid19-coronavirus.
6. "Why Digital Transformation for Education" [Online], https://www.al-enterprise.com/-/media/assets/internet/documents/digital-transformation-faq-en.pdf.
7. "Policy Brief: Education during COVID-19 and Beyond" [Online], https://www.un.org/development/desa/dspd/wp-content/uploads/sites/22/2020/08/sg_policy_brief_covid-19_and_education_august_2020.pdf.
8. "UAE Public Urged to Join COVID-19 Contact Tracing App Alhosn to Protect Themselves, Communities" [Online], https://www.mohap.gov.ae/en/MediaCenter/News/Pages/2422.aspx.
9. "The Use of IoT Technologies to Identify and Control the COVID-19 Pandemic in Urban Areas" [Online], https://www.frontiersin.org/research-topics/14707/the-use-of-iot-technologies-to-identify-and-control-the-covid-19-pandemic-in-urban-areas.
10. Emiliana Vegas, "School Closures, Government Responses, and Learning Inequity around the World during COVID-19" [Online], https://www.brookings.edu/research/school-closures-government-responses-and-learning-inequality-around-the-world-during-covid-19/.
11. Donna Griffiths, "The Growing Importance of Health and Wellbeing at Work" [Online], https://www.westfieldhealth.com/resources/blog/the-growing-importance-of-health-and-wellbeing-at-work.
12. Tom, "The History of Online Education" [Online], https://www.petersons.com/blog/the-history-of-online-education/.
13. "Online Education (Self-Made Survey)" [Online], https://www.surveymonkey.com/r/J2CQLW3.

14. "Self-Made Picture" [Online], https://www.canva.com.
15. "Why Cybersecurity Needs to Be a Priority for the Education Sector" [Online], https://
    swivelsecure.com/solutions/education/why-cybersecurity-needs-to-be-a-priority-for-
    the-education-sector/#:~:text=Education%20institutions%20need%20to%20make%20
    cybersecurity%20a%20priority.&text=It's%20an%20unfortunate%20fact%20
    that,to%20protect%20students%20from%20harm.
    "Why Cybersecurity Needs to Be a Priority for the Education Sector" [Online], https://
    swivelsecure.com/solutions/education/why-cybersecurity-needs-to-be-a-priority-for-
    the-education-sector/#:~:text=Education%20institutions%20need%20to%20make%20
    cybersecurity%20a%20priority.&text=It's%20an%20unfortunate%20fact%20
    that,to%20protect%20students%20from%20harm.
16. Thomas Reisinger, "Zoom Security: Here's What You Need to Know" [Online], https://
    techxplore.com/news/2020-05-zoom-security-here-what-you.html#:~:text=A%20
    number%20of%20issues%20with,codes%20could%20easily%20be%20identified%20.
17. Rae Hodge, "Zoom Security Issues: Zoom Buys Security Company, Aims for End-to-
    End Encryption" [Online], https://www.cnet.com/news/zoom-security-issues-zoom-
    buys-security-company-aims-for-end-to-end-encryption/.
18. Jeff Melnick, "5 Tips for Hardening Microsoft Teams Security" [Online], https://blog.
    netwrix.com/2020/04/16/microsoft-teams-security/.
19. Tara Seals, "Beyond Zoom: How Safe Are Slack and Other Collaboration Apps?" [Online],
    https://threatpost.com/beyond-zoom-safe-slack-collaboration-apps/154446/#:~:
    text=A%20failure%20to%20lock%20down,way%20to%20shrinking%20the%20risk.
20. Molly McLaughlin, Juan Martinez, and Daniel Brame, "Adobe Connect Review"
    [Online], https://www.pcmag.com/reviews/adobe-connect.
21. Christian Cawley, "3 Skype Security Issues and Threats You Should Know About"
    [Online], https://www.makeuseof.com/tag/3-skype-security-issues/.
22. Shanhong Liu, "Number of Daily Active Users (DAU) of Microsoft Teams Worldwide
    as of April 30.2020 (in millions)" [Online], https://www.statista.com/statistics/1033742/
    worldwide-microsoft-teams-daily-and-monthly-users/#:~:text=Microsoft%20
    Teams%3A%20number%20of%20daily%20active%20users%202019%20and%20
    2020&text=The%20number%20of%20daily%20active,million%20as%20of%20
    April%2030.

Index